Harold Innis on Peter Pond

Harold Innis

on Peter Pond

Biography, Cultural Memory,

and the Continental Fur Trade

Edited by

WILLIAM J. BUXTON

McGill-Queen's University Press

Montreal & Kingston · London · Chicago

© McGill-Queen's University Press 2019

ISBN 978-0-7735-5860-1 (cloth)
ISBN 978-0-7735-5861-8 (paper)
ISBN 978-0-7735-5975-2 (ePDF)
ISBN 978-0-7735-5976-9 (ePUB)

Legal deposit fourth quarter 2019
Bibliothèque nationale du Québec

Printed in Canada on acid-free paper that is 100% ancient forest free (100% post-consumer recycled), processed chlorine free

We acknowledge the support of the Canada Council for the Arts.

Nous remercions le Conseil des arts du Canada de son soutien.

Library and Archives Canada Cataloguing in Publication

Title: Harold Innis on Peter Pond : biography, cultural memory, and the continental fur trade / edited by William J. Buxton.
Names: Innis, Harold A. (Harold Adams), 1894-1952, author. | Buxton, William, 1947- editor.
Description: Includes bibliographical references and index.
Identifiers: Canadiana (print) 20190188731 | Canadiana (ebook) 20190188790 | ISBN 9780773558618 (paper) | ISBN 9780773558601 (cloth) | ISBN 9780773559752 (ePDF) | ISBN 9780773559769 (ePUB)
Subjects: LCSH: Pond, Peter, 1740-1807. | LCSH: Fur traders—Northwest, Canadian—Biography. | LCSH: Explorers—Northwest, Canadian—Biography. | LCSH: Fur trade—Canada—History. | LCGFT: Biographies.
Classification: LCC FC3212.1.P65 155 2019 | DDC 971.2/01092—dc23

In memory of Paul Heyer

Contents

Preface and Acknowledgments | ix
Introduction: Peter Pond: Requiem for a Fur Trader
  and Adventurer | xiii

1 INNIS'S WRITINGS ON PETER POND AND THE FUR TRADE

"The North West Company," *Canadian Historical Review* 8
  (1927) | 3
"Peter Pond in 1780," *Canadian Historical Review* 9 (1928) | 18
"Peter Pond and the Influence of Capt. James Cook on Exploration
  in the Interior of North America," RSC Trans. [Royal Society of
  Canada Transactions], 3rd ser., 22 (1928), s. ii | 20
The Fur Trade in Canada. Toronto: University of Toronto Press,
  1930 | 32
Peter Pond: Fur Trader and Adventurer. Toronto: R.S. Irwin &
  Gordon, 1930 | 47
"Some Further Material on Peter Pond," *Canadian Historical
  Review* 16 (1935) | 130
"A Note on Recent Publications on the Fur Trade," *Canadian
  Review of Economics and Political Science / Revue canadienne
  d'Économique et de Science politique* 2 (4) (November 1936) | 135

"Alexander Mackenzie, Peter Pond, David Thompson," in *Les explorateurs célèbres*, ed. André Leroi-Gourhan. Paris: Éditions d'art Lucien Mazenod, 1947 | 149

2 CANNON-INNIS CORRESPONDENCE

Introduction | 159
Mrs LeGrand Cannon to Harold Innis, 11 September 1932 | 161
Harold Innis to Mrs LeGrand Cannon, 15 September 1932 | 162
Mrs LeGrand Cannon to Harold Innis, 25 September 1932 | 162
Mrs LeGrand Cannon to Harold Innis, 18 October 1932 | 163
Harold Innis to Mrs LeGrand Cannon, 21 October 1932 | 164
Mrs LeGrand Cannon to Harold Innis, 1 November 1932 | 165
Mrs LeGrand Cannon to Harold Innis, 28 April 1935 | 166
Harold Innis to Mrs LeGrand Cannon, 21 May 1935 | 166

3 R. HARVEY FLEMING MATERIAL

Harold Innis, R. Harvey Fleming, and the North American
Fur Trade | 175
R. Harvey Fleming, "Trading Ventures of Peter Pond
in Minnesota" | 198
Documents | 201

Glossary | 215
References | 221
Index | 245

Preface and Acknowledgments

This book is a testament to the Cheshire cat's famous maxim: "If you don't know where you want to go, then it doesn't matter what path you take" (Carroll 1865). But aware of Marshall McLuhan's sage advice that one should not "look at the present through a rear view mirror" (McLuhan and Fiore 1967, 74–5), I wished to avoid the cul de sacs and potholes that have bedevilled the routes previously taken by commentators on Innis, marked with well-intended but largely misleading signposts. Yet, as the late Paul Heyer pointed out, Innis's own pathways could not easily be captured by this cartographic landscape (Heyer 2004, 2013). Seemingly eschewing materialist, macroscopic claims, Innis evinced an intense interest in exploring biography, most markedly in his largely neglected memoir on Peter Pond (Pond and Innis, 1930). The desire to account for this incongruence between standard views on Innis and his extensive biographical work animated my research. It quickly became evident to me that Pond was more than a passing interest for Innis; charting the life of the fur trader preoccupied him for more than two decades, intersecting with his ongoing studies of the fur trade itself. The more that I delved into Innis's engagement with Peter Pond, the more convinced I became that this endeavour could help shed light on the life and times of the (still largely) "unknown Innis" (Cooper 1977).

The line of argument for the introductory essay was developed in talks given at meetings of the Canadian Communication Association and the

Canadian Historical Association and at a conference ("Excavating Media: Devices, Processes, Apparatuses") held at Cambridge University. In addition, I benefited from the responses to invited presentations given at the John F. Kennedy Institute of North American Studies (Die Freie Universität Berlin), at the Frankfurt Memory Studies Platform (Johann Wolfgang Goethe-Universität, Frankfurt am Main), at the International Research Institute for Cultural Techniques and Media Philosophy (Bauhaus-Universität Weimar), at Le Centre de recherche interuniversitaire sur la communication, l'information et la société (l'université du Québec à Montréal), and at the Bill Smiley Archives (Prince Albert Historical Society). I am very grateful for the kindnesses afforded to me by those who made arrangements for these events, particularly James Gabrillo and Nathaniel Zetter (Cambridge), Astrid Erll and Jarula Wegner (Frankfurt), Harald Wenzel and Regina Wenzel (Berlin), Gabriele Schabacher and Claudia Tittel (Weimar), Oumar Kane and Lena Huebner (Montreal), and Ken Guedo (Prince Albert).

I am also indebted to the help and support provided by the staff at numerous library and archival sites in both Canada and the United States. These include Chelsea Shriver (Rare Books and Special Collections, University of British Columbia); Patrick Hayes (University Archives and Special Collections, University of Saskatchewan); Carla Reczek and Dawn Eurich (Detroit Public Library); Laura Weber, Erin Schultz, Jenny McElroy, Steve Nielsen, and Charles Rogers (Minnesota Historical Society); Ed Surato (Whitney Library of the New Haven Museum); Deirdre Bryden (Queen's University Archives); Harold Averill, Loryl MacDonald, and Barbara Edwards (University of Toronto Archives and Record Management Services); Nathalie Vallières, Denise Guindon, Paula Clark Mann, and Kimberly Catraneo (Parks Canada); Elizabeth Ridolfo and John Shoesmith (Thomas Fisher Rare Book Library); Richie Sue Allen (Library and Archives Canada); Elerina Aldamar (Oregon Historical Society), and a representative of the Neville Public Museum of Brown County, Green Bay, Wisconsin.

Given that issues related to the continental fur trade, cultural history, Canadian historiography, and biography-writing were largely *terra incognita* for me, I have learned a great deal about these and related subjects through exchanges with those with much more expertise on these subjects than I, including Michael Stamm, Arthur Ray, David Wilson, Carolyn

Preface and Acknowledgments

Podruchny, Donald Wright, Agnes Ladon, Scott Flemming, Jeffrey Brison, Nicole St-Onge, Jean Barman, Liam Young, and Deidre Simmons.

In my efforts to make better sense of Peter Pond – through the lens of Harold Innis's writings – I have been helped enormously by a number of colleagues and institutions. Anne Innis Dagg, on behalf of the Harold Innis estate, has kindly provided permission to republish some of Innis's writings and correspondence in this volume. Peter Pond's "Memorandum of Goods Rec[ei]ved from Mr Shaney [Jacques Chénier], Lea bay [La Baye] 22 May 1775" has been published courtesy of the Burton Historical Collection, Detroit Public Library. Ryan Scheiding has been of enormous assistance in making Innis's rendition of Peter Pond's memoir more intelligible. Catherine Burns kindly provided me with three original letters sent by Innis to Florence Pond Cannon. Marian Scott, through her efforts to have Pond's legacy given greater recognition by cultural institutions, has given me insights into the extent to which the fur trader's importance for Canadian history has largely gone unrecognized (Scott 2018). Barry Gough and Bill McDonald have unfailingly responded to my endless queries about Peter Pond's life and activities. It should be emphasized, of course, that I bear full responsibility for any shortcomings or oversights the final work may have.

It would have been impossible to complete this project without the solid and unstinting institutional support of Concordia University and l'Université Laval. In particular, I wish to acknowledge my gratitude to Carmen Taranto, Mary Melnyk, Donna Stewart, Sheelah O'Neill, Mircea Mandache, Michele Kaplan, Frederick Clayman, Charles R. Acland, Véronique Nguyen-Duy, Catherine Savard, and Arnaud Anciaux.

I have also been privileged to draw on the publishing expertise of the staff at McGill-Queen's University Press, who have worked diligently to have this volume see the light of day. They include Jonathan Crago, Kathleen Fraser, Finn Purcell, and Jennifer Roberts. Ian MacKenzie's copyediting of the (rather unwieldy) manuscript has been exemplary in every respect. My preparation of this volume was funded by an Insight grant (#435-2017-0937) of the Social Sciences and Humanities Research Council of Canada.

Manon, Océane, and Jesse Lee, besides filling my life with love, joy, and their passionate enthusiasm, have patiently endured the constant presence of two mysterious historical figures in our household for what must have seemed to have been an interminable length of time.

Finally, as the manuscript for this book was nearing completion, I was heartbroken to learn of the death of my friend, colleague, and co-author, Paul Heyer. It was through Paul's sterling example that I first became acquainted with the history of media and communication thought. And it was his pioneering work on Innis's "history from the inside" that originally inspired me to explore the latter's biographical engagement with Peter Pond. While I was very saddened that Paul was suddenly and tragically taken from us, my hope is that the dedication of this book to the memory of him might in some small way help to keep that memory alive.

Introduction
Peter Pond: Requiem for a Fur Trader and Adventurer

Innis's Biographical Work

Harold Innis has long been considered as someone whose discussions of political and social life were marked by an emphasis on material factors – with particular reference to technology. Such an analysis, according to commentators, pervaded not only his early work on political economy but also his later writings on communication. All were thought to be characterized by an emphasis upon structure, with little emphasis given to issues of agency and the place of the individual in history.[1]

This neglect of Innis's engagement with biography is an artefact of how his oeuvres have been characterized. Not only has it been assumed that he was preoccupied with staples (and then communication technology), but also that his contributions were defined by the production of major staples tomes, each produced over ten-year spans (Creighton 1957). His biographical work has largely been ignored because of these biases.

Departing from most treatments of Innis, Paul Heyer gave close attention to the extent to which biography was a central part of his oeuvres (2003, 2004, 2013). His own biography of Innis interweaves discussions of Innis's treatment of individual life narratives into his examination of Innis's work and career (2003). In particular, Heyer discusses at some length Innis's biographies of Andrew McPhail (McPhail and Innis 1940), Peter Pond (Innis 1930c), and Simeon Perkins (Perkins and Innis 1948).[2] He demonstrates how Innis's biographical treatments arose of out of his broader interests in staples economies: Pond for the fur trade, McPhail for the wheat economy[3] and Perkins for timber, leather, and the fisheries (Heyer 2003, 2004). According to Heyer, Innis's well-known concern with the "material, technological, and broad social conditions of history" was complemented by his interest in what could be called "'history from the inside' – an approach that acknowledges the role of the individual as a witness to history" (Heyer 2013, 72).[4]

While Heyer has been able to identify the importance of biography for Innis, he has provided little detail about what he means by "history from the inside," and how it relates to Innis's wide-ranging engagement with biographical studies. In particular, he treats Innis's biographical work as somehow separate from his broader structural concerns, rather than intersecting with them in some way. This is likely rooted in his assumption that Innis's approach was detached and contemplative, with little attention given to the broader stakes involved in choosing to do biographical work on particular figures. However, if one views biographical writing as a form of intervention – with implications for the construction of cultural memory – I argue, it becomes possible to understand how structure and biography intersected in Innis's writings.

This would involve examining Innis's intellectual practice as informed by civic engagement, generating new institutions, reconfiguring old ones, recasting public opinion, as well as redirecting political and social practices. My contention is that Innis's life-long project was informed by the French possibilist tradition of cultural geography (Berdoulay and Chapman 1987), which eschewed environmental determinism in favour of an approach that emphasized the interplay between geography and human endeavour. Innis's intellectual practice, I argue, could be seen as a form of engaged possibilism, as reflected in his efforts to help reconfigure time and space through his research, pedagogy, and administrative work.[5] His activities as an intellectual, I argue, went well beyond making his views known to the public on the important political and social issues of the day (Salter and Dahl 1999). He did not confine himself to intervening in the public sphere, but rather sought to shape public life through a diverse series of intersecting and overlapping knowledge initiatives.[6] Innis's intellectual practice as it pertained to the building of knowledge systems was by no means static. His thought and engagement became increasingly reflexive as he became more aware of how

Introduction

the production of knowledge by social scientists was inherently tied into the reality they purported to study.

Innis's intellectual practice, as embodied in his historical studies, was very much geared to excavating the foundations that had set the terms for contemporary civilization (Buxton 1998). He could be viewed as an advocate of "public history" *avant la lettre*,[7] a central aspect of which was his biographical work, which involved shaping cultural memory by bringing to light life narratives that had been neglected. Innis's engagement with biography underpinned his involvement with commemoration through official channels.

Biographies for Innis represented the constitutive aspect of his engagement with broader structures and practices. From his early days as a soldier until his untimely death in 1952, Innis was very much concerned with biography and individual experience in relation to larger contexts. His very first publication examined how the lives of soldiers were bound up with economic issues (1918a). Along the same lines, his master's thesis dealt with the problems faced by soldiers returning to Canada (1918b, Innis et al. 2016). Throughout his career he wrote numerous obituaries (largely for former colleagues) that characteristically addressed their contributions to scholarship and/or public life.[8] He also penned forewords and prefaces to biographical works.[9] His narrative about the temporal and spatial aspects of settlement in northern Canada was grounded in thoughts he had distilled from various memoirs, diaries, and recollections (Buxton 2013; Audette-Longo and Buxton 2014). Along the same lines, he recurrently reviewed biographies written about persons whose work was familiar to him[10] as well as published versions of journals and diaries.[11] In his view, biographies worked in concert. If a cluster of biographies related to a particular theme or issue could be written, this would allow one to better understand the meaning and significance of a particular life.[12]

In line with Thomas Carlyle's "great man" theory of history (Carlyle and MacMechan 1904), he contended that it was at least in part by virtue of the actions taken by key individuals that major transformations took place. More often than not, his discussions of major industries or currents of thought also involved an examination of the thought and practice of leading figures. His *History of the Canadian Pacific Railway* (1923) formed the backdrop for the short entries he wrote a decade later for the *Encyclopedia of the Social Sciences*[13] as well as a review of a book written about Lord Strathcona, the railway magnate (1926; MacNaughton and Vaughan 1926).

Innis's approach involved shedding light on the foundations of a particular field or practice through the lens of a particular individual's contributions to them. Having realized the importance of Thorstein Veblen's views for his own emergent analysis of industrial society, he assembled a bibliography of the institutionalist economist's major works, which included an insightful biographical statement (1929a). His interest in the Western cooperative movement led him to annotate Andrew McPhail's diary and to write introductions and conclusions to the volume (McPhail and Innis 1940).[14] In order to gain insights into life in colonial Nova Scotia he edited a volume (1766–80) – with an introduction and notes – of Colonel Simeon Perkins (Perkins and Innis 1948). As part of his early interest in the history of the newspaper industry in nineteenth-century Britain, he examined the biographies of figures who had taken a leadership role in journalism (Buxton and Dickens 2006; Innis 2006). His massive history of communications manuscript, compiled in the last dozen years of his life, contains extensive biographical material. This served as an ideographic counterpoint to the fulsome items pertaining to the material aspects of the development of paper and printing from antiquity to early modernity (Innis 2015). Finally, during the summer of 1952 (months before he passed away), Innis wrote a memoir of his own life covering the years 1894 to 1922. While not very revealing about his personal and emotional life, it does provide a good deal of information about his family background as well as what he considered to have been the major events of his life up to his early years as a faculty member at the University of Toronto (Innis 2016).

And what about the fur trade? While Innis was attentive to the biographies of those whose activities had shaped the industry (e.g., 1935d, 1935e), he gave particular attention to Peter Pond. Innis, however, was not interested in Pond's biography for its own sake. He largely eschewed detailed interpretations of his personality, character, values, and motivations – the usual stuff of biographical work.[15] Rather, Pond's biography represented a point of entry into understanding the origins and development of precursors to the North West Company, which originally came to dominate the North American fur trade. Indeed, Innis went so far as to claim that Pond could be viewed as a "father of Confederation," ranking

Introduction xvii

with the political figures that hammered out the Charlottetown accord.[16] Through charting Pond's activities in time and space, Innis sought to provide insights into the extent to which the organization of the early fur trade had implications for subsequent patterns of communication, settlement, and governance.

Genealogy of the Peter Pond Memoir

Innis did not simply write about Pond; he helped to shape the process through which Pond's memoir was published and assessed. His work with the document was very much informed by earlier efforts to bring it to the attention of various publics. The key figures in having Pond's journal see the light of day were likely Mrs Nathan Pond (née Sophia Matilda Mooney, 1836–1920), and her husband Dr Nathan Gillette Pond (1832–1894).[17] Born in New York, Dr Pond was the great-nephew of Peter Pond and the great-grandson of Charles Pond (Peter's brother). Both were avid amateur historians and were very interested in the Pond family's history. Sophia is credited with having rescued Pond's manuscript from destruction. According to her account, the "ancient manuscripts were found by me in 1868, about to be destroyed with waste paper in the kitchen of the home of Hon. Charles Hobby Pond." Evidently a member of the family was in the process of "tearing off pages from an old time-stained document." She felt that it looked interesting and asked what it was. She was told that it was "nothing but old 'Sir' Peter Pond's journeys [and was] not worth anything." Sophia Pond was "welcome to it" (Mrs N.G. Pond and McLachlan 1906, 235).

Taking advantage of this serendipity was consistent with her "habit of devouring everything that looks interesting." Even though she was not herself a descendent of Peter Pond, she was intrigued by the "old Manuscripts [which were] almost undecipherable." She felt that they were "of much import" and could throw "a strong clear light on one of the most important periods in American history." She took it upon herself to decipher the "musty sheets," fascinated by "the quaint diction and phonetic spelling." She marvelled at the document, which in her view chronicled the "daring adventures of the old pioneer fur trader who had so picturesquely narrated the story of his life in the Northwest wilderness of America" (235).

While Mrs Pond believed the journal to be a "contribution to history" and to be of "value," she did not immediately look into having it published. Rather, it languished for over two decades before she began doing research about its significance. Evidently aware of Peter Pond's later career north of the great lakes, Mrs Pond wrote to "Hon. David R. McCord M.A. B.C.L. of Montreal, Canada, one of the best authorities on questions of Canadian history" who "gave [her] much data" (236). External circumstances may also have played a role in prompting Mrs Pond to see the document through to publication. Her husband, Dr Nathan Pond, who had left a business career in New York to devote himself to cattle breeding and genealogical work at a country estate near Milford, completed a number of initiatives that were designed to highlight the contributions of some of the town's most notable residents. Probably the most long-lasting and visible of his biographical efforts was the memorial bridge dedicated in 1889, which honoured the founders of the town and commemorated the 250th anniversary of its settlement (N.G. Pond 1987). Dr Pond not only "conceived the idea of the 'Memorial bridge'" but prepared "ancestral tablets" that adorned it. These were considered to be "remarkable to their completeness and ... invaluable to their fortunate possessors."

It could be seen as "a fitting monument to one who laboured long and faithfully to accomplish it" (N.G. Pond 1906, 161). In line with the memorial-bridge project, during the town's commemorative year, he published a book on its tombstones (N.G. Pond 1889). Together with Sophia Pond and George Clark Bryant, he compiled a collection of materials on "Old Milford Families" (Bryant, Pond, and Pond, n.d.). However, his most detailed and painstaking biographical undertaking related to Milford was a genealogy of the Pond family from the time of the town's settlement to the present generation. Unfortunately, Dr Pond was not able to finish the project, as he passed away in 1894. However, Sophia Pond took on the responsibility of seeing the genealogy through to publication, binding it together with her ongoing work on Peter Pond's journal. She returned to her research on the document in the year after her husband's death by contacting Robert Wallace McLachlan, a prominent antiquarian and numismatic authority in Montreal.[18] She was able to secure evidence from him that she felt proved her belief that Pond was one of the creators of the famous "North West Company."

Introduction   xix

Quite taken with Washington Irving's account of the company in *Astoria*, she viewed Pond as a founder of an organization that "for a time held lordly sway over the wintry lakes and boundless forests of the Canadas almost equal to that of the East India Company over the voluptuous climes and magnificent realms of the 'Orient.'"

Mrs Pond's romantic reading of the journal most likely informed not only her selection of an outlet for it, but also how it was ultimately framed and presented. Given that she viewed Pond as a figure who would have broad popular appeal by virtue of his colourful life, and that she was broadly interested in how family genealogy related to the broader community, it made sense for her to seek publication in a journal that sought to make history accessible to the general public. That outlet was the *Connecticut Magazine*, published on a quarterly basis in nearby New Haven. As it was described in notes from its publisher (quoting from the *Bridgeport Standard*) that appeared in one of the early issues, "This publication is worthy of the hearty support of the people of Connecticut, as it serves as a medium for the interchange of opinions and facts upon our state history, which is one to be proud of, and offers a suitable repository on a historic, genealogical, and antiquarian lore that is or ever will be of interest to the inhabitants of Connecticut."[19]

It is noteworthy that Pond's journal did not appear entirely on its own. It was paired with a revised version of Nathan Gillette Pond's genealogy of the Pond family of Milford, which had appeared in the previous issue of the magazine. It covered seven generations of the Pond family in New England, beginning with John and William Pond, who accompanied John Winthrop when the latter arrived in Salem, Massachusetts, with the "great fleet" in 1630. It ended with an entry on Charles Hobby Pond (1807–1860) and his four progeny, including himself. In between, he provided brief biographical entries on members of the Pond family in succeeding generations, along with much longer entries on those he considered to be of greater importance (or perhaps had left more information about their lives).[20] Among these was Captain Charles Pond (1744–1832), a fourth-generation family member whose exploits in the American War of Independence are described by Dr Pond in minute detail (leaving space in the entry for the results of "future work"). And what of Charles Pond's elder brother Peter (1740–1807), author of the journal that had fallen into his widow's hands?

Nathan Pond confused him with Peter Pond Jr (1763–1813), claiming that in 1779 he accompanied his brother on the "'new Defence,' a small brig built at Guilford, but fitted and equipped in New Haven" (N.G. Pond 1906, 165). Yet as Chapin points out, it was seventeen-year-old Peter Pond Jr who had joined the *New Defence* as "sailing master's mate with Captain Charles Pond of Milford" (his uncle) (2014, 183). The young Pond's father, Peter Senior, by that time had been northwest of the Great Lakes for more than four years, including the winter of 1778–79 in the Athabasca territory. It was evident that Nathan Pond had given little attention to his great-uncle's diary and was able to only remark in his genealogy of Milford's Pond family that he "was evidently of a roving, speculative disposition" (N.G. Pond 1906, 163).[21]

Even though the manuscript was in an unfinished state, Sophia Pond – with the assistance of the eminent genealogist Charles L.N. Camp – prepared it for publication.[22] Unfortunately, they did not notice the erroneous material on Peter Pond, nor did they try to revise his entry so that it would better reflect the extent to which he was important. However, a note from the editor included after Pond's entry stated that his journal was "an important historical document in connection with this Pond genealogy and will be published in the second part of this compilation" (163). And at the end of the document another editor's note announced that the following issue of the magazine would include "*The Journal of Peter Pond* from whom the Ponds of Milford, Connecticut, directly descend" (176).

The virtual absence of Peter Pond from his great-nephew's genealogy of the Milford Pond family would seem to explain – at least in part – Sophia Pond's framing of the Peter Pond journal. Given that the entry on him in Nathan Pond's account was in equal measure mistaken and cursory, this meant that in providing a portrait of Pond she was largely working with a tabula rasa and could define him in any way she saw fit. Inspired as she was by Washington Irving's *Astoria* (1836), she chose to link his experiences to the "very romantic period" of the early fur trade, whose pioneers, in seeking "rich peltries of the North … penetrated at once, in defiance of difficulties and dangers, to the heart of savage countries; laying open the hidden secrets of the wilderness" (Mrs N.G. Pond 1906, 235).

At the same time, perhaps in an effort to demonstrate that Pond's accomplishments were not confined to the United States, she included after

Introduction xxi

her own introduction a statement written by R.W. McLachlan, with whom she had communicated both a decade earlier and just prior to preparing the Pond material for publication.[23] As reflected in the title given to his brief article ("Connecticut Adventurer Was a Founder of Famous Fur Trust in 1783"), McLachlan stressed that the trading pool that he formed was the "beginning of what afterwards became the powerful Northwest Fur Company" (*sic*). McLachlan also provided an assessment of Pond's character, disposition, and abilities. He conceded that he was "haughty and arrogant and suspicious in his dealings not only with his opponents but with his partners." But at the same time he described his character as "most energetic and his courage and activity as truly wonderful." He stressed above all that Pond was very diligent, in that he "employed his spare time in useful works and in studying the topography of the country." While the map of the Northwest that he produced was "very inaccurate," it revealed his "natural ability, close attention to detail, and keen observations." Finally, perhaps as a way of providing Pond with the patina of civilization, McLachlan noted that he was a charter member of the prestigious Beaver Club founded in Montreal in 1785. This was a very exclusive group; its criterion for membership was having spent at least two winters "in the wilds of the Northwest." Yet the rewards for having undergone this experience were far removed from the ordeals of coping with life in the wilderness. Each member was entitled to receive a gold medal "engraved no doubt by a local artist" and was "enjoined to wear [it] at the club meetings," which were highly convivial events held fortnightly during the winter months. Given that Dr Pond's genealogy of the Pond family gave particular attention to external forms of recognition (such as prestigious positions, military honours, and awards), McLachlan's references to the North West Company and the Beaver Club medal served to offset the vulgarity and illiteracy that characterized the document that followed. They also ensured that Peter Pond could be considered as a worthy addendum to the genealogy of the Milford Pond family that had largely ignored him (McLachlan 1906, 236–7).

In preparing the document for publication, Sophia Pond simply transcribed what Pond had written (in his highly idiosyncratic orthography), making no effort to provide clarification of what he meant by his frequently inaccessible vocabulary and phrasing. She also did not provide any annotations. However, she (or perhaps the magazine's editor) provided headings and subheadings that broke up the text into a series of sections, rendering Pond's journal into what was likely considered to be a thrilling and compelling narrative. The story told was one replete with adventure and exotic encounters with different "savages" in the wilderness.[24] The text was also accompanied by two wood engravings by Octavius Carr Darley taken from John W. Deforest's *History of the Indians of Connecticut* (Forest and Darley 1851).[25] At the end of the text – following an explanation of why it ended to abruptly and reiterating how the "ancient manuscript" was discovered – was a photograph by "Randall" entitled "The American Indian." Its subject matter was a statue located at the Corning Fountain in Bushnell Park, Hartford.[26] Given that Peter Pond's encounters with Connecticut indigenous people received little, if any, attention in his journal, one can only conclude that the purpose of the inclusion of these images was to connect Pond's text with the knowledge and experience of the magazine's readers during a time when American frontier life was coming into prominence.[27]

All the same, the images and their captions were for the most part at odds with the rather lurid headings that had been inserted into the text, which largely reflected Washington Irving's romantic depictions of frontier life; these had served Sophia Pond as a point of reference for understanding Peter Pond's diary. Instead, they presented a very sympathetic representation of the plight of the American Indian, emphasizing how their way of life had been destroyed by their encounter with white-settler colonization.[28] That Peter Pond's text was subject to tugs and pulls such as this demonstrates the extent to which its meaning and significance have been contested over time, depending on the outlooks and interests of those involved in making the document available to the public.

The original manuscript, its various incarnations notwithstanding, has survived largely intact. It was passed from the son of Sophia and Nathan Pond (Harold Gillette Pond) to the son of their niece (Florence Atherton Pond), LeGrand "Lee" Cannon Jr, a well-known author.[29] He had two sisters, one of whom (Laura Tuttle Cannon, BA, Vassar 1918) had been enrolled in the Graduate School at Yale in 1919–20. Evidently Florence Cannon not only arranged to have a photostat copy[30] of the original memoir made (and sent to Innis, as we shall see) but took it upon herself to have

Introduction

xxiii

the entire memoir copied into more legible handwriting. It was her daughter Laura (Tuttle Cannon) Burns who completed this task.[31] The original of the memoir was donated to Yale University in 1947. The current whereabouts of Ms Burns's transcription is not known.

The next effort to publish the manuscript occurred two years after Sophia Pond's version appeared in the *Connecticut Magazine*. Reuben Gold Thwaites, secretary and superintendent of the Wisconsin State Historical Society, was in the process of editing an extensive series of volumes, each comprising primary documents related to the history of Wisconsin.[32] These were presented more or less chronologically and organized into thematic clusters, each reflecting the regime that was dominant at the time. Interspersed among these were clusters of documents that shed light on particular historical phenomena. Volume 18 of the series was made up of three such sections: "The French Regime in Wisconsin – 1743–1760,"[33] "The British Regime in Wisconsin – 1760–1800," and "The Mackinac Register of Marriages – 1725–1821." Since Wisconsin had received statehood only in 1848, the series of volumes was painted on a broader canvas, covering developments in what was called the "upper Great lakes region," of which the state of Wisconsin was historically and geographically a part.

While putting together the section on the British Regime in Wisconsin (in volume 18 of the series), Reuben Thwaites had become familiar with the journal of Peter Pond that had been published in the *Connecticut Magazine*. In his view, the rationale for its original publication was that it represented a "curious example of orthography," and that it described "the adventures of a Connecticut native in the far West." Thwaites's somewhat dismissive assessment of the reasons for the journal's publication seemed to rest on the assumption that Sophia Pond and the magazine's editor viewed it primarily in terms of its entertainment value and its contributions to Connecticut collective life. What Thwaites had in mind for the journal was something quite different. "Impressed with its value as one of the earliest English descriptions of Wisconsin," he sought and obtained permission to publish it (Thwaites and State Historical Society of Wisconsin 1908, 314). More specifically, the journal was included within the chronological narrative provided by primary documents related to the British Regime in Wisconsin during the late eighteenth century. Given that the memoir covered the period from 1740 to 1775 and included a good deal of material on Pond's childhood and early years in colonial America, it did not fit readily into the section that had been designated for it. Rather than treating the journal as a marker for the entire period it covered (which would have meant ignoring other important items), Thwaites placed it as a spanning document, overlapping with the previous material (going back to the beginning part of the section "The British Take Command") and dovetailing with the item that followed it – a letter from Maj. A.S. De Peyster to Charles Langlade, dated 4 July 1776 (355). Pond's journal ended abruptly in 1775, shortly before he departed for the British-controlled region north of the Great Lakes. As for Pond's life and career prior to entering the upper Mississippi region, Thwaites simply ignored it in an early synoptic footnote, perhaps because he did not deem this material relevant to the Upper Great Lakes / Wisconsin focus of the section. However, he did provide a detailed and cogent account of Pond's life after he had "entered the Northwest fur trade" (314).

Finally, referring to the Pond genealogy that had been published in the *Connecticut Magazine*, he politely corrected the erroneous information that it had included about Peter Pond. According to the genealogy, Thwaites wrote, "he [Peter Pond] married Susanna Newell, and had at least two children, of whom Peter (1763–1813) must have accompanied his uncle Charles in naval operations during the Revolutionary War. Peter Pond the elder was in the Northwest during the entire Revolutionary period" (315).

The *Wisconsin Historical Collections* version of the journal dropped all of the headings, subheadings, and images that had been added to the *Connecticut Magazine* version.[34] Unlike the earlier iteration of the journal, the new version contained what the editor considered to be the correct spelling for the words that Pond was using. These were enclosed within square brackets following the Pond misspelling in question (e.g., Capatalasion [capitulation]). Moreover, the Thwaites-edited version, unlike its predecessors, contained numerous footnotes. These appear to have been written to serve purposes such as tracing the origins of the manuscript, outlining the later life and career of Pond, providing information about key figures, places, and events mentioned in the text, suggesting sources for more detailed accounts of particular issues, and clarifying passages in the text. Overall, the footnotes served to distil from Pond's sometimes unwieldy memoir insights into the workings of the British regime in the upper Great Lakes region

Introduction

during the late eighteenth century. They also provided a means for linking Pond's journal to the earlier documents that had appeared earlier in the series, thereby contributing to its coherence and continuity.

Pond in the Innis Oeuvres

While Innis was familiar with both earlier published accounts of Pond's journal, he decided to use the Wisconsin rather than the Connecticut version. Indeed, in deciding whether or not he could rely on the journal for his ongoing research on Peter Pond, he noted that its "details which have been checked by its editor, the late R.G. Thwaites leave no doubt as to its accuracy and authenticity" (Innis and Pond 1930, 144). And while he shared with Sophia Pond and Reuben Thwaites an enthusiasm for the document, he approached it in a manner that was quite at odds with their respective efforts. In both cases, the journal had been of interest for what it revealed about the emergence and development of state-centred collectivities, namely those of Connecticut and Wisconsin. But at the same time, because the journal ended abruptly before Pond had left the upper Mississippi for the territory northwest of the Great Lakes, the two American editors were not able to make the case for Pond's historical significance, based on his somewhat limited accomplishments in the United States. Hence they both relied on Pond's later activities as a fur trader (as well as founder of the North West Company), explorer, and mapmaker in order to elevate the importance of Pond in cultural memory. In effect, Pond's later activities in the Northwest became the background to the foreground of his earlier life and career in colonial America.

Innis essentially reversed this equation: Pond's career in Canada became the foreground and his earlier life served as the background. Moreover Innis's examination of the trajectory of Pond's life in Canada was bound up with his ongoing study of the early fur trade, with particular reference to how the North West Company had emerged and developed, eventually becoming a continent-wide operation. And since Innis's study of the fur trade was not confined to *The Fur Trade in Canada* but encompassed numerous other writings and interventions spanning almost a quarter century, this meant that his work on Pond by necessity was emergent as well. His biography of Pond was not a "one-off" piece; his engagement with the fur trader and adventurer resulted in an evolving body of work, consisting of a number of writings related to Pond, exploration, and the fur trade that appeared between 1928 and 1947 – prior and subsequent to his major biography of 1930.[35] Arguably Innis's engagement with Pond can be divided into two periods – that preceding his 1930 biography and that subsequent to it. His early work was grounded in his commitment to Canadian nation-state building, with particular reference to configuring its time and space. In the second period, which spanned 1932 to 1947, his emphasis had shifted to what can best be described as a form of "continentalism" (Bélanger 2011; Wright 2015). with a focus on how Pond, exploration, and the fur trade could best be viewed within a North American context.[36]

The origins of this engagement can be found in Innis's first major publication, *A History of the Canadian Pacific Railway* (1923). This text has often been dismissed as piece of juvenilia dealing with a subject matter that Innis abandoned in favour of the more promising staples industries – grounded in Canada's geographic make-up.[37] However, it not only makes numerous references to the fur trade but also lays out a framework – namely the "drainage basin" theory of development – that Innis was to use with great effect in some of his later writings (e.g., Innis and Lower 1933). In his view, the origins of Canada were rooted in the settlements that developed in the drainage basins of the Pacific Coast, Hudson Bay, and the St Lawrence River (1923, 74). Within this compass, Pond is given brief mention for having founded Fort Athabasca in 1778 (24). By acknowledging Pond in this manner, however, Innis was undermining the drainage-basin framework that anchored his first monograph. Pond's fort, often considered to have been the first settlement in the vast Athabasca territory, was located not within the Hudson Bay drainage basin, but within the Mackenzie River basin, which was mentioned but not examined in the volume. Innis's first major "dirt research" venture, which took place shortly after the publication of his railway history, can be seen as a corrective to this oversight. Accompanied by his former McMaster classmate (and fellow Great War veteran John Long), Innis travelled to Edmonton and Waterways by rail and then made his way up to the mouth of the Mackenzie River by canoe and steamship. The research conducted on this trip provided Innis with material initially used for a fourth-year seminar he was teaching as part of

Introduction xxvii

the University of Toronto Commerce course, and subsequently for his two monographs on the fur trade (1927b, [1930] 1956).

This suggests that Innis's early projects were shaped by his efforts to make sense of Canada's shifting place in the world. His history of the Canadian Pacific Railway stemmed from his interest in understanding how Canadian sub-civilizations in various drainage basins had been linked through railway technology (1923, 1–3). His work on the fur trade began with an exploration of how the industry functioned in the modern era, with particular reference to Canada (1927c). The extensive research he conducted in 1927 on mining and forestry / pulp and paper was intended to contribute to the building of a "New Ontario," premised on the province's exploitation of its abundant natural resources (Lower and Innis 1936; Nelles 2005). His visit to western Hudson Bay and northwestern Manitoba in 1929 was prompted by an interest in how the Hudson Bay railway could potentially reconfigure the transportation infrastructure of Canada's north and beyond (1930b; Audette-Longo and Buxton 2014).

After *The Fur Trade of Canada* (1927b), Innis plunged into completing the projected historical backdrop to the contemporary fur trade, culminating in *The Fur Trade in Canada* ([1930] 1956). The editor at Yale University Press responded favourably to the manuscript in the spring of 1928.[38] The final version of the manuscript was submitted to Yale University Press in May 1929.[39] After negotiation with a number of publishers, his volume *Select Documents* was published by the University of Toronto Press (1929b). He also oversaw the publication of the journal *Contributions in Canadian Economics*, which appeared from 1928 to 1933 (Drummond 1983, 74–5). The first two issues featured overviews by Innis of key works in the field of economics (Audette-Longo and Buxton 2014).

That Innis was becoming involved with a broad range of initiatives related to research in Canadian history was evident in his decision to become a member of the Champlain Society, an organization responsible for compiling and publishing key documents of relevance to the history of Canada.[40] He also became involved with the Public Archives of Canada and contributed to its efforts to acquire the Henry Kelsey papers (Kelsey 1929).[41]

His work on Pond seemed to have emerged from the research he had conducted in writing *The Fur Trade in Canada* ([1930] 1956). In his effort to understand the role played by the North West Company in the development of the early fur trade, he turned his attention to the company's precursors, namely the Montreal-based independent traders. Among these, the one who stood out for Innis – by virtue of his organizational accomplishments – was Peter Pond. In order to expand his knowledge related to these concerns, Innis corresponded with a number of persons and institutions. He sought to learn more about pemmican by consulting with his former student and colleague Owen Merriman,[42] as well as Clark Wissler of the American Museum of Natural History.[43] Photostats of various maps were acquired from the Library of Congress.[44] Inquiries were made about "the early History of Detroit and other parts of Michigan,"[45] and he acquired material related to the early American fur trade from both the Burton Historical Collection of the Public Library in Detroit[46] and the Minnesota Historical Society in St Paul, Minnesota.[47]

His first publication in this area was a detailed account of early efforts by independent traders to co-operate, which would eventually lead to the formation of the North West Company (1927c).[48] Using Masson's *Les Bourgeois de la Compagnie de Nord-Ouest* (1889) as a point of departure, he sought to unravel the agreements that had been reached by trading partners prior to the formal constitutions of the early nineteenth century. This involved not only tracing the number and distribution of shares, but also discerning the factors that underpinned the various amalgamations. Noting that the traders had come to recognize the importance of cooperation, he argued that "the North West Company of 1783–4 emerged as the result of the increased strength necessary to prosecute the trade in the Athabaska country, of the pressure toward the north which followed the dislocation of trade to Detroit incidental to the American Revolution, and of the disappearance of Albany as a rival base to Montreal. The Company of 1787 was a result of the impossibilities of competition in the trade" (1927c, 313–14). Central to Innis's analysis was the need of the North West Company to follow "the extension of trade into the Athabaska country." This drive to the north set in motion "small independent traders who combined in defensive groups" in order to get a piece of the action (315). This led to difficulties, given that the trade to the south was gradually disappearing. Since Pond had played such a pivotal role in opening up the Northwest to the fur trade, it is not surprising that Innis singled him out for attention.

Introduction   xxix

In a brief follow-up note he sought to correct an error he thought he had made in stating Pond's movements and whereabouts in 1779–81 (1928b).[49] Having examined the John Askin Papers held at the Detroit Public Library, he had determined that Pond had not returned to Montreal "after his first trip to Athabaska"; he had remained in the Northwest: while "licences were made out in Pond's name at Montreal in the spring of 1780 ... apparently he was not present" (333). Innis had thought it important to make this correction in order to be able to determine the origins of the North West Company with more precision.

Innis and Canadian Biographical Writing

Innis's biographical work on Pond can be understood as part of a strong current of biographical writing that was sweeping Canada in the late 1920s. In 1926 a flurry of biographical material appeared. As part of a revised "Makers of Canada" series (see W. Stewart Wallace 1926b) a new encyclopedia of Canadian history was included (Burpee 1926); Wallace's own *Dictionary of Canadian Biography* (1926a) also appeared. The new Makers of Canada series was an updated version of an initiative of the same name that had been published by George M. Morang from 1903 to 1907, edited by Pelham Edgar and Duncan Campbell Scott. Considered as the "first cooperative venture in Canadian historical writing," it embodied the idea that "each of the great figures of our history will be dealt with in a single volume ... each will be treated by a writer who is best fitted ... to deal with the particular topic" (Wallace 1926b, 325). Influenced by the thought of Thomas Carlyle (Carlyle and MacMechan 1904), biography had enjoyed a vogue after the turn of the century: it was perceived as "an unusually popular and successful form of expression for Canadian historians" and was "probably the most accessible form of history from the point of view of the general reader." Indeed the biography was viewed as an important means for educating the general public about broader political and social developments; it was claimed that "the history of an individual is often the history of a nation" (Klinck et al. 1976).[50] As Klinck et al. note, the Makers of Canada series embodied the Whiggish historiography of the day, which was preoccupied with particular periods, in particular the "conquest of New France" and the "struggle for responsible government" (1976). It neglected, however, "the movement for the union of British North America." This move towards confederation was viewed as "a corollary to responsible government, a natural outcome of the achievement of internal colonial liberty" within the framework of the British nation." Arguably, the new version of the Makers of Canada series retained the Whiggish orientation of its predecessor, but viewed the culmination of Canadian history not to be responsible government as a colony, but emergent sovereignty as an autonomous nation.[51] Hence, the original series was reworked, with some titles dropped and others added.[52] That Innis's views on biography were in line with the "neo-Whiggism" espoused by the volumes of the new Makers of Canada series was evident in his review of one of the volumes that had been added to the series, namely MacNaughton's and Vaughan's *Lord Strathcona* (1926). It is instructive that Innis chose this volume for review; Lord Strathcona (aka Donald Smith) was not only a major figure in the development of Canadian railways, but also had been a major figure in the fur trade. Echoing the thoughts of Buckingham and Ross on Alexander Mackenzie (1892), Innis felt that this work was "much more than a biography of Lord Strathcona"; it "was a history of the Dominion of Canada." In his view, "no one has approached [the authors in their] grasp of the main principles which have been behind the movement toward Confederation." While the text was "not in any sense the final word on the background of Canadian development ... it is the first volume which has shown an appreciation of the lines of the foundation." Indeed, "MacNaughton has performed in some sense for Canadian history a task similar to that which Lord Strathcona performed for Canadian expansion" (Innis 1926, 349).[53]

As we will now examine, Innis's point of reference for his subsequent biographical work on Pond was the historical ferment that accompanied Canada's 1927 Diamond Jubilee of Confederation. With its emphasis on how and to what extent Canada had progressed in the sixty years subsequent to Confederation, the Diamond Jubilee had adapted Whiggish views to Canadian realities in the late 1920s.

The Diamond Jubilee of Confederation

The Diamond Jubilee of Confederation placed particular emphasis on cultivating the history of Canada.[54] In line with his view that Canada had "too

Introduction xxxi

much geography and not enough history" (Osborne 2001), Prime Minister Mackenzie King remarked, during the summer of 1927, that "nothing had the Diamond Jubilee been more fruitful in than in the encouragement it has given to the study of Canadian history" (Kelley 1984, 53).[55] As Kelley noted, "Three major aspects of Canadian history were put to use – the exploration of the New World, the importance of the Fathers of Confederation, and the evolution of nationhood for Canada" (54). For Canadian historians, this meant abandoning the "imperial context" in favour of a national one. Theories that addressed events from the past in specific Canadian terms were to be deployed. In order to cultivate patriotism, historians were to stress the "role played by great and daring Canadians of the past." Along the same lines, the national committee of the Diamond Jubilee encouraged the creation of tableaux at the local level that "were tributes to the explorers, railway engineers ... nation builders of the past (54)."

This emphasis was evident in the handbook prepared for local committees about pageants, floats, and tableaux in which biographical material was prominently featured (Canada, National Committee ... and Lagacé 1927). In a section on historical biography it gives particular attention to the "new edition of The Makers of Canada," along with others thought to be of "special interest and importance." These included the material produced by the Champlain Society in the form of "narratives of such famous explorers and travellers as Champlain, Lescarbot, La Vérendrye, Hearne, and Thompson." In addition there were "many works devoted to the discoveries of LaSalle [as well as] Jacques Cartier." Finally, "Masson's *Les Bourgeois de la Compagnie du Nord-Ouest* (1889) contains the narratives of a number of the western fur traders" (44–5).

One of the local pageants that articulated this emphasis on biography was that directed by Amy Sternberg. Entitled *Historical Pageant* and produced for the IODE (Imperial Order Daughters of the Empire), it "premiered at Massey Hall in Toronto on Wednesday, 22 June and was performed for three consecutive nights plus a Saturday matinee." Consisting of "nine scenes and accompanying *tableaux vivants* ... [it] implied that the country had been shaped primarily by men like Jacques Cartier, Samuel de Champlain, Generals Wolfe and Montcalm, and the Fathers of Confederation" (Lindgren 2011, 2–3). Biographical portraits figured prominently in the various tableaux, perhaps most vividly in the penultimate tableau 7, "Fathers of Confederation," "modeled after Robert Harris's 1884 painting Conference at Québec in 1864, to settle the Basics of a Union of the British North American Provinces ... (also known as The Fathers of Confederation). One by one the actors portraying the Fathers of Confederation rose from the tableau and recited brief excerpts from the Confederation Debates" (10).

As orchestrated by the two Diamond Jubilee subcommittees, an emphasis was thus placed on historical enactment. On the academic and publishing side, the confederation served as a point of reference for defining both the present and the future. This involved extensive use of the biographical form in texts, but also through circulating images, such as those produced by C.W. Jefferys (1927). Commercial enterprises became involved, sponsoring exhibitions and texts with historical themes (Canadian Pacific Limited and ... Edward 1927; David Spencer Ltd 1927). Miniaturized versions of this could be seen in postage stamps, which stressed progress in pictorial forms, with particular reference to the fathers of Confederation (Martin 2015) and to forms of transportation. Echoing the Makers of Canada series, numerous biographies appeared, which dealt with figures thought to be central to Canadian progress. A crucial element of the jubilee year was the performing of parades and pageants, featuring representations of figures considered to be of significance for the development of the country (Cupido 1998; Lindgren 2011). At the local level, celebrations held on the Dominion Day weekend placed great stock in honouring descendants of "fathers of Confederation" as well as members of the community who had lived for the longest time in the area.[56]

Diamond Jubilee and Academic biography

This concern with biography was no less evident in the 1927 meetings of the Canadian Historical Association (CHA) – the year of the Diamond Jubilee of Confederation – that took place in Toronto from May 27 to 28. These were held in conjunction with a ceremony held at noon on 23 May 1927 at the Mount Royal Cemetery in Montreal. This involved the unveiling of a memorial to the explorer David Thompson, whose body had originally been placed in an unmarked grave belonging to someone else, seventy years earlier ("David Thompson Monument" 1927). The memo-

Introduction

rial was a "simple, but dignified fluted pillar surmounted by a sextant ... about nine feet in height" sculpted by Henri Hubert. The members of the CHA had figured prominently in the planning and carrying out of the unveiling ceremony. Not only had the CHA raised a special fund to defray the expense of the monument, but its president, Professor G.M. Wrong, presided at the event. The unveiling itself was conducted by the Bank of Montreal president, Sir Frederick Williams-Taylor, who gave a short address that "emphasized Thompson's personal qualities of modesty, idealism, and determination." Finally, J.B. Tyrrell "then read a paper dealing at some length with the nature and extent of Thompson's achievements." He claimed that "Thompson was the greatest practical and geographer the world has produced ... His geographical genius" was evident in the fact that "his location of points, measurements of distances, and estimates of altitudes ... show an uncanny accuracy when checked by modern surveyors" (*Canadian Historical Review* 1927).[57]

The annual meeting of the CHA was held in Baldwin House in Toronto (Burpee 1927b; Cochrane 1926; Cochrane and Doughty 1927; "List of Members and Affiliated Associations" 1927).[58] It featured a Friday-night dinner in the Great Hall of Hart House, a presidential address delivered by Professor G.M. Wrong, "and concluded with a review of significant publications on Canadian affairs during the past year" (G.M. Wrong 1927). Wrong's address examined the problems facing historical research "under modern conditions" and how the field related to other domains of inquiry and described the relations of history with allied subjects such as anthropology, economics, and philosophy. Most notably, the papers all dealt with themes "appropriate to the celebration of the Diamond Jubilee of Confederation." To this end, papers dealing with "the Confederation movement" across the country were prominently featured.[59]

This cluster of papers addressing Confederation from a spatial perspective was followed by one that was concerned more with "various problems of Canadian national life."[60] In line with the Thompson monument event, a list was prepared of historic and prehistoric sites that had been / would be commemorated (Canadian National Parks Branch 1928). In the series of general papers, Stewart Wallace traced the growth of national feeling from the foundation of the "Canada First" movement to the organization of a Canadian ministry at Washington.

Paralleling these meetings, the same theme was addressed at the Royal Society of Canada Meetings, held in May 1927,[61] which included papers pertinent to the Diamond Jubilee by Francis J. Audet (1927), Pelham Edgar (1927), Marius Barbeau (1927), Robert Falconer (1927), Fred Landon (1927), and William Renwick Riddell (1927). Audet's Section 1 (French) presidential address traced the progress of French Canada since Confederation. In Edgar's Section 2 (English) presidential address, he noted that, given that this was "Confederation year," he had been "urged almost authoritatively to trace the history of our intellectual growth from its inception to the present more full-statured hour" (1).

Innis's effort to champion the cause of Pond thus took place against the backdrop of historians invoking aspects of Canada's "progress" since Confederation to commemorate the Diamond Jubilee. The celebrations involved not only a special event honouring David Thompson, but also a number of activities placing Alexander Mackenzie at the centre of an emergent definition of Canada's path to nationhood.[62] The Diamond Jubilee parade in Ottawa featured a float honouring Alexander Mackenzie. Moreover, on 26 August 1927, the Historic Sites and Monuments Board of Canada dedicated a memorial cairn to "one of the earliest monuments in the history of the Pacific Northwest," namely "Mackenzie's Rock," the site ("scientifically determined by engineers") where Sir Alexander Mackenzie had reached the Pacific coast on 21–2 July 1793 after having travelled overland[63] (Canadian National Parks Branch 1928). Echoing the celebration of Mackenzie as the first person to cross Canada from east to west, the Jubilee Celebration held in Ottawa on 1 July 1927 was broadcast nationwide by radio, the first time that the entire country had been able to listen to a broadcast simultaneously.

Innis's writings on Pond, which appeared in the aftermath of the onslaught of books and events honouring Mackenzie,[64] made the case that the grizzled explorer had not received the attention he deserved, and that this lack of recognition could be attributed at least in part to Alexander Mackenzie. According to Innis, Mackenzie, in his accounts of the precursors to the North West Company (1927) – which were viewed as authoritative – "[took] the opportunity not only to neglect the importance of [Pond's] work but actually to malign him" (Innis and Pond 1930, 114). In Innis's view, then, "History has not been kind to Peter Pond. It has taken the word of the chief chronicler of his activities without question" (114).[65] After pointing out the extent to which Mackenzie's version was in fact very questionable, Innis went on to chronicle the important contributions made by Pond to both the North West Company in general and to Canadian development in particular.[66] These included his mapmaking activities and his status as the first white man to traverse the Methye portage, which linked the drainage basin of Hudson Bay with that of the Mackenzie River, thereby extending the fur trade across the upper tier of North America. Innis went so far as to say that by virtue of his contributions, "Pond warranted a general appreciation of his position as one of the fathers of Confederation," a recognition that had been denied to him because "the vilification of his enemies has up to the present made this estimate impossible" (Innis and Pond 1930, ix).

Innis's work on Pond likely came in response to the surfeit of books on Mackenzie that appeared in 1927 in conjunction with the Diamond Jubilee of Confederation.[67] Obviously weary with the onslaught of Mackenzie-related material, he vented his frustrations in a review of a new edition of Mackenzie's *Voyages* that was published by the Radisson Society (Innis 1927e; Mackenzie 1927). Remarking that this was "the *fourth* [emphasis mine] volume on Mackenzie to appear in 1927[68] and the most recent of the editions of his *Voyages*," he found it difficult to understand why this book was chosen for publication, seemingly incredulous about the editor's claim that it was selected "'not so much for its literary style and significance [but] for its historical and informative importance.'" While he agreed that "a new edition of Mackenzie's *Voyages* carefully edited and annotated, is badly needed from the 'historical and informative point of view,'" he believed that "the publishing of this volume will seriously delay a new edition such as the Champlain Society might bring out." He found the volume lacking in many respects. Its introduction by Prof. [Charles W.] Colby was not only "general and superficial" but "rather out of line with recent work on the North West Company." It made no mention of Wade's (1927) work on "Mackenzie's early history and its bibliography was inadequate." Finally, it had been proof read in haste and its pen sketches were not "historically accurate in detail" (1927d, 65).

In his effort to clarify some issues related to the maps of Pond – and his relationship to Mackenzie – Innis contacted Lawrence Burpee, who had dealt with these questions in his pioneering work on the exploration of the Northwest (Burpee 1908). Burpee, however, had difficulty recalling what he had intended, so largely failed to address Innis's queries. Innis's relationship with Burpee went beyond their exchange of letters about Peter Pond. Burpee was also scheduled to submit Innis's paper on Pond and James Cook to the 1928 Royal Canadian Society Meetings to be held in Winnipeg in May.[69]

However, as it turned out, Burpee was not able to attend the meetings and submit Innis's paper; he was going to Europe instead. He had requested that Prof. D.C. Harvey of the University of Manitoba serve as a replacement for him. As he had been "extremely pressed for work" he had "not been able to go into the details of [Innis's] study of Peter Pond." Nevertheless, he found it to be an "admirable piece of work [with] very great interest and value to students." However, as he was "not clear if [Innis] intended this particular copy to be presented to the Royal Society, or a corrected copy," he was sending it back to him. He asked that Innis send Harvey a copy of the paper when it was ready. He warned Innis that it would "not ... be possible to print such a long paper in the Transactions" [of the Royal Society of Canada] and suggested that he might wish to make his own publication arrangements.[70] Evidently, Innis was able to eventually produce a paper of acceptable length, as it appeared in the Royal Society *Transactions* of that year (1928a).[71]

Innis made it quite clear at the beginning of the paper why he believed that Pond was deserving of more attention: "It is perhaps altogether fitting and proper, in consideration of the recently celebrated sixtieth anniversary of the Dominion, that the work of students in Canadian history should centre so largely on the development of responsible government and the formation of Confederation" (1928a, 1). He was most likely referring to the CHA and Royal Society meetings of the previous year, which had largely examined the meaning and significance of Canada's Diamond Jubilee in terms of constitutional arrangements. This echoed the sentiments he expressed in his introduction to the *Select Documents in Canadian Economic History* (1929b), which was published the following year: "The constitutional history of Canada has been traced in its outlines, but the economic history, is, or the most part, an uncharted sea" (Innis 1929b, vii). He was most likely referring to the volume produced by Arthur Doughty and Adam

Introduction xxxvii

Shortt of the Public Archives of Canada, as well as that of his colleague, W.L.M. Kennedy (Doughty and Shortt 1907; Kennedy 1922).[72] That Innis had some reservations about Shortt's approach is evident in a review he wrote on the latter's two-volume collection of documents related to currency, exchange, and finance during the French period (Shortt 1925–6):

> These facts strengthen a further impression that Dr Shortt approached the field as a constitutional historian. The volumes are definitely and obviously a most effective introduction to the constitutional history of the colony, and are an integral part of the work of Dr Shortt as a constitutional historian. For these reasons the work appears to deal with economic history secondarily and in spite of Dr Shortt's first intentions. It is consequently the most significant work which has appeared for some time, since it is an indication that a foremost worker in constitutional history has caught the vision of an unbroken field of economic history which lies beyond. (Innis 1927a, 64)

He also took issue with Shortt's tendency to focus on post-confederate developments, while neglecting the prior and subsequent periods (62). In giving his attention to the period 1763 to 1821, Innis's critique of the constitutional/juridical approach of Doughty, Shortt, and Kennedy was implicit in his Royal Society paper on Pond and Cook. Innis was making the claim that it was mistaken to understand Canada's unity exclusively on the basis of the 1867 constitutional arrangements; rather one must examine "the organization of greatest importance to Canadian interests in the prosecution of the [fur] trade [namely] the Northwest Company and ... pay especial attention to the activities of an individual who played an important role in its formation" namely, Peter Pond.[73] Anticipating his line of argument from *The Fur Trade in Canada* (Innis [1930] 1956), he claimed that the borders for Canada more or less coincided with the territory controlled by the North West Company (1928a, 131).

After providing a brief biographical sketch of Pond (drawing on material from the latter's memoir covering the period up to 1775), Innis then turned to Pond's activities in the Northwest, with particular reference to "developments leading to the formation of the Northwest Company." He gave particular attention to Pond's contributions to solving "the problems incidental to the establishment of trade in" Athabasca (135). He then addressed the controversies surrounding his later activities and sketched how he came to leave Canada for good, returning to his native United States. Innis then attempted to summarize Pond's contributions to the organization of the fur trade, as well as to exploration and mapmaking. Finally, he related Pond's efforts to map and explore the Northwest to both Alexander Mackenzie and Captain James Cook (139–40).[74]

Innis examined Pond's activities in the Northwest in *The Fur Trade in Canada* as part of a broader discussion of how the fur trade was conducted by the North West Company. Having been able to pinpoint Pond's movements and whereabouts in the late 1770s and early 1780s (1927c, 1928b), he could now use him as a point of entry for examining the trading practices of the North West Company on the Saskatchewan: "The quantity of furs brought to the fort (des Prairies) was very great and from twenty to thirty Indians arrived daily ... Thomas Frobisher returned with the Indians in the summer of 1776 and wintered, according to Peter Pond's map, on Isle à la Crosse lake, going out in 1777. According to the same source, Pond wintered in 1776 and 1777 on the north branch of the Saskatchewan" ([1930] 1956, 195).

Innis could also elaborate on how Pond was able to establish himself as such a pivotal figure in the Western fur trade: "According to Mackenzie, traders on the Saskatchewan in 1778 pooled their stock to send Pond to the Athabasca country following the success of Thomas Frobisher the preceding year" (Innis [1930] 1956, 196). "In any case, Pond crossed the height of land at Portage la Loche and wintered on the Athabasca River about forty miles above Lake Athabasca. He came out in 1779 but was obliged to return in the same year for a cache of furs he had left."

Innis drew on various records to establish how the shares in the proto–North West Company were divided: according to an agreement reached in Quebec and dated 24 April, 1780 Pond was to be allocated 4 canoes; in 1781, Pond, McBeath, and Graves each was allocated 4 canoes as well. However, he noted that subsequently (in 1783–4) "the Northwest Company ... probably included Peter Pond, one share (taken in 1785)" (197–8).

Innis's attention to Pond was also implicit in how he conceived of the fur trade in relation to the development of Canada and allows us to better understand what he meant by the two sentences that have become synec-

Introduction

doches for the entire volume: "The present Dominion emerged not in spite of geography but because of it. The significance of the fur trade consisted in its determination of the geographic framework" ([1930] 1956, 393).

While the first sentence has been cited in mantra-like fashion, the significance of the second sentence has been largely overlooked. It reveals that Innis did not believe geography in and of itself to be determinant for the development of Canada as a nation state. Rather, he claimed that the fur trade *determined* geography.[75] *The Fur Trade in Canada* did not treat the fur trade in a monolithic fashion; he addresses a number of different fur-trade regimes, each of which had different characteristics (including those of initial contact in the Atlantic region, New France, the Hudson's Bay Company, and the North West Company). The latter two are discussed in the most detail and are viewed by Innis as representing diametrically opposed ways of conducting the fur trade. The centralized London-based Hudson's Bay Company operated from trading posts surrounding the western and southern shores of Hudson's Bay (to which natives brought their furs to trade). On the other hand, the Montreal-based North West Company (and its predecessors) worked in a more decentralized fashion through a network of trading posts that ultimately extended from eastern Canada to the Athabasca region and the Mackenzie River drainage basin. While Innis argued that through their merger in 1821 the two approaches were combined, he was of the view that the North West Company's organizational structure, by virtue of its "space-binding" capacity, made possible the emergence of Canada as a nation state. As he emphasized, much of the North West Company's success could be attributed to the skills and activities of Peter Pond. These included mapmaking, developing the logistics for long-distance trade through the use of pemmican, caches, extended supply lines, intercultural skills, and the ability to organize pooling of resources.[76]

Peter Pond: Publishing History

Innis incorporated sections of his Royal Society paper in his biography of Pond that was published by Irwin and Gordon of Toronto in 1930 (Innis and Pond 1930).[77] As a young academic, he had not been in any position to publish his work with established presses (which, in any case, were relatively limited). *History of the Canadian Pacific Railway* was finally accepted by P.S. King & Son Ltd of London, but only with little compensation for Innis.[78] Its circulation was quite restricted and was not even available in Canada.[79] *Fur Trade of Canada* did not fare much better.[80] It was eventually published in a limited edition through the Department of Political Economy after a subsidy was negotiated through the university publication committee. His arrangement to have Peter Pond published arose through his efforts to find a firm willing to publish *Fur Trade of Canada* and *Select Documents*. He approached the small company of Irwin and Gordon, which had only recently begun operations. While it was not interested in publishing his book on the contemporary fur trade, the co-owner of the firm, J.S. Gordon, notified Innis that the Pond manuscript was the "sort of thing we wish to publish judging by your description of it." He added that he and his partner Irwin would "give it most careful attention" and told Innis that it was "kind of [him] to think of the young firm so frequently."[81] They also had an interest in publishing the *Select Documents* manuscript, and in the spring of 1928 Gordon suggested that they "talk over both books" at a place convenient to Innis.[82] Sometime during the next year an agreement was reached to publish the book, and negotiations about the form and content of the text were well underway in the period from March to May 1929. In May 1930 Gordon informed Innis that Innis was being sent "final proofs of Peter Pond." All was thought to be "correct except for the last page," where a mistake had been made "in setting the new material regarding Pond's alleged complicity in the murder of Ross & Waden."[83] Publication of the book, however, was further delayed because of difficulties that arose in displaying the maps.[84] Also, Printer's Guild Ltd, the firm responsible for putting the book into production, was not clear that the cost for binding the book (24 cents a volume "in lots of one hundred") was acceptable and contacted Innis to make sure that it was.[85] Finally, in the fall of 1931, well after Innis had begun negotiations with Irwin & Gordon (and a year after the listed publication date), the book finally saw the light of day, selling for $1.50 a copy.[86]

Peter Pond: The Text

The volume had a total of 153 pages, on fine paper with deckled edges on the top and bottom, evidently unusual for the time.[87] The text was printed in single space, with a narrow margin in the middle and wide margins on

Introduction   xli

the other sides, and had a pale purple cover. For the most part, Innis used the version produced for the Wisconsin series, reproducing the corrections in spelling but replacing upper-case letters with lower-case ones in material he quoted. He also did not make use of Thwaites's extensive footnotes, replacing them with a small number of his own. The first section was based largely on Pond's journal (which covered the period up to 1775).[88]

Innis alternated between Pond's words (indicated with quotation marks) and his own commentary. Proceeding in this manner, he succeeded in incorporating about 80 per cent of Pond's journal into the biography.

The second section, covering the period until Pond's return to the United States, was based largely on whatever sources Innis could find (some of which were later considered to be unreliable). The preface provided context to the volume, as did the bibliography, which effectively situated the book in relation to primary sources. Written after the book had gone to press, it made reference to a number of sources that had subsequently come to Innis's attention.

The book was dedicated to T.W. Harris[89] and J.A. Long.[90] Both had figured prominently in Innis's 1924 visit to Athabasca country, the area that Pond helped to open up to further exploration and settlement. In his acknowledgements he also thanked Lawrence Burpee for his "kindness in arranging for the presentation of part of this study before the Royal Society of Canada at Winnipeg, in May 1928, as well as for other kindnesses" (Innis and Pond 1930, ix).[91] As he stated in the preface, he wished to challenge the "common assumption that ... more important traders and explorers were born in Scotland." He emphasized rather the "formative period of the trade," namely that "following the Conquest" (ca 1760) and prior to the formation of the North West Company (ca 1775). During this period he was of the view that "traders born in the Colonies occupied an important place." Both Pond and Alexander Henry[92] were significant for their "profound influence on exploration and trade in the northwest." But while Henry had received a good deal of attention (Henry and Gough 1992), Pond, according to Innis, had been "almost forgotten." This could be attributed to the fact that he was poorly educated and largely illiterate. But in Innis's view, Pond deserved to be remembered, as his biography served as a window into the "early history of the Northwest Company." In particular, through a study of Pond's life, one could gain insights into the "organization of the technical side of the trade [which] made possible the evolution of the North West Company." And since the company was a "crucial organization" for the development of Canada, one could better appreciate "his position as one of the fathers of Confederation."[93] Such an estimation had hitherto been impossible, largely because of the "vilification of his enemies" (vii–ix). Moreover, because the works discussing Peter Pond were both "scanty" and "unreliable," writing his biography proved to be challenging. Most of the later works addressing Pond were "unsatisfactory" and based on material that was of dubious authenticity. This was the case with David Thompson's narrative (Thompson and Tyrrell 1916), which he thought should be "used with caution." In Innis's bibliography he drew attention to items of relevance that had come to his attention after the main text had gone to press. These included "various accounts and memoranda relating to Peter Pond" in the Detroit Public library, and some documents that had been copied by his former student R. Harvey Fleming from the Phyn Ellis papers in the Buffalo Historical Society Library.[94] Finally, he had come across additional material related to Pond's murders of Waden and Ross, which he felt strengthened his conviction that the evidence against him was extremely slight (Innis and Pond 1930, 144–53).

Distribution of *Peter Pond*

On the basis of archival correspondence related to the book, one can estimate that about 500 copies were printed. Evidently, around the middle of November, the publisher distributed a number of page-proof copies to newspapers and journals, and reviews of the book began to appear shortly thereafter. Distribution of the book began, but sometime in early 1932, Irwin and Gordon went bankrupt, and Innis was not able to receive any royalties for books that had been sold. He hired the firm of Gregory, Armstrong, & Kemp, Barristers and Solicitors, to help him deal with the legal questions involved and to provide assistance with securing the remaining unsold books.[95] As of 10 May 1932, 110 copies had been sold, with 24 still on the Irwin & Gordon premises.[96] At the end of May, Innis wrote to Dr Lorne Pierce, managing editor of Ryerson about what he described as "a personal matter." Because of the bankruptcy of Irwin and Gordon (of which Pierce was aware), Innis noted that *Peter Pond* did not have a distributor. He informed Pierce that the book's printer, Hunter Rose Co., was in possession of 400 copies of the book. Since they belonged to him, Innis was "anxious to have a reputable publishing firm handle it on the usual basis of ten percent commission." He concluded by asking Pierce if Ryerson Press would "consider a possible arrangement" and if he would provide him with advice and suggestions.[97] On behalf of Ryerson, Pierce agreed to distribute the books, proposing that the publisher receive fifty cents per copy (to which Innis agreed). Innis informed Pierce that his solicitor, Frederick Kemp, would contact him about the delivery of the unsold books in possession of the printer and the "receiver." He also planned to send Pierce a list of reviews as well as "a copy of the publications to which reviews were sent." Finally, he requested that "three complementary copies [be] sent to Prof. R.B. Thomson[98] Dept. of Botany, University of Toronto, Dr. George Walton,[99] Churchill, Man., and Dr. C.W. Jefferys,[100] York Mills."[101] By the summer of 1932 the book had shifted to Ryerson's list and was showing some sales.[102] While the shift from Irwin & Gordon to Ryerson was an inconvenient experience for Innis, it allowed him to arrange for the publication of a collection of his articles as *Problems of Staple Production in Canada* (Innis 1933c), which was intended to anchor a new series on staples.[103] Its first volume was Ruth Grant's *The Canadian Atlantic Fishery* (1934), for which Innis provided an introduction. While this series never really materialized, it did provide the foundation for the much more extensive Canadian-American series, published simultaneously by Ryerson and Yale University Press, funded by the Carnegie Endowment for International Peace. Innis served as Canadian editor for the series, produced some volumes for it (e.g., Innis 1954; Ruddick et Innis 1937), and had his hand in producing some of the others (e.g., Innis, Ware, and Logan 1937; Innis and Jacobson 1936).

Reception

That Innis was proud of his text and wished to share it with his friends is evident in the fact that he sent out a number of copies upon the book's publication. The recipients included T.W. Harris (to whom the book was dedicated),[104] Andrew Semple,[105] Dr Frederick Winnett,[106] and Louis Hamilton of Berlin. The reviews began to appear in the autumn of 1931. While some were little more than announcements[107] or short descriptions (*Toronto Globe* 1931), most were quite positive, complimenting Innis on the approach that he had taken to his subject matter. The reviewer for the *Manitoba Free Press* was particularly effusive, noting that Innis deserved congratulations for "making available the important record and the unique journal of [someone] who did so much toward the opening up of the West." Not only were Pond's achievements "surprisingly various and diverse," but his journal was "remarkable, naïve, direct, altogether delightful." Despite the fact that the journal "is without benefit of orthodox spelling, it is not without benefit of acute observation and accurate description [as] habits, ceremonies, customs of Indian tribes interested [Pond] endlessly" (*Manitoba Free Press* 1931).

Duncan McArthur, editor of the *Queen's Quarterly*, judged it to be "a comprehensive study of the work of Peter Pond, the 'wild man' of the early North-West trade." He noted that "Professor Innis ... has already done most significant pioneer work in the history of the Canadian fur trade." At the same time, the review pointed out a number of the book's deficiencies: "Two or three minor defects detract from the pleasure that should be given for the reading of the book and from its usefulness to the student of history." Given that "commonly accepted rules of punctuation [are] generously disregarded ... the author's meaning is at times obscure." Moreover, "proof sheets have not been carefully read." Overall, there would seem to be little justification for depriving the student of the valuable aid that even a "name and place" index would provide. McArthur also called into question Pond's character, noting that the "Pond escutcheon is not free from stain," given his confession that his opponent in a duel in fought at Detroit "was unfortunate." He took issue with Innis's claim that "the evidence of Pond's complicity in the murder is extremely slight" (McArthur 1931).

A review in the *Mail and Empire* raised the possibility that another controversy might arise from the book, given Innis's claim that Pond ought to be given credit for Alexander Mackenzie's various "discoveries" (*Mail and Empire* 1931).[108] In a review published in the *Toronto Globe* on the same day, Innis's discussion of the relationship between Pond and Mackenzie was examined from a slightly different angle: "Peter Pond was a pioneer explorer in the far Northwest of Canada, but the work of ... Mackenzie has been so well set forth by Mackenzie himself and others that Pond has

Introduction

received less than justice ... Innis sets out to correct the perspective of modern students and readers. By liberal use of quotations from Pond's own narrative ... we learn of the personality back of a long career of trading and exploration" (*Toronto Globe* 1931).

The book was described in a colourful and evocative review that appeared in the *Toronto Star*:

> Deckled edges, bad spelling and a folded map have never been embedded in one book until the publication of *Peter Pond*. The diaries as published in this fascinating volume have the bold freshness of Trader Horn[109] the quaint simplicity of Don Quixote and the naiveté of Robinson Crusoe. The editor of the volume who compiled and wisely refrained from correcting the diaries, adds to his own interpretation to make a continuous narrative valuable as a new angle on part of Canada's romantic history. (*Toronto Star* 1931)

The reviewer for the *Montreal Star* was impressed by the book's aesthetics and overall production values: "From the standpoint of a sample of Canadian craftsmanship in the art of book-making, Mr. Innes' [*sic*] volume leaves very little to be desired. In binding, typography, general format and materials employed, it is something to which the publisher may justly point with considerable pride" (*Montreal Daily Star* 1932).

Most notably, one can detect in the reviews a tendency to frame their evaluations of the book in terms of its relevance to the reviewer's own concerns. Viewing the text from the standpoint of "the student of Canadian history," McArthur believed that "its fourth and fifth chapters which discuss Pond's activities as explorer and trader in the Saskatchewan and Athabasca country" were of particular significance, as they "conclude with an appraisal of the value of his work ... Here for the first time is presented a detailed account of Pond's activities, year by year; of his association with the smaller traders in the farther west; and of his connection with the group of Montreal traders which finally formed the northwest company ... Innis is of the opinion that Pond fired Mackenzie with the possibilities of discovery down the Mackenzie and gave him the information necessary to enable him to accomplish that feat" (McArthur 1931).

xlvi

After summarizing what the book tells us about Pond's early career, A.S. Morton turned to what he considered to be "the most valuable part of the volume," namely that dealing "with Pond's career in the Canadian Northwest." Despite the fact that the available material on Pond is "so slight and disjointed," he believed that Innis's examination of Pond "has been accomplished ... with complete success. All future writers will turn to this volume for authoritative guidance in dealing with Peter Pond." While Morton believed that Pond's career in Athabasca was "ably described" by Innis,[110] he shared McArthur's reservations about how capably Innis addressed the two murders that Pond was accused of committing (Morton 1932).

Grace Lee Nute, a noted historian of exploration and the fur trade, acknowledged the importance of Pond, "the enigmatic Yankee [notable for] his illiterate spelling, his dry humor, his vigorous and picturesque language, and his extraordinary gift for exploration." Indeed, she was of the view that he was an individual who "influenced the history of the whole continent" by virtue of his "unusual vitality, powers of adaptation, and vision." She felt, however, that Innis's biography left a good deal to be desired. To be sure, it "summarized very well Pond's achievements," making it plain that "Pond was an explorer of the first rank." However, it offered "few new data" and "assumed a good deal of historical knowledge on the part of his readers." The volume would have been more readable had he "placed behind his picture of Peter Pond a background depicting the tremendous force at work in western North America to open up the fur regions and to find a Northwest passage." Moreover, Innis could have better elucidated "all of his characters" as well as "the rivalry between the Northwest Company and the Hudson's Bay Company." In particular, she felt that Innis should have made better use of the available maps attributed to Pond. Overall, she felt that his biography was far too compressed and hoped that he "would do him full justice in a more leisurely narrative" (Nute 1932). Reviewing the book for *Minnesota History*, Charles Gates not surprisingly highlighted the aspects of the text that would be of "especial interest to Minnesota readers," namely the years Pond spent (1773–75) "on the St Peter's, or Minnesota River," where he "was one of the first traders to take bales of goods to the Sioux living in that region." In particular, part of the book tells "the story of the experiences of these years, descriptive as it is

Introduction   xlvii

of many of the customs of the Indians." However, he noted that "perhaps the most significant thing about the book is the attempt by the author to evaluate Pond's services as explorer and trader, and to correct the unfavorable portrayal of his personality that has come down to us from associates unfriendly to him." However, echoing the criticisms of Nute, Gates noted that "no serious effort is made to untangle the complications surrounding the various original maps drafted by Pond and the copies that were later made from them. Nor does the author deal with questions of textual criticism in the case of explanatory material in French accompanying certain of the extant copies of the Pond maps." But overall, he found the book to be "a scholarly biographical study by a recognized authority in the field" (Gates 1932).

Reviewing the book for the *Oregon Historical Quarterly*, T.C. Elliot cautioned the journal's readers that "there is little in this book which directly concerns the Oregon audience." But all the same, the reviewer felt that "students of our history will welcome many items of interest drawn from original sources." In order to make the case for Pond's relevance to the state, the reviewer underscored the point that Pond shared features in common with Jonathan Carver, one of Oregon's most celebrated pioneering figures: "Peter Pond was a Connecticut Yankee as was Jonathan Carver, and both served in the colonial army in the French-Indian war. Carver spent two years in the Wisconsin-Minnesota country, where the name Oregon was used by the natives. A year or so later Pond engaged in the fur trade on the Mississippi and St Peters rivers." The reviewer pointed out that the comments made by Pond "on the career of Carver are pertinent and reliable." The review went on to elaborate how Pond was able to transfer his trade "to the undeveloped fields of the Saskatchewan and Athabaska watersheds through the Grand Portage gateway." It was there that Pond became "connected with the Montreal capitalists and organizers of the North West Company." According to Elliot, "this book contains much valuable information as to the personnel and growth of the company ... and reveals some astonishing facts; one as to the amount of rum used in the trade then." In line with some of the other reviews, it judged Innis to be "well qualified to assemble and edit the facts [the book] contains" and praised it as "an exhibit of fine paper and fine printing" (Elliott 1933).

Innis's Responses to Reviews of *Peter Pond*

Given that Innis's project on Pond – as bound up with the North West Company and the North American fur trade – was a work in progress, it was not surprising that he sought to bring his research up to date for both the scholarly community and the general public. This took the form of an article that appeared in the *Canadian Historical Review* (Harold A. Innis 1935b).[111] Noting that "additional material [had] been made available from a variety of sources," he felt that a "brief discussion" was warranted. This material corresponded to the two divisions of the text; the early part was based on the journal and may have been linked to the review of *Peter Pond* by Charles Gates (1932). The material related to the post-1775 material represented a direct response to the review of Morton (1932) and others (1935b, 61): "The scepticism expressed by various reviews of my book, including that by Professor A.S. Morton in the REVIEW of June, 1932, as to Pond's probable innocence in the murders of John Ross in 1787 and Étienne Waden in 1782, warrants a brief review of the evidence, particularly as additional material has come to light since the publication of the volume."

In particular, Morton had taken issue with Innis's claims that the accusations made against Pond of having committed two murders in the North West were unfounded: "Pond's career in Athabaska is ably described. His efficiency and the intellectual interest taken by him in the country which he saw and in its relation with the Pacific make one wish that those two murders – of Jean Etienne Waden (1782) on Lac la Ronge, and of John Ross of the Gregory-Pangman interest on the Athabaska River (1787) – were not associated with his name" (Morton 1932).

Morton went on to make the case that for the Waden murder, all of the available evidence was not taken into account, and there is no record of Pond having been "tried and convicted." As for the "matter of the Ross murder," Morton argued that Innis treated it "lightly." Not only did he put too much stock in statements made by Roderick McKenzie, but the "all important papers" and documents were still wanting.

Obviously stung by the criticism of Morton and others, Innis cited some new evidence that pointed to others, rather than Pond, as having responsibility for the two murders.[112] Innis also drew on new material to

Introduction · xlix

provide greater precision about Pond's activities and movements (Tyrrell 1934)[113] and about his mapping activities.[114] In terms of the pre-1775 material, he reported that "Mrs Le Grand Cannon of New Haven, Connecticut, a descendant of Peter Pond, has confirmed minor points and has been good enough to arrange for photostats to be made of the journal in the possession of Mr Le Grand Cannon, Jr. These are now in the possession of the University of Toronto library" (61)[115] Specifically, in two letters she wrote to him in 1932, she discussed the arrangements for sending the Photostats, answered his questions about the diary of Yale president Ezra Stiles (in which Pond was mentioned) as well as the status of Pond's donations to Yale.[116] That Innis felt it necessary to contact Mrs Cannon and clarify a number of matters suggests his sense that the biography was incomplete in a number of respects. His exchange reveals that Innis was now thinking of Pond primarily as a North American figure, rather than someone whose main claim to fame was his contributions of helping build Canadian nationhood.

Reframing Pond, the North West Company, and the Fur Trade

By virtue of its abandonment of the established genres of celebrating politicians and the same cast of adventurers, *Peter Pond* could be seen as a revisionist work. Subsequent to the publication of the text, Innis put some effort into clarifying how the biographies of figures including Lord Selkirk, Alexander Mackenzie, and William McGillivray intersected with that of Pond (1932b). In the early thirties, moreover, Innis began to frame Pond more broadly, using North America as a point of reference.[117] This may have been related to the new availability of primary material on the fur trade, which drew on materials spanning national borders. Among these was Ernest Voorhis's (1930) exhaustive compilation of data about "Historic Forts and Trading Posts of the French Regime and of the English Fur Trading Companies," which Innis found to contain a "vast amount of easily accessible information" (1931c, 212).

Arguably Innis's growing embrace of continentalism could also be attributed to conjunctural factors.[118] At the time that Innis originally engaged with Pond, the fur trade, and the North West Company, Canada was in the throes of moving from "colony to nation" (Lower and MacLean 1946). The Balfour Report of 1926 (which arose out of the Imperial Conference of 1923) defined Britain and the dominions as "autonomous Communities within the British Empire, equal in status, in no way subordinate to one another in any respect of their domestic or external affairs." As such, they were "freely associated as members of the British Commonwealth of Nations" (Thompson and Seager 1985, 49).

In effect, the Diamond Jubilee year of 1927 and its immediate aftermath could be viewed as a liminal zone within which disparate versions of Canada's birth as a nation-state competed with one another. A number of these were in evidence in the meetings of the Canadian Historical Association and the Royal Society, both attended by Innis. Innis's championing of Pond and the North West Company precursors as constitutive of Canada (both institutionally and in terms of borders) was directed against both those who focused on Confederation and its immediate aftermath as crucial, and those who singled out particular explorers and fur traders (most notably Thompson and Mackenzie) as the most important nation-builders having that calling. However, once the ferment of the Diamond Jubilee / Balfour declaration era had dissipated, Innis no longer had the need to make the case for Pond as a "father of Confederation." Rather, he could turn his attention to helping redefine the emergent Canadian nationhood within a North American context. This involved posing a challenge to the centralization of power he had discerned in the *Fur Trade in Canada,* and becoming an advocate of various Canadian regions (the north, the prairies, the Maritimes) within a continental framework.

That Innis was moving in this direction is evident in a Canadian Historical Association conference paper he presented entitled "An Introduction to the Economic History of the Maritimes (including Newfoundland and New England)" (1931b). He noted that he was "more immediately concerned with the area which has been dominated by the fishing industry ... four separate governments are interested in the fisheries of the North Atlantic ... United States in New England, Canada in the Maritime provinces ... France ... Newfoundland" (85). In the 1932 American Historical Association conference held in Toronto, Innis presented a paper on the interplay of the fur trade between the United States and Canada, revising it for publication the following year (Innis 1933b).

Introduction   li

While he made considerable mention of Canada in this paper, his focus rather was on the relationship between the Canadian fur trade and that of the United States. Expanding on the approach he had developed elsewhere in relation to Canada, he noted that "the drainage basin continued as an important geographical and trade unit; mastery over the main entrance to the drainage basin was therefore of vital importance" (324). More broadly, his point of reference was the continent-based framework involving a geographically dispersed pattern of trade of staple products:

The fur trade of the North American continent was an index of wide movements. It persisted in space and time with greatest continuity in the forested areas of the Precambrian formation and in relation to the support of a highly industrialized area and a metropolitan market. Throughout the history of the continent the territory restricted in diversity of product and dependent on a staple commodity steadily drifted into the control of a metropolitan market dependent on cheap all the year round water transportation. Cod from Newfoundland, beaver from Canada, and sugar from the West Indies depended on commercial and industrial England. In the face of this drift Spain, Holland, and France disappeared from North America, and because of this drift the United States emerged as a separate entity. (324)

He was particularly concerned with elucidating the dynamics of the shifts and changes (anticipating the cyclonics model he would elucidate by the end of the decade). For instance, he explained the expansion of the La Vérendrye–led expansion into the Northwest by referring to "pressure from the north and from the center by English trade." Subsequently, he noted that the "disturbances of the Americans" resulted in traders moving from the Revolutionary United States. As a result of these disturbances, "traders moved from Albany to Montreal." Fortified with British manufactured goods and West Indian rum they were able to "control ... trade from the St Lawrence to the interior" in almost a monopoly fashion. Eventually, because of hostilities, "they crowded to the far Northwest and in 1778 Pond penetrated to the Athabasca region and opened the trade to the Mackenzie River drainage basin." The eventual emergence of the North West Company as "the first large scale continental organization in North America" had implications south of the border, as fur-trade magnate John Jacob Astor sought to develop "a similar organization in the United States." Moreover, Innis called attention to the Americans' reliance on "Canadian boatmen" whose skills far surpassed those of the local workforce. He saw the influence also working the other way, as in the case of the "speculative boom ... centered about the New York market," which arguably contributed to the "expansion of the Hudson's Bay Company and to its present difficulties." At the same time, Innis also emphasized that "the fur trade of the United States gradually evolved as independent of British control." Because of factors unique to the United States such as labour migration, particular cultural traits of indigenous peoples, and the lack of ready access to manufactured goods, "development along a different line than was characteristic of the Canadian trade" occurred in the United States. Overall, he observed that "lack of continuity, Indian wars, the control exercised by one man or one family as in the case of the Astors, characterized the American rather than the Canadian trade." Above all, the America fur trade, because of the settlement patterns referred to by Frederick Turner, had an "an essentially frontier aspect, whereas the Canadian fur assumed a permanent and not a transient phase" (331–2).

This continentalist approach to the fur trade was evident in an entry on the fur-trade industry that Innis wrote for the New York–based *Encyclopedia of the Social Sciences* (1931a). He noted that "with the lengthening of transport lines to the interior, competition threatened from adjoining drainage basins, first that of the Richelieu River and later of the Mohawk route to Lake Ontario and Hudson Bay. The centralized organization of the colony dependent on the fur trade faced serious direct losses of trade and military expenditures to check competition."

Such an interdependence was evident in the area of marketing in relation to communications: "Cheaper furs ... have been sold to an increasing extent in new marketing centres, in North America, such as St Louis, New York, Montreal, and Winnipeg.... Improvements in communication, especially the radio, and in transportation have contributed in hastening important changes in marketing structure (*Encyclopedia of the Social Sciences* 1931a, 534). Overall, he claimed that "the fur trade is an index of the decreasing disparity between the cultures of the northern hemisphere resulting from the spread of industry" (536).

Introduction

Innis's emergent continentalism was evident in his review of *The Investor Pays*, by Max Lowenthal (1934a). He noted that the implications of the book for Canada "are of fundamental importance." In particular, it revealed the extent to which Canada and the United States were bound up together: "The basic New York–Chicago railway rate is a key to the Canadian as well as to the American rate structure. Canadian roads are in competition with American roads and the rate structure on both sides is tied to a competitive situation." In terms of Canadian government activity, the book drew attention to the fact that "construction of the St Lawrence canals [placed] Montreal on a basis of equality with New York." In this respect "waterways have played a central role in Canadian development and Canadians will continue to be unable to appreciate the conclusions of American works on transportation." Overall, "disturbances in the United States are reflected directly in Canada." Indeed, "the trend of monetary policy in the United States will strengthen more definitely the trend of monetary policy in Canada" (1934a, 150).

This continentalist approach also informed a review Innis wrote of recent publications on the fur trade, in the midst of the Great Depression.[119] He noted that "problems of continental organization have become conspicuous during the present depression, on the one hand in the emergence of regionalism, and on the other in the emphasis on centralization: for example, the agitation for amalgamation of the railways. These problems have been to a large extent a result of the difficulties of the Prairie Provinces and it is suggestive that they appear in the fur trade in the same regions and in territory far distant from the St Lawrence" (1936, 562).

This review article presented Innis with the opportunity to summarize some of the recent work on the history of the fur trade and to call attention to some of the archival collections housing material in need of further examination. He also was of the view that a number of recent studies pertaining to the North West Company made it possible to better understand its origins.[120] In particular, they revealed some new insights into the role Pond played in some of the early pooling arrangements: "Pond arrived at Cumberland House on May 26 with five large canoes loaded with goods. 'He is going to penetrate into the Athopuskow country as far as he can possibly go and there to stay this next winter.'[121] For the first time apparently a general concern had been maintained throughout the winter and had been sufficient to support Pond's expedition to Athabaska. The North West Company in the interior may be said to have been established in 1777" (568).

He went on to note that "the organization in the North-west and in Montreal had a strong tendency toward unification. Pond's return on July 2, 1779, with a small quantity of furs (but leaving a large quantity in the Athabaska) made an addition to the returns of the general concern of 1777–78 and of 1778–79. The general concern enabled him to bring out the supply in 1779–80 ... In the period preceding the emergence of the North West Company, and indeed throughout the history of the Company, the difficulties of achieving unity are striking and significant" (571–2).

He was particularly enthusiastic about a memoir by former fur trader Philip Godsell (1934), which was "a biographical account of his life in the fur trade since 1906." For an account of the discovery and partial use of the documents published herewith, see Innis and Pond (1930, 150–3) and a "contribution of first importance to the history of the trade." It served to link more recent trends to Innis's research on Peter Pond and the early fur trade. It also had a strong performative component in that in 1924 Godsell sought to open up new posts in the Western Arctic. This was the same year that Innis had visited the Northwest and the Mackenzie River Delta. In the same way that Innis had exhaustively described Pond's contributions to the organization of the fur trade, he was able to glean from Godsell's book important aspects of how the contemporary fur trade functioned. He noted that the "volume is important for its description of the organization and personnel of the Hudson's Bay Company and of rival organizations." Godsell, in his view, "describes at first hand the limitations and qualifications of commissioners of the HBC and rival companies." He recognized "difficulties of organization as a result of the high prices and disturbances of the war and post-war periods." Overall, it was a "most illuminating document" that was able to address problems of conservation and includes appendices on the muskoxen, caribou, mineral discoveries, and natives. Moreover, "Its end maps, photographs [and] excellent appendix increase the value of the book indispensable to the student of the recent trade" (1935a, 199).

Introduction   lv

Convergence with Bolton and Brebner

Innis was not alone in his embrace of a continentalist perspective in the fourth decade of the century. His views mirrored those of ex-patriot Canadian historian (and friend) J. Bartlet Brebner, as well as the eminent University of California historian Herbert Bolton. As the decade progressed, the intersections of their work became increasingly pronounced.

That Innis was already moving in the direction of continentalism by the late 1920s was remarked on by Brebner in his review (1930) of Innis's *Select Documents* (1929b). Brebner underscored the importance of Innis's volume, in terms of the shift that it represented from an emphasis on "constitutional history" to "economic history." In line with Canada's change in status from colony to nation, Brebner noted that "Canada has become the fifth nation in the world in international trade." Innis, in his view, was knowledgeable about "North American geography and has studied its influences," as well as "loyal to the continental interpretation of Canadian history." Hence, his collection was important to all students of North American history." He [Innis] was well aware that it was "seldom possible to think of Canada in isolation," as evident in the workings of a range of industries, including "fisheries ... fur trade, settlement, labor, shipbuilding, agriculture, lumbering, building, mining, petty industry, [and] transportation." It was hoped by Brebner that if he were to go "into the more complex Canadian, North American, and World economic relationship of the years after 1783, Mr Innis will be able to keep up the high standard he has set himself here" (882–3).

That Brebner shared Innis's views was evident in a paper he presented in the CHA meetings held in Ottawa in 1931. Entitled "Canadian and North American History," the paper argued that "the method of applying North American ... continental contours to the histories of Canada and the United States is very useful ... North American generalizations emerge from the written histories of both countries, in spite of the tendency of their histories to lock their findings in impermeable national compartments" (1931, 37). The main exemplar he provided for the continental approach was that of Professor Herbert Bolton at the University of California: "The better educational institutions in both countries teach North American history as a whole or in closely related parts. Indeed Professor

Bolton at the University of California groups in his teaching the history of all the Americas and his text-books and guides have won followers elsewhere" (38).[122] Among the works he cited as illustrating this tendency was Innis's *Fur Trade in Canada* ([1930] 1956): "As Professor Innis has shown their [fur traders'] entry to the Northwest was not an occupation, but a circumvention of the Hudson's Bay Company in quest of ever-receding castor gras" (39).

Bolton's approach became better known to Canadian historians by virtue of his notable presence at the American Historical Association meetings, held in Toronto in December 1932.[123] As president of the association, Bolton not only delivered a major address but was presented with a two-volume Festschrift and was awarded with an honorary doctorate by the University of Toronto. Brebner followed up on his 1931 paper by drawing extensively on Bolton's approach in assembling his overview, *The Explorers of North America, 1492–1806* (1933). He not only extensively cited Bolton as well as an influential work of one of his students, Gordon C. Davidson (1918), but included detailed biographical references, in line with the Boltonian approach.

The extent to which Bolton and Innis converged in their assessments of the book is quite striking. In his review of the text, Bolton (1935) described it as "an excellent book, admirably conceived and well executed" (517). The editors of the Pioneer Histories series of which it was a part, Bolton judged, took a "comprehensive view of early European overseas expansion ... an outlook quite in harmony with that of a rapidly growing group scholars on this side of the Atlantic.... The volumes will do much to help Americans of the different nations to correct the shortcomings of the narrowly nationalistic treatment of Western Hemisphere history which used to be in vogue" (518). Bolton went so far as to claim that the book could serve as a synthesis of "large historical units" that would serve to reveal "gaps in the monographic literature of a field" (518). He believed that the book would "give new meaning to the special researches of all students of North American exploration.... We need other books thus broadly conceived and treating of other aspects of the transit of European civilization to the Western Hemisphere" (518).

Along the same lines, it was evident that Innis was also very enthusiastic about Brebner's Bolton-inspired account of North American exploration,

Introduction

lvii

which mirrored his own emergent views: "This is a volume dear to the heart of the present reviewer. For the first time exploration is linked to the economic expansion of the continent." Mirroring Bolton's view that Brebner's text should be viewed as a significant point of reference for future research, he claimed that "it supersedes immediately all previous volumes on the history of the exploration of North America and provides a basis of approach with which future volumes must begin. The author has planned his study in relation to the continent as a whole with valuable results" (1934c, 71).[124]

Around the same time, Innis acknowledged his debt to *Five Fur Traders of the Northwest,* sponsored by the Minnesota Society of the Colonial Dames of America, which included an annotated version of Pond's memoir along with four other diaries (Gates 1933). He noted that "Canadians, and particularly students of the fur trade, are brought under fresh obligations to American scholars for this additional contribution to a field of common interest." These diaries were "of interest to the state of Minnesota but perhaps of even greater interest to Canada," as they pertained to "Canadian territory adjacent to the state of Minnesota." Innis was struck by how effectively the diaries captured every life of the period: "References are made to births and deaths and frequent illnesses with blood letting, emetics, purges and Turlington balsam. Fears of Indian uprisings and of damage as a result of drunkenness are mingled with the joys of celebration on Christmas and New-Year's and on all occasions capable of being celebrated by a dance." He remarked on how the diaries converged on the notion that "wives were acquired without difficulty" (1934b).

One can chart the direct lineage from Brebner's 1931 paper through to the series funded by the Carnegie Endowment for International Peace. By virtue of "the germ of the idea for a series on Canadian-American relations" Brebner was able to convince his "friend and mentor" James T. Shotwell to support the initiative. "The series was approved in 1932 with funding in 1933; Shotwell was general editor with Brebner serving as 'chief advisor and planner of the historical volumes'" (Campbell 2013, 329).[125] As Donald Creighton (1966) observed, the "new method" that Brebner suggested, "the continental approach to Canadian history," was the "direct inspiration of the long series of volumes," The Relations of Canada and the United States, "a great co-operative work completely realized." While this approach was "not so novel as he had imagined, it was ... very closely and sympathetically in tune with his times and expressed an attitude which was very fashionable at the time" (xvii).[126] Indeed, as Creighton claimed, it was quite in line with "King's heroic crusade for what used to be called 'dominion status' ... about to be completed ... crowned by the passage of the Statute of Westminster." As such, the continentalists viewed it as a "modest Canadian equivalent to the great and glorious American war of independence" (xviii). All the same, Creighton was quick to point out that the series "never quite became that imposing and integrated a demonstration of continentalism that some Canadians may have expected" (xix). He attributed this to the fact that Harold Innis, the Canadian editor of the series, "had little belief in continentalism ... *The Fur Trade in Canada* went far to demolish the geo-political bases on which continentalist theories where founded" (xix). Creighton argued that "by virtue of Innis's editorial leadership – at least in part, the result was a somewhat unsystematic series, with a few unaccountable gaps and some dubious inclusions" (xix).

As Brebner's comments on the same Innis text make clear, a continentalist reading of *The Fur Trade in Canada* is at least plausible.[127] But even more damaging to Creighton's interpretation of Innis's approach is the body of work that the latter had produced on Pond, the fur trade, and economic history in the 1930s, much of which took North American metropolitanism as its point of reference. Innis, like Brebner, was very much in tune with the times and was moving in a continentalist direction, in accord with the Boltonesque framework that informed Brebner's 1931 paper (39).[128]

That Innis viewed the work of Bolton favourably is evident in his own extensive citing of Bolton's student Gordon Davidson in one of his major monographs ([1930] 1956).[129] He also wrote a very positive review of Edmund Robert Murphy's (1941) book on the Mississippi fur trader Henry de Tonty (1942). "Written by a graduate student following the stimulus received in a seminar under Professor Bolton of the University of California," Innis noted, the text was "a tribute to the ability of the author and the zeal of the instructor. The study is a detailed, painstaking account based on a critical ... use of a wide range of sources" (154).

Innis believed that the study afforded "an interesting supplement to the work of Professor Nef on the mercantile system of France" with its treat-

Introduction

ment of "attempts to establish an outpost of the St Lawrence on the upper Mississippi" (154). This was in line with Innis's growing interest in examining the North American fur trade as a whole, which led him to claim that the text "offers suggestive parallels to the history of attempts by Radisson and Groseilliers to establish posts on Hudson Bay." All the same, he thought that a "broader treatment, particularly with reference to problems of strategy in North America," would have been preferable" (155).

Moreover, Innis wrote the foreword (1943b) to a book by a former student from the University of Toronto, Murray Lawson, based on a dissertation at University of California, Berkeley, supervised in part by one of Bolton's former students, Lawrence A. Harper. However, rather than using the foreword to introduce the material in the book, Innis advanced in it a line of argument that was not evident in Lawson's text, which was concerned primarily with examining the North American fur trade in relation to British mercantilism. To be sure, Innis shared Lawson's view that the North American fur trade must be examined holistically, rather than considering it from the standpoint of separate national or trading interests. But rather than addressing in detail Lawson's claims about the impact on the fur trade of British mercantilism – with particular reference to the hatting industry – Innis uses his foreword to provide an overview of the fur trade based not on the contours of geography but rather on political considerations and how they shaped the pattern of the development of the North American fur trade – one in which national boundaries were immaterial, for the most part. His point of departure was how the fur trade was rooted in the sub-civilizations that had grown up around particular drainage basins.[130] However, in this latter iteration, Innis examined how the contending forces in the fur trade sought to expand beyond their original fiefdoms. The conflict that ensued served as a constraint, resulting in patterns of development that were not necessarily sustainable in the long run. He noted that "in each of the major drainage basins facing the Atlantic, European groups representing separate nationalities or separate groups in the same nation attempted to dominate the region and became engaged in a struggle with adjacent drainage basins" (vii). "In this regard, trade from the drainage basin of the St Lawrence was extended against enormous handicaps" (ix).

He suggested that the expansion of the fur trade under the New France regime had less to do with continental geography, and more to with the political competition posed by its rivals: "Competition from the Hudson River drainage basin and from the Mississippi River basin with the French and from Hudson Bay left only the territory northwest of Lake Superior" (x).

This made for the extension of the fur trade "over vast areas," which were difficult to control administratively (xi). After the French regime fell, the Montreal-based traders occupied the "region formerly occupied by the French" and were forced to penetrate "into new territory in the Mackenzie River drainage basin in 1788." Implicit in this analysis was his contention that it was largely through the initiatives of Peter Pond that "partnership agreements were formed" (accompanying Pond's effective deployment of pemmican, caches, and networking with native groups).[131] Eventually, its successor organization, the North West Company, was able to extend its operations all the way to Columbia. But like the French regime before it, this extension engendered "strains comparable to the collapse of the French" (xiii). In his subsequent analysis, Innis sketches how these strains were manifest, and how the North West Company was ultimately unable to compete with American fur interests and settlement in the Pacific Northwest and was forced to withdraw north of the border. It is instructive that, unlike his classic works on the fur trade, Innis was now framing his discussion of the industry more holistically, with North America rather than Canada as his point of reference. Arguably the original impetus for this was at least in part his growing conviction (based on his engagement with Pond's memoir and the reception to it) that the fur trader and explorer needed to be recast not merely as a father of Canadian confederation but as a harbinger of North American continentalism.[132]

Commemorating Pond

By virtue of his engagement with the commemorative activities related to the Diamond Jubilee celebrations of 1927, Innis became increasingly aware of the extent to which figures thought to be crucial to Canada's emergence as a nation-state had been commemorated. Indeed, as we have examined, his advocacy on behalf of Peter Pond's role in history could be seen as a cor-

Introduction   lxi

rective to the tendency to celebrate other fur-trader-explorers like Thompson and Mackenzie while neglecting Pond. That Pond still had a key place in cultural memory in Canada was driven home to Innis during a 1933 visit to Prince Albert, Saskatchewan, when he learned of the ongoing discussions about Pond as well as the efforts to find the traces of his fort on the Sturgeon River. It also became evident to Innis through his contact with members of the Minnesota Historical Society that Pond was considered to be significant figure in American fur trade and exploration history, as evident in the inclusion of his memoir in the volume *Five Fur Traders of the Northwest* (Gates 1933).

Innis received further confirmation of ongoing efforts to commemorate Pond through his correspondence with Florence Pond Atherton Cannon.[133] As an aside in a letter thanking Innis for sending her some Pond-related "pamphlets" (and providing support for Innis's claim that Pond had been unfairly accused of murder), she informed him of "two circumstances which are the result of your 'Peter Pond Fur Trader and Adventurer.'" The first was a stone to be placed in memory of Peter Pond in a memorial bridge to be built in Milford commemorating "the three hundredth anniversary of the settlement of the town." The second was Joseph Lawrence Pond of Milford naming his son Peter (two years old at the time of the letter) in honour of his ancestor.[134] In his response, Innis noted that he was "tremendously pleased to learn of the memorial that has been planned to commemorate Peter Pond." He added that Pond "of course left important memorials to his work in Canada but they are of a more intangible form." He stressed that "the interest in Canadian history and especially the history of Western Canada renders recognition of his work more and more certain as time goes on." Obviously concerned that the activities to be held in Milford might be too limited in their focus, Innis conveyed his hope that "the tribute which has been planned will pay adequate respect to his international contributions." He also informed Mrs Cannon that the Minnesota Historical Society had requested "a mimeograph copy of the journal which you were good enough to send us" and that W. Stewart Wallace, the University of Toronto librarian, had arranged to have a copy made and had sent it to her. Finally, Innis found it "nice to hear that his name is being perpetuated in the family."[135]

There is some evidence that Mrs Cannon's observations reflected a growing recognition in Milford of Peter Pond's significance. The memorial bridge she mentioned was but one aspect of the tercentenary commemorations that were taking place. This involved, among other things, the production of a history of the town from 1639 to 1939, compiled and written as part of a WPA-sponsored Federal Writers project.[136] Pond was singled out as "one of the adventurous spirits" of the colonial period whose "restlessness and desire for adventure" ultimately led him to ultimately establish the "initial unit of the powerful Northwest Fur Company, comparable to the East India Company in financial strength and influence." This was likely "his greatest exploit" (Milford Tercentenary Committee and Federal Writers' Project 1939, 39–40). Pond also gained attention through the efforts of local historian, Dr De Witt Baldwin Nettleton, who presented a paper on Peter Pond during the town's Tercentenary Celebration (1939).[137]

Innis's expressed interest in how Pond was being commemorated was very likely related to his involvement during the 1930s with the activities of the Historic Sites and Monuments Board of Canada. While Innis had no formal position in the organization, he was asked by a friend and colleague, Judge Frederick W. Howay, to serve as a consultant for the board on a number of occasions.[138] His initial request from Howay was for assistance in determining the origins and location of Fort Maurepas in Manitoba. Given Innis's expertise on "the history of the early fur-trade," Howay posed a series of questions to him about the fort's site, who built it, and where he stood on the conflicting claims about the fort's origins. As the person on the board responsible for the drafting of the inscription, Howay wished to "keep on the rails" and make sure that the statement on the commemorative tablet was accurate.[139] Expressing his disagreement with an article written by Nellis M. Crouse (1928), Innis was of the view that "old Maurepas was abandoned" and "the new interest centred on Lake Winnipeg" replaced it. He believed that this was part of a broader "expansion to the Saskatchewan and to the north of Lake Winnipeg," a dynamic that had been missing in Crouse's analysis. In effect, Innis viewed the exploratory and fur-trading activities of La Vérendrye under the French regime as setting the stage for the later initiatives of Peter Pond and other Montreal-based traders further west on the Saskatchewan. Through tracing the genealogy of the French system of forts as it pushed towards the

Northwest, it would then be possible to link this to the later endeavours of the Montreal peddlers and the nascent North West Company, thereby defining the overall arc of their expansion towards the Athabasca.[140]

Innis's contribution to helping Howay determine the origins of Fort Maurepas may have prompted the judge to invite Innis to accompany him at the unveiling ceremony for "a memorial marking the end of the overland telegraph" at Quesnel, British Columbia, in August 1933.[141] On the way back from Quesnel to Vancouver by train, Innis was able to have a discussion with an elderly man, named William Adams, who had spoken at the ceremony. As it turned out, he had originally come from Dumfries Township in Ontario and was a cousin of Innis's mother. Innis took notes about their conversation and ultimately drew upon them in his research (Innis 2016).

Howay also requested that he comment on the draft of a statement that was to appear on the commemorative plaque for the Methye Portage in Fort McMurray, Alberta. Innis's rewording of the inscription – emphasizing the specific timing of Pond's activities – was essentially the version that appeared on the plaque when it was dedicated at Fort McMurray in 1937.[142]

Unfortunately, however, Peter Pond got lost in the shuffle. In Howay's address at the unveiling of the commemorative plaque, he downplayed the importance of Pond and emphasized rather the extent to which the Methye Portage embodied the pioneer spirit in the region.[143]

"Les Explorateurs Célèbres": Mackenzie, Thompson, and Pond

Innis's final commentary on Pond (accompanied by short essays on Thompson and Mackenzie) could be seen as something of a coda for his examination of exploration in North America in relation to the fur trade. It appeared in a comprehensive volume on world exploration, *Les Explorateurs Célèbres* (Leroi-Gourhan 1947)[144] "intended to celebrate the great explorers of the world, from ancient times until the present, with a particular focus on the exploration of the main non-European land masses of the world: Africa, North and South America, Asia, Australia, the Arctic, and the Antarctic." It not only could be seen as a compilation of knowledge about world exploration, but also a commemorative gallery

lxiv   Introduction

of the explorers' accomplishments in relation to those of other "hommes célèbres" (Brunet 1948, 374). Innis's essays in the volume, which had been translated into French, appeared among the eleven contributions in the section on North America" (Buxton 2004).[145] If read collectively, the three statements can be viewed as an effort by Innis to shift prevailing perspectives on the trio. Indeed, it constituted a final reckoning for his interventions on Pond, the fur trade, and the North West Company that he had begun some two decades earlier. In light of his subsequent work on Pond, as well as the considerable intervening scholarship on Thompson and Mackenzie, he sought to provide a capsule assessment of how their legacies should be viewed in relation to one another.

This involved denigrating Mackenzie's accomplishments while at the same time making the case that Pond had largely been given a "raw deal" by commentators, and that Thompson's work had been largely unappreciated. Innis's essay on Mackenzie was more of an exercise of damning with faint praise than a celebration of the explorer's achievements (1947b). While he acknowledged that Mackenzie was likely the first white person to descend the river that now bears his name, Innis underscored that this project was among others that had originally been conceived of by Peter Pond. Innis had the same view of Mackenzie's discovery of a route to the Pacific in British territory. In this case, Innis emphasized that this would not have been possible without the earlier solid work of his competitors. Indeed, he suggested that Mackenzie's contribution to the fur industry in the Northwest was limited because he preferred to remain in Montreal and devote himself to resolving organizational issues in order to assure himself a greater share of company benefits. In any case, Innis believed that he had little influence on the North West Company after he left North America and was uncertain to what extent this was the result of the antagonisms he had created in the company himself. All the same, Innis pointed out that he had made significant accomplishments in the domain of exploration, such as discerning the real character of the Mackenzie River, and bringing to light the impracticality of using the Fraser River as a route to the Pacific Ocean (154).

Not unexpectedly, Innis was much more lavish in his praise of Peter Pond (1947c). After having provided a concise, yet nuanced biography of the explorer, he sought to demonstrate that his contributions to geographical knowledge of North America had been underappreciated because of his

Introduction

lack of literacy. Since Pond's memoir covered only the period of his life up until 1775, accounts of his later career had been based largely on the recollections of other explorers. Most notably, according to Innis, the description of him provided by Alexander Mackenzie in his journal was highly prejudiced. His lack of formal education and crude mapmaking skills notwithstanding, by virtue of his linguistic abilities, his understanding of indigenous commerce, and his organizational capacities Pond was able to play an important leadership role in the extension of the fur trade across the North American continent. For the most part, however, it was his successors who reaped the benefits of his efforts, as he lacked the capacity to counter their ambitious manoeuvres to take advantage of his weaknesses and to deprecate his efforts. In fact, Innis contended, he was dragged into the difficulties of commercial competition and suffered the consequences. Not only was his position weakened, but the jealousies he aroused led him to be blamed for biasing the process of determining the boundary between the British North America and the United States. Innis stressed, however, that the honour of realizing the economic organization of the Mackenzie Basin could not be denied to him; without this achievement, the work of his successors would not have been possible.

In his discussion of David Thompson, Innis made no mention of jealousy or criticism directed towards him (as was the case on his account of Peter Pond) (1947a). He emphasized, rather, the extent to which Thompson's accomplishments in the area of cartography were late in receiving the recognition that they deserved. As with Mackenzie and Pond, Innis provided a fulsome account of Thompson's career and peregrinations. However, rather than dwelling on his activities in the fur trade, he focused on how his extensive work as a mapmaker left its mark on North American governance and society. In particular, Innis noted that Thompson was able to disentangle representations of the extremely complex watershed of the Columbia River's drainage basin. In his view, it was because of Thompson's interest in technical problems of geography that he was slow in reaching the Pacific and was only able to bequeath Britain weak land claims in the Columbia River region. According to Innis, this could also account for the neglect he may have given to his business affairs and why he left Western North America soon after the occupation of the Columbia district by the Americans. Nevertheless, it was thanks to Thompson, Innis contended, that the North

West Company was able to expand to the Pacific. And overall, Innis underscored the point that it was due to his efforts that knowledge of North American drainage basins was given greater precision.

The volume could be seen as carrying out the contention of both Innis and Bolton that Brebner's *Explorers of North America* could serve as an overarching point of reference for further studies of particular figures. The volume actually went further, with its examination of the accomplishments of myriad adventurers throughout world history. The inclusion of Innis's short essays on the trio of Canadian explorers could also be seen as testament to Canada's history being taken seriously on the global stage, with Pond, Mackenzie, and Thompson joining the ranks of the likes of Marco Polo, Christopher Columbus, and Vasco da Gama.

Innis's Peter Pond: Unwitting Self-Betrayal / Sly Self-Substantiation?

Innis's biographical work on Peter Pond represented much more than an effort to write his life story. By illuminating his activities and accomplishments, he sought to reveal how Pond, working in concert with other Montreal-based peddlers, put in place the infrastructure that provided the basis for trade and settlement from the St Lawrence valley to the Athabasca region. Pond's biography thus served as a window to understanding not only the early fur trade and exploration but also the origins of Canada as a nation-state. Mirroring his later remarks on the diary of Simeon Perkins, Pond's memoir (and material related to it) could be seen as a "quarry for the study of economic political, and social institutions" (Perkins and Innis 1948, preface).

Given that making sense of these historical underpinnings was very much in flux at the time (with new materials and insights constantly being made available), Innis's project on Pond was very much part and parcel of an international collective effort, inherently bound up with the efforts of others to examine the intersections between biography and the early fur trade. Innis's frame of reference for interpreting Pond gradually expanded from pre-Confederation Canada to North America (before and after the American Revolution), and finally to the world-historical stage, where Pond was to find his place among other "explorateurs célèbres."

Yet the stakes were much greater than merely adding some new biographical insights into the academic mix. Innis was acutely aware that the formation of nationhood was rooted in cultural memory and a strongly shared sense of what had made a country's emergence possible. His initial work on Pond can be seen as an intervention into ongoing discussions about Canada's origins – a bid to have him included as a major point of reference for Canada's collective identity. And once Canada had emerged from its colonial status and gained recognition as a sovereign power, Pond's status for Innis shifted from that of an erstwhile "father of Confederation" to one of the pre-eminent architects of trade and exploration for the entire North American continent.

This project was not without its challenges. The memoir left by Pond was not only lacking in literary niceties, it also represented only a fragment of his life. And other documentation for Pond was not entirely reliable. Innis appeared to have addressed these difficulties by treating his project on Pond as a tentative work in progress, subject to correction and revision as new material became available, the product of an ongoing dialogue with others having a stake in the Pond material. Also, since he viewed Pond as bound up with the broader fur trade and exploration, advances on this front had reverberations for how Pond himself should be understood. The project was also layered and complicated, as it involved a reworking of conventions of autobiography and biography; taking a memoir as a point of departure for constructing a biography, somehow meshing the two without losing Pond's own voice in the process. While Innis largely took him at his word – as his own witness – he made extensive use of third-party sources to put Pond's revelations into perspective. He accomplished this by constantly changing modes of address, recurrently disrupting Pond's own narrative by situating his subjective views within broader, more objectively based circumstances.

Innis's strategy of transforming subjective memoirs into more objective biographies led inexorably to a powerful reflexive element in the renditions of the life narratives that he produced. For in abandoning the subjective standpoint of the biographee, he was obliged to establish another point of reference, which more often than not coincided with his own life experience. This reflexive standpoint was revealed in a review he wrote of a biography of John Maynard Keynes: "We can agree with George Jean Nathan that 'the most pointedly personal autobiography of a biographer is the biography that he has written of some other man,' and that all biography is 'a form of unwitting self betrayal or sly self substantiation'" (1951b, 553).

There is some evidence that Innis unwittingly betrayed himself through his biographical work. And in doing so, he substantiated himself in ways that were likely more than circumstantial. For Innis, the biographical enterprise went beyond making sense of the lives of particular individuals. His fascination with them could not be separated from his passion for the causes that they espoused and their efforts to bring their ideals to fruition. Heyer points out that Innis had a great deal in common with Alexander McPhail (1883–1931), farm leader, agricultural reformer, and first leader of the Saskatchewan Wheat Board. Both had Scottish ancestry, had rural backgrounds, and served in the military. Innis observes that McPhail "'loathed ... pomposity ... admired brains ... and respected honesty.'" Moreover, he disliked wasting time, had a good sense of humour, avoided "emotionalism," was not fond of publicity, and was an avid reader, "particularly biography" (2004, 163). Heyer was struck by the extent to which Innis seemed to identify "with McPhail's character and personality," as revealed by the self-descriptions he provided in his autobiographical memoir" (Innis 2016). It was evident that Innis was also an advocate of the cause dear to the heart of McPhail, namely the Western cooperative movement in grain marketing. Innis had come to embrace the standpoint of Western grain-growers during the summer of 1915 when he lived with a rural family while teaching in central Alberta. Heyer notes that "McPhail's assiduous labours on behalf of the co-operative movement obviously impressed him" (2004). Hence, through his efforts to frame McPhail's diary as a biography, Innis was also articulating the goals and convictions of the prairie cooperative initiative.

The same coupling of advocacy and diary appeared to have also been at work in his biography of Simeon Perkins (1735–1812), Nova Scotia militia leader, merchant, diarist, and politician. In this case, Innis had become more familiar with Maritime issues when he began to study how the decentralized Atlantic economy could be seen as a contrast to the more centralized fur-trade and railway industries (1931b). He was able to further develop his views on this question through his membership on the royal commission to examine the Nova Scotia economy (Nova Scotia 1934). He

Introduction   lxix

also spent much of the 1930s undertaking research on the East Coast cod fisheries (1954). It was through this study that he became familiar with the diary of Simeon Perkins, which he cites on a number of occasions. As with Alexander McPhail, Innis likely saw a good deal of himself in Perkins. Not only did Perkins exhibit discipline, curiosity, and public engagement through assiduously keeping a diary over the course of many years, he also successfully managed to juggle a variety of pursuits, including involvement with fisheries, lumber, leather goods, merchandising, local militias, and civic politics. Moreover, as Innis was becoming increasingly disenchanted with American cultural imperialism in relation to Canada during the Cold War (1952a), he likely found himself identifying more closely with Perkins, who led the resistance against a variety of foreign intrusions during the colonial period.[146]

His identification with Pond arguably went even further. Innis remarked that "a biography of an economist by an economist will emphasize the views of the author which coincide with the views of the subject of the biography" (1950b, 553). In this case, the biography of an explorer by an inveterate traveller undoubtedly led to some overlap in viewpoints. Innis and Pond had more in common than a love of experiencing new territory. Neither waxed poetically about landscape but both revelled in the subtleties of human settlement. Both had humble origins and were lacking in pretension. By virtue of his curiosity and hands-on approach to the acquisition of knowledge, Pond was a quintessential dirt researcher in the Innisian mould. While both were fascinated by geography and how it could be represented pictorially, both eschewed conventional mapmaking – Pond by circumstance and Innis by choice. They shared the conviction that a major purpose of maps was to usefully convey knowledge about particular territories. For Pond this took the form of preparing maps that included notes about the area in question. For Innis, this involved working with government officials to prepare maps that captured the distribution of staples resources. These in turn were to be made available for classroom use.

While Pond continually chafed under military authority, he still managed to perform the tasks assigned to him in a workmanlike fashion. Like Innis, he identified very much with the rank-and-file soldier and often found military leadership to be wanting. Innis was obviously quite taken with Pond's organizational skills and planning abilities (that had been honed in his military service), mirrored by his own enthusiasm for the logistics that made possible the taking of Vimy Ridge and the building of the Hudson Bay Railway (Innis 2016). His propensity to work collectively echoed Pond's evident skill at networking and pooling resources for a common cause. Harbouring resentment for having been passed over for various honours and recognitions, Innis eagerly took up the cause of countering the claims of Pond's detractors, bending over backwards to find and present exculpatory information about him. Well aware of his own literary shortcomings, he believed that what Pond had to say was much more important than how he said it. Finally, his motto "Push on – Keep moving" could have been written for Pond. Throughout his life Pond abjured a sedentary existence, the continual impediments to his movements notwithstanding. His travels knew no boundaries; he was troubled by neither allegiances nor fear of the unknown. Innis, by all accounts, was as intrigued by his journeys as he was by spending time in his planned destinations. In his efforts to track Pond's movements in time and space with exactitude, he was also defining the contours of his own activities and perambulations: "In retracing the fur-trade routes of Pond and others, Innis experienced part of the relationship between early exploitation of the Canadian North and the land upon which it took place" (Heyer 2013, 72). Pond's legacy likely loomed large in Innis's engagement with northern Canada, as described with eloquence by Matthew Evenden: "Innis imagined the North before arriving there, grafted ambitions onto the region, inscribed ideas in field notes and represented the North to popular audiences in southern Canada on his return. In the process of creating a northern vision that stressed the importance of the North as a frontier for industrialism and a binding agent for national unity, Innis adopted and refashioned popular ideas of Canada's northern regions and remade himself as a public intellectual and nationalist thinker" (Evenden 2013, 74).

Arguably, his engagement with those he met on his various journeys also helped to make him something of an organic intellectual who came to identify with those who had been marginalized. To be sure, much of his time during episodes of "dirt research" was spent with political, economic, and religious elites. Yet Innis not only sought to meet a wide range of persons involved with everyday activities, he also made a point of doing various jobs himself, including working as a deckhand and trying his hand at placer min-

Introduction lxxi

ing. This point of reference very much informed his historiographical sensibility. In this regard, his preface to Mary Quayle Innis's *Economic History of Canada* (1943a) can be viewed as something of a manifesto for the reconstruction of Canadian cultural memory, articulating the vision that was emergent in his biographical work on Peter Pond. Continuing the line of argument he had developed attendant upon Canada's 1927 jubilee, he noted that "intensive work in Canadian history has been concerned primarily with constitutional developments, and important outposts have been pushed into finance and money." He argued that Mary Quayle Innis's text represented "an attempt ... to advance from the geographic and technological approach toward work done in the constitutional field and to stake out a broad field for the study of Canadian cultural growth." The lengthy sketch of elements that followed was presented as a corrective to the forgetting that Innis viewed as rampant. According to Innis, not only had whole classes of people been forgotten "(... fishermen ... Indians ... voyageurs ... slaves ... farmers ... lumbermen ... navvies ... miners)" but also areas "(Hudson Bay ... Precambrian formation ... fishing banks)," commodities "(... beaver, iron, brandy, rum, cod, square timber, potash ... placer gold)," and equipment "(... canoe ... Durham and York boats ... stern-wheel steamboat ... sluice box)." This ode to the reconstruction of cultural memory was grounded in the practice of biography, with its "interest ... in the continuous labour of Canadians who have shifted the scenes, rather than on those who have been engaged in the unseemly rush to take the curtain call." Our major institutions, he argued, "reflect the energy, patience and initiative of a people who did the country's work" (1943a, v–vi). Peter Pond, by virtue of his organizational abilities, planning capacities, and interpersonal skills, was viewed by Innis as exemplary in this respect. While Innis did not make much headway with his colleagues in having Peter Pond recognized as a founding figure for Canada, he did have much better luck keeping the fur trader's name alive in some of the continent's "forgotten" outposts.

Pond and His Biographers

While Innis's biographical work on Pond certainly helped to rescue him from obscurity, it in no way succeeded in making him into a household name. To be sure, he was frequently mentioned (most of often in passing) in works discussing the history of the fur trade and exploration in North America (Burpee 1908, 1927a; Brebner 1933; Chalmers 2003; Clancy 1978; Cooke 1974; Fedirchuk 1990; Hayes 2002; Kellogg 1935) and was even the subject of a short biography (Wagner 1955) as well as an entry in the *Dictionary of Canadian Biography* (Gough n.d.). But he has never been able to join the ranks of figures such as David Thompson and Alexander Mackenzie in the Canadian imagination. Recently, however (and quite unaccountably), the tide of cultural memory has been flowing more in Pond's direction. Not only has he been the subject of two full-scale biographies (Chapin 2014; Gough 2014) but he is the central figure in a novel written about his involvement in the Canadian fur trade (McDonald 2018).[147]

While these recent biographical accounts of Pond make reference to a range of Innis writings on Pond, they largely fail to recognize the extent to which his perspective on the fur trader/adventurer was bound up in his evolving views on the North American fur trade (1933b, 1936, 1942, 1943b). This means that they tend to focus on Innis's early Pond-related writings (informed by Canadian nationalism) while ignoring his later (more continentalist) reflections on the North American fur industry (to which Pond made a major contribution). Despite their neglect of this aspect of Innis's work on Pond, they come to similar conclusions on their own. On the basis of their extensive research using both primary and secondary sources, they both underscore the notion that Peter Pond's contributions should be viewed as having significance that transcends national boundaries.

Even though Chapin and Gough both use Innis as an important point of reference for their examinations of Peter Pond's life, their approaches to biography differ from that of Innis, albeit in much different ways. In his preface to *Peter Pond* (Innis and Pond 1930), Innis notes that his "attention was attracted to [his] work through a study of the early history of the Northwest Company." In his view, "the organization of the technical side of the trade which followed the expansion to the Saskatchewan and especially to Athabasca and which made possible the evolution of the Northwest Company was to a large extent a result of the efforts of Peter Pond." Hence, "to understand the history of the fur trade during the formative stages of the Northwest Company [he] found it necessary to attempt a biography of Peter Pond." By virtue of Pond's contributions to the development of Canada as linked to the North West Company, Innis believed that "a gen-

Introduction

eral appreciation of his position as one of the fathers of Confederation" was warranted. Underlying Innis's historical efforts on behalf of Pond was his contention that "the vilification of his enemies up to the present has made this estimate impossible" (Innis and Pond 1930, viii–ix).

As we have argued, Innis's biographical work on Pond could be seen as an intervention into discussions about Canadian cultural memory that were occasioned by the 1927 Diamond Jubilee of Confederation. In trying to make the case that Pond should be considered as a "father of Confederation," Innis emphasized Pond's activities in his capacity as a founding figure of the North West Company. This meant that his discussion of Pond's work and career was centred on his involvement with the Canadian fur trade with his earlier and later life experiences south of the border receiving less attention. Moreover, in focusing on Pond's organizational activities, Innis tended to avoid examining some of the usual components of biographical discussions, such as character, motivation, and personality.

In his biographical work on Pond,[148] Barry Gough makes frequent and explicit reference to Innis. He notes in his preface to *The Elusive Mr Pond* that Innis's *Peter Pond* (as an effort to elucidate the North West Company's history) was a "pioneering biography" and "a considerable achievement" (2014). His praise for Innis was qualified by his claim that parts of his Pond biography "were shown to be unreliable and it also left many questions unanswered."[149] Nevertheless, in examining the period covered by Pond's memoir, he adopts the same periodization of Pond's life deployed by Innis, adding some flesh on the bones laid bare by Innis. Overall, Gough paints on a broad canvas, seeking to understand Innis in relation to eighteenth-century geopolitics. From his standpoint as a historian of British Columbia, he has a particular interest in what insights Pond's activities provide into Western exploration. Despite the paucity of documentation coming from Pond or the North West Company, Gough has declined the seduction of engaging in "creative non-fiction," aside from some speculations on Pond's appearance (xvi). To be sure, when solid background information is available, he does offer conjectures about why Pond acted the way he did.[150] When faced with the difficulty of making sense of Pond's decisions and activities, Gough deftly provides insightful overviews of the historical backdrop to his actions. A case in point is his chapter on Robert Rogers, Jonathan Carver, and the Northwest Passage. While he makes scant mention of Pond in the chapter, he argues persuasively that Pond was eventually able to benefit from the British military regulation that was put in place in Michilimackinac. This set the stage for his later discussion of Pond's views on Carver (64), which allows him to provide insights into how Pond assessed his own travels and activities. Overall, Gough offers support for Innis's claim that Pond was unfairly vilified by his enemies: "[He] had to battle the views of conniving rivals for pre-eminence and fame, and these rivals were prepared to sweep him away by categorizing him as of an old and less scientific breed than they were. It is an old story and victims stalk the stages of history reminding us that winners should not always write the great chronicles" (7).

Like Gough, Chapin cites a number of Innis's works on Pond throughout his text. However, in contrast to Gough, his debt to Innis appears to be more implicit than explicit. Unlike Gough, he rarely quotes from Innis or engages with his interpretations. And while Gough largely relies on Innis's *Peter Pond* (Innis and Pond 1930) when he wishes to make use of Pond's memoir, Chapin prefers to refer to the second Gates version (1965). At first glance, his approach to writing a biography of Pond differs from that of Innis. He notes that his focus is on "Peter Pond's personal story and his individual experiences" (x). However, he also emphasizes that "one cannot tell Pond's story without telling the story of the North American fur trade. Pond was part of a generation of traders who came of age while English-speaking people were extending their influence and their trade across North America." He goes on to stress that "Pond's story is a story of exploration, both geographic and cultural." Aside from his emphasis on recounting Pond's personal story and experiences, his account appears to be very much in line with Innis's biographical work on the fur trader and explorer. Mirroring Innis's penchant for combining "dirt research" with what might be called "dust research," Chapin not only visited numerous archival sites, but also made a point of traversing the routes taken by Pond and the places where he lived. And in the same way that Innis was intensely interested in issues of commemoration and cultural memory, Chapin's visits to historical sites involved conferring with "dedicated people preserving the memory of the places Pond knew well" (xi).

In probing Pond's cultural exploration, Chapin frames his discussion in terms of Pond's curiosity and quest for knowledge. Like Innis, he is much

Introduction

more interested in Pond's nascent intellectual and practical skills than in his literary and cartographical shortcomings. He shares with both Innis and Gough the frustration that Pond's paper trail is thin, uneven, and meandering. He has been able to overcome the dearth of direct documentary material on Pond by providing numerous detailed accounts of the contexts that were pertinent to his life and career. In instances for which evidence about an aspect of Pond's life is clear, Chapin uses a simple declarative style ("when Mary Hubbard Pond died she left behind at least three children"). However, in instances where there is more uncertainty about what transpired, Chapin writes in a more conjectural register: "Peter *would also have had to* tend to his father's shop, which his mother *would have been* running during her husband's absence. His brothers *should have been* of some help ... Charles had enlisted ... in the army in early April and *would not be* discharged until December. No record of Zachariah or Phineas ... *Perhaps they were in Milford* helping their older brother ... *perhaps one or both were with their father* on his trading mission to Detroit" (34).

This approach allows Chapin to make use of the available evidence in a fruitful manner, conveying as precisely as possible the degree of certainty with which he can make statements pertinent to Pond's biography. It also means he is able to examine the interplay between Pond's activities and broader tendencies. This can be seen in his discussion of Pond's travels in relation to the smallpox epidemic: "By the winter of 1778–79, when Pond had reached Athabasca ... smallpox was in New Orleans. In the summer of 1779 when Pond travelled east to Montreal, smallpox travelled west to Mexico City ... Like Pond, the *variola major* virus followed trade routes across vast North American distances" (189).

While Chapin does not provide any direct evidence of the impact of smallpox on Pond (and vice versa), he is able to hypothesize (by virtue of the striking spatial-temporal parallels) that the spread of smallpox most likely accompanied Pond's travels and exploration (Chapin 2014, 189). By virtue of contextual material such as this, one can make better sense of numerous aspects of Innis's biographical work on Pond.[151]

Unlike Gough, who has largely steered away from "creative non-fiction," Chapin's account at times relies more on imagination than evidence, such as in his speculative rendering of Pond's brigade traversing the Methye Portage. Chapin likely used the material as the introduction to his book in an effort to evoke the "structure of feeling" of the times. While the event is framed as if it had actually taken place ("five large birch bark canoes glided across a quiet lake"), the text is sprinkled with references that are more conjectural ("white pelicans may have skimmed the water ... the guide perhaps informed them ... Pond likely noted that the cool fresh water would be appreciated") (1–3). Chapin concludes his re-enactment of the traversing of the Methye Portage by speculating about how a member of the canoe party might have felt about what he had experienced: "Perhaps they found some satisfaction ... in knowing that they were pioneering a new route that would play an important part in a global network of trade. If not, at least they knew they were acquiring stories to tell and feats to boast of on their next trip north" (3).

At this point Chapin largely abandons the approach of imaginatively reconstructing particular historical events in favour of one based more on historical reportage, drawing effectively on primary and secondary sources with the life and times of Peter Pond as his focus.

For the most part, both Gough and Chapin use Pond's memoir as their point of reference for constructing Pond's biography from his birth in 1740 to the point at which he was about to leave the upper Mississippi area to the region north of the Great Lakes.[152] Moreover, their respective renditions of the key events in this period closely follow the periodization used by Innis.[153] Rather than going off in directions differing from those of Innis, they mostly add flesh to Innis's somewhat barebones account of this period of Pond's life, relying mostly on his memoir.

This involves, *inter alia*, adding additional information about Pond's genealogical background and upbringing, clarifying the background to Pond's military service (through discussions of enlistment patterns, troop movements, victories and defeats), discussing the fate of the fur trade and exploration in what had become the new province of Quebec in British North America, emphasizing the role played by Robert Rogers and Jonathan Carver in searching for the Northwest Passage, elaborating how Michilimackimac was a British military and trading stronghold, as well as summarizing Pond's specific techniques for conducting diplomacy with native peoples.

Innis's next chapter, "The Northwest Company," is again divided into two sections: "The Explorer" (1775–78) and "The Organizer" (1778–90).

Introduction

The first of these charts his movements as related to the fur trade, encompassing Pond's early explorations, culminating in his journey to the Athabasca territory in 1778; the second focuses more on his organizational and administrative activities in relation to the incipient North West Company. Neither Chapin nor Gough separates Pond's activities as explorer and administrator in this fashion. Rather, while both place Pond's movements at the centre of their narratives, these are always viewed in the context of Pond's organizational work, initially as an independent trader and eventually as a founding figure of what was to become the North West Company. Most notably, each examines Pond's excursion to the Athabasca territory separately from his other travels. While Innis's account of the expedition itself is rather sketchy (largely relying on a letter written from Alexander Henry to Joseph Banks, 18 October 1781), the descriptions offered by Gough and Chapin are much more nuanced and detailed, likely because of their access to sources that were unavailable to Innis (Morse 1979; E.E. Rich and Johnson 1951).

Innis was extremely tentative about the conclusions he could reach on the fur trade from 1778 to 1783. He noted that "the sources of information are meagre and in many cases biased." In a previous efforts to disentangle the shifting membership of the emergent organization (1927c), he concluded that "the problems are extremely complex" (91). This section on Pond as "organizer" paralleled the section he had written on Pond as "peace maker" for the period when he was on the upper Mississippi (47–66). In this case, Innis claimed that Pond had been very successful in his mediation between warring Indian tribes. However, Innis believed that Pond was much less successful in his later role as an organizer; he was largely unable to effectively mediate the struggles between the larger and the smaller groups of traders on the Saskatchewan – precursors to the North West Company. According to Innis, these ongoing and unresolved tensions underpinned the murders of Waden and Ross, which came to cast a shadow over Pond's reputation (92–3).

Along the same lines, Innis traces how in the early stages of the North West Company Pond was at odds with the others about how the shares in the emergent organization should be allocated (104). Perhaps because they were less preoccupied than Innis was with Pond's relationship to the early

North West Company, both Gough and Chapin do not focus on these organizational tensions; their examinations of this aspect of Innis's biography tend to downplay the structural conflicts at issue.

Innis's summation chapter, "The Man and His Work," ties directly into his preceding one on the North West Company. He emphasizes that because the fur trade was "productive of bitter enmities," Pond's chief chronicler (i.e., Alexander Mackenzie) not only neglected "the importance of his work" but actually maligned him (113–14). Innis claims that this rancour was rooted in the fact that Mackenzie's account of the fur trade "was written from the standpoint of that small band of traders who never surrendered." Hence, "the hostility of the small traders to the North West Company was never overcome." The remainder of the chapter chronicles Pond's activities after returning from Athabasca, with a few final pages dedicated to the period after his return to Milford in 1790. Neither Gough nor Chapin has much more to add about Pond's final years, which are mired in obscurity. However, in their assessments of Pond's overall significance, they disagree with Innis, who concluded that Pond's achievements were "not of a sensational nature," attributing this to his many disadvantages, including his illiteracy and lack of technical training. In effect, rather than springing to Pond's defence, Innis appears to have taken the criticisms of his detractors to heart.

Gough and Chapin, however, judged that the achievements of Pond, if not sensational, were certainly remarkable and significant, particularly in light of his circumstances. Arguably they were able to reach this conclusion because of the abundant insights found in Innis's writings on Peter Pond and on the fur trade. Most notably, Innis focused on Pond's activities as trader, explorer, diplomat, mapmaker, organizer, and, to a lesser extent, as collector and philosopher. Through their respective research efforts, Chapin and Gough have been able to add detail, depth, and nuance to this profile. This has involved not only drawing on sources that were unavailable to Innis, but also reinterpreting material that he himself had used. By virtue of this material, we are able to better understand three periods of Pond's life referred to by Innis: his trading on the upper Mississippi (1775), his leadership of the English River Fort (1786), and finally, his later explorations based in the Athabasca region, which set the stage for extensive discussion in the late eighteenth century (1787–89).

Introduction

The first item in question did not take the form of new material; it was an article that offered a re-evaluation of the meaning and significance of Pond's memoir as discursive intervention bound up with his dual position as a frontiersman at work in the hinterlands and a person aspiring to become a published author (Greenfield 2002). While Innis makes extensive use of Pond's memoir in crafting his biography, for the most part he takes the document at face value as a retrospective description of the fur trader's life. However, as Greenfield points out, the memoir is a product of what happens when someone with considerable life experience but minimal literary skill sought to gain access to the "urban centers where texts were published and from which they were diffused" (415). Pond, he argues, was seeking to join the likes of fellow explorers such as Alexander Mackenzie and Jonathan Carver who sought to "inform readers about the distant reaches of empire [and] to present themselves in terms of the vast distances and cultural frontiers they had crossed" (415–16). Indeed, "the publishing successes of his fur-trade contemporaries were part of the flourishing state of travel publishing during the later eighteenth century … [T]hey perhaps helped foster Peter Pond's ambition, despite his rudimentary literacy, to author a book." According to Greenfield, by virtue of the dualism that combined living "in close contact with the native communities" with writing for the Euro-American publishing world in the late eighteenth century produced a particular kind of subjectivity (417). Specifically, he claims that the life Pond lived "can be understood through reference to [Richard] White's (2011) concept of 'the middle ground,' the two-way verbal/cultural accommodation that developed among the French (and later the English) and the mainly Algonkian-speaking Indians of the region [pays d'en haut or upper country]" (427). In Gough's view, by framing Pond's interactions with members of the Winnebago village in terms of the "middle ground," Greenfield is able to make "important observations" about how Pond is able to position himself on the group's periphery while still maintaining emotional contact with unfolding events (61–2). This positioning, Greenfield claims, was an artefact of Pond's desire to provide a description that would capture the feelings he shared with his hosts, but at the same time gain accessibility to a literary readership. This line of argument, by shedding light on the dynamics of Pond's relations to native Americans of the Great Lakes region, serves to give more depth and nuance to Innis's commentary on the episode in his biography of Pond.

In terms of new sources referred to by either Gough or Chapin, one of the most revealing is *The English River Book: A North West Company Journal and Account Book of 1786* (Duckworth and North West Company 1990). This is a published version of a parchment-bound ledger with the title "1786 English River Book R.R.R." While the author's name is not included, one can surmise that the person responsible for it was Peter Pond's clerk, Cuthbert Grant. Included in the ledger is "a short journal of daily activities from April 1 to May 31, 1786 at Pond's fort on the Athabasca River" (Chapin 2014, 255). The first entries chronicle the activities of the fort during the spring trading season when small groups of first nations people – particularly Crees and Denes – arrived at the fort to exchange their furs. The journal reveals the management style used by Pond in dealing with both the visitors and his clerks (suggesting that Grant chafed at Pond's authoritarian manner). Chapin judges that "Pond certainly comes across as an overly controlling boss who could exhibit curmudgeonly behaviour at times" (2014, 256). Pond also was not above using force to make sure rules of conduct were followed. On one occasion he cut a Beaver Indian on the head with his dagger in order to stop a threat of violence. However, it was apparently typical that after incidents like this Pond would attempt to reconcile with the aggrieved by providing that person with a gift. As Chapin observes, Pond's action was not out of line, as "the use of physical violence to maintain discipline was the norm throughout the English-speaking world" (256). Grant also describes some of Pond's less dramatic activities, including negotiating contracts and providing "influential Dene leaders" with gifts in order to secure their loyalty. More generally, the journal describes the day-to-day activities of the fort (such as packing furs and making canoes), providing insights into the organizational life that Pond was overseeing. This material serves to flesh out what Innis had to say about Pond's efficacy as a fur-trade administrator.

Subsequent to the publication of Innis's *Peter Pond*, closer attention was given to a pair of letters written by residents of Quebec City to persons in London, recounting what Peter Pond had told them during meetings with them in the late autumn of 1789: Dr J. Mervin Nooth in Quebec City to Joseph Banks, London, 4 November 1789; Isaac Ogden, Quebec City, to David Ogden, London, 7 November 1789.[154] As Isaac Ogden noted to his father, David Ogden,[155] having been frustrated by the lack of accuracy in common

Introduction

lxxxi

knowledge about the size of Canada, a state of affairs that was not satisfactory to a "Philosophic Mind," he was grateful to "have had an opportunity of seeing a Map or Chart of that Country made by a Gentleman of observation and Science [Peter Pond], who has actually traversed it and made his Map in it." He was able to have "several Conversations with the map before [him]" (Dillon and Nooth 1951, 324–5). While he had not made a copy of the map, he had made "copious notes" of it and was able to describe to his father with great detail the co-ordinates given to him by Pond for numerous geographical features of the North American continent.[156] He made mention of Pond, having observed a "Species of Buffaloes, that have no tails ... smaller than the common buffaloes" and referred to a "great Chain of Mountains approach to the Verge of Slave Lake and River." He reported that according to Pond, in 1787 "Indians from the Lake penetrated North ... where the Waters ebb and flow ... At the Northern Ocean they met & killed a number of Eskimaux Indians, which ... are to be found only on the Banks or Boundary of the Ocean from the Labrador Coast Northward" (324).

Innis was well aware of this letter, having seen a published version of it (1889), finding that "the account leaves much to be desired" (Innis and Pond 1930, 146). However, in the absence of Pond's own reflections on whether Cook's River could be located in the West, he was obliged to gain insights into Pond's views by examining the "second-hand" information provided by Ogden in his letter. He found the report "extremely difficult to follow [with] its comments suggestive as to Ogden's confusion." After itemizing a number of errors that he believed Ogden had made, he did concede that his "observations on Pond's conversations ... in the main ... were probably accurate." However, it is unclear from his discussion whether he believed that Pond's account was off base or whether Ogden had misconstrued what he had been told.

Innis, however, was not familiar with the letter from Nooth to Banks, written a few days before the letter from Isaac Ogden to his father. Had he known about this letter, he might have responded differently to the later correspondence. The letter from Nooth to Banks was one of several that he wrote in the fall of 1789, accompanied by samples of botanical material he had collected, such as "Seeds of the Zizania aquatica" and a "Quantity of the Folle Avoine" (Dillon and Nooth 1951, 329). Nooth not only wished to convey to Banks what Pond had told him about his geographical discoveries, but also to let him know what Pond had to say about the flora, fauna, and geological material he had observed. Nooth described as Pond as "a very singular person" who claimed that he had "discover'd an immense Lake [Great Slave Lake] nearly equal to Great Britain that communicates in all probability with Cook's River or Sandwich Sound [Alaska]." In addition to describing a meeting with "Indians that had undoubtedly seen Cooks [*sic*] Ships & who had with them a variety of European Articles evidently of English manufacture," Pond spoke of the level landscape "abounded with Timber" and "very luxuriant grass," as well as "an infinite Variety of Fossils" they had collected from riverbanks.[157] Mirroring what was reported in the Ogden letter, Pond noted that the most common animals they saw were "Buffaloes" and even claimed that he had discovered "a new species of Buffaloe that wants a tail." In terms of "mineral substances," all that they could find was "Iron, & this was chiefly Bog Ore such as abounds in the neighbourhood of Three Rivers" (Dillon and Nooth 1951, 329).

The interpretations of these letters by Gough and Chapin were very much inflected by the fact that the two were treated as a tandem in Dillon and Nooth's 1951 article, in which Nooth's letter – likely because of its novelty – was the point of reference. This suggested that Pond should not be narrowly viewed as an explorer and would-be mapmaker, but as someone with a driving curiosity to make sense of both the natural and human worlds. In Chapin's view, both Ogden and Nooth described Pond as a "man who had embraced the scientific milieu of the Enlightenment – a man for whom the collection of new knowledge about the natural world was its own reward" (276). By virtue of drawing on Nooth's letter to examine Pond in a more holistic fashion, both Gough and Chapin also added to the range of activities that could be associated with the intrepid adventurer and explorer. Taken in concert, their two texts had already provided evidence that the list of Pond's activities should be expanded to include eighteenth-century variants of reconnaissance, logistics, market analysis, personnel management, investment, intercultural communication, as well as authorship. On the basis of Nooth's letter, one could also add botanist, biologist, geologist, and collector.

Introduction

In writing the bibliography for Peter Pond, Innis complained that "the works dealing with the activities of Peter Pond are extremely scanty and in most cases very unreliable" (Innis and Pond 1930, 144). Through engaging with sources not available to Innis, attending closely to Pond's everyday life, and examining him through new lenses, Gough and Chapin have been able to demonstrate the extent to which Pond was something of a jack-of-all-(fur)trades, combined with an aspiring polymath whose myriad activities were determined both by necessity and passion.

Yet the arc of Pond's development is not captured by the range and variety of his endeavours. As Greenfield describes his efforts to refashion himself as an author, "Pond's experiences on a local ground, which occurred in accordance with the discourses of that ground, are narrated in a voice that asserts community with early nineteenth-century readers, a physically and experientially distant group, through adoption of the conventions of the printed discourses of that community" (2002, 430).

Arguably, the same dynamic was at work in Pond's later-life aspirations to become part of the knowledge-making community: "Pond collected and transported knowledge as well as goods. He recorded the plants and animals he encountered. He collected fossils and minerals. He learned about Algonquian, Siouan, and Athapascan people. He talked with them about their customs and asked them about the places they had traveled. He drew maps that showed the remote areas he visited and the places beyond about which he heard" (Chapin 2014, 8–9).

As evident in the letters of Nooth and Ogden, Pond delighted in sharing his knowledge with others. Their inaccuracies notwithstanding, Pond's ideas and maps, along with verbal reports of his recollections, became part and parcel of discussions that were taking place in "the highest levels of the European and North American scientific worlds."[158]

As Gough and Chapin note, international interest in Pond's maps and ideas proved to be short-lived. And on the home front, Innis noted that Pond's ending in Canada was a sad one. He left the country "with all his later conclusions disproved. Had the conjecture proved correct he would have been accorded a place among the great discoverers of Canadian history. But it was proved wrong and his former friends and supporters probably regarded him as a traitor" (Innis and Pond 1930, 140). Unfortunately, Innis's assessment of Pond's place in history was overly influenced by the criteria used by his detractors, leading him to claim that his achievements "were not of a sensational nature." But had he assessed Pond's contributions more broadly on the basis of criteria of his own making, his conclusions might have been much different. Moreover, not only was he unable to take advantage of the vast storehouse of primary material that was to eventually become available, but his project on Peter Pond and the fur trade was cut short because of other pressures and commitments.

However, in framing their respective discussions in terms of Pond's activities – à la Innis – Chapin and Gough have been able to make a convincing case that Pond's "achievement placed him among the greats of early North American history" (Gough 2014, 170) and that "through his life we see the landscape of eighteenth century North America through a wider lens" (Chapin 2014, 9).

NOTES

1 According to Daniel Drache, "Innis focused on the *longue durée*, the history of events and epoch-making forces that transformed economies, states and civilizations" (Innis 1995, xiv). Meyrowitz observes that Innis "rewrites human history as the history of communication technologies" (Meyrowitz 2014, 52).

2 While A. John Watson, in his compendious biography of Innis (2006), claims that Innis was of the view that "the continuous vitality of western civilization depended on the efforts of individual thinkers" (23), he makes no mention whatsoever of Innis's work on Pond, McPhail, and Perkins. Similarly, Donald Creighton's otherwise thorough discussion of Innis's work (1957) does not address the biographical dimension of Innis's research.

3 See also Britnell (1939).

4 Heyer (2004, 159) notes that Innis "considered the epistle, memoir, and especially the diary as revealing sources for understanding history – a way of glimpsing it from the inside." This is evident in "some surprisingly unconventional sources" that he drew upon in *Bias of Communication* ([1951] 1964):

Thomas Constable's *Archibald Constable and His Literary Correspondents*; Harold Spender's *Fire of Life: A Book of Memories*; Brand Whit-

Introduction lxxxv

lock's *Forty Years of It*; John Maynard Keynes' *Two Memoirs*; W.R. Inge's *Diary of a Dean*; *The Journals of André Gide*; George Gissing's *Private Papers of Henry Rycroft*; Norman Hapgood's *Changing Years: Reminiscences*; E.L. Goodkin's *Reflections and Comments*; *The Letters of Ezra Pound*; *Further Extracts from the Notebooks of Samuel Butler*; *The Autobiography of Leigh Hunt*; J.H. Harper's *I Remember*; Melville Stone's *Fifty Years a Journalist*; E.P. Mitchell's *Memoirs of an Editor* (185); Mark Pattison's *Memoirs*; Cyrus Redding's *Fifty Years' Recollections*; *The Journal of Sir Walter Scott*; Frederick Harrison's *Autobiographic Memoirs*; and A.M. Thompson's *Here I Lie*.

5 Innis was quite familiar with the writings of French theorists of human geography, such as Albert Demangeon, Jean Brunhes, Vidal de la Blache, André Siegfried, as well as the work of Quebec authors working in this tradition, such as Raymond Tanghe and Benoit Brouillette (Buxton 2004).

6 This in line with Blondheim's claim that Innis "maintains that societies are capable of balancing their time-space act through appropriating communication technologies that would counter the monopolizing tendencies of entrenched media." Hence, "he emerges as a through and through social constructivist, holding that technological change is engineered and affected by society's strategies and choices." Arguably, his view of the "strategies and choices" of intellectuals (including himself) was based on the same premise (Blondheim 2004, 128).

7 This involved the elevation of the public good through historical practice (Dick 2009; Conrad 2007).

8 Each obituary typically was followed by a brief bibliography of the deceased's contributions. These included those written for Stephen Butler Leacock (1869–1944) (Innis 1944); Edward Johns Urwick (1867–1945) (Innis 1945); William T. Jackman (1871–1951) (Innis 1952b); Charles Norris Cochrane (1889–1945) (Innis 1946); Arthur James Glazebrook (1861–1940) (Innis 1941); and William Burton Hurd (1894–1950) (Innis 1950a).

9 These included Sage (1927), Davis and Davis (1934), and Hutchins (1952).

10 These included reviews of MacNaughton and Vaughan (1926) (Innis 1926); Porter (1931) (Innis 1932a); Murphy (1941); Garnett (1949) (Innis 1950b); and Rolph (1950) (Innis 1951).

11 These included editions of *Journals and Letters of Pierre Gaultier de Varennes de La Vérendrye and His Sons* (La Vérendrye, Burpee, and Le Sueur

1927) (Innis 1928d); *Journals of Samuel Herne and Philip Turnor* (Innis 1935d); *Documents Relating to the North West Company* (W. Stewart Wallace 1934) (Innis 1935b); *Holland's Description of Cape Breton Island and Other Documents* (Holland and Harvey 1935) (Innis 1935c); *The Journal of Duncan M'Gillivray of the North West Company …* (M'Gillivray and Morton 1929) (Innis 1935e); *The John Askin Papers* (Askin and Quaife 1928) (Innis 1928c); and *Voyages from Montreal on the River St Laurence through the Continent of North America …* (Mackenzie 1927) (Innis 1927e).

12 In the conclusion to the diary of Andrew McPhail he maintained that it "will not be possible to appraise the work of McPhail until we have had biographies of such men as [L.C.] Brouillette … [G.W.] Robertson … [Henry Wise] Wood, [Premier John Edward] Brownlee, [J.I.] McFarland,… and of [C.H.] Burnell and [P.F.] Bredt" (McPhail and Innis 1940). In a later review of a biography of Wood (1951), he provided some sense of how one could draw on one biography to make better sense of others, and in doing so to shed light on broader questions:

> The diary of A.J. McPhail is suggestive in pointing to the way in which Mr Brownlee continued to keep the pool on tenterhooks by considering appointment as general manager, and the question arises as to whether this was a device to keep the political party under his control and to keep Wood from exercising too much control in the political and economic field…. McPhail complained also of the tendency of Alberta to play a lone hand in the determination of pool policy…. Again we need a life of the Hon. T.A. Crerar if we are to appreciate the extent to which he was driven from the economic to the larger field of federal politics. (578)

This might explain why Innis wrote short biographies of three railway magnates and wrote a review of a biography on another and why the numerous obituaries he wrote had more or less the same format.

Subsequent to a 1933 visit to Prince Albert Saskatchewan with J.B. Tyrrell (to give talks to the local historical society and to search for and examine remains of fur-trade forts), he sent a copy of his Peter Pond biography to their main host, Rev. J.A. MacDonell and his wife. In his response, MacDonell noted that they not only appreciated "the book itself and the spirit behind it" but also "the trouble [Innis] took to insert the additional notes from Turnor's journal." Rev. W.A.

Introduction

lxxxvii

MacDonell to Harold Innis, 22 September 1933. In his talk, Tyrrell had read from the journal (which he was editing for publication) (1934). University of Toronto Archives (hereafter UTA), Department of Political Economy papers (hereafter DPE), A76-0025, box 5, file 2. This would suggest that Innis considered Pond to be *primus inter pares* among early fur traders and explorers.

13 These included those on Hugh Bart Allan (1810–1982) (1930a), Sir William Mackenzie (1849–1923) (1933d), and George Stephen, First Baron Mount Stephen (1829–1921) (1933a).

14 He notes that McPhail "gave the initiative which led to the establishment of a farmer's government in Alberta and to the establishment of the first wheat pool" (McPhail and Innis 1940, 265).

15 The litany of opinions of Pond's character is summarized by Gough (2014, 141–2, 155, 168–70).

16 Heyer (2013) describes this as an example of Innis's penchant for "provocative overstatement in order to draw our attention to the substance of an argument he wished to make" (69).

17 They were married in 1856 in New York.

18 Evidently it was David McCord who had given Sophia Pond McLachlan's address. McLachlan noted the he saw him "occasionally" and considered him "a great talker." However, he believed that he was not a "good correspondent," which he thought accounted for the fact that he had not written to her lately. R.W. McLachlan to Sophia Pond, 18 December 1905. New Haven Museum, "Old Milford Families: Pond Collection," box 9, folder e, coll. 96-B.

19 *Connecticut Magazine*, vols 3–4, 1897. Publisher's notes, 425.

20 The not-so-hidden agenda of Dr Pond was to draw attention to the strength of the Pond bloodline. His own pedigree was highlighted in the editorial notes to his article: "third in descent from Charles Pond of revolutionary fame; ... sixth in descent from Sir Charles Hobby, colonel in the Port Royal Expedition, 1710 and knighted ...; — sixth in descent form Captain John Miles ... served under Major Robert Treat in the great swamp fight; ... seventh in descent from Theophilus Eaton ... first governor of New Haven Colony." His overlapping interests in cattle breeding and genealogy was a profile that one often found for those interested in eugenics (Kevles 1985, 61).

21 It is quite startling that Dr Pond, whose research for the genealogy had

been so painstaking, made the egregious error of confusing Peter Pond with his son. Pond's memoir had been right under his nose since its discovery by his wife in 1868, and even a cursory reading of it would have set him straight about the life and times of his great-uncle. Perhaps as a member of the Society of Colonial Wars as well as the Society of the Cincinnati (both consisting of proud descendants of those who had fought against the British in the Revolutionary War), he could not bear the thought of being descended from someone who had fled colonial America just at the time that revolutionary fervour was breaking out. Instead, he was much more comfortable with the notion that Peter Pond served in the Revolutionary Navy under the command of his younger brother, Captain Charles Pond.

22 Camp was responsible for conducting the "Genealogical Department" of the "Studies in Ancestry" section of the *Connecticut Magazine*. Its purpose was to answer genealogical queries submitted by readers. It followed directly after Nathan Pond's genealogy in the same issue of the magazine. She had hope to have the genealogy ready for the "Christmas Magazine" (i.e., vol. 10, no. 4, 1905), but had to wait until the next issue because it was not completed in time. She did promise to send McLachlan her articles once they were published. Sophia Pond to R.W. McLachlan, 15 December 1905. New Haven Museum, "Old Milford Families: Pond Collection," box 9, folder e, coll. 96-B.

23 While McLachlan was pleased to be of assistance to Sophia Pond, he emphasized that although he was "interested in antiquities," she should put him down as "a full private." He went on to add, "My special line of study is numismatics. I have probably the largest collection of coins in Canada and am connected with several numismatic societies, both in America and Europe. I am Honorary Curator of the society whose name appears at the head of this letter [The Numismatic and Antiquarian Society of Montreal] and as such have had a good deal to do with establishing the Chateau de Ramezay Museum which has a reputation on this continent."

McLachlan's assessment of his lack of expertise in "antiquities" as opposed to his great knowledge about numismatics explains why his account of Pond's Beaver Club medal was much more trenchant than were his observations on Pond's life. R.W. McLachlan to Sophia Pond, 18 December 1905. New Haven Museum, "Old Milford Families: Pond Collection," box 9, folder e, coll. 96-B.

Introduction

24 These included "Adventure into Indian Camp during Burial Ceremony," "Courtship and Marriage among American Indians," "Experiences with the Savages on the Plain of the Dogs," and "Indians Mystified by Wandering French Magician."

25 These were "The American Indian as he appeared when the White man invaded his land and bartered European trinkets for his rich furs" and "The Red Man pleading for his rights before the White Invader."

26 It was originally intended as a "rare tribute to the American Indian" (Yenckel 1987). "Corning Fountain stands as a tribute to the American Indian tribes who originally inhabited the area around Hartford" (Coo Boutique n.d.).

27 The readers of the *Connecticut Magazine* would have already had a good deal of exposure to popular representations of indigenous societies and their encounters with American "civilization." The Buffalo Bill Cody Wild West Show, for instance, had visited New Haven no less than sixteen times between 1874 and 1916 and Hartford twenty-two times during the same period (Buffalo Bill Museum and Grave 2010).

28 Given that the work had been commissioned by the Connecticut Historical Society, the images and captions were more consistent with an endeavour that was public-minded rather than commercial.

29 A 1920 graduate of Yale, Cannon (1899–1979) completed an MBA at Harvard the following year. After working in business, he embarked on a career as a writer in 1927. He is best known for his novel *Look to the Mountain* (Cannon 1942), an account of settler life in the New England wilderness.

30 This is a photographic print of a document using a special "copying camera." The process of photostatting was invented in Kansas City by Oscar T. Gregory in 1907. The Photostat brand machine was further developed by the Commercial Camera company, which evidently became the Photostat Corporation around 1921. The brand became so widespread that its name was genericized; photostat or photostatting was used in the same way that Xerox or Xeroxing came to refer to a copy that was made using electrostatic photocopying.

31 Laura Burns also was the recipient of Florence Cannon's letters, which in turn were passed on to her daughter-in-law, Catherine Burns. Among these letters were three from Harold Innis, which Ms Burns has kindly sent to me. I am arranging for them to be added to the Innis papers, filed with the

letters from Cannon to him. The entire set of eight letters has been included as in this volume (immediately following the introduction).

32 This series was by no means unique. Numerous historical societies had formed at the state level in the nineteenth century and were also compiling · collections of pertinent collections of historical documents.

33 This was part 3 of a series of sections on the French Regime in Wisconsin. Parts 1 (1634–1727) and 2 (1727–48) had appeared in volumes 16 (1902) and 17 (1906), respectively.

34 While fourteen illustrations had been included in the volume, none accompanied Pond's journal. The images used were largely of artefacts, maps, letters, contracts, portraits, and photographs.

35 These included: 1927, 1928a, 1928b, (1930) 1956 (195–203), 1935b, and 1947c. Gough, in his own biography of Pond, judged Innis's version to be a "pioneering biography" and "in its day ... a considerable achievement." However, he was of the view that the text had been "rushed ... into print," with the result that he "had to publish a number of articles correcting, retracting, or defending his position, especially against his detractor ... Arthur Silver Morton." While Innis did indeed write three articles that related directly to Pond, only one appeared after his biography had been published. There is no evidence that the biography was rushed into print. (If anything, it had a relatively long gestation period. He seemed to have begun working on Pond in 1927. The biography appeared to have been more or less ready to go by 1930 but did not see the light of day until late 1931.) Gough (2014, xiv) is somewhat correct in suggesting that in the one article that appeared after Peter Pond's publication, Innis sought to clarify his position (partially in response to Morton's review). But aside from raising issues about Innis's interpretation of Pond's accusations of murder, Morton's review (1932) was quite positive.

36 The year 1932 has been used as the dividing date because although *Peter Pond* was officially published in 1930, it did not actually appear until the end of 1931. The reviews that came out in late 1931 appear to have been based on page-proof copies of the text.

37 Watson (2006, 95, 102) claims that Innis sought to "move *back* to a more rudimentary examination of the economic history of Canada," which involved "underlying geographical features that had given rise to the country."

38 Malcolm Davis, editor, Yale University Press, informed Innis, had "been

Introduction xci

carefully considered by several readers here," and it was "of much interest." The press "should like to come ... to some arrangement ... for its publication." However, he felt that it needed "to be condensed [with the] French sections rendered into English." If this were to be done, the press would "be prepared to reconsider the whole work, with a view to its recommendation." Davis to Innis, 17 April 1928. UTA, DPE, A76-0025, box 4, file 3.

39 E. Holliday, Yale University Press, to Innis, 9 May 1929. UTA, DPE, A76-0025, box 4, file 4.

40 To this end, he took over the place of his colleague, W.P.M. Kennedy, as a member of the society. Julia I. Jarvis to Innis, 10 March 1927. UTA, DPE, A76-0025, box 3, file 3.

41 A.S. Doughty to Innis, 31 March 1927. UTA, DPE, A76-0025, box 3, file 2.

42 R. Owen Merriman to Innis, 5 September 1927. UTA, DPE, A76-0025, box 3, file 3.

43 Clark Wissler to Innis, 5 September 1927. UTA, DPE, A76-0025, box 3, file 3.

44 J.L. Farnum to Innis, 3 November 1927. UTA, DPE, A76-0025, box 3, file 3.

45 William Renwick Riddell to Innis, 21 September 1927. UTA, DPE, A76-0025, box 3, file 3.

46 G.B. Krum to Innis, 14 October 1927. UTA, DPE, A76-0025, box 3, file 3.

47 Grace Lee Nute to Innis, 14 October 1927. UTA, DPE, A76-0025, box 3, file 3.

48 This volume, pp. 3–17.

49 This volume, pp. 18–19.

50 These were the words used to describe the significance of Alexander Mackenzie by his biographers (Buckingham and Ross 1892, 1), cited in Klinck et al. (1976, 243).

51 The volumes could be seen as a form of literary pantheon, a divine set of works in which only exemplary volumes were included. They were imbued with an aura, by virtue of their attractive binding; the sets were intended to be collectors' items.

52 These changes were met with approval with one of the leading contributors to biography, W. Stewart Wallace. In his view, the old Makers of Canada series was of "unequal quality," and he believed that it could be "said most emphatically that the new series is a much more creditable

performance than the old" (1926b). Similar trends of historiography could be discerned in writings that appeared in the *Canadian Historical Review* during the 1920s. In a review that appeared in one of the first issues of the journal, Wallace wrote that "'*no doubt* the constitutional aspect is the most important aspect of the history of Canada'" (Careless 1970, 50). Careless described the "sentiment reflected in the pages of the *Canadian Historical Review*" as one of "optimistic, evolutionary nationalism. Emphasis in articles was heavily on political, constitutional, or imperial themes" (50).

53 Innis's claim that the biographies of key figures involved in industries were in line with the emergent national narrative was evident in the three entries he wrote for the *Encyclopedia of the Social Science*: 1933a, 1933d.

54 Quite surprisingly, two of the main overviews of twentieth-century Canadian history (Bothwell, Drummond, and English 1990; Thompson and Seager 1985) – as well as an otherwise thorough survey of Canadian nationalism in the 1920s (Vipond 1993) – make no mention whatsoever of the Diamond Jubilee.

55 The Diamond Jubilee marked a sea change in Canadian historiography. Arguably, the shift towards Confederation as the point of reference could be attributed to the periodization inherent in the Diamond Jubilee, which stressed the "progress" Canada had supposedly made since 1867 embodying the growth of national feeling alluded to it by Wallace (1927) (Kelley 1984). Hence the emphasis was now on key events and processes of nation-state-building over the sixty-year period, with particular attention given to those who were being singled out as "Makers of Canada." Biography had been a central part of nation-building in both English and French Canada (Gordon 2014) as a flexible canon of inclusion and exclusion.

56 This was evident in the celebrations in Winnipeg, as described by Robert Cupido (2010, 68): "The pageant opened with the customary nostalgic salute to the 'old-timers,' the earliest homesteaders from Ontario and Great Britain, since 'nothing was more pleasing than to bring together the children and the veterans who led the way in community development.' The historical section of the parade was led by the float of the Lord Selkirk Society, which featured the eight-year-old great-granddaughter of John Sutherland, the leader of the opposition in Manitoba's first Parliament."

57 As recounted on the "Find a Grave" website (2001): "When Tyrrell visited

Thompson's grave, he was embarrassed by the modest marker. He arranged for the one [consisting of] four iron rods sticking out of the top of the white pillar on the marker; these originally supported a large decorative iron sextant. At some point, it was vandalized, or vandalism was feared, and the sextant is now in 'safekeeping' in a storage shed at the cemetery."

58 This was the location of the Department of Political Economy, the University of Toronto. Innis was a member of the department at this time.

59 These included papers on the Maritimes by D.C. Harvey (1927); Quebec by The Abbé G. Robitaille (1927); Ontario by Frank H. Underhill (1927); British Columbia by Judge Frederick Howay (1927); and the Prairie Provinces by Chester Martin (1927). Finally, Reginald Trotter presented a paper on the relationship between British finance and the Confederation movement (1927).

60 This group of papers seemed to have been framed by W.S. Wallace's influential article that had appeared a few years earlier in the *Canadian Historical Review* (1920). That it now had become something of a leitmotif to the 1927 Diamond Jubilee year was a testament to its resonance and timeliness (1927). The other papers explored the "national feeling" theme from different angles: "The French Canadians under Confederation," by N.-A. Belcourt (1927); "The Development of Imperial Relations," by W.T. Waugh (1927); and "Canadian Cultural Development," by J.C. Webster (1927). Edgar's presidential address on Canadian writing and modernity largely side-stepped the issue, making mention of only two Canadian writers (Mazo de la Roche and Martha Ostenso) while using trends in Britain as his point of reference. These papers were all printed in the 1927 annual report of the Canadian Historical Association.

61 Founded in 1882, the Royal Society of Canada was made up of members who had been elected for "distinguished contribution to Canadian intellectual life." During the 1920s it was considered to be the "genuine focal point of Canadian intellectual life" (Vipond 1993, 448–9). See also Berger (1996a).

62 The Balfour Declaration of 1926 set in motion events leading to the de jure recognition of Canada's law-making autonomy through the Statute of Westminster in 1931.

63 Canada's Historic Places (n.d.).

64 He may have been responding to the flurry of biographies on Mackenzie

(Wade 1927; Woollacott 1927; H.H. Wrong 1927), along with a new edition of his diary (Mackenzie 1927).

65 That Innis's assessment had merit is evidenced by the fact that no mention is made of Pond in the statement about Mackenzie and his legacy that was written for the latter's commemorative plaque.

66 Napoleon Belcourt, in a paper presented at the 1927 annual meeting of the Canadian Historical Association (the theme of which was the Diamond Jubilee of Confederation), was of the same view: "The men who really discovered the Mackenzie [and] brought the great explorer to it [were] men of French Canadian blood: Étienne Lucière, Joseph Gervais, Louis Labonté, Pierre Bleques." All were employees of the Hudson's Bay Company (1927, 30).

67 These works notwithstanding, Donald Creighton believed there had been little tradition of biographical writing in Canada, looking to developments in the United Kingdom instead. He described Canadian biographies as "'solemn works of commemoration, usually in two fat funereal volumes'" (Wright 2015, 175).

68 The other three biographies to which Innis referred were likely (Wade 1927; H.H. Wrong 1927; and Woollacott 1927). In addition, another version of *Voyages* appeared in 1927 (Garvin and Mackenzie 1927), as well as numerous articles on the explorer (e.g., Baker 1927). The books by Wade, Woollacott, and Wrong were reviewed by Lawrence Burpee in the *Canadian Historical Review* (1927c).

69 Innis (1928a). The session also included papers by F.W. Howay (1928), J.B. Tyrrell (1944), and W.J. Wintemberg (1928). (The last was an elaboration of the theme of a paper that had been published anonymously by the CHA the previous year.)

70 The following year, Burpee published a short work (1929) on Pond and Alexander Henry.

71 Lawrence Burpee to Innis, 19 April 1928. UTA, DPE, A76-0025, box 4, file 1. (See this volume pp. 20–31.)

72 He was most likely referring to the volume produced by Arthur G. Doughty and Adam Shortt of the Public Archives of Canada (1907), as well as his colleague, W.L.M. Kennedy's constitutional history of Canada (1922). Kennedy had drawn extensively on the Doughty and Shortt collection in preparing his text.

Introduction

73 Innis's claims on behalf of Pond were very much in line with the guidelines adumbrated for the historical work encouraged for the Diamond Jubilee.

74 In highlighting the connection between Cook and Pond, Innis appeared to agree with Howay's views, as expressed in his reflections on Cook and Nootka Sound (Clayton 1999; Scholefield and Howay 1914; Howay 1925; Sage 1925).

75 In this regard he echoed Trotter's view that the Canadian Shield posed considerable barriers to movement and settlement in Canada (1939). However, he claimed that it was by virtue of the efforts made to overcome these barriers through technological and other means that Canada was unified. The Methye portage, as a formidable barrier, belies the notion that Canada was unified by its waterways. It was only through ingenuity, logistics, and sheer effort that it became a workable means for moving from one drainage basin to another (Morse 1979). In his searching account of how this barrier was overcome, McKinnon (2008) seems to support this contention, even though he cites Innis's famous passage about geography unifying the country. (See also Kupsch 1977.) These notions underpinned Ells's view that the significance of the portage was what it said about pioneers. He had become intimately familiar with the portage over the years, and even sketched it and wrote poetry about it (1938).

76 W.L. Morton (1966) explained the success of the North West Company with a line of argument similar to what Innis argued in both *Peter Pond* and the *Fur Trade in Canada*.

77 Indeed, in reviewing his correspondence with the publisher as well as Burpee, it would appear that the book manuscript had already been completed by the time the Royal Society meetings took place in May 1928.

78 "We shall be willing to publish this book at our own risk and expense and pay you a royalty of 1s per copy after 600 sales." Horace H. King to Innis, 16 December 1927. UTA, Innis Papers (hereafter IP), B72-0003, box 4, file 9.

79 G.P. de T. Glazebrook to Innis, 14 June 1931. UTA, DPE, A76-0025, box 4, file 7. Glazebrook was a member of the History Department at the University of Toronto.

80 He had better luck with *The Fur Trade in Canada*. Yale University Press likely agreed to publish it because of its potential appeal to Canadian audiences, and because Yale University had a longstanding interest in Canadian issues.

81 H.K. Gordon, Irwin and Gordon Ltd to Innis, 16 December 1927. UTA, DPE, A76-0025, box 4, file 1.

82 H.K. Gordon, Irwin and Gordon Ltd to Innis, 28 March 1928. UTA, DPE, A76-0025, box 4, file 1.

83 H.K. Gordon, Irwin and Gordon Ltd to Innis, 25 April,1930. UTA, DPE, A76-0025, box 4, file 6.

84 John S. Irwin to Innis, 13 March 1931. UTA, DPE, A76-0025, box 4, file 7; Innis to John S. Irwin, 13 March 1931. UTA, DPE, A76-0025, box 4, file 7.

85 F.C. Annesley to Innis, 10 September 1931. UTA, DPE, A76-0025, box 4, file 8.

86 This was only after a final problem had been resolved, namely whether Innis was in agreement with the estimated cost of binding the volume, and that Irwin and Gordon – rather than the printer – would be responsible for selling it. F.C. Annesley to Innis, 10 September 1931. UTA, DPE, A76-0025, box 4, file 8.

87 Prior to the nineteenth century, when sheets of paper were produced individually on a deckle, the natural artefact of this process was the production of rough-cut pages. With advances in paper-making technology, deckled edges were no longer standard. However, some publishers (such as Irwin and Gordon) made use of them, evidently to give their books higher aesthetic value.

88 While presented as a biography, the text actually combined features of biography as well as autobiography. The latter consisted of extensive portions of Pond's memoir, presumably based on the version available in the Wisconsin Historical Collections. Innis draws heavily on the "journal" for the first three sections (the time period covered by Pond in his journal); the final two sections are based on other sources Innis was able to locate). He did not include the entire journal, but selected passages that he thought were relevant, while not including others. Some change of order was made, and a map was included. Innis corrected only the most unrecognizable instances of Pond's tortured prose, and added a few explanatory footnotes.

89 Indian agent at Fort Simpson, NWT.

90 John Alexander Long (1891–?). Holding a 1915 BA from McMaster, he enlisted in the Divisional Signal Company as a sapper. He became friends with Innis, socializing with him in Toronto during the early 1920s and accom-

panying him on his trip to the mouth of the Mackenzie River in 1924, for which he took photographs. He later became a faculty member of the Ontario Institute for Studies in Education.

91 He was likely referring to the advice Burpee had given him about maps. It is noteworthy that Thwaites also thanked Burpee in the preface to the volume he edited containing Pond's journal (Thwaites and State Historical Society of Wisconsin 1908, xxv). Lawrence Johnston Burpee (1873–1946), civil servant, librarian, and author, was a founder of the Canadian Historical Association and honorary secretary 1926–35 and president 1936–7 of the Royal Society of Canada. He published many articles and works on Canadian studies, including a number important works on the fur trade and exploration (Burpee 1908, 1910, 1927a).

92 Alexander Henry (1739–1824). American-born in New Jersey, like Peter Pond, he also was an important figure in the early fur trade. His memoir (2010) had a sizable circulation.

93 In making this claim, Innis may have been using a reductio ad absurdum. If one accepts this line of argument, the whole notion of father of Confederation collapses, as Pond was not only a Yankee lacking in literacy, but his contributions were inseparable from the building of the fur trade through the North West Company. Above all he lacked the quality that seems to be a requisite for those considered to be fathers of Confederation, namely vision. Pond, rather, was a man of action. If his actions were in any sense foundational, Canada was largely just an unintended consequence. In departing from the perspective of the "fathers of Confederation" in this pointed manner, Innis was in line with others questioning this notion at the 1927 Canadian Historical Association meetings (e.g., Trotter 1927; Howay 1927). The suggestions of Innis and the other dissenters mirrored the extent to which the national plans for pageants had gone awry. This reflected the fact that there was some degree of overlap between the leading figures in history, and those providing directives to the pageants, most notably Wrong and Doughty. Cupido (1998) draws attention to the extent to which local pageants did not correspond to the prescribed model. This could be seen in the widespread failure to make mention of the fathers of Confederation and to emphasize pre-Confederation elements instead. See also Morgan (2016).

See Martin (2015) for a searching critique of the notion of the fathers of Confederation, with particular reference to its deployment as part of the

1927 Diamond Jubilee of Confederation celebrations. Pelletier (2010) provides a good account of how the fathers of Confederation figured in the Jubilee celebration with particular reference to John A. MacDonald. In Hammond's (1917) survey of Confederation and its leaders, only those who attended the Quebec Conference of 1864 are listed.

94 See Fleming (1932).

95 Innis eventually paid Kemp's firm ten dollars for acting for him in the matter of his claim against Irwin and Gordon Ltd, as well as for "investigation," "advising," "arranging for the transfer of unsold copies," and "interviews with Pierce." Frederick Kemp to Innis, 13 December 1932. UTA, IP, A76-0025, box 4, file 15.

96 Frederick Kemp to Innis, 3 May 1932. UTA, IP, A76-0025, box 4, file 12. A few weeks earlier, Innis had written to Lorne Pierce appending a list of seventy-seven books that had been sold, mostly to public libraries. Harold Innis to Lorne Pierce, 19 April 1932. Queen's University Archives (hereafter QUA), Pierce Papers (hereafter PP).

97 Harold Innis to Lorne Pierce, 30 May 1932. QUA, PP.

98 This was Robert Boyd Thomson (1870–1947), a professor of plant morphology in the Department of Botany at the University of Toronto, perhaps best known for his field guide to plants and weeds in Canada and the United States (Thomson and Sifton 1922). Innis may have come to know Thomson through his (Innis's) research on pulp and paper during the 1927–8 academic year.

99 This was George Rutherford Walton, who had a long career as the city medical health officer in Regina. Like Innis, he had served with the Canadian expeditionary forces during World War I, and was discharged because of a wound suffered in combat (at Passchendaele). He subsequently graduated with a BA in medicine from the University of Toronto in 1923. After practising medicine in rural Saskatchewan, he was appointed medical officer to the federal Department of Railways and Canals. As he wrote of his experience as a government employee, "I was in charge of a small hospital which the government built at Churchill to care for the men employed by the government to construct a harbour there. I was the entire medical staff of the hospital. I was also the police magistrate, a post I was made to assume." Innis had likely met him when he (Innis) spent time in Churchill,

Introduction   xcix

after having travelled there on the Hudson Bay Railway (Canadian Public Health Leader 1961).

100 This was Charles William Jefferys (1869–1951), a Canadian painter, illustrator, author, and teacher best known for his representations of Canadian history. Innis wrote that "no one has done more to unearth and record in permanent form the obscure but fundamentally vital facts of Canadian history than Jefferys" (Cinefocus n.d.). Jefferys's depiction of historical figures was very much in line with Innis's efforts, beginning with the 1927 Diamond Jubilee, to shift attention away from those involved in constitutional matters to those who worked in staples industries. Innis may have known Jefferys through their respective publishing ventures with Ryerson Press or through the latter's exhibitions at Hart House. See Campbell (1995, 2013).

101 Harold Innis to Lorne Pierce, 16 June 1932. QUA, PP. Innis followed up on this request later in the summer, also asking that review copies be sent to presses as well as to "Herr Louis Hamilton, 4A Lutherstrasse, Lichterfelde Ost, Berlin," who reviewed "Canadian books for various German periodicals." (Hamilton had been in touch with Innis a few weeks before and had asked that a review copy be sent to him.) Harold Innis to Lorne Pierce, 3 September 1932. QUA, PP; Louis Hamilton to Harold Innis, 29 July 1932. UTA, IP, A76-0025, box 4, file 13. Hamilton was sent the review copy, as well as one of *Problems in Staple Production* (Innis 1933a), for which he thanked Innis. Hamilton to Innis, 24 April 1933. UTA, IP, A76-0025, box 4, file 15. It is not known if Hamilton was successful in placing reviews in any German journals.

102 One copy had been sold in July 1932, and six more had been sold by the end of August.

Ryerson Press to Harold Innis, 30 September 1932. UTA, IP, A76-0025, box 4, file 8. The modest sales of the book in the summer of 1932 was a portent of things to come; *Peter Pond* did not prove to be one of Ryerson Press's best sellers. As Pierce informed Innis in the early post–World War II period, "We have on hand 134 copies of Peter Pond and we don't seem to be able to move them, although we have carried the book in the catalogue for several years." He suggested that Ryerson Press "distribute these among a number of colleges and universities" and offered to take care of this. Pierce to Innis, 7 December 1945. QUA, PP.

103 Sometime in the summer of 1932 Pierce had evidently broached the possibility of putting together a series of this kind. Obviously enthusiastic about this proposal, Innis told Pierce that he would be "glad to go over ... the suggestions [he was] good enough to send on regarding the series on staples." Innis to Pierce, 3 September 1932, QUA, PP.

104 Writing from Fort Good Hope, NWT (where he was head of the HBC post), Harris noted that he was "much pleased with the receipt of 'Peter Pond,' and also with the kind thought which caused [Innis] to associate [his] name with John Long on the title page." Harris to Innis, 7 December 1931, UTA, IP, A76-0025, box 4, file 8.

105 Innis had stayed with Semple and his family during the summer of 1915 when he taught school in rural Alberta. After thanking Innis for the book, Semple asked "If he could only see this continent now. What an effort some of these old fellows made to gain riches and adventure. We don't care to exert ourselves quite as much now and look for more returns." Semple to Innis, 10 December 1931. UTA, IP, A76-0025, box 4, file 6.

106 He may have been Innis's family physician. Winnett to Innis, 13 January 1933. UTA, IP, A76-0025, box 4, file 14.

107 See "Peter Pond: Fur Trader and Adventurer," *New York Times*, 29 November 1931.

108 "Peter Pond Receives Credit for Mackenzie's Discovery," *Mail and Empire*, December 1931.

"Peter Pond receives credit for Mackenzie's discovery: Professor H.A. Innis of Toronto University, in a small but important historical book, hails Pond as Great-Grandfather of Confederation." A reviewer for the *Canadian Baptist* indeed reported that the *Mail and Empire* review predicts the book will launch a controversy, for the gist of it is the transfer from Alexander Mackenzie to Peter Pond of the credit for the opening of the northwest, for the discovery of Lake Athabasca and the Mackenzie River, and for the first knowledge of the Yukon. "Peter Pond" (*Canadian Baptist*, 10 December 1931).

109 *Trader Horn* was a rather salacious film of 1931 (directed by W.S. van Dyke), depicting the adventures of trader Alfred Aloysius Horn in sub-Saharan Africa. It was based on his memoirs that had been published as *The Life and Works of Alfred Aloysius Horn. III, The Waters of Africa*, edited by Ethelreda Lewis (1929).

110 This was in line with the *Canadian Baptist* reviewer's observation that Pond had "special title to fame as a pioneer in western agriculture. As early as 1787 he had a kitchen garden containing turnips carrots, parsnips, and potatoes at a spot 100 miles beyond the northern limit of any present railway in Alberta" (*Canadian Baptist*, 10 December 1931).

111 See pp. 130–4 this volume.

112 For Ross, Innis agreed with the view that "he was shot, really by accident, from a gun in the hand of a voyageur named Peche." For Waden, Innis agreed with "the examination and report of Joseph Fagniant of Berthier," who claimed "that a scuffle had occurred and that Toussaint Sieur had been implicated in the fatal shots" (1935f, 63). In reaching these conclusions, Innis may have been buoyed by Mrs Cannon's contentions that the evidence against Pond was not convincing.

113 Innis also conferred with J.B. Tyrrell, who provided insights into the two murders:

> Thank you for kindly sending me the Report of the Special Committee, 1788, which I read with a great deal of interest, and I have taken the liberty of copying that portion which refers to Nadeau and Le Compte. Have you any idea whether the statements of these two men are in existence and available or not? They would probably tell their story of the fight which seems to have been very definitely told though both Alexander and Roderick Mackenzie must have known the full details of it. There was evidently a conspiracy of silence about this whole matter ... Could you tell me where the piece is mentioned in the "Shoe and Canoe" (Bigsby 1850). (J.B. Tyrrell to Harold Innis, 21 September 1932. UTA, DPE, A76-0025, box 4, file 13.)

114 Here he relied on a discovery of a map by Grace Lee Nute, which had been reproduced in Davidson's *North West Company* (1918).

115 Mrs LeGrand Pond Cannon to Innis, 28 February 1932, 28 April 1935. UTA, IP, 76-0025, box 4, file 13. (See Cannon-Innis correspondence in this volume.)

116 See Cannon-Innis correspondence in this volume.

117 Indeed, Pond can be viewed as a continentalist fly in the nationalist ointment. That Innis championed Pond as a father of Confederation belies the widely held view that Innis was a hard-and-fast Canadian nationalist claiming that Canada's origins were geographically determined (Klinck

et al. 1976). Rather, Canada was very much shaped by the organizational acumen of a Yankee fur trader and explorers whose activities spanned the continent.

Arguably, during the late 1920s and 1930s, the field of history itself was quite continentalist in orientation – at least in the circles in which Innis moved. There was close contact between proto-public historians like Innis and their American counterparts. This was evident in the interchanges they had with historical societies such as those in Minnesota and Wisconsin, as well as Archives at the Burton Collection at the Detroit Public Library. While much has been made of the community fostered in the Public Archives of Canada during the 1920s (Wright 2005), much less attention has been given to how international archival relationships took form. Notes and articles in journals on both sides of the border made frequent mention about important developments in the other country. Published works in both countries served as reciprocal points of reference. These included not only the works of Innis and Brebner, but also Stevens (1926), Davidson (1918), and Lower (1938). Compilations and commemorations were important to both. Canadian students commonly did graduate work in the United States (e.g., Davidson, Lower, Lawson, Fleming). A number of figures served as conduits between the two countries. These included Brebner, Innis, Nute, and George Brown, as well as Albert Corey and Reginald Trotter.

118 See Carl Berger's analysis of the continentalist turn (1986b).

119 See pp. 135–48 this volume.

120 These included Askin and Quaife (1928); Wallace (1934); Montgomery (1934); Godsell (1934); Fleming (1932); Ermatinger (1833).

121 Innis quoting Tyrrell (1934, 51).

122 In support of this claim, Brebner cites Bolton and Marshall (1920) and Bolton (1926).

123 Innis attended this conference and presented a paper there.

124 Brebner would go on to write a series of monographs examining historical tendencies from a continentalist perspective. These included 1937, 1945, 1960, 1973.

125 The series inspired by Brebner's paper "eventually included twenty-five volumes," with Brebner's own *North Atlantic Triangle* (1945) becoming its final text (Brebner 1945, note on the author). Innis served as the Cana-

Introduction ciii

dian editor for the series, and Ryerson Press was chosen as the Canadian publisher.

126 Aside from Brebner, and Goldwin Smith, Creighton does not divulge those he considered to be in the continentalist camp. According to Creighton biographer Donald Wright, the "continentalists" in question were Arthur Lower and Frank Underhill (e-mail from Wright, 27 November 2017). A more detailed examination is provided by Bélanger (2011).

127 Innis shared a continentalist perspective with that of Mackintosh (1923). Indeed, Innis's statement that Canada was created because of geography, not in spite of it, reflects similar sentiments to those of Mackintosh, if one includes the qualifying line that follows. In terms of Careless's conception of historiography, both fit squarely into the continentalist, environmental camp, with Innis having less in common with Creighton's Laurentian school (Careless 1954).

128 Bolton's influence on Canada extended well beyond the work of Brebner and Innis.

UBC historian Walter Sage underscored the significance of Bolton's work in reviewing the two volumes that were presented to him on the occasion of his presidential address: "It was fitting that the historian of greater America should be thus honoured on Canadian soil. In his long career Dr Bolton has been a pioneer in two fields: the history of the Spanish borderlands and the history of the two Americas. His address 'The Epic of Greater America' was a comprehensive survey of the development of the Western Hemisphere. During his long connection with the University of California, Bolton has trained more than fifty doctors of philosophy and two hundred and fifty masters of arts (1933)."

In a letter to Bolton (with whom he had had contact during a summer spent in Berkeley), Sage averred, "We here in BC regard the Toronto view of Canada just as you do the New England tradition in the history of the U.S." More generally he believed that Canadian historians had been "slow to recognize Canada as a North American nation rather than as a British colony" (quoted in Reimer 2009, 105). He most likely did not include Innis (a member of his PhD committee) among these Toronto-centric historians, as the latter had spent considerable time in the province during the mid 1930s and was very appreciative of how "BC's problems … might be interpreted as a struggle against mountains, rocks, and forests" (110). Innis's view of British Columbia was in line with his continentalism, which emphasized how barriers to settlement were overcome through effective organizational practices and the deployment of technology. Most notably, Innis wrote the foreword to the published version of Sage's dissertation (1927) that developed this line of argument.

Queen's historian Reginald Trotter, "who took a comparative approach looking at the Spanish, French, and English experiences in the New World ... found a place for a broader approach to Canadian history that coincided with Bolton's concept of the study of the Americas" (Magnaghi and Bolton 1998, 67). Innis's history colleague, George W. Brown, "was also a strong proponent of the Americas idea," maintaining that "historians have been far much disposed to study the colonies of some one nation rather than colonial America as a whole" (68). He took part in an international symposium as part of the annual meetings of the American Historical Association held in Chicago on 29 December 1941, "in a session devoted to the general subject of 'The History of the Americas.'" The papers, including that of Brown (1942), were published the following year in the *Canadian Historical Review*. (They were later republished as part of a volume addressing the "Bolton Theory" [Hanke 1968].)

129 Gordon Charles Davidson (1884–1922) received an MA and PhD in history from University of California, Berkeley. Canadian-born, he served with the Canadian Expeditionary Force in World War I. It was during this time that his PhD thesis (edited by Bolton) was published by the University of California Press (1918). It became what is considered to be the definitive work on the North West Company. Davidson taught briefly in the History Department at the University of British Columbia and committed suicide in 1922, apparently because of the depression occasioned by the wounds he suffered in World War I.

130 This approach had been elaborated in some of his earlier works, most notably (Innis 1923, [1930] 1956; Innis and Lower, 1933). However, rather than the two Canadian drainage basins that he deployed in *Fur Trade*, he now discusses a multiplicity of drainage basins located on the North American continent.

131 Colpitts (2014, 44) challenges Innis's singling out of Pond "as the genius

Introduction cv

behind solving the pemmican puzzle," arguing instead that the Nor'westers more likely had appropriated the practice from subarctic Chipewyan. Evidently Innis may have had second thoughts about claiming that the use of pemmican for the fur trade originated with Pond, as he wrote to both Clark Wissler and Owen Merriman requesting clarification about pemmican's origins.

132 Innis's emergent continentalism was in line with his own growing familiarity with the continent through both research and travel. In addition to engaging with the north and the Atlantic region, he also became more knowledgeable about the West Coast, beginning in the late 1920s. In 1926 he travelled to the Yukon and Alaska by ship from Seattle (Gibb 1934). He supervised Walter Sage's thesis on BC history. He taught summer school at UBC in 1933 and kept a diary of his trip. He travelled with Howay that year to witness the commemoration of the Overland telegraph in Quesnel, which impressed upon him the extent to which BC was becoming integrated into world communications via telegraphy. He began to attend meetings organized by the IPR and wrote on the Panama canal.

133 See Cannon-Innis correspondence in this volume.

134 Cannon to Innis, 28 April 1935. UTA, IP, A76-0025, box 4, file 13. Cannon to Innis, 28 April 1935. (See Cannon-Innis correspondence in this volume.) Bill McDonald, head of the Peter Pond Society of Milford, was not able to confirm either of these claims. He did, however, know the later Peter Pond, who, as it turned out, was brought in to dedicate the Peter Pond monument near Prince Albert, Saskatchewan, in 1955.

135 Innis to Florence Cannon, 21 May 1935. UTA, PP (See Cannon-Innis correspondence in this volume).

136 The younger Peter Pond (six years old at the time) was also featured in a performance that took place as part of the Milford Tercentenary. (*Connecticut Circle: The Magazine of the Nutmeg State* 1939.)

137 The paper was based largely on Innis's Pond biography. Nettleton presented a copy of it to the younger Peter Pond. On the cover page of the paper he listed the names of those persons from the previous generations linking the younger Pond to the original Peter Pond, as well those persons from previous generations linking him to the original Pond. Both were descended from Captain Charles Pond, Peter Pond's brother. The Milford tercentenary

events notwithstanding, Nettleton would later maintain that Pond has been "forgotten by the people of the town which gave him birth and was witness to his last days." This reflection seemed to have been prompted by a request from a "member of the Historic Sites (and) Monuments Board of Canada," who resided in "Battleford, Saskatchewan, Canada." Specifically, Nettleton had been asked to provide "a proper birth and death date of Pond, which would be inscribed on a monument erected in his memory by people of that rugged Canadian province." Nettleton was struck by the fact that "in the half-tamed country of Saskatchewan, there is a lake Peter Pond, on the shores of which this illustrious son of Milford dealt with the savages. But in Milford, where he was born and died, there is slight remembrance of him." Nettleton took advantage of the occasion to draw attention to "Milford's least remembered hero." Describing him as a "fiery figure of the fur trade in the Northwest of Revolutionary days," Nettleton noted that "Pond lived a life as dangerous as any fiction hero, more than once being forced to kill an opponent in duel," but was recognized as perhaps the shrewdest member of the North West Company (*New Haven Register* 1953). Given that Nettleton had presented the younger Peter Pond with a copy of the paper he had written in 1939 on the original Peter Pond, he may have played a role in having Pond's descendant (by that time twenty-two years old), come to Prince Albert in 1955 to unveil the plaque commemorating Pond's founding of Fort Sturgeon (the ruins of which were just outside the town). (*Prince Albert Herald* 1955.)

138 Innis had likely been able to spend more time with Howay during the summer of 1933 when he taught a summer-school course at the University of British Columbia.

139 Frederick Howay to Harold Innis, 10 February 1933. University of British Columbia, Rare Books and Special Collections (hereafter UCBRB), Frederick Howay Papers (hereafter HP).

140 Innis to Howay, 27 February 1933. UCBRB, HP.

141 Innis was at the West Coast at the time, teaching at the University of British Columbia, and travelled to Quesnel with Howay by rail to attend the event.

142 Harold Innis to Frederick Howay, 24 October 1933. UCBRB, HP.

143 Frederick Howay. Address given at the Unveiling of Methye Portage Commemorative Plaque, Fort McMurray, Alberta, 15 September 1938. UCBRB, HP.

Introduction

cvii

144 This was part of a series of texts celebrating various pursuits and professions. It included "Les peintures célèbres," "les musiciens célèbres," "les medecins célèbres," and "La galerie des hommes célèbres."

145 It featured essays by a number of leading scholars who had worked on issues relating to exploration and the fur trade, including those with whom Innis was closely familiar (such as J.B. Brebner, Marcel Giraud, Benoit Brouillette, and Grace Lee Nute). It was organized by Brebner and Giraud (with whom Innis had had numerous intellectual exchanges – most often through published reviews of each other's work). Giraud hosted Innis during his visit to Paris in 1951, and Brebner had worked with him in such ventures as the Carnegie Series and the assessment of Canadian humanities in the post-war period. It is noteworthy that that the volume began with the contributions of ancient explorers (organized by civilizations), followed by accounts of global exploration (by Europeans and by the Russian, Bering), as well as accounts of exploration of the non-Euro-Asian continents. It concluded with an essay on future outer-space exploration.

146 He noted that those interested in the history of Nova Scotia have attached importance to the diary, particularly for what it reveals about "the problem of the position of the colony during the Revolutionary War." He pointed to the fact that Nova Scotia "remained loyal to Great Britain when the colonies rebelled. An American colony became a British province." He noted that the diary was drawn upon by both Brebner (1937) and Thomas Raddall in his novel (1942) and that "these volumes provide a valuable background to an understanding of its significance" (Perkins and Innis, 1948, xxxiii).

147 Bill McDonald, the author of the novel, established the widely circulated Peter Pond newsletter in 2000. A former journalist and resident of Pond's hometown, Milford, CT, McDonald was the driving force behind a successful campaign to erect a monument to Pond in the city.

148 These include 2004, 2013, 2014.)

149 Gough does not reveal which aspects of the biography he considered to be unreliable. However, in addressing "one of the unanswered questions left to us," namely Pond's relationship with Mackenzie, he appeared to side with Innis's claim that Mackenzie had worked to vilify him (2014, xiv).

150 For instance, he suggested that Pond may have written his memoir in response to Dr Stiles's pleadings or "would have seen in [Baron de] Lahontan's pages the places of his own early travels" (Gough 2014, 162–3).

151 Gough (2014, 109–10) also provides valuable insights into the smallpox epidemic, albeit drawing on other forms of evidence.

152 While Gough uses the memoir as rendered by Innis in Peter Pond, Chapin refers to the 1965 Gates version.

153 "Early Life and the Army," "The Apprentice Trader." The section on the Mississippi was divided into two sub-sections: "The Trader," 1773–4, and "The Peacemaker," 1774–5.

154 Both letters were published in Dillon and Nooth (1951).

155 Isaac Ogden was a "judge of the Admiralty court in Quebec" as well as "acting clerk of the Crown" (Gough 2014, 133). He wrote the letter to his father, David Ogden, also a judge, who "had become King's Counsel in New Jersey. As a Loyalist, he was obliged to seek refuge, and moved London." However, the commentary by Gough and Chapin would suggest that Innis was perhaps too hasty in dismissing Ogden's letter. When read in conjunction with that of Nooth, it is quite revealing.

156 Gough discerned from the letter that "Pond knew, or at least speculated, that the river that drained Slave Lake flowed to the Arctic." This was *De Cho*, the River Big, as the Dene called it, the Mackenzie River" (134).

157 Gough concluded from Nooth's account that Pond was describing what Sir John Franklin would later call "the barrens" and found it striking that Nooth made no mention of Pond having viewed any mountainous terrain (2014, 133).

158 As Gough observes, Alexander Dalrymple, the hydrographer to the East India Company who became hydrographer to the Admiralty in 1795, was well aware of Pond's contentions, but believed that the North West Company had no right to act on them (2014, 127, 130). Banks, who had been elected president of the Royal Society in 1778, had been told about Pond by Captain Bentinck in 1788, and had received a letter about Pond from Alexander Henry in 1781 (Henry 1908). Ogden's letter was published in the March 1790 issue of *Gentleman's Magazine* along with the version of Pond's map that accompanied it (Gough 2014, 130).

1

Innis's Writings on
Peter Pond and the Fur Trade

H.A. Innis, "The North West Company,"
Canadian Historical Review 8 (1927):
308–21

The North West Company

The early history of the series of partnerships known as the North West Company is a fascinating, but little known, field. The agreements of 1802 and 1804 given in L.R. Masson, *Les Bourgeois de la Compagnie de Nord-Ouest* (Quebec, 1890), Vol. II, pp. 459–481 and 482–499 respectively, were presented as the only constitutions the organization possessed and so far as I am aware, the following agreement[1] of 1790, to which M. Pierre-Georges Roy, the archivist of the province of Quebec, has drawn my attention, is the first constitution of an earlier date to come to light. Some general items of this agreement were given in a letter[2] from Alexander Mackenzie to Roderick Mackenzie dated Lac la Pluie, August, 1791, but little was known of the detailed character of the concern.

From the information presented in this document it has been possible to determine, with approximate accuracy, the proportion of the shares held by different partners in the amalgamation of 1787. The members of the opposition company[3] formed in 1784–5, which included John Gregory, Peter Pangman, John Ross, Alexander Mackenzie, and Normand McLeod (dormant partner) had been reduced to four in number through the murder of John Ross in the winter of 1786–7, and these were given one share each in the amalgamated company. The remaining sixteen shares were divided as follows: McTavish, Frobisher and Co., seven; Robert Grant, two; Nicholas

Montour, two; Patrick Small, two; Peter Pond, one; George McBeath, one; and William Holmes, one.

Having determined the allocation of shares in the amalgamation of 1787 and the number of shares owned in the new company by members of the old company of 1783, I had hoped to discover the number of shares held by the original partners in 1783–4, but the changes from that year to 1787 are uncertain. In a copy of the Frobisher letter book in the Canadian Archives it is shown that Benjamin Frobisher died on April 15, 1787; that S. McTavish, in a letter dated Montreal, April, 1787, suggested a partnership of equal shares; that Joseph Frobisher accepted the arrangement; and that the partnership of McTavish, Frobisher and Co. was completed on Nov. 19, 1787. McTavish stated that this arrangement gave the firm one-half the concern, after deducting the shares of Small and Montour. From this information the conjecture is submitted that the sixteen shares of the partnership of 1783–4 were divided as follows: Peter Pond (who refused to accept the share allocated to him, but a year later agreed) had one share; Grant, Montour, Small each held two shares and Holmes one share in the amalgamated concern of 1787, and it is probable that they held the same number of shares in the agreement of 1783–4; according to the Frobisher letter book, McBeath held two shares, one of which was apparently sold in 1787 to McTavish, Frobisher and Co.; the remaining six shares were evenly divided between S. McTavish and B. and J. Frobisher. The number of canoes for each license in that year supports the conclusion that the two shares each held by Montour and Small were under the control of B. and J. Frobisher and S. McTavish respectively. Each canoe was roughly represented by one share. In partnerships those supplying the capital secured the larger shares – McBeath two and Pond one, Grant two and Holmes one, McTavish three and Small two, and Frobisher three and Montour two.

This suggestion as to the probable distribution of shares in the agreement of 1783–4 is supported by an analysis of the developments of the preceding period. The beginnings of trouble with the American colonies and the increasing competition in southern areas, as well as the prospect of large profits to be obtained from trade in the Northwest led to a great movement to that territory. Peter Pond, who had traded on the Mississippi in 1773 and 1774, and Alexander Henry, with his partner Cadotte, decided to venture to the Northwest in 1775. Masson[4] and Bain have suggested that the

"The North West Company" 5

North West Company began with the joint stock arrangements on the Saskatchewan in that year, and later evidence confirms this position. The first hint of concentration appeared at Montreal in that year in the grant of one license[5] to James McGill, Benjamin Frobisher, and Maurice Blondeau to take twelve canoes to Grand Portage, licenses for the remaining sixteen canoes to that point being divided among six other grantees of whom Lawrence Ermatinger was the largest, with six canoes. Following this concentration of the trade in Montreal, Alexander Henry described the new alignments in the interior. Arriving[6] "at Cumberland House, the parties separated." Pond took two canoes to Fort Dauphin, and Cadotte, Henry's partner, four canoes to Fort des Prairies. Joseph and Thomas Frobisher and Alexander Henry joined their stock, "Messrs. Frobisher retained six [canoes] and myself four." They wintered at Beaver Lake and built a post on the Churchill River in the spring of 1776. Thomas Frobisher followed this successful venture by wintering at Isle à la Crosse Lake in 1776–7. On his visit to Fort des Prairies in the winter of 1715–16, Henry found four different interests, probably James Finlay, Patterson representing McGill and Patterson, Holmes representing Holmes and Grant, and, lastly, Cadotte, who had "fortunately this year agreed to join their stock, and when the season was over, to divide the skins and meat." The amalgamation of interests was evident at Montreal and in the Saskatchewan. License returns for 1776 are missing, but in the following year concentration was also evident in the license to J. Bte. Adhémar with James McGill guarantor, for ten canoes valued at £5100.

The existence of a distinct organization at this date, was generally assumed, as is shown in the following extracts. Lieutenant-Governor Sinclair in letters from Michilimackinac dated February 15, 1780, wrote:[7] "The North West Company are not better than they ought to be, their conduct in sending an embassy to Congress in '76 may be traced now to matters more detrimental." Lawrence Ermatinger referred to the North West Company in a letter dated November 28, 1776. In 1778 John McGill and Frobisher despatched twelve canoes presumably for the Company, since John Askin, in a letter[8] dated Michilimackinac, June 13, 1778, to these men wrote, "As I'm informed that you have to transact the business of the N.W. Co. this season"; and in a letter[9] of June 14, 1778, to Todd and McGill, he wrote, "As to the supplying of others with rum, corn, etc. after I have made sure of what will be wanted for the great Co. (as we must now term them for distinction sake)." Hostilities incidental to the American Revolution and the decline in furs to the south were increasingly responsible for a shift of traders from Detroit to the north. Simon McTavish had been interested in forwarding supplies from Albany to Detroit in 1774. In 1775 his name with that of McBeath appears as the owner of a vessel of thirty tons. He was engaged in trade to Grand Portage in 1776, but it was not until 1778 that his name appeared among the grantees of licenses to that point, when he was given permission to take eight canoes. An increase in the number of interests trading from Grand Portage led to renewed attempts to discover new territory. In 1778 several interests combined[10] to support Pond in an expedition of four canoes to the Athabaska country to repeat the success of Thomas Frobisher in the preceding year. The chief interests were represented by the two houses of Frobisher and McTavish, and this arrangement was probably the direct forerunner of the North West Company of 1783–4. The expedition was very successful and Pond came out in 1770 to Montreal. In 1779[11] those concerned in the Northwest "joined their stock together and made one common interest" of the whole, sixteen shares being divided as follows: the larger interests – Todd and McGill two shares; B. and J. Frobisher two shares; McTavish and Co. two shares; McBeath and Co. two shares; and the independent interests possibly, Holmes and Grant two shares, and Waden and Co. two shares; Ross and Co. one share, Oakes and Co. one share. Apparently Waden, as a representative of the small independent interests, was sent as a compromise choice by the amalgamated concern during Pond's absence, as he wintered in 1779 at Lac la Ronge. According to one account[12] the agreement of 1779 was renewed in 1780 for three years, but discontinued in two years. The licenses granted at that time support this conclusion. In 1780 a license was granted to Frobisher and Frobisher for eight canoes, in 1781 to Todd and McGill, B. and J. Frobisher, and McGill and Patterson for twelve canoes, in 1782 to B. and J. Frobisher for ten canoes. In 1783 the agreement was apparently broken and licenses for large shipments to Grand Portage were granted as follows: B. and J. Frobisher, 5 canoes valued at 3500 livres; S. McTavish, 6 canoes valued at 4500 livres; Holmes and Grant, 3 canoes valued at 1800 livres; and to Lake Superior, McBeath and Pond, 3 canoes valued at 2000 livres.

"The North West Company" 7

In any case Pond was granted a license for four canoes to Grand Portage in 1780, and apparently returned to winter in Athabaska and collect the furs he had been obliged to leave in 1779. He was at Grand Portage in 1781, and was selected[13] presumably by the larger interests as a representative to trade a joint stock with Waden, who apparently spent the summer at Lac la Ronge. Waden was killed in March, 1782, as a result, it has been suggested, of quarrels over policies in which Waden represented the small independent interests and Pond the larger interests. Pond is reported[14] to have met the Indians from the Athabaska country, traded with them and warned them of the smallpox among the Indians below. In the same year the agreement of the fur traders appears to have broken up, possibly as the result of the news of Waden's death, and two parties were sent to establish posts in Athabaska of which one probably representing the small independent traders was successful in reaching the district only to find that the smallpox had preceded them. They secured only seven packs of furs. There is reason to believe that Pond did not reach the district in 1782, but undoubtedly he was in Athabaska in 1783 and secured favourable returns. Meanwhile McTavish and the Frobishers gradually emerged as the strongest independent interests, and, the advantages of co-operation having been realized, a new agreement was made in 1783–4, which has been regarded as the beginning of the North West Company. The omission of the small independent traders was a feature of the agreement which led to the formation of the small company and to the period of competition from 1785 to 1787, when amalgamation followed. The success of the amalgamation has been questioned, and it is probable that Alexander Mackenzie as the chief representative of the small traders never became reconciled to the policies of the larger organization. The North West Company of 1783–4 emerged as the result of the increased strength necessary to prosecute the trade in the Athabaska country, of the pressure toward the north which followed the dislocation of trade to Detroit incidental to the American Revolution, and of the disappearance of Albany as a rival base to Montreal. The Company of 1787 was a result of the impossibilities of competition in the trade.

The agreement of 1790 occupies an important position in the evolution of the organization. According to article one, "McTavish, Frobisher and Co. shall do all the business of this concern at Montreal." The trade was carried on through Montreal importing firms, which in turn had connections with English firms. Again conjectures may be made as to the interrelationship of these firms at that time. From information in the Frobisher letter book it appears that McBeath's two shares were supplied by Forsyth in Montreal and in turn by Phyn and Ellice in London. According to a letter dated 1787 from John Richardson to John Porteous, McBeath was obliged to assign the affairs of McBeath, Grant and Co. to the hands of trustees, and he had undertaken a debt due by Sutherland and Grant to Phyn and Ellice "which will, of course, insure his ruin." These difficulties apparently necessitated the sale of at least one share to McTavish, Frobisher and Co., and Pond and McBeath's two shares were then supplied by Phyn and Ellice. Holmes and Grant was supplied by Blackwood. B. and J. Frobisher was supplied by Brickwood, Pattle and Co., and S. McTavish by Dyer, Allan and Co. The new firm of McTavish, Frobisher and Co. of 1787 was supplied equally by Brickwood, Pattle and Co., and Dyer, Allan and Co. In 1788 Dyer, Allan and Co. transferred their share to Brickwood, Pattle and Co. In the following year McTavish, Frobisher and Co. secured the right to supply McBeath and Pond's shares, and the share of Dyer, Allan and Co. acquired by Brickwood, Pattle and Co. was transferred to Phyn and Ellice in England. Phyn and Ellice were represented in Canada by the firm of R. Ellice and Co. which was chiefly interested in the southern trade. This firm disappeared on April 1, 1790; and a new firm, Forsyth, Richardson and Co., was formed which made provision for Forsyth who had been eliminated from the Northwest trade. The supply business of the North West Company in Montreal had come into the hands of the single firm of McTavish, Frobisher and Co., and that of the southern trade into the hands of Forsyth, Richardson and Co. In England, McTavish, Frobisher and Co. was supplied by Brickwood, Pattle and Co. and by Phyn and Ellice, the latter also acting as a supply house for Forsyth, Richardson and Co. These arrangements were strengthened in the agreement of 1790 which began with the first outfit for the year 1792 and ran for seven years to 1798, when it was superseded by the agreement of 1795, which began with the first outfit for 1799. The agreement of 1790 is important as it represents the first charter in which consolidation from London to the Northwest had become effective. Gregory and McLeod had been disposed of in the amalga-

"The North West Company"   9

mation of 1787, and Forsyth, Richardson and Co. were chiefly concerned in the Detroit trade. In 1792 McTavish, Frobisher and Co. was supreme in the Northwest. The basis of the organization preceding the marked expansion of 1798, and of 1802, was laid down in the agreement of 1790.

The centre of disturbance to the entire trade structure was in the southern trade. A state of equilibrium had been reached by 1790, but it was of short duration. In a letter dated September 23, 1789, John Richardson[15] wrote to John Porteous complaining of the decline of the Detroit trade and stating:

> I have made some arrangements here [Michilimackinac] this year which will produce an extension of our business in that quarter and I hope a safe one, –Mich'a is far preferable to Detroit as being more out of the way of either military or commercial interference from the States.

Forsyth, Richardson and Co. and Todd, McGill and Co. wrote to Dorchester in a letter dated Montreal, August 10, 1791, asking for protection in the country south of Detroit following the burning of a Miami village. In a letter dated August 15, 1793, further complaints were made of a decline in trade. "F.R. and Co. are most severe sufferers by last year's shipments. May all the curses of Emaulphus fall upon these *Sans Culottes* Villains of France." A storm was precipitated with the Jay Treaty. Small firms[16] such as Grant, Campion and Co. disappeared. The firm of Forsyth, Richardson and Co. became an important competitor for the Northwest trade in its merger with other groups in the X Y Co., especially after 1798 and after Alexander Mackenzie had joined its ranks following his release from the North West Company at the end of the 1700 agreement.

The North West Company had its origin in the demand for increasing capital following the extension of trade into the Athabaska country. Its difficulties throughout the period prior to 1804 were largely the result of gradual disappearance of the trade to the south and the struggle of small independent traders who combined in defensive groups to obtain a share of the rich fur trade of the Northwest. Alexander Mackenzie was an important figure in both of the struggles waged by the small groups from 1785 to 1787 and during the later history of the X Y Co. The hostilities of the

American Revolution and the Jay Treaty had their effects on the North West Company's agreements from 1775 to 1787 and in the formation of the X Y Co. at a later date.

H.A INNIS

[Copy compared with the original preserved in the archives of the Seminary of Quebec, by Amédie Gosselin, archivist of the Seminary of Quebec and of Laval University]

Articles of agreement[17] entered into at the Grand Portage between Mc-Tavish Frobisher & Coy, Nicholas Montour, Robert Grant, Patrick Small, William McGillivray, Daniel Sutherland, John Gregory, Peter Pangman, and Alexander Mackenzie, for the purpose of carrying on a Trade on their joint Accounts, to that part of the Indian Country commonly called the North West, or elsewhere as the Parties may hereafter agree; to be divided into twenty shares of which McTavish Frobisher & Coy are to hold six twentieths, Nich Montour two twentieths, Robert Grant two twentieths, Pat Small two twentieths, Will McGillivray[18] one twentieth, Daniel Sutherland one twentieth, John Gregory, two twentieths, Peter Pangman two twentieths, and Alex. Mackenzie, two twentieths, in all profits and loss arising from thence; to commence with the first outfit for the year 1792, and to continue there after for the full and complete term of seven years.

Article first,

That McTavish, Frobisher & Coy, shall do all the business of this concern at Montreal, and import the goods necessary for the supplies, charging[19] 5 per cent at the bottom of the invoice, and interest from the time they fall due in England, at the rate of 5 per cent p. annum, with 4 per cent on the amount of the whole outfit, at the close of each year, the goods, men, wages, provisions, (wherever they may be purchased), cash disbursements, etc, to be included, and interest at 6 per cent p. annum on all advances, imports excepted.

"The North West Company" 11

Second.

That the furs shall be shipped to England by McTavish Frobisher & Coy on account of this concern, for which they are to be allowed a commission of one half p. cent on the amount. The neat [net] proceeds whereof are to be credited each individual of the company in proportion to the share or shares, he or they hold, so soon as they are carried to the credit of McTavish Frobisher & Coy in England.

Third.[20]

That Mr Montour & Mr Pangman shall winter and transact the Company's business at Forts des Prairies, Mr Small, Mr McGillivray & Mr MacKenzie, shall winter and transact the business at the English River, and Mr Rob Grant shall winter and transact the business at the Red River; subject however to such changes, as the majority of the Concern present in the summer at this place, shall think most for their interest. But that two of the parties may winter below, each year, in rotation, or as they may agree amongst themselves, upon paying the salary of an able clerk each, to take their places, and to return the year following to their stations, cases of sickness only excepted: Or otherwise to relinquish the one half of what share, or shares, he or they may hold in the concern in favor of such deserving clerk or clerks, as he or they so relinquishing may judge proper, provided they are such as are approved of by the Company; if not, to be settled by ballot; and the person or persons so retiring may retain the other half of his or their share or shares in the concern, without any attendance to the business: it is further understood, and agreed to by the parties who may so relinquish, that the clerks in whose favor they resign shall have the shares on the same principle, as the property is at present calculated to cost at the different posts.

Fourth.

That for the conducting of the business, one of the house of McTavish Frobisher & Coy, John Gregory and Daniel Sutherland, shall come up annually to this place, unless Mr McTavish's presence in England, shall be found more for the interest of this concern, in which case, the former are to be exempted. And as it is thought necessary for the interest of the present

North West concern,[21] that Mr McTavish should go to England this autumn, that the parties belonging to that concern, subscribing to this agreement, give their assent thereto, on condition of McTavish Frobisher & Coy making over to Daniel Sutherland[22] one of their twentieth shares, for the two remaining years of said concern, in order to give him weight, to represent their interest in assisting Mr Gregory to manage the Company's affairs here.

Fifth.

In case of the death of any of the parties hereto, before the expiration of this agreement, his or their executor, or executors, may nominate another person, in his or their place to be approved of by the concern; who shall in every respect conform to this agreement.

Sixth.

If all the parties herein, choose to retire from the business at the expiration of this agreement, a small assortment of goods shall nevertheless be sent to the Portage, if judged necessary, but not otherwise, in order to realize, and bring to final close in the most advantageous manner, the remaining business of this adventure, and whatever the clerks, guides, and canoemen, may be then indebted, shall be considered as debts due to this concern, and not otherwise.

Seventh.

The contracting parties most solemnly declare that in the respective departments, in which they may be employed in the management of this business, they will keep faithful and exact accounts of all and every part of their transaction, so far as they are able, and will oblige all clerks and others under their direction to do the same, and further, they shall use every exertion, within the reach of the industry and abilities to promote on every occasion the interest of this concern.

Eighth.

That as all the parties hereto, have or may have other concerns in trade, in no wise connected with this business, and the present agreement being solely for the purpose of carrying on a joint adventure to the North West;

"The North West Company" 13

in order therefor to prevent any of the parties from being involved, or in any manner responsible for one another, it is stipulated, and provided, that on no pretence whatever, shall any of the parties sign for, or contract debts for account, or in the name of any of the other parties, without a special power for that purpose.

Ninth.

All persons of what denomination soever, whether principals, or others, who winter in the interior country, or elsewhere, shall deliver, or send to the Portage annually, an exact account of the goods, or other property they had remaining, as also of the peltries and canoemen, they may have left in the country, and as far as they are able, shall produce faithful accounts of their transactions, and the expenditure of the goods, committed to their care the preceding year. The principals who winter, as well as those who come up from Montreal (while on the voyage, and at this place) shall be allowed their personal necessaries, out of the commons stock of the concern, and no more, every thing exceeding this limitation, they are required to keep an account of, and either send or bring the same to the portage annually, in order that it may be charged to their accounts.

Tenth.

All difficulties that may arise in conducting this business shall be decided by the votes of twelve shares, which, in such case shall be considered as unanimous in every matter of what nature soever, and the contending party or parties, shall be obliged to submit to it; but in any case where the votes are under twelve, it shall be left to the arbitration and decision of four disinterested persons, men conversant in this business, who, if they cannot agree, shall chose an umpire, and the award signed by such five persons, or any three of them, shall be binding to all parties.

Eleventh.

All persons interested in this concern shall not upon any account, enter into any new engagements, during the term of this agreement, to the detriment of this concern. This article shall be equally binding upon any one of the concern, who disposes of their share to any other person.

Twelfth.

In case this agreement is dissolved at the end of seven years, and that all the parties choose to continue in this business, on their separate account, or otherwise, without renewing this concern, in such case, all the goods remaining on hand, clerks, guides and canoemen, who are indebted to the company, whether at the Grand Portage, or in the interior Country, shall be equally divided, according to the different shares. The forts, buildings, and fixed property at the Grand Portage, to be sold in four lots, at public sale, to the highest bidder, and those in the interior country, to be sold in like manner, in single lots, for each post.

Thirteenth.

That whenever either of the parties become worth more money than what it requires to carry on their proportion of the outfits; if left in the hands of Messrs McTavish, Frobisher & Coy, they are only to be allowed interest on the surplus at the rate of five per cent per annum.

Fourteenth.

That the accounts of each year's outfit, shall be made up in November, after the goods are forwarded from Montreal, and accounts current with each of the parties to be signed and interchanged yearly.

Fifteenth.

That Mr MacKenzie shall pay to George McBeath a premium of three hundred and fifty pounds current money of the province of Quebec, over and above the stock that will remain on hand in the name of George McBeath in spring 1792, at the prices agreed upon by the article third, upon his relinquishing all pretentions to any interest in the concern, and, that Mr Gregory and Mr Pangman, shall satisfy Normand McLeod[23] and William Holmes, for the good will of the shares, which they hold in the present North West concern, and which form two of their shares in the new concern.

Sixteenth.

That whereas it is judged necessary by the parties hereunto subscribing, to have no witnesses to this agreement, it is nevertheless hereby, most ex-

"The North West Company"   15

pressly understood and solemnly declared, to be equally valid, and binding on all parties, in every respect, as if the same had been duly executed in form by a notary public, any law or usage to the contrary notwithstanding.

Seventeenth.[24]

For the true performance of all and every part of the foregoing articles, each party binds himself unto the others, in the penal sum of five hundred pounds, current money of the province of Quebec, for every twentieth share, to be paid by the party failing to the party observing, or willing to observe, the same.

In witness whereof we have hereunto set our hand and seals at the Grand Portage, this twenty fourth day of July one thousand seven hundred and ninety.

McTavish Frobisher & Co.
Nicholas Montour
Robert Grant
Pat. Small
Will. McGillivray
D. Sutherland
John Gregory
John Gregory by power of attorney for
Peter Pangman
Alex. MacKenzie

NOTES

1 A comparison of this agreement with that of 1802 shows striking similarity and indicates the extent to which the organization had been built up in 1790.

2 L.R. Masson, *Les Bourgeois de la Compagnie du Nord-Ouest*, I, 38–9.

3 Reminiscences by the Honourable Roderick Mackenzie, *ibid.*, 10.

4 *Ibid.*, 11.

5 Return of trade licenses – photostat copies in the University of Toronto library included in the material issued under the direction of Professor Wayne Stevens and the auspices of the Minnesota Historical Society. The

mass of information in these returns is bewildering, but it gives several hints which make possible a tentative reconstruction of the early history.

6 James Bain, ed., *Travels and Adventures in Canada and the Indian Territories between the years 1760 and 1776 by Alexander Henry* (Toronto, 1901), 263. This paragraph is ambiguous, but Masson and apparently Bain interpret the joint stock as affecting the whole part and not Henry and the Frobishers only. It is probable, however, that Pond did not join the venture.

7 Extracts of letters from Lieutenant-Governor Sinclair concerning the trade and traders to Michilimackinac and the Northwest, February 15, 1780. Canadian Archives, *Series Q*, Vol. 17, Pt. I, 256–7.

8 *Wisconsin Historical Collections*, XIX, 245.

9 *Ibid.*, 248.

10 Alexander Mackenzie, *Voyages from Montreal through the Continent of North America* (Toronto, n.d.), I, xxxv.

11 Memorandum of Charles Grant to Haldimand, dates Quebec, April 24, 1780. *Canadian Archives Report*, 1888, 59–61.

12 *Sketch of the Fur Trade of Canada, 1809,* in the Canadian Archives. This is a photostat copy of an original which was apparently in an early draft of the work *On the Origins and Progress of the Northwest Company of Canada* (London, 1811), supposedly written by Nathaniel Atcheson. The phrasing of the *Sketch of the Fur Trade*, and of the *Origin and Progress* is in many cases identical. The work was possibly the result of contributions by several important traders brought into final shape by Atcheson.

13 Alexander Mackenzie, *Voyages*, I, xl. Mackenzie's account is most unsatisfactory. He has given the date of Waden's death as 1780–1, whereas it was March, 1782 (Canadian Archives, *Haldimand Papers*, B. 129, pp. 113–5). From this error the remainder of his account is thrown out of line.

14 *Ibid.*, xli.

15 Copies of *Richardson Correspondence*, Canadian Archives.

16 Copies of *Baby Papers*, Canadian Archives.

17 "We are all bound upon honor not to make it public before a future period that might be agreed upon. I shall make no other apology for keeping it from you." Alexander Mackenzie to Roderick Mackenzie, Lac la Pluie, August 2, 1791 (L.R. Masson, *Les Bourgeois de la Compagnie du Nord-Ouest*, I, 38).

18 "Mr. McGillivray paid Mr. Pond £800 for his share" (*ibid.*).

"The North West Company" 17

19 "The goods to be imported on account of the concern paying the house below 5 per cent at the foot of the invoice; the rest of the expenses as usual, etc." (*ibid.*).

20 The importance of English River and the Athabaska country is shown very clearly – five shares were represented in this district; four shares in the Fort des Prairies section of the Saskatchewan, an important provision district supplying the English River country; and two shares in the Red River district which supplied provisions for the transport to Grand Portage.

21 An illustration of the interrelation of agreements in which the agreement of 1790 changed the agreement of 1787.

22 Reducing the seven shares of McTavish, Frobisher and Co. to six. "Sutherland gets his share out of McTavish, Frobisher and Co. through the latter's interest" (Masson, *Les Bourgeois de la Compagnie du Nord-Ouest*, I, 38–9). Daniel Sutherland was apparently from the firm of Sutherland, Grant and Porteous which traded in the Temiscamingue district under various names from 1769 to 1785.

23 "The latter [McLeod] disposed of his for £200 per annum for I suppose three of four years; the former [Holmes] is not settled with" (*Ibid.*, 38–9).

24 An important article explaining the effectiveness of the agreement.

H.A. Innis, "Peter Pond in 1780," *Canadian Historical Review* 9 (1928): 333

In my article on the North West Company, in the CANADIAN HISTORICAL REVIEW, December, 1927, pp. 308–321, I stated (p. 312), that Peter Pond came back to Montreal in 1779 after his first trip to Athabaska, which was begun in the previous year, and that he returned to Athabaska in 1780 (p. 313). This statement was based on the appearance of Pond's name in the list of licenses issued in Montreal in the spring of 1780. Recent material noted in the Askin papers (Detroit, 1928), and copied by Courtesy of the Detroit Public Library throws further light on Pond's movements. The log-book of His Majesty's armed sloop Welcome, Capt. Alexander Harrow, has two items in this connection. The first is dated Mackinac, Sunday November 26, 1780: "This evening Mr. Pond with seven engagees arrived in a batteau from Lake Superior." The second has reference to the new fort which was being built on Mackinac island in 1781: "Thursday 10th May. This day borrowed a small batteau from Mr. Pond, a merchant, for the vessel's use."

Obviously Pond wintered at Mackinac in 1780–1, and not, as I have suggested, in Athabaska. The evidence supports the conclusion that Pond did not come down to Montreal in 1779, but came down only as far as Grand Portage, and returned directly to bring out the furs which, as Alexander Mackenzie notes, had been left in Athabaska. Pond came out late in the season of 1780, wintered at Mackinac in 1780–1, and returned to winter with Waden at Lac la Rouge in 1781–2. The licenses were made out in Pond's name at Montreal in the spring of 1780, but apparently he was not present. This is written as a correction, and in the hope that it will afford one more certain link to the history of the uncertain years from 1778 to 1783.

HAROLD A. INNIS

H.A. Innis, "Peter Pond and the Influence of Capt. James Cook on Exploration in the Interior of North America," RSC Trans. [Royal Society of Canada Transactions], 3rd ser., 22 (1928), s. ii: 131–41

Presented by LAWRENCE J. BURPEE, F.R.S.C.

It is perhaps altogether fitting and proper, in consideration of the recently celebrated sixtieth anniversary of the Dominion, that the work of students in Canadian history should centre so largely on the development of responsible government and the formation of Confederation. This paper is not an attempt to disparage the importance and value of that work but rather to insist that equally important work remains to be done in Canadian history both earlier and later than the period 1840–1867. It is concerned especially with the period after the Conquest, or roughly the early and crucial part of the period 1763–1821.

From the standpoint of Canadian history this period witnessed the conquest of the French on North America, the revolt of the American colonies, and the approximate determination of the boundary lines of those portions of North America which were destined to remain British. Considerable attention has been paid to the difficulties, especially the geographic difficulties, under which Confederation has been achieved. Comparatively little attention has been paid to the period in which the northern part of North America, apparently without serious difficulty, became a distinct unit under the control of Great Britain. Canadian unity was developed from the Atlantic to the Pacific from 1763 to 1821, and it is a part of the plan of this paper to inquire into the causes which were at work. Ordinarily the British army and the navy have been given most of the credit for the outcome of the American Revolution and of the War of 1812, but work done recently and notably by Mrs. K.B. Jackson [as M.G. Reid, "The Québec Fur Traders

"Peter Pond and the Influence of Capt. Cook"

and Western Policy, 1763–74] and Professor Wayne Stevens [*The Northwest Fur Trade, 1763–1800*] has shown, however, that the fur trade and the importance of British manufacturers to the trade have been of very great importance in the diplomatic arrangements which finally determined the boundaries during this period. The organization of greatest importance to Canadian interests in the prosecution of the trade was the Northwest Company, and it is proposed to pay especial attention to the activities of an individual who played an important role in its formation.

Peter Pond, adventurer and fur trader, was born in Milford, in the county of New Haven in Connecticut, on January 18, 1740. Interestingly enough Alexander Henry, his contemporary, was born in New Jersey in August, 1739. Both these men were present at the Surrender of Fort de Lévis in 1760, Pond as a commissioned officer and Henry as a merchant supplying the commissariat. In 1775 these men made their first voyages by Grand Portage to the Northwest. Alexander Henry is a well known figure in the fur trade, but Peter Pond has suffered relative obscurity.

The reasons for the obscurity were apparently lack of an ordinary education and consequent bad spelling, which meant that his journal was partly destroyed and the remaining fragment published only at a very late date in the Wisconsin Historical Collections. Nevertheless, it has a flavour not found in any other fur trader's journal. From the available evidence Peter Pond was a descendant of William Pond of Groton, Suffolk, England, a neighbour of John Winthrop. Two sons of William Pond arrived at Salem, Massachusetts, and it is probable that Peter was a descendant of one of these sons, probably Samuel Pond. In any case Peter Pond was the eldest son of nine children of Peter Pond and Mary Hubbard. His father appears to have been a shoemaker by trade, as the son enlisted on April 17, 1759, with the Suffolk County Regiment as a shoemaker. His journal begins with entry into army life. At the age of 16, in 1755, he enlisted under Capt. David Baldwin in the seventh company of the Connecticut regiment. He was engaged during the summer on the Fort George front but saw no hard fighting. In the autumn he returned to Milford and did not enlist in the following year. However, in 1758, he joined the army under Col. Nathan Whiting of the second Connecticut regiment and was engaged in the fiasco at Ticonderoga under Abercromby. His account of the campaign is conclusive evidence of the validity of his journal. In 1759 he joined the Suffolk County regiment and was engaged in the successful attack on Niagara. Again he returned to Milford at the end of the season's campaign, but enlisted the following year with a commission. As already shown he was present at the attack of Fort de Levis, and also at the capitulation of Montreal. In 1760 he had served in three campaigns and he was twenty years of age.

Six of the succeeding twelve years were spent in the fur trade at Detroit, but unfortunately the journal gives little information as to his activities, We do know, however, that after his return from the army he went in 1761 on a voyage to the West Indies and returned to find that his father had joined the rush of traders to Detroit after the Conquest and that his mother had died. He assumed charge of a large family until his father returned (probably 1762) and at some time during the next three years married Susanna Newell, by whom he had at least two children. His father apparently had little success in the Detroit venture, probably because of the disturbances prior to the Pontiac wars – he died insolvent in 1764. The following year Peter Pond engaged in the Detroit trade, and practically nothing is known of his success in the next six years except that toward the end of the period he disposed of an enemy in a duel. Certainly he was at Detroit in 1767, as along with Isaac Todd and other traders he signed a petition on November 26th of that year asking for restrictions on the trade in rum. On August 13, 1770, he is recorded as having purchased 120 acres of land on Grosse Point. He probably extended his activities to Michili-mackinac, as there is reason to believe he wintered there in 1770–71. After his duel in 1771 he returned to Milford and made another trip to the West Indies in 1772.

With his return from the West Indies, a long and unbroken connection with the fur trade begins. He received a letter from Mr. Graham[1] of New York, an Albany trader, who had been engaged in the trade of Michili-mackinac at least as early as 1767, offering to arrange a partnership in trade from Michilimackinac. Pond was presumably to supply the experience and Graham the capital. In 1773 a cargo valued at 4,600 pounds was made up and Pond departed for Montreal to secure goods for the trade not available in New York, while Graham took the boat loads of merchandise to Oswego and by the lakes to Michilimackinac. Pond's goods were taken up the Ottawa by the well known route to Michilimackinac in the

"Peter Pond and the Influence of Capt. Cook" 23

canoes of his old acquaintance, Isaac Todd and of James McGill. At Michili-mackinac he completed arrangements to take twelve large canoes and nine clerks for various points on the Mississippi. He reached Green Bay, crossed over the Fox Portage and from Prairie du Chien despatched the clerks to various districts. Pond wintered on St. Peter's river apparently above the point at which Carver had wintered in 1766–7. In the spring of 1774 he returned to Prairie du Chien and in company with his other canoes pro-ceeded after a successful winter, to Michilimackinac where he met Mr. Graham with a new supply of goods. His success warranted his buying out Mr. Graham[2] and in the following year he returned on his own venture. In 1774 after completing his cargo, and before leaving for a return visit to the Mississippi, news arrived of an outbreak of trouble between the Sioux and the Chippewas. Pond, in addition to his activities as a trader was despatched also as a peacemaker. He reached his old wintering place on St. Peter's river and spent a successful winter including a visit to the Yank-tons, a band of the Sioux. In the spring he left St. Peter's river and took with him some of the chiefs of the Sioux preparatory to arranging a peace at Michilimackinac. With his return in 1775 the journal, unfortunately, comes to an end.

After his return to Michilimackinac, Pond, for various reasons, decided to proceed to Grand Portage[3] and the Northwest and to abandon the Mis-sissippi country. In the same year Simon McTavish appears to have decided on a venture to the same district. Also we learn that Alexander Henry made his first visit to that region. It is necessary to inquire at this point into the general reasons for the northwest migration. The significant changes relate to those who had traded from Albany. McTavish had been a forwarder from Albany. The firm of Phyn and Ellice with headquarters at Albany left for Montreal and London. So too, Pond who had obtained his goods from Albany began to rely on Montreal. Several causes may be assigned for the change. The supplies of fur of the Mississippi country were being worked out and reports were abroad of tremendous profits to be obtained from the better furs of the north-west. Finlay wintered on the Saskatchewan in 1768. In 1771, Thomas Curry had wintered at Cedar Lake, and in 1772 took down large quantities of furs. But probably more important as a cause of the migration was the rumour of the outbreak of troubles in the colonies and the advisability of depending on Montreal as a base of supplies in the event of the cutting of the Albany route, and of retreating to territory beyond the pale of disturbance.

The significance of the movement from Albany may be shown in its relations to later developments leading to the formation of the Northwest Company. Albany traders had depended on lake transportation and the use of boats to carry goods along Lake Ontario, Lake Erie and Lake Huron. For this reason important capital investment was involved in providing transport facilities. The Albany traders, especially Phyn and Ellice and McTavish, acquired substantial capital interests as a result of the methods by which the trade was conducted and the substantial profits available as a reward. The importance of the Ellice family and of McTavish and McGillivray, which persists throughout the history of the Northwest Company and its successor, the amalgamated Hudson's Bay Company, was a result of the capital acquired in the early trade from Albany prior to 1774.

On August 18, 1775, Alexander Henry, en route to the Saskatchewan, was joined on Lake Winnipeg by Peter Pond with two canoes. They were obliged to proceed slowly because of storms on the lake and because of the necessity of constantly stopping to fish to get a supply of food. On the seventh of September they were overtaken by Joseph and Thomas Frobisher and Mr. Patterson, and on October 26th they reached Cumberland House which had been established the preceding year by Hearne for the Hudson's Bay Company. After this long and trying journey, plans were made for the winter – Henry and the Frobishers went to the North, Peter Pond dropped down stream to Cedar Lake, portaged to Lake Winnipegosis and proceeded to Lake Dauphin on the shores of which he built his fort. Several reasons may have persuaded Pond to winter at this point. He may have joined with the other traders and acted in concert with them, taking his smaller outfit to the point which would prevent the Indians from the south going to Hudson Bay. Or he may have realized that acting as an independent this was the only plan left open for him. The post gave him access to the buffalo country and he was able to trade with the Assiniboines with whose language he was already familiar. In the spring of 1776 he probably returned, certainly to Grand Portage and possibly to Michilimackinac, to dispose of his furs and secure a new supply of goods. It is known that Simon McTavish had a small boat on Lake Superior in 1775 and that he brought down some

"Peter Pond and the Influence of Capt. Cook"

£15,000 worth of furs, most of which was probably from Grand Portage in 1776. It is quite possible that McTavish had taken Pond's goods to Grand Portage for him in 1775 and that he met Pond at that point to receive his furs in 1776. The partnership of McTavish and McBeath owned a boat of thirty tons on the Upper Lake in 1775. In 1777 McBeath took out a license for five canoes to Grand Portage.[4] For this license Alexander Ellice acted as guarantor. It is quite probable that the goods taken up by McBeath to Grand Portage in that year were intended for Peter Pond.

After Pond's visit to Grand Portage or to Michilimackinac in 1776, he decided upon a change in his plans and wintered beyond the posts of Canadian traders above the Forks on the North Saskatchewan. In the same year the Hudson's Bay Company had decided on a post in the same locality to check the Canadian traders, and Tomison was directed to build a post near the present site of Prince Albert, called Hudson's House. Pond remained at this post two years, but possibly as a result of Hudson's Bay Company competition and smaller profits decided in 1778 to attempt a trade to the Athabasca district.

Pond's chief contribution was the solution of the problems incidental to the establishment of trade in this distant area. Alexander Henry and Thomas and Joseph Frobisher had been extremely successful in 1775–6 in meeting the Indians from Athabasca on their way to trade at Hudson Bay or at Cumberland House. In 1776 Thomas Frobisher proposed to accompany the Indians on their return to Athabasca, but wintered on Isle à la Crosse Lake. The problem of Athabasca was incidental to the lack of food supply and the short season. Canoes were the feasible method of travel in the difficult waters of the Churchill and only a small quantity of food could be carried. To reach Athabasca it was necessary to start early in the season to give sufficient time to fish along the route for a supply of food and to get in before the season closed. It was impossible at that time, with no organization of the food supply, to reach the district from Grand Portage in one season.

Several factors contributed to solve the problem. In the first place the traders on the Saskatchewan had reached an agreement among themselves, at least as early as 1775, for a pooling of supplies of dry meat. Ample supplies of food were necessary to support the trip to Grand Portage from the Saskatchewan, and the buffalo were drawn upon as the chief source. This pooling of resources which began apparently in reference to the meat supply, was the beginning of co-operation which was at the basis of the Northwest Company. Competition on the Saskatchewan from the Hudson's Bay Company affected not only Pond but other traders as well. In 1778 it was agreed that the merchandise left over should be pooled, and that surplus meat should be used to support Pond in a venture to Athabasca. It was a tribute to Pond's organizing ability and to his trading ability that four canoes were entrusted to him to open the trade. The success with which he carried out the expedition with the honour of being the first white man to enter the Mackenzie River drainage basin by the Methye Portage, was evidence that the trust was well placed. He established a post on the Athabasca river about forty miles above Lake Athabasca, acquired a supply of food for the return voyage and a large quantity of furs, a portion of which he was obliged to leave in cache until the next season.

The development of trade in Athabasca was fundamental to the Northwest Company. The distance from Montreal necessitated the closest co-operation between all the traders concerned. Larger quantities of capital were necessary to finance the trade. It was necessary to organize supplies of food from the Detroit area for the canoes at Grand Portage and from the Saskatchewan area for the canoes at Cumberland House. Corn and grease had been adapted to the fur trade in the Grand Portage area and pemmican in the Saskatchewan. The source of pemmican, contrary to general belief, has not been definitely located. There is some reason to believe that it was a cultural trait of the Chipewyans or of the northern Indians of Athabasca, and that the Plains Indians prior to the coming of the white man had subsisted on dried meat. It is possible that Pond made a valuable contribution in adapting the pemmican which he found in use among the Athabascan Indians to the development of the trade from the Saskatchewan. The production of ample supplies of pemmican in Athabasca and the Saskatchewan was basic to the conduct of the trade in Athabasca and to the organization of the Northwest Company.

After a successful venture to Athabasca in 1778, Pond came down to Montreal in 1779.[5] In that year as a result of the lateness of the season in which the passes were issued, a formal agreement was made between the important traders at Grand Portage. Waden was selected to represent the partnership in the Athabasca district and wintered in Pond's absence

"Peter Pond and the Influence of Capt. Cook" 27

at Lake la Ronge in 1779–80. In the partnership, McBeath and Company probably including Pond, held two shares. In 1780 Pond took out two licenses at Montreal for two canoes each for Grand Portage, and with these he apparently returned to Athabasca to bring out the furs he had left in cache in 1779. In 1781 he probably came down to Grand Portage with these furs and secured the goods brought up from Montreal in four canoes under a license to McBeath, Pond and Graves; Waden was apparently still at Lac la Ronge in the summer of 1781 representing the minor interests in the trade to Athabasca. Pond was consequently chosen at Grand Portage to represent the larger interests and to trade on a joint account with Waden. Difficulties developed between the two men, probably as a result of the conflicting policies which they were chosen to represent, and Waden was killed in 1782. Mackenzie's account of the murder is unreliable and inaccurate, as shown in a sworn statement of a voyageur in Montreal. In any case Pond was acquitted. After the death of Waden, Pond sent his clerk, Toussaint Sieur, to meet the Indians on their way from Athabasca to Hudson Bay and to warn them of the dangers of smallpox, which was at that time raging on the plains. After the trade Pond came down to Grand Portage with the news of Waden's death. This news apparently led to a disruption of the agreement and two parties were sent to establish posts at Athabasca, only to find that the smallpox had preceded them, and to return with only seven packages of beaver. Pond apparently arrived too late to get into the district and wintered at Isle à la Crosse Lake. It is probable that he did not go down to Grand Portage in the summer of 1783, but proceeded directly to Athabasca. In any case he wintered in Athabasca and came down to Grand Portage and Montreal in 1784.

The difficulty of carrying on trade to Athabasca and the large quantities of capital involved made competition intolerable and in the autumn of 1783 Montreal interests had apparently decided on a merger. Pond arrived at Grand Portage in 1784 to find that he had been allotted one share in a sixteen share concern. Considering the importance of his work in facilitating the formation of the Company, he was disappointed at not receiving an additional share, and resolved to join a small opposition group. He was soon to discover that his affections were still with his old friends in the larger group and decided to accept the share which had been left vacant for him. In the winter of 1784–5 he probably spent some time at his old home in Milford. On March 1st, 1785, he presented his famous map to Congress. On April 18, 1785, he signed a memorial at Quebec and later in the year returned to Grand Portage and Athabasca. He found himself in opposition in Athabasca to John Ross the representative of the small group, which had secured the support of Gregory and McLeod of Montreal. His immediate problem was that of establishing posts and organizing the district. In the summer of 1786 he apparently surveyed the district and decided on building a post on Peace River above Vermilion Falls and a post on Slave Lake to the east of the entrance of Slave River. In the winter of 1786–7 competition became more severe and in the summer of 1787 word arrived that Ross "had been shot in a scuffle with Mr. Pond's men." The small opposition group amalgamated to form the Northwest Company in that year. Alexander Mackenzie, who had been a member of the small company was dispatched to Athabasca in 1787 to take Pond's place. The latter retired from Athabasca in 1788 and in the agreement of 1790, sold his share in the Northwest Company to William McGillivray for £800. In March, 1790, he returned to Milford and severed his connection with the fur trade forever.

His contribution to the fur trade was important. He bridged the difficult gap between Cumberland House and Athabasca and left the Athabasca district an organized department. From this organization the Northwest Company was able to expand its activities to New Caledonia in British Columbia and eventually to the Pacific Coast. The most profitable department of the Company was that of Athabasca. Its organization was an important factor leading to the formation of the Northwest Company. Pond was a pioneer and an organizer and in a very real sense a father of the Northwest Company.

We have attempted to this point to indicate Pond's contributions in the development of fur trade organization. There remains the task of appraising his work and influence on exploration. As already shown he was the first white man to cross the Methye Portage to the Mackenzie River drainage basin, and it is in reference to the Mackenzie River drainage basin that his later work in exploration was concerned. His work in exploration was very much handicapped through the lack of a scientific training and the lack of accurate instruments. He apparently learned something of the methods of taking observations from his experience in the army and his voyages to the West Indies. According to David Thompson, Pond used a compass and for distances adopted those of the Canadian canoe men in leagues, reckoning a league as three miles whereas it should have been two. Consequently his maps were very inaccurate from the standpoint of longitude, but quite accurate from the standpoint of latitude. To offset these disadvantages he possessed an amazing facility for acquiring accurate information from the Indians. In spite of the demands made by the fur trade he was able to extend very appreciably the existing knowledge of the Mackenzie River drainage basin. Indeed, without his organization of the trade in Athabasca, the later voyages of Mackenzie could not have been accomplished at such an early date.

From information which Pond had acquired in 1778–9, in 1779–80 and 1783–4 he was able to construct his first important map of the Northwest. To that time he had apparently not been below Lake Athabasca and yet his map of 1785 shows the main features of the Northwest with surprising accuracy. The locations of Slave Lake, Bear Lake, and of the Arctic Coast line and the route of the Mackenzie River are shown to be approximately correct. There can be no doubt that he had gained a clear conception of the topographical features of the country chiefly through his reliance on information supplied by the Indians. In a memorandum, of which a copy is included in the Appendix to Davidson's *Northwest Company*, he gives much valuable supplementary information to that which is included on the map. The map of 1785 is undoubtedly his most important and permanent contribution to geography and exploration.

In 1785 he returned to Athabasca apparently with the intention of verifying his information and continuing his exploration of the lower river. Before discussing his later work it is necessary to review briefly the general developments in exploration on the Pacific Coast. He had learned in Montreal of Cook's voyages and had apparently read the volume by W. Ellis, *An Authentic Narrative of a Voyage Performed by Captain Cook and Captain Clarke. (London, 1782).* He had noted the locations of Prince William Sound and King George's Sound, of Cook's Inlet, Bering Strait and other points. He was especially impressed with the information that Cook's Inlet was the mouth of a very large river. The importance of this information impressed not only Pond but other traders, including Alexander Henry. The profitable fur trade of the Pacific Coast was an incentive to American traders in Boston and New York. In this, Montreal traders were anxious to share. From this information it is not surprising that Pond decided that Cook's Inlet was probably the outlet of the Mackenzie River. Should this prove to be the case the traders of the Athabasca would have an outlet to the Pacific for their furs, which would greatly reduce costs of transport of furs and supplies and enable them to share in the profitable trade of the Pacific! Pond had returned to the Athabasca department, already an old man for the fur trade, to attempt a solution to the problem.

His movements are difficult to follow but he apparently visited Slave Lake in July, 1787, and he may have proceeded to the entrance of Mackenzie River in the same year. Alexander Mackenzie arrived in the district in the autumn of 1787. In the winter of 1787–8 we learn that Alexander Mackenzie in a visit to Patrick Small spoke of "the wild ideas Mr. Pond has of matters, which Mr. Mackenzie told me were incomprehensibly extravagant. He is preparing a fine map to lay before the Empress of Russia." There is evidence that Pond had decided to go down the Mackenzie River after he had visited Grand Portage in 1788, as Small writes that he gave orders to him "to go with or after the packs but represented to him that he required to be expeditious if he intended returning after seeing the Grand Portage." Arriving at Grand Portage he found it necessary to go on to Montreal and the partners apparently decided that Mackenzie should be sent in his place in 1789 the following summer. Mackenzie had also become inspired with the possibilities of the expedition and made his famous voyage only to find that he had travelled down the River Disappointment which emptied into the Arctic and not into Cook's inlet on the Pacific. While the partners had decided that Mackenzie should take Pond's place in his voyage down the Mackenzie in 1789, it was also decided that Pond's presence in Montreal was very much needed to interest the government in the possibilities of exploration. The Montreal traders were enthusiastic over the possibility of discovering the route to the Pacific. Pond gave Ogden, among others, a detailed account of the country, which was written to his father in London and forwarded to Evan Nepean on January 23, 1790. Alexander Dalyrymple suggested on February 2nd, 1790, that two vessels be sent, "one round Cape Horn without delay and another to Hudson's Bay, and the Hudson's Bay Company have expressed their readiness to co-operate

"Peter Pond and the Influence of Capt. Cook"   31

with government." The Hudson's Bay Company were [*sic*] extremely anxious to co-operate and if possible to share in the profits of the new route and in 1790 dispatched Philip Turnor to Athabasca to determine the locations. He met Alexander Mackenzie on his way out after his return from the disappointing journey. As late as July 25th, 1790, Captain Holland in a letter to Evan Nepean, suggested plans for exploration in the following year. These bubbles came to a sudden end with the news of Alexander Mackenzie's failure, Pond was discredited. Unfortunately he was too old to return to the attack, whereas Alexander Mackenzie was still a young man and able to vindicate himself by his determined voyage to the Pacific in 1793.

Pond's difficulties were the result of his inaccurate determination of longitude. He returned to Milford in March, 1790. He visited Ezra Stiles, the President of Yale University, who fortunately made a copy of the map which he had apparently planned to present to the Empress of Russia. Little is known of his later days but they were apparently spent in writing his journal, in reading other accounts of the countries in which he travelled and in musing over an eventful life. He is said to have died in poverty in Boston in 1807.

NOTES

1 Information discovered since this paper went to press shows that Pond and Felix Graham were partners in 1771.

2 The partnership of Graham and Pond was replaced by the partnership of Pond and Williams.

3 This adventure from Grand Portage was undertaken by Pond and Greves [Graves], and Pond was at Grand Portage July 22, 1775.

4 In 1777 the partnership of Pond and Williams is replaced by the partnership of Pond and McBeath.

5 Later evidence shows that Pond probably returned to Athabasca in 1779 and came out to Michilimackinac in 1780, returning to winter with Waden in 1781. See *Canadian Historical Review*, Dec. 1928.

H.A. Innis, *The Fur Trade in Canada*. Toronto: University of Toronto Press, 1930, 195–201, 252–3, 262, 390–3

H.A. Innis, *The Fur Trade in Canada*, 195-201

The quantity of furs brought into the fort was very great and from twenty to thirty Indians arrived daily, laden with packs of beaver skins. Thomas and Joseph Frobisher and Alexander Henry with forty men wintered on Beaver Lake. On April 12, 1776, Thomas Frobisher and six men went to Churchill River to build a fort at Portage du Traite, where he was joined by the remainder of the party on June 15. They started up the Churchill to find the Indians and met them at the entrance of Isle à la Crosse Lake. These Indians were from Athabasca and they traded "twelve thousand beaver skins, besides large numbers of otter and marten." The returns of the general joint stock of that year were apparently very successful.

Thomas Frobisher returned with the Indians in the summer of 1776 and wintered, according to Peter Pond's map,[1] on Isle à la Crosse Lake, coming out in 1777. According to the same source, Pond wintered in 1776 and 1777 on the north branch of the Saskatchewan. In that bitter year licences were granted for Grand Portage to Venant Lerner St. Germain and to Charles Paterson for one canoe each and to Jean Étienne Waden and C. Chaboillez for three canoes each; to George McBeath, with Alexander Ellice guarantor, for 5 canoes, 32 men, 790 gal. beverages, 40 rifles, 1,200 lb. gunpowder, 12 cwt. of shot and ball, valued at £2,000; to F. Oakes, with L. Ermatinger guarantor, for 7 canoes, 49 men, 1,350 gal. beverages, 64 guns, 1,500 lb. powder, 18 cwt. shot and ball, valued at £2,000; to William

The Fur Trade in Canada

Kay, with John Kay guarantor, 7 canoes, 41 men, 1,376 gal. beverages, 88 rifles, 2,400 lb. of gunpowder, 30 cwt. ball and shot, valued at £2,600; and J. Bte. Adhémar, with James McGill guarantor, 10 canoes, 94 men, 440 gal. beverages, 112 rifles, 3,700 lb. gunpowder, 47 cwt. bali and shot, valued at £5,100. There is evidence to show that each of these traders took out licences to Grand Portage in the previous year (1776) but the returns are not available.[2] According to Mackenzie, traders on the Saskatchewan in 1778 pooled their stock to send Pond to the Athabasca country following the success of Thomas Frobisher the preceding year.[3] There is no indication as to the names of the traders involved but St. Germain, Waden, McBeath, Paterson, Adhémar, McGill, Frobisher, McTavish, and Oakes were probably interested. In any case Pond crossed the height of land at Portage La Loche and wintered on the Athabasca River about forty miles above Lake Athabasca. He came out in 1779 but was obliged to return in the same year for a cache of furs he had left.

The licences for 1778[4] which were for 2 canoes each, included Charles Chaboillez, guarantors B. Frobisher and T. Corey; W. and J. Kay and D. Rankin, guarantors G. Phyn and Jas. McGill. J.E. Waden had a licence for 3 canoes guaranteed by R. Dobie and J. McKindlay; Holmes and Grant, 4 canoes, guarantors, R. Grant and Porteous; McBeath and Wright, 6 canoes, guarantors, G. Phyn and Jas. McGill; Forrest Oakes, 6 canoes, guarantors, Oakes and Ermatinger; McTavish and Bannerman, 8 canoes, guarantors, McTavish and J.B. Durocher; and John McGill and Thomas Frobisher, 12 canoes. In a report of Charles Grant it was stated,[5]

> Last year the passes for the Indian goods were given out so late, that it was impossible to forward goods to the places of destination especially in the North-west. For that reason those concerned in that quarter joined their stock together and made one common interest of the whole, as it continues at present in the hands of the different persons or companies as mentioned at the food of this ...
> Quebec, 24th April, 1780.

Todd & McGill	2 shares
Ben. & Jos. Frobisher	2 do.
McGill & Paterson	2 do.

McTavish & Co.	2 do.
Holmes & Grant	2 do.
Wadden & Co.	2 do.
McBeath & Co.	1 do.
Ross & Co.	1
Oakes & Co.	1

The North West is Divided into Sixteen Shares All Which Form but One Company at This Time

The returns for the passes in the same year included George McBeath, 2 canoes; St. Germain, 3 canoes; W. and J. Kay, 2 canoes; McTavish and Bannerman, 4 canoes; Porteous, Sutherland and Co., 2 canoes; J. Ross, 1 canoe; B. and J. Frobisher, 6 canoes; F. Oakes, 2 canoes; Paterson and Frobisher, 4 canoes. It is difficult to reconcile the two returns but Grant's report includes the supply firm of Todd and McGill; and probably Waden & Co. included St. Germain; Holmes and Grant included Porteous, Sutherland & Co., and F. Oakes included W. and J. Kay. Licence returns in 1780 included J. Lecuyer, 1 canoe; Frobisher and Patterson, 8 canoes; Holmes and Grant, 5 canoes; Waden and St. Germain, 5 canoes; Peter Pond, 4 canoes; Ross and Pangman, 4 canoes; F. Oakes, 3 canoes; S. McTavish, 5 canoes; W. and J. Kay, 2 canoes; B. and J. Frobisher, 2 canoes.[6] According to one account the agreement of 1779, called "the nine parties' agreement," was renewed in 1780 for three years but discontinued in two years. The following licence arrangements tend to support that conclusion. In 1781 Todd and McGill, B. and J. Frobisher, and McGill and Paterson under one licence sent 12 canoes; S. McTavish, 4 canoes; McBeath, Pond, and Graves, 4 canoes; Holmes and Grant, 4 canoes; Waden and St. Germain, 4 canoes; B. and J. Frobisher, 1 canoe; F. Oakes, 2 canoes; 1782, F. Oakes, 1 canoe, S. McTavish, 6 canoes; Charlebois and Morel, 1 canoe; Chamailant and Dassu, 1 canoe; Waden and St. Germain, 4 canoes; Holmes and Grant, 2 canoes; B. and J. Frobisher, 10 canoes; and George McBeath and Co., 4 canoes; 1783, B. and J. Frobisher, 5 canoes; S. McTavish, 6 canoes, Holmes and Grant, 3 canoes; and Desjerlais and Plante, 1 canoe. The North West Company of 1783–84 probably included Peter Pond, one share (taken in 1785); McBeath, one share; Grant, two shares; and Holmes, one share; S.

The Fur Trade in Canada   35

McTavish, three shares, with two additional shares held by Small; and B. and J. Frobisher, four shares, with two additional shares held by Montour.[7]

During the period of uncertainty following the war with the United States and the severe restrictions placed on trade, a combination of interests became inevitable. Larger numbers of traders including Pond and Henry and McTavish became interested in the Northwest trade immediately following the outbreak of hostilities. To compete with the Hudson's Bay Company it was necessary to combine as shown in the arrangements of 1775. To carry on trade across the difficult country between Grand Portage and the Saskatchewan,[8] depots for the production of dried meat and pemmican were essential. Co-operation had been essential to support Pond on the journey from the Saskatchewan to Athabasca. The capital requirements of this extended trade to Athabasca were an important contributing factor in the formation of the North West Company. In 1781 Pond was at Grand Portage and a joint enterprise was arranged for the prosecution of trade with Indians coming down the Churchill River. Waden had wintered at Lac la Ronge during the first year of amalgamation in 1779 and probably also in 1780, while in 1781 Pond was entrusted to represent other interests in a joint stock with him. In March of 1782 Waden was killed. Trade was carried on with the Churchill River Indians and they were persuaded to abandon the trip to Hudson Bay through fear of the smallpox which had been disastrous in the south. News of Waden's death probably led to a break up of the agreement in 1782. Pond may have been the trader to proceed "with one canoe strong handed and light loaded" to winter in the Athabasca country in 1782, but more probably he arrived too late at Portage la Loche and being preceded by representatives of the other interests, wintered at Clear Lake. Unfortunately smallpox had spread to the Athabasca country and returns were light in 1783 (seven packages of beaver). Pond continued to Athabasca in that year, however, and brought out large quantities of fur to Grand Portage and to Montreal in 1784. In 1785 he returned[9] to the Athabasca country and in the summer of 1786 sent Cuthbert Grant to establish a post at the mouth of the Slave River. John Ross also went into the Athabasca country in 1785[10] for the opposition company which had been formed that year at the instigation of Peter Pangman, who was dissatisfied with the arrangement of 1784, and probably sent Laurent Leroux to establish a post in opposition to Cuthbert Grant.[11] John Gregory, Peter Pangman, John Ross, Alexander Mackenzie, and Normand McLeod (dormant partner) were partners of the new company. Opposition between Ross and Pond in the Athabasca country became so severe that Ross was murdered "in a scuffle with Mr. Pond's men" in the winter of 1786–87.[12] This precipitated an amalgamation in a new concern in 1787 with the following shares: John Gregory, Peter Pangman, Alexander Mackenzie, and Normand McLeod, one share each; McTavish, Frobisher & Co., seven shares; Robert Grant, Nicholas Montour, and Patrick Small, two shares each; Peter Pond, George McBeath, and William Holmes, one share each; a total of twenty shares.

The amalgamation permitted the consolidation of interests in the trade as a basis for further expansion. General interest had been aroused at this time as to the possibilities of a northwest passage from Athabasca to Cook's Inlet. As a result of the amalgamation it was possible to explore Mackenzie River, and Alexander Mackenzie was immediately dispatched in 1787 to Athabasca department to relieve Pond for that expedition. In a letter dated Athabasca, December 2, 1787, the former wrote that he had arrived on October 21. Following the amalgamation, economies were suggested in the department and Leroux was ordered to abandon Slave Lake. St. Germain arrived too late to take goods to the Peace River country and Grant, with two canoes for Slave Lake, was stopped by ice on Lake Athabasca. As a result it was decided to establish Lac la Pluie as an advance depot from Grand Portage. Alexander Mackenzie went out in 1788 to Lac la Pluie and Pond went to Grand Portage to receive final instructions regarding his voyage down the Mackenzie. Apparently it was decided that Pond's assistance would be of more value in Montreal to enlist the support of the government in the expedition and that Alexander Mackenzie should be sent down the Mackenzie in his place in 1789. On Mackenzie's return to Athabasca with Roderick Mackenzie, the latter established Fort Chipewyan on Lake Athabasca. In 1789 Alexander Mackenzie undertook the trip to Cook's Inlet.[13] Laurent Leroux accompanied him with a trading outfit[14] to the houses erected in 1786 on Slave Lake and across the lake to the north arm, where trade was prosecuted during the summer with the Copper Indians and the Slave Indians around Lac La Martre. Leroux wintered on Slave Lake. Mackenzie returned to report failure for his expedition and went out

The Fur Trade in Canada 37

to Grand Portage in 1790 where he signed the new agreement giving him two shares out of twenty, and returned to Fort Chipewyan.[15] Determined to reach the Pacific he went to England in 1791 and returned in 1792 preparatory to the voyage up the Peace River in 1793. The earliest establishment on Peace River[16] was apparently made under Pond's direction in the neighbourhood of the present Fort Vermilion above Vermilion Falls in 1786. This was replaced by a fort below Carcajou and higher up the river at least as early as 1792. In that year Alexander Mackenzie established a post at the forks of the Peace and the Smoky[17] and in the following year continued the journey to the Pacific.

Although contrary to Pond's expectations, no feasible transport route to the Pacific had been found, Mackenzie's expeditions successfully mapped out the northern fur fields and provided for a rapid extension of trade.

H.A. Innis, *The Fur Trade in Canada*, 252–3

In 1778 they combined to support Pond's expedition to Athabasca. The restricted number of passes was referred to as the cause of joint stock operation in 1779. Difficulties with the Plains Indians at posts near Eagle Hills in the Saskatchewan in 1780 and the desolation caused by the smallpox were noted by Mackenzie as a cause of cooperation. After the Revolution a threatened encroachment from the United States on the boundary line from Lake Superior to Lake of the Woods was given as a reason for concerted action. "Their first object was to prepare the necessary supplies and provide against any interruption to their business from the United States by discovering another passage from Lake Superior to the River Quinipigue."[18] In 1784 Edward Umfreville was dispatched to discover a better route than that by Grand Portage. In these cases a common task presented itself and it could only be performed by co-operative effort.

In the latter stages of development co-operation appears less important as a factor tending toward concentration, and the ruinous effects of competition under conditions of heavy overhead costs became a driving force in favour of amalgamation. Reference has been made to the competition of the small Montreal Company from 1785 to 1787, formed at the suggestion of Pangman, Ross, and Pond following disagreement with the 1784 arrangement under the auspices of Gregory, McLeod & Company. The competition of this small organization began with the outfit of 1785.[19] In that year the Northwest Company sent to Grand Portage and Detroit, 25 canoes and 4 bateaux with 260 men in canoes and 16 men in bateaux carrying 6,000 gal. of rum, 340 gal. of wine, 300 rifles, 8,000 lb. of powder, 120 cwt. of shot, all of which was valued at £20,500, whereas Gregory and McLeod sent 4 canoes with 50 men, 400 gal. of rum, 32 gal. of wine, 63 rifles, 1,700 lb. of powder and 20 cwt. of shot, valued at £2,850, and Ross and Pangman took up the same number of canoes, 40 men, 350 gal. of rum, 32 gal. of wine, 36 rifles, 1,600 lb. of powder, 18 cwt. of shot, valued at £2,775. In 1786 the Northwest Company increased their outfits to include 30 canoes and 300 men, 2 bateaux and 9 men, 3,000 gal. of rum, 500 gal. of wine, 500 rifles, 9,000 lb. of powder, 120 cwt. of shot, valued at £25,500, whereas Gregory and McLeod sent 8 canoes, 3 men, 1,600 gal. of rum, 64 gal. of wine, 104 rifles, 2,800 lb. of powder, 45 cwt. of shot, valued at £4,500. Finally, in the year of amalgamation the Northwest Company sent 25 canoes and 250 men, 4 bateaux and 20 men, 5,300 gal. of rum, 786 gal. of wine, 500 rifles, 7,000 lb. of powder, 106 cwt. of shot, valued at £22,000, and Gregory and McLeod sent 9 canoes, 90 men, 1,600 gal. of rum, 54 gal. of wine, 150 rifles, 3,400 lb. of powder, 45 cwt. of shot valued at £4,700.

The small company in 1785 placed John Ross in charge of the Athabasca district, Alexander Mackenzie of English River, Peter Pangman of Fort des Prairies and Mr. Pollock, a clerk, of Red River. It was obliged to build new posts at Grand Portage and in the interior. The "guides, *commis* men and interpreters were few in number and not of the first quality." The success of Pollock against Robert Grant[20] and William McGillivray in the Red River department would probably not be important.

H.A. Innis, *The Fur Trade in Canada*, 262

The organization of the Northwest Company, adapted to expanding trade over wider areas, became a serious handicap with changed conditions in which new territory was no longer available. W.F. Wentzel, an unrewarded clerk, in a letter to Roderick Mackenzie dated Bear Lake, March 6, 1815, wrote: "Notwithstanding these gloomy appearances [in the Athabasca district] squires are manufactured yearly with as much speed and confidence

The Fur Trade in Canada 39

as Captains, Lieutenants and Ensigns were in His Excellency, Sir George
Prévost's time when I was two years ago in Montreal."[21]

As control within the Northwest Company became more concentrated
and the inability to adapt itself to a permanent trade became more conspicuous, control in the Hudson's Bay Company became less concentrated and
the ability to adapt itself to an expanding trade became more conspicuous.

By 1821 the Northwest Company had built up an organization which
extended from the Atlantic to the Pacific. The foundations of the present
Dominion of Canada had been securely laid. The boundaries of the trade
were changed slightly in later periods but primarily the territory over
which the Northwest Company had organized its trade was the territory
which later became the Dominion. The work of the French traders and
explorers and of the English who built upon foundations laid down by
them was complete. The fur trade had pushed beyond the St. Lawrence
drainage basin to the north and the northwest along the edge of the Pre-
Cambrian shield and the forest regions, and had organized the bases of
provisions in the more fertile territory to the south at Detroit, the Assiniboine, the Saskatchewan, the Peace, and lastly, the Columbia. The Northwest Company was the forerunner of confederation and it was built on
the work of the French *voyageur,* the contributions of the Indian, especially
the canoe, Indian corn, and pemmican, and the organizing ability of
Anglo-American merchants.

H.A. Innis, *The Fur Trade in Canada,* 390–3

The increasing distances over which the trade was carried on and the increasing capital investment and expense incidental to the elaborate organization of transport had a direct influence on its financial organization.
Immediate trade with Europe from the St. Lawrence involved the export of
large quantities of fur to meet the overhead costs of long ocean voyages and
the imports of large quantities of heavy merchandise. Monopoly inevitably
followed, and it was supported by the European institutional arrangements
which involved the organization of monopolies for the conduct of foreign
trade. On the other hand, internal trade, following its extension in the interior and the demand for larger numbers of *voyageurs* and canoes to undertake the difficult task of transportation and the increasing dependence

on the initiative of the trader in carrying on trade with remote tribes, was, within certain limits, competitive. Trade from Quebec and Montreal with canoes up the Ottawa to Michilimackinac, La Baye, and Lake Superior could be financed with relatively small quantities of capital and was consequently competitive. Further extension of trade through Lake Superior by Grand Portage (later Kaministiquia) to Lake Winnipeg, the Saskatchewan, Athabasca, the Mackenzie River, and New Caledonia and the Pacific coast involved heavy overhead costs and an extensive organization of transportation. But the organization was of a type peculiar to the demands of the fur trade. Individual initiative was stressed in the partnership agreements which characterized the Northwest Company. The trade carried on over extended areas under conditions of limited transportation made close control of individual partners by a central organization impossible. The Northwest Company, which extended its organization from the Atlantic to the Pacific, developed along lines which were fundamentally linked to the technique of the fur trade. This organization was strengthened in the amalgamation of 1821 by control of a charter guaranteeing monopoly and by the advantages incidental to lower costs of transportation by Hudson Bay.

The effects of these large centralized organizations characteristic of the fur trade as shown in the monopolies of New France, in the Hudson's Bay Company, and in the Northwest Company were shown in the institutional development of Canada. In New France constant expansion of the trade to the interior had increased costs of transportation and extended the possibilities of competition from New England. The population of New France during the open season of navigation was increasingly engaged in carrying on the trade over longer distances to the neglect of agriculture and other phases of economic development. To offset the effects of competition from the English colonies in the south and the Hudson's Bay Company in the north, a military policy, involving Indian alliances, expenditure on strategic posts, expensive campaigns, and constant direct and indirect drains on the economic life of New and old France, was essential. As a result of these developments, control of political activities in New France was centralized and the paternalism of old France was strengthened by the fur trade. Centralized control as shown in the activities of the government, the church, the seigniorial system, and other institutions was in part a result of the overwhelming importance of the fur trade.

The Fur Trade in Canada 41

The institutional development of New France was an indication of relation between the fur trade and the mercantile policy. The fur trade provided an ample supply of raw material for the manufacture of highly profitable luxury goods. A colony engaged in the fur trade was not in a position to develop industries to compete with manufactures of the mother country. Its weakness necessitated reliance upon the military support of the mother country. Finally the insatiable demands of the Indians for goods stimulated European manufactures.

The importance of manufactures in the fur trade gave England, with her more efficient industrial development, a decided advantage. The competition of cheaper goods contributed in a definite fashion to the downfall of New France and enabled Great Britain to prevail in the face of its pronounced militaristic development. Moreover, the importance of manufactured goods to the fur trade made inevitable the continuation of control by Great Britain in the northern half of North America. The participation of American and English merchants in the fur trade immediately following the Conquest led to the rapid growth of a new organization[22] which was instrumental in securing the Quebec Act and which contributed to the failure of the American Revolution so far as it affected Quebec and the St. Lawrence. These merchants were active in the negotiations prior to the Constitutional Act of 1791 and the Jay Treaty of 1794.[23] As prominent members of the government formed under the Quebec Act and the Constitutional Act, they did much to direct the general trend of legislation. The later growth of the North West Company assured a permanent attachment to Great Britain because of its dependence on English manufactures.

The northern half of North America remained British because of the importance of fur as a staple product. The continent of North America became divided into three areas: (1) to the north in what is now the Dominion of Canada, producing furs, (2) to the south in what were during the Civil War the secession states, producing cotton, and (3) in the centre the widely diversified economic territory including the New England states and the coal and iron areas of the middle west demanding raw materials and a market. The staple-producing areas were closely dependent on industrial Europe, especially Great Britain. The fur-producing area was destined to remain British. The cotton-producing area was forced after the Civil War to become subordinate to the central territory just as the northern fur-producing area, at present producing the staples, wheat, pulp and paper, minerals, and lumber, tends to be brought under its influence.

The Northwest Company and its successor the Hudson's Bay Company established a centralized organization which covered the northern half of North America from the Atlantic to the Pacific. The importance of this organization was recognized in boundary disputes, and it played a large role[24] in the numerous negotiations responsible for the location of the present boundaries. It is no mere accident that the present Dominion coincides roughly with the fur-trading areas of northern North America. The bases of supplies for the trade in Quebec, in western Ontario, and in British Columbia represent the agricultural areas of the present Dominion. The Northwest Company was the forerunner of the present confederation.

There are other interesting by-products of the study which may be indicated briefly. Canada has had no serious problems with her native peoples, since the fur trade depended primarily on these races. In the United States no point of contact of such magnitude was at hand and troubles with the Indians were a result. The existence of small and isolated sections of French half-breeds throughout Canada is another interesting survival of this contact.[25] The half-breed has never assumed such importance in the United States.

"The lords of the lakes and forest have passed away" but their work will endure in the boundaries of the Dominion of Canada and in Canadian institutional life. The place of the beaver in Canadian life has been fittingly noted in the coat of arms. We have given to the maple a prominence which was due to the birch. We have not yet realized that the Indian and his culture were fundamental to the growth of Canadian institutions. We are only beginning to realize the central position of the Canadian Shield.

3. The Forest Industries

Canada emerged as a political entity with boundaries largely determined by the fur trade. These boundaries included a vast north temperate land area extending from the Atlantic to the Pacific and dominated by the Canadian Shield. The present Dominion emerged not in spite of geography but because of it. The significance of the fur trade consisted in its determination of the geographic framework. Later economic developments in Canada were profoundly influenced by this background.

The Fur Trade in Canada 43

The decline of the fur trade in eastern Canada which followed the export of furs from the Northwest through Hudson Bay after 1821 necessitated increased dependence on other staple exports. Wheat and potash had become increasingly important but they were overshadowed by the rise of the lumber trade. The transport organization and personnel of the fur trade and its capitalistic beginnings were shifted to the development of new lines of trade.[26] An extended financial organization under the fur trade was attested by the plans for the first establishment of a bank in Canada with the strong support of Phyn and Ellice[27] and the establishment of the Bank of Montreal in 1817[28] with John Gray, an old fur trader, as president and John Richardson of Forsyth, Richardson & Company, as a strong supporter. McGill University persisted as a memorial to the wealth acquired by James McGill. Edward Ellice became an important figure in London with strong colonial interests and Simon McGillivray retained an interest in colonial activities. On this basis, with the advantages of preference in England and abundant and cheap shipping after the war, the lumber exports to Great Britain increased rapidly in the face of Baltic competition.

As with the fur trade the development of the lumber trade depended on water transportation. A bulky commodity, it was restricted in the early period to the large rivers. The buoyant softwoods could be floated in rafts down the St. Lawrence and the Ottawa to Quebec for shipment to England. The largest and best trees were in demand for the square timber trade. Square timber was in demand in England for the wooden shipbuilding industry, exports of which reached a peak in 1845.[29]

NOTES

1 See map in G.C. Davidson, *The North West Company*, p. 32.

2 In 1777 Graves, McCormick, Bruce, Montour, Pangman, Pond and B. Blondeau were at Sturgeon River Fort. In November, 1777, Francis killed an Indian there. *Journals of Hearne and Turnor*, p. 54. Apparently St. Germain in partnership with J.B. Nolin bought Michipicoten with 1 canoe of goods in 1778 from Alexander Henry for 15,000 livres. The first winter they got 23 packs of furs. In 1779–80 they got 44 packs in which there were 34 packs of beaver, 3 of otter, 3 of cats, 1½ of marten, 2½ of bear, musquash etc. In 1780–81 the trade was not half so good. They proposed to go in

1781–82 to build a post at Me-caw-baw-nish Lake. *Ibid.*, p. 301. Turnor said that Holmes was highest up the Saskatchewan in 1776–77. *Ibid.*, p. 231. Was his the house the ruins of which Turnor passed on March 13, 1779, noting that it had been built by Holmes in trust for Frobisher and Co.? *Ibid.*, p. 217.

3 Alexander Mackenzie, *Voyages from Montreal*, I, xxxv–xxxvi.

4 In 1778 B. Blondeau with a canoe and 6 men on Pine Island Lake got 11 packs of furs, mostly cats, beaver and marten, chiefly from Indians in debt to Hudson's Bay Company. *Journals of Hearne and Turnor*, pp. 214, 234.

On March 7, 1779, Philip Turnor met Canadians from Blondeau's upper post going to Pine Island Lake. Turnor arrived on March 17 at two houses, one of them inhabited by Blondeau, the other by Robert Grant. His journal entry for March 19 mentions a house in possession of Gibosh (Gibeau?) in trust for Waden, one in possession of Holmes and Graves, and one in possession of Nicholas Montour in trust for Blondeau. The upper settlement on the Saskatchewan in 1779 belonged to McCormick, Graves, Pangman, Blondeau, Holmes, Grant, and Gibosh. It was first settled by Pangman, Mc-Cormick, and Gibosh. Graves, "having a great number of men, hauled his goods up as soon as the river set fast. They found they should have ruined each other had they not entered into a General Partnership." Blondeau had not entered the partnership but he expected to come in. In 1778 Blondeau and Pangman were partners and Graves, Holmes, and Grant. Robert Long-moor of the Hudson's Bay Company accepted one of Blondeau's houses. (Pond linked with Graves, Holmes, and Grant?) Blondeau was interested in four sites besides the vacant house lent to Longmoor. On the Saskatche-wan in 1778–79 were (*ibid.*, p. 253):

Blondeau	6 canoes	63 packs
McCormick	6	46
Gibosh (Waden)	3	31
Pangman	5	36
Graves	5	118
Holmes & Grant	5	____
		294

Among the Canadians, Graves and Jacobs were from Great Britain, Robert Grant was a North Briton, McCormick and Holmes were natives

The Fur Trade in Canada 45

of Ireland (*ibid.*, p. 232). Traders were driven out in the spring of 1779 by the murder of John Cole (*ibid.*, p. 224).

About 10 canoes went to Churchill 1778–79. Blondeau planned to winter in 1779–80 north of Cumberland House and left Tute to act for him on the Saskatchewan. Graves sent 2 canoes of goods in to Athabasca in 1779. *Ibid.*, pp. 233–234.

5 "North West Trade," *Report on Canadian Archives*, 1888, p. 61.

6 In 1780 no canoes had passed Michipicoten by June 26 though they usually passed in May. *Journals of Jearne and Turnor*, pp. 299–300. In 1780 Bruce and Boyer fought at Fort aux Trembles against the Indians. Bruce and Tute died of smallpox in 1781–82. *Ibid.*, p. 159n.

7 See H.A. Innis, "The North West Company."

8 In 1779 traders were driven out of the Saskatchewan by Indians and probably began to go to Athabasca. Large returns were expected from that area and difficulty as to the rights of the Hudson's Bay Company was overcome. *Journals of Hearne and Tunor*, pp. 224–235. Cole had left the Hudson's Bay Company (*ibid.*, p. 230) apparently to go with Graves. Frobisher was probably linked to Holmes, Grant, Graves, and Pond.

9 L.-R. Masson, *Les Bourgeois de la Compagnie du Nord-Ouest*, I, 94.

10 *Ibid.*, pp. 10ff.

11 Apparently wrong. Cuthbert Grant was with Gregory and McLeod, Leroux with the Northwest Company. *Journals of Hearne and Turnor*, p. 370.

12 The shooting of Mr. Ross "made the other company who was most powerful readily join them in partnership to prevent too great inquiry into the affair; if it had not happened Mr. Ross's party would soon have been ruined but they now trade as they please having no opposers." Philip Turnor, July 22, 1791; *ibid.*, p. 417.

13 G.C. Davidson, *The North West Company*, p. 44.

14 Alexander Mackenzie, *Voyages from Montreal*, I,194.

15 H.A. Innis, "The North West Company."

16 Alexander Mackenzie, *Voyages from Montreal*, I, 348ff.; see J.N. Wallace, *The Wintering Partners on Peace River*, chaps. ii, iii.

17 Alexander Mackenzie, *Voyages from Montreal*, I, 284–285; II, 160–161.

18 Can. Arch., Haldimand Papers, B.217, p. 470; also Frobisher Letter Book, p. 60; see letters to the government on the subject of the boundary line,

"North West Trade," *Report on Canadian Archives,* 1888, pp. 63ff.; also petition of merchants, February 6, 1783, Can. Arch., Shelburne MSS, LXXII, 288–293. See requests for exclusive privileges and charters, Memorial of the Northwest Company, Montreal, October 4, 1784; Benjamin and Joseph Frobisher to General Haldimand, Montreal, October 4, 1784; and Memorial of Peter Pond, Quebec, April 18, 1785, "North-Western Explorations," *Report on Canadian Archives,* 1890, pp. 48–54; E. Umfreville, *Nipigon to Winnipeg.*

19 L.-R. Masson, *Les Bourgeois,* I, 10.

20 Robert Grant and Peter Pangman retired in 1793; *Five Fur Traders,* pp. 95–96.

21 L.-R. Masson, *Les Bourgeois,* I, 115.

22 See Mrs. K.B Jackson (as M.G. Reid), "The Quebec Fur-Traders and Western Policy, 1763–1774."

23 See W.E. Stevens, *The Northwest Fur Trade, 1763–1800.*

24 *Ibid.*

25 See Marcel Giraud, *Le Métis canadien.*

26 F.W. Howay, "The Fur Trade in Northwestern Development."

27 Appendix G. For an advertisement of the Canada Banking Company, R.M. Breckenridge, *The Canadian Banking System, 1817–1890,* p. 18.

28 See *Centenary of the Bank of Montreal, 1817–1917.*

29 See A.R.M. Lower, "A History of the Canadian Timber and Lumber Trade," master's thesis (University of Toronto Library).

H.A. Innis, *Peter Pond: Fur Trader and Adventurer*. Toronto: R.S. Irwin & Gordon, 1930

In writing his biography of Peter Pond, Innis drew heavily on the version edited by R.C. Thwaites that appeared in Wisconsin Historical Collections, incorporating much of it into his text.* The portions that he cited were enclosed within quotation marks. Subsequent to the publication of Peter Pond in 1930, two successively improved versions of the text, both edited by Gates, were produced by the Minnesota Historical Society.† The volume contained not only Pond's memoir but a number of other first-hand accounts of the early fur trade in North America. The 1965 version is likely the definitive version of the text of Pond's journal, as it was thoroughly edited and annotated by June D. Holmquist, Anne A. Hage, and Lucile M. Kane, based on a completely new transcription of the document, held at Yale University. In that edition, many of the idiosyncratic spellings and phrasings used by Pond were accompanied by more accessible wordings,

---

* R.C. Thwaites, ed., "1749–75: Journal of Peter Pond," *Wisconsin State Historical Society Collections*, 18 (1908): 314–54.

† Charles M. Gates, ed., *Five Fur Traders of the Northwest: Being the Narrative of Peter Pond and Diaries of John Macdonell, Archibald N. McLeod, Hugh Faries, and Thomas Conner* (Minneapolis: Pub. for the Minnesota Society of the Colonial Dames of America, The University of Minnesota Press, 1933); Charles M. Gates, ed., *Five Fur Traders of the Northwest: Being the Narrative of Peter Pond and Diaries of John Macdonell, Archibald N. McLeod, Hugh Faries, and Thomas Conner*, with an introduction by Grace L. Nute and a foreword by Theodore C. Blegen (St Paul: Publications of the Minnesota Historical Society, 1965).

and the footnotes providing information about persons, places, and events mentioned in the text were revised and expanded.

In this edition of the text, we have added the citations from Pond's journal, using their locations in the authoritative 1965 edition in square brackets next to the cited passage. Ryan Scheiding has written commentary on Innis's approach to editing portions of the Pond memoir.

Contents

Chapter

	Preface
	Preface
I.	Early Life and the Army
II.	The Apprentice Trader
III.	The Mississippi:
	(a) The Trader, 1773–74
	(b) The Peacemaker, 1774–75
IV.	The Northwest Company:
	(a) The Explorer, 1775–78
	(b) The Organizer, 1778–90
V.	The Man and His Work
VI.	Bibliography

Preface

It has been a common assumption among writers on the fur trade that the more important traders and explorers were born in Scotland but in the formative period of the trade immediately following the Conquest and previous to the formation of the Northwest Company, traders born in the Colonies occupied an important place. Two of these traders, Alexander Henry, born in New Jersey in Aug. 1739, and Peter Pond, born in Milford in the county of New Haven in Connecticut on Jan. 18, 1740, exercised a profound influence on exploration and trade in the Northwest. They were born within a year of each other and there were two interesting coincidences in later life. At the surrender of Fort de Lévis in 1760 and on the journey down the St. Lawrence to the attack on Montreal, Peter Pond was a commissioned officer under General Amherst, and Alexander Henry

Peter Pond: Fur Trader and Adventurer 49

was a merchant engaged in supplying the commissariat. In 1775 Alexander Henry proceeded from Michilimackinac to Grand Portage and to the Northwest on his first visit and on Aug. 18 of that year on Lake Winnipeg he was joined by Peter Pond who was also on his first visit to that country. The work of Alexander Henry has been generally known through the editions of his *Travels and Adventures in Canada and the Indian territories* but the name of Peter Pond has been almost forgotten. This neglect has been due largely to the scarcity of material concerning him. His crowded life left little room for a formal education and his illiteracy was a serious handicap to the attainment of a permanent place in Canadian history. His journal was apparently written in the latter part of his life probably after he was sixty years of age and after he had ceased to have any connection with the fur trade. Apparently a large part of it has been destroyed but the remainder which has been printed in the Wisconsin Historical Collections and elsewhere is an extremely interesting and valuable record of the activities of his early life. From a study of this record it is possible to gain an insight into the later life of the man, a knowledge of which must be gleaned from scanty and biased information supplied by contemporaries.

My attention was attracted to the work of Peter Pond through a study of the early history of the Northwest Company. The organization of the technical side of the trade which followed the expansion to the Saskatchewan and especially to Athabaska and which made possible the evolution of the Northwest Company was to a large extent a result of the efforts of Peter Pond. He was the first white man to cross the Methye Portage to the drainage basin of the Mackenzie river. To understand the history of the fur trade of the Northwest during the formative stages of the Northwest Company I found it necessary to attempt a biography of Peter Pond. His contributions to Canadian development, and the Northwest Company was [as?] a crucial organization, appeared to warrant a general appreciation of his position as one of the fathers of Confederation. The vilification of his enemies has up to the present made this estimate impossible.

I should like to thank Mr. L.J. Burpee for his kindness in arranging for the presentation of a part of this study before the Royal Society of Canada at Winnipeg, in May 1928, as well as for other kindnesses.

H.A.I.

I. Early Life and the Army

Peter Pond wrote regarding his ancestry "It is well known that from fifth gineration downward we ware all waryers ither by sea or land"[18] and the available evidence in the Pond genealogy lends support to his statement. The date of arrival of the first Pond in New England has not been definitely established, but it is probable that he was one of two sons of William Pond, a neighbor of John Winthrop, of Groton, Suffolk who arrived with the latter at Salem, Massachusetts in the "great fleet" of 1630. Winthrop refers in one of his letters to John Pond and it is probable that the other son was Samuel and that he migrated from Salem with various Dorchester settlers to Windsor, Connecticut. In any case a Samuel Pond married Sarah Ware at Windsor on November 18, 1642, and a son, named Samuel Pond, was born on March 4, 1648. Six years later on March 14, 1654 the father died leaving his widow a small estate of 130 pounds. She apparently moved to Branford, Connecticut, and on July 6, 1655 married John Linsley at that place. The son became one of the charterers of Branford and in 1672 became a freeman at Hartford. He was deputy to the General Court for Branford in 1678, 1682–3 (seargeant of "ye trainband" in the latter year), and 1687, and was made lieutenant in 1695. On February 3, 1669 he was married to Miriam Blatchley of Hartford and on July 1, 1679, a son, Samuel Pond, the third, was born. On June 8, 1704 this son was married to Abigail Goodrich, of Branford, a daughter of Bartholomew Goodrich, who had been made lieutenant in 1695. A son, Peter Pond, was born at Branford on January 22, 1718. The latter married Mary Hubbard, a daughter of Zachariah Hubbard of Boston, probably in 1739, and Peter Pond, the second, was born in Milford on Jan. 18, 1740 the eldest of nine children. His mother died on June 16, 1761 at the age of thirty seven and his father in 1764.

Little is known of the early life of Peter Pond. According to the rolls of the Suffolk County Regiment he enlisted on April 17, 1759 as a shoemaker by trade and it is probable that his father was a shoemaker also. At the age of sixteen he writes that his parents forbade him to join the army "and no wonder as my father had a larg and young famerly I just began to be of sum youse to him in his afairs."[18] The spelling of this

Peter Pond: Fur Trader and Adventurer

journal warrants the conclusion that little time was available to acquire a formal education. The son of a shoemaker in a large family probably suffered from handicaps.

His account of his early life begins with enlistment in the colonial army. In 1755 Braddock was killed on the banks of Monongahela river with heavy losses to his troops. Pond writes "A part of the British troops which ascaped cam to Milford."[18 (edited to remove additional details)] Attracted by tales of adventures in the service he was determined to enlist. "Toward spring government began to rase troops for the insewing campaign aganst Crown Point under the comand of General Winsloe. Beaing then sixteen years of age I gave my parans to understand that I had a strong desire to be a solge. That I was detarmind to enlist under the Oficers that was going from Milford and joine the army. – the same inklanation and sperit that my ancesters profest run thero my vanes. – and indead so strong was the propensatey for the arme that I could not with stand its Temtations. One Eaveing in April the drums an instraments of Musick were all imployed to that degrea that they charmed me. – I found miney lads of my acquantans which seamd detarmined to go into the Sarvis. I talkt with Capt. Baldwin and ask him weather he would take me in his Companey as he was the recruiting offeser. He readealey agread and I set my hand to the orders." [18–19 (sentences rearranged to make more sense)]

Peter Pond was a recruit in the seventh company of the Connecticut regiment under Capt. David Baldwin. "My parans was so angry that thay forbid me making my apearance at home. I taread about the town among my fello solgers and thought that I had made a profitable Exchange giting a rigimintal coate – At length the time came to report. Early in June we imbarked on bord a vessel to join the arme at the randivoere. We sald from Milford to New York proceeded up North river and arrived safe at Albany. I cam on smartly as I had sum of my Bountey money with me. I did not want for ginger bread and small bear and sun forgot that I had left my parans who were exseedingley trubled in minde for my well-fair. After taring thare sum weakes the Prinsabel part of the Armey got togather and we proceaded up to the Halfmoon and thare lay til the hole of the Armey from differant parts of the hole countray got to gather. In the meantime parties and teamsters ware imploid in forwarding provishon from post to post and from Forte Eadward to the head of Lake George. It was supposed that we should crose Lake George and make a desent on ticondaroge but before that coud be a Complished the sumer ended. Fall of year Seat in and we went to work at the fort George which lay on the head of the Lake by that name. In November it Groed two cold to sleap in tents and the men began to Mutanie and say that thay had sarved thare times out for which thay ware inlisted and would return home after satisfying them with smooth words thay ware prevailed on to prolong the campaign a few weakes and at the time promest by the Gineral the camp broke up and the troops returned to thare respective plasis in all parts of ye country from which thay came. But not without leaving a grate number behind which died with the disentary and other diseases which camps are subjet to appesaley [especially] among raw troops as the Amaracans ware at that time and they Beaing strangers to a holesome Mod of cookeraray it mad grate havock with them in making youse of salt provisions as they did which was in a grate part Broyling and drinking water with it to Exses."[19–20]

This introduction to army life had satisfied him for the time and the following year did not find him anxious to enlist. "The year insewing which was 57 I taread at home with my parans so that I ascaped the misfortune of a number of my countrey men for Moncalm came against fort George and capterd it and as the Amaracans ware going of for fort Edward a Greabel to ye capatalasion [capitulation] the Indians fel apon them and mad grate Havack."[20]

But in spite of the disasters of that campaign two years of inactivity proved unbearable. "In ye year 58 the safety of British Amaraca required that a large arme should be raised to act with the British Troops against Cannaday and under the command of Gineral Abercrombie against ticonderoge. I found tareing at home was too inactive a life for me therefore I joined many of my old Companyans a secont time for the arme of ye end of the Campain under the same offisers and same regiment under the command of Cornl Nathan Whiting" – of the second Connecticut regiment. "In the Spring we embarked to gine the arme at Albany whare we arrived safe at the time appointed. We ware emploid in forwarding Provishuns to Fort Edward for the youse of the Sarvis. When all was readey to cross Lake George the armey imbarked consisting of 18000 British and Provincals in about 1200 boates and a number of whalebotes, floating battery,

Peter Pond: Fur Trader and Adventurer 53

Gondaloes, Rogalleyes and Gunbotes."[20–1 (Innis provides context on who Whiting is, corrects minor spelling issues, and changes written numbers into numerals)]

"The next day we arrived at the north end of Lake George and landed without opposition. The french that were encampt at that end of the Lake fled at our appearance as far as Ticonderoge and joined thare old commander Moncalm and we ware drawn up in order and divided into collams and ordered to March toward Moncalm in his camp before the fort – but unfortunately for us Moncalm like a Gineral dispatched five hundred to oppose us in our landing or at least to imbarres us in our March so he might put his camp in some sort of defense before our arme could arrive and thay did it most completely. We had not Marcht more than a mile and a half befoare we meat the falon [forlorn] hope for such it proved to be. The British troops kept [the] rode in one collam the Amaracans marcht threw ye woods on thare left. On ye rite of the British was the run of water that emteys from Lake George into Lake Champlain. The British and French meat in the open rode verey near each other befoar they discovered the french in a count of the uneaveneas of the ground. Lord How held the secont place in command and beaing at the head of the British troops with a small sidearm in his hand he ordered the troops to forme thare front to ye left to atack the french. But while this was dueing the french fird and his Lordship receaved a ball and three buck shot threw the senter of his brest and expired without spekeing a word. But the french pade dear for this bold atempt. It was but a short time befoare thay ware surounded by the hole of the Amaracan troops and those that did not leape into the rapid stream in order to regan thare camp ware made prisners or kild and those that did went down with the Raped curant and was drounded. From the best information I could geat from ye french of that partea was that thare was but seven men of ye five hundred that reacht the campt but it answered the purpas amaseingly."[21–2 (shortened to omit repeated/unnecessary information) added paragraph break]

"This afair hapend on thirsday. The troops beaing all strangers to the ground and runing threw the woods after the disparst frenchmen night came on and thay got themselves so disparst that thay could not find the way back to thare boates at the landing. That nite the British did beatter haveing the open rod to direct them thay got to ye lake Sid without trubel.

A large party of ye amaracans past the nite within a Bout half a mile of the french lines without noeing whare thay ware til morning. I was not in this partey. I had wandered in ye woods in the nite with a bout twelve men of my aquantans – finealey fel on the Rode a bout a mile north of ye spot whare the first fire began. Beaing in the rode we marched toward our boates at ye water side but beaing dark we made but a stumbling pece of bisness of it and sun coming among the dead bodeyes, which ware strewed quit thick on the ground for sum little distans. We stumbled over them for a while as long as thay lasted. At lengh we got to the water just before day lite in the morn."[22; added paragraph break]

"What could be found of the troops got in sum order and began our march a bout two a clock in ye afternoon crossing the raped stream and left it on our left the rode on this side was good and we advansd toward the french camp as far as the miles [mills] about a mile from the works and thare past the night lying on our armes."[22; added paragraph break]

"This delay gave the french what thay wanted – time to secure thare camp which was well executed. The next day which was Satterday about eleven we ware seat in mosin [were set in motion?] the British leading the van it was about. [?] They ware drawn up before strong brest work but more in extent then to permit four thousand five hundred acting. We had no cannon up to the works. The intent was to march over this work but thay found themselves sadly mistaken. The french had cut down a grate number of pinetrease in front of thare camp at some distance. While som ware entrenching others ware imployed cuting of the lims of the trease and sharpening them at both ends for a shevo dufrease [chevaux de frise] others cuting of larg logs and geting them to the Brest works. At length thay ware ready for our resaption."[22–3; added paragraph break]

"About twelve the parties began thare fire and the British put thare plan on fut to march over the works but the lims and tops of the trease on the side for the diek stuck fast in the ground and all pointed at upper end that thay could not git threw them til thay ware at last obliged to quit that plan for three forths ware kild in the atempt but the grater part of the armey lade in the rear on thare fases til nite while the British ware batteling a brest work nine logs thick in som plases which was dun without ye help of canan tho we had as fine an artilrey just at hand as could be in an armey of fifteen thousand men but thay ware of no youse while thay ware lying on thare

Peter Pond: Fur Trader and Adventurer

fases. Just as the sun was seating Abercrombie came from left to rite in the rear of the troops ingaged and ordered a retreat beat and we left the ground with about two thousand two hundred loss [actually over nineteen hundred] as I was informd by an officer who saw the returns of ye nite wounded and mising."[23 (fixed spelling of "Abercrombie," added paragraph break)]

"We ware ordered to regain our boates at the lake side which was dun after traveling all nite so sloley that we fell asleep by the way. About nine or tenn in the morning we were ordered to imbark and cross the lake to the head of Lake George but to sea the confusion thare was the solgers could not find thare one botes but imbarked permisherley [promiscuously] whare ever thay could git in expecting the french at thare heales eavery minnet. We arrived at the head of the lake in a short time – took up our old incampment which was well fortefied."[23 (fixed spelling of "fortified," added paragraph break)]

"After a few days the armey began to com to themselves and found thay ware safe for the hole of the french in that part of the country was not more than three thousand men and we about fortee thousand. We then began to git up provishan from fort Edward to the camp but the french ware so bold as to beseat our scouting party between the camp and fort Edward and cut of all the teames, destroy the provishun, kill the parties and all under thare ascort. We past the sumer in that maner and in the fall verey late the camp broke up and what remaned went into winter qaters in different parts of the collanees thus ended the most ridicklas campane eaver hard of."[23–4]

Pond's account of the campaign corroborates the general views which have been held by various writers. The clumsiness of General Abercromby, the loss of Lord Howe, and the fatal attack on the French without the support of artillery are the points stressed in explanation of the British defeat.

Pond had been engaged in two campaigns as a soldier on the Lake George–Lake Champlain front. In the first campaign he had endured the ennui of camp life and in the second campaign he had seen his first severe fighting with heavy casualties. He had no liking for a third campaign in this territory. "The year 59 an armey was rased to go against Niagaray to be commanded by Gineral [Prideaux]. As the Connecticut troops ware not to be imploid in that part of the armey I went to Long Island and ingaged in thot sarvis"[24] – joining the Suffolk County regiment on April 17, 1759.

"In the Spring we repaired to Albany and gined the armey as that was the plase of Rondevuse. We ware imploid in geating forward provisons to Oswego for the sarvis of the Campain. When we asemled at Osawaga Col. Haldaman took part of the troops under his command and incampt on the Ontarey side but the troops that ware destind to go against Niagara incampt on the opaset side of the river under the command of General [Prideaux]. But the Company I belonged to was not ordered over the lake at all but Col. Johnston [Col. John Johnstone] who was in the Garsea [Jersey] Sarvis sent for me in partickler to go over the lake. I wated on him and inquired of him how he came to take me the ondley man of the Company out to go over the lake. He sade he had a mind I should be with him. I then asked him for as maney of the companey as would make me aseat of tent mates. He sun complid and we went and incampt with the troop for that sarvis. Capt. Vanvater [Thwaites suggests Capt. Van Veghte] commanded the company we joined."[24–5 (added paragraph break)]

"We sun imbarkt and arived at Nagarey. In a few days when all ware landead I was sent by the Agatint Mr. Bull as orderly sarjant to General [Prideaux]. I was kept so close to my dutey that I got neither sleape nor rest for the armey was down at Johnsons landing four miles from the acting part of the army. I was forced to run back and forth four miles nite and day til I could not sarve eney longer. I sent to Mr. Bull to releave me by sending another sargint in my plase which was dun and I gind my friends agane and fought in the trenches aganst the fort."[25 ("shot" changed to "fought," added paragraph break)]

"Befoar we had capterd the fort the Gennarel had gind the arme and himself and my frend Col. Johnson ware both kilt in one day and Col. [Thodey] of the New York troops shot threw the leag. This was a loss to our small armey – three brave offesars in one day. We continued the seage with spereat under the command of Sir William Johnson who it fell to after the death of [Prideaux]. I was faverd – I got but one slite wound dureing the seage. At the end of twenty-five days the fort capatalated to leave the works with the honners of war and lay down thare armes on the beach whare thay ware to imbark in boates for Schanactady under an escort. After apointing troops to garsen the fort we returned to Oswego and bilt a fort cald fort Erey [Fort Ontario]."[25–6 ("Braduck" changed to "Prideaux," added paragraph break)]

Peter Pond: Fur Trader and Adventurer

He began to realize that war meant the loss of friends and he writes, "At the close of the Campain what was alive returned home to thare native plases but we had left a number behind who was in thare life brave men. On my arival at Milford I found maney of the prisners I had bin so industres in captering ware billeated in the town. I past the winter among them."[26 (added paragraph break)] Pond's knowledge of French was probably acquired at this time.

In the siege at Niagara and Pond's third campaign he had begun to impress his superior officers with his ability and was singled out for promotion. He had reached maturity. We find him writing "in 1760 I receaved a Commission and entered a forth time in the army. We then gind the armey at the old plase of Rondavuse and after lying thare a few weakes in camp duing Rigimental dutey General Armarst [Amherst] sent of in pourshen to carre the baggage to Oswego whare part of the armey had all readey arived. I was ordered on this command four offesers and eighty men. On our arrival at Oswego the Genarel gave the other three offesers as maney men as would man one boate and ordered them to return to thare rigiment. Me he ordered to incamp with my men in the rear of his fammerley til farther orders with seventy men til just befoar the armey imbarkt for S[wegatchie] and then gind my regiment. Sun after thare was apointed a light infantry companey to be pickt out of each regiment – hats cut small that thay mite be youneform. I was apointed to this Company."[26 (corrected spelling of "Oswego," added paragraph break)]

"When orders ware given the armey about nine thousand imbark in a number of boates and went on the lake towards Swagochea whare we arived safe. Thare we found Pashoe [Pouchot] that had bin taken at Niagarey the sumer before commanding the fort and semed to be determined to dispute us and give us all the trubel he could but after eight or a few more days he was obliged to comply with the tarmes of our victoras armey a second time in les than one year."[26–7 (added paragraph break)]

"We then left a garrson and descended the river til we reacht Montreal the ondley plase the french had in possession in Canaday. Hear we lay one night on our armes. The next day the town suranderd to Gineral Amharst." [27 (added paragraph break)]

With the capture of Montreal the work of the army in the conquest of New France was finished. Peter Pond at the end of the campaigns was twenty years old. During the space of four years he had joined as a raw young recruit, had been engaged as a private in two campaigns, those of 1756 and 1758 on the Ticonderoga front, had become a sergeant at Niagara in 1759, and obtained his commission in 1760. He had become inured to the hardships of army life and to its discipline and had gained favour in the eyes of his superior officers. He acquired a knowledge of the army in a remarkably short space of time. He appears to have had an extraordinary physique. He had seen life at its worst but there stands out clearly in this part of his life his great loyalty to his friends. He rejoined the same company in 1758, he asked for a set of tent-mates to go with him to Niagara, he wanted to be returned to the ranks at Niagara, and he was a man who won his commission because of his ability to command men. These were impressionable years as one can gather from the detailed character of his description of the campaigns.

II. The Apprentice Trader (1761–1773)

The conquest was over and for Peter Pond there came the problem of adjustment to civil life. "All Canaday subdued I thought thare was no bisnes left for me and turned my atenshan to the seas thinking to make it my profesion and in sixtey one I went a Voige to the islands in the West Indees and returned safe but found that my father had gon a trading voig to Detroit and my mother falling sick with a feaver dide (on June 16, 1761) before his return."[27 (added date of Pond's mother's death)] For the time Pond found it necessary to curb his restless temperament which army experience had intensified. He writes, "I was oblige to give up the idea of going to sea at that time and take charge of a young fammaley til my father returnd."[27] After his father's return "I bent my mind after differant objects and tared in Milford three years."[27] No information is given in his journal as to his activities but according to records he was married during this interval to Susanna Newell by whom he had at least two children, one of whom, Peter Pond, the third, was born in 1763. These family ties explain his three year sojourn at Milford. "Which was the ondley three years of my life I was three years in one place sins I was sixteen years old up to sixtey."[27]

Peter Pond: Fur Trader and Adventurer

Information on the activities of his life in the decade after 1763 is extremely scanty. His father apparently joined the numbers of traders in 1761 who rushed to the west after the conquest of New France. He may have returned in 1762 and doubtless found prospects had suffered through the uncertainties of Indian trade previous to the outbreak of Pontiac's war in 1763. It is known that he died insolvent in 1764 and that his principal creditors were Captain John Gibb and Garrett Van Horn Dewitt. With the close of the Indian wars and possibly assuming his father's debts Peter Pond decided to follow in his father's footsteps. In 1765 he left Milford to engage in the Detroit trade. Little is known of his activities in the six years of his residence in the Detroit country. He writes in his journal "I continued in trade for six years in different parts of that countrey but beaing exposed to all sorts of Companey. It hapend that a parson [person] who was in trade himself to abuse me in a shamefull manner knowing that if I resented he could shake me in peaces at same time supposing that I dare not sea him at the pints or at leas I would not but the abuse was too grate. We met the next morning eairley and discharged pistels in which the pore fellowe was unfortenat. I then came down the country and declard the fact but thare was none to prosacute me."[27] It is probable that like other traders he was under the close supervision which Sir William Johnson exercised over the southern posts. Along with other traders at Detroit, including Isaac Todd, he signed a petition[1] on 26th November, 1767, asking Sir William Johnson to restrict the amount of rum brought by traders to 50 gallons in each 3 handed battoe load of dry goods and also to permit the petitioners to trade beyond the fort of Detroit since otherwise the trade was lost to small unscrupulous traders. He appears to have wintered at some time at Michilimackinac since he mentions the fishing at the straits of Mackinac in winter. "I have wade a trout taken in by Mr. Camps with a hook and line under the ice in March sixtey six pounds wate."[32] Again he writes "I was at Mackinac when Capt. George Turnbull comanded."[34] Turnbull apparently went to Mackinac in 1770 and left for the West Indies with his regiment in 1773. Probably Pond was at Michilimackinac in the winter of 1770–1. His main interest during the period centred about Detroit, during the later years, extending his trade to outlying points as at Michilimackinac. With the extension of trade beyond the posts regulation became less effective and it was inevitable that Pond should meet numbers of rough characters who were notorious in the trade at that time. That Pond was not prosecuted for the results of the duel is evidence that these events were not uncommon.

In 1771 he came down to Milford and made another "ture to ye West Indies"[28] in 1772. On his return he received a letter from a Mr Graham in New York asking him to come down to arrange for a partnership to venture in the trade from Michilimackinac. This invitation was evidence that Pond's apprenticeship in the Detroit trade had ended. He had acquired wide experience in the trade and probably some capital. Graham had apparently been engaged in the Michilimackinac trade for several years, as his name appears as an Albany trader at that point in 1767. In the intervening period he had probably acquired a substantial supply of capital from the trade by Green Bay to the Mississippi, and in 1773 he appears to have been one of the largest traders to that district. It was significant of the impression which Pond had made on his fellow traders as to his ability as a trader, and his honesty and integrity, that he should have been chosen as the active partner for this important venture. No higher tribute could have been paid to him.

He had acquired at the end of this period a thorough grasp of the demands of the trade. He knew the character of goods required for a successful trade. He probably knew the Indian languages and had a knowledge of French. From his voyages to the West Indies and his army experience he had probably acquired a knowledge of astronomy and navigation sufficient to enable him to determine latitude and longitude. He had prepared himself for the active years which were to follow. He was a master trader at thirty-one. [Innis appears to have written this section of the biography based on information found outside the Gates memoir. He largely ignores what Pond wrote in this section.]

III. The Mississippi

A. The Trader (1773–1774)

A partnership with Graham was formed and a cargo weighing 4600 pounds was made up. It is probable that Graham furnished the major share of the capital and that Pond was the active partner. In 1773 at the age of thirty-

Peter Pond: Fur Trader and Adventurer 61

three Peter Pond entered his majority in the fur trade. In April he left Milford not to return for at least twelve years.

After the Conquest, traders from New York and Albany pushed westward to Detroit and Michilimackinac. New York became a more important depot for the fur trade at the expense of Montreal which had dominated the trade in the French regime. The advantages of New York were shown in the character of the route by which goods were sent by the Great Lakes to the interior. Pond gives a valuable description of the Albany route which he had reason to know thoroughly from his experience in forwarding supplies to Oswego in 1759 and 1760 and to Detroit in later years. Mr. Graham took the goods to Michilimackinac by this route but Pond was not less qualified to describe it. The goods were shipped from New York to Albany and freighted in wagons fourteen miles from Albany to Schenectady. At this point they were loaded on batteaus and hauled up the Mohawk River to Fort Stanwix. The batteaus and goods were hauled over land for the distance of one mile to Wood Creek. From Wood Creek they went through Oneida Lake down the Oswego river to Lake Ontario. The boats were taken along the south shore of Lake Ontario to the landing place at Niagara and hauled over the nine mile portage above the rapids and the falls to Fort Schlosser. From that point they were taken up the Niagara to Fort Erie and along the south side of the lake to Detroit across Lake St. Clair and along the west side of Lake Huron to Michilimackinac. Goods could be taken in comparatively large boats and the transport costs from New York by the Great Lakes favoured the development of trade from that point.

But Montreal had the advantage of experience in the trade such as had been gained in the long period of the French regime. Pond writes for example, "I wanted some small artickles in the Indian way to compleat my asortment which was not to be had in New York."[29] Consequently he took a boat through Lake George and Lake Champlain to Montreal, "whare I found all I wanted."[29] Again he was familiar with the route to the foot of Lake George from the unsuccessful attack on Ticonderoga. It was fifteen years since Pond had been engaged in the memorable battles around Lake George and thirteen years since he had been at the capitulation of Montreal. He was able to purchase the necessary goods and he found the fur trade already well organized under English auspices following the collapse of French trade after the Conquest. Several canoes were outfitting in the spring of 1773 for Michilimackinac, some of them owned by the firm of his old acquaintance of Detroit, Isaac Todd, and James McGill. He arranged with these two men to have his goods taken in their canoes and with them he embarked in a canoe from Lachine to Michilimackinac by the Ottawa River.

The route from Montreal by the Ottawa to Michilimackinac was new to Pond. It has been described in numerous fur trading journals in great detail. Pond apparently found little to interest him on the long up stream journey on the Ottawa to Lake Nipissing, down the French river to Georgian Bay, along the north shore of Lake Huron until they were opposite Mackinac, and across the strait to the island on which the British garrison was located. The incident of the trip which interested him greatly as it did other travellers was the ceremony at the church of St. Ann on the Lake of Two Mountains. The voyageurs deposited a small sum and "by that meanes thay suppose thay are protected"[30] by St. Ann, their patron saint. No one but a fur trader would have noticed that "while absent the church is not locked but the money box is well secured from theaves."[30] Pond arrived at Michilimackinac "where I found my goods from New York had arived safe."[30]

Michilimackinac was the outfitting depot for traders going to winter in the interior around Lake Michigan, Green Bay, and the Mississippi, or around Lake Superior. "Thare was a British Garason whare all the traders assembled yearley to arang thare afaires for the insewing winter."[29] "Hear I met with a grate meney hundred people all denominations."[30] At various periods Pond spent considerable time at this depot and his description of Mackinac is worthy of addition to the large number of descriptions already in existence. He begins "This place is kept up by a Capts. command of British which were lodged in good barracks within the stockades whare thare is some french bildings and a commodious Roman church whare the French inhabitants and Ingasheas [engagés] go to mass."[31] Pond was much impressed with the French Catholics and their religion. "Befoare it was given up to the British thare was a French Missenare astablished hear who resided for a number of years hear. While I was hear thare was none but traveling one who Coms sometimes to make a short stay but all way in the Spring when the people ware ye most numeras then the engashea often went to confes and git absolution."[31] The district had a

Peter Pond: Fur Trader and Adventurer

large floating population, and Pond was impressed by the number of people who had come from Quebec. "Most of the frenchmen's wives are white women."[32] "The inhabitans of this plase trade with the natives and thay go out with ye Indians in the fall and winter with them – men, women and children. – In the Spring thay make a grate quantity of maple sugar for the youse of thare families and for sale som of them."[31–2 (note that Innis separates the previous quote from this one to make the account read more easily)] Michilimackinac was primarily a trading locality. "The land about Macinac is vary baran – a mear sand bank – but the gareson by manure have good potaters and sum vegetables. The British cut hay anuf for thare stock a few miles distans from the gareson and bring hom on boates. Others cut the gras and stock it on the streat [strait] and slead it on the ice thirty miles in ye winter."[32] Fish was important as a staple food, and the traders were to a large extent dependent on this resource. Pond writes "I have wade a trout taken in by Mr. Camps with a hook and line under the ice in March sixty six pounds wate. I was present. The water was fifteen fatham deape. The white fish are ye another exquisseat fish. They will way from 2-1/2 to 9 and 10 pound wt."[32]

Alexander Henry has described the village of the Ottawas at L'Arbre Croche from which he obtained supplies of Indian corn and sugar. Pond notes the existence of these Indian villages some twenty or thirty miles distant "whare the natives improve verey good ground. Thay have corn beens and meney articles which thay youse in part themselves and bring the remainder to market. The nearest tribe is the Atawase and the most sivelised in these parts but drink to exses. Often in the winter thay go out on a hunting party. In ye Spring thay return to thare villages and imploy the sumer in rasein things for food as yousal. But this is to be understood to belong to the women – the men never meadel – this part of thare bisness is confind to the females ondley. Men are imployd in hunting, fishing and fouling, war parties etc. These wood aford partreages, hairs, vensen fixis and rackcones, sum wild pigins."[32] During the summer tribes from the surrounding territory and from "a grate distance"[30] came to Michilimackinac to trade, bringing furs, skins, maple sugar, "dride vensen, bares greas and the like which is a considerable part of trade."[30]

Pond's immediate task at Michilimackinac was that of rearranging the goods which had arrived by boats, purchasing canoes, provisions and supplies, and hiring men and loading the bales in the canoes. Equipments were made up for the different parts of the country. He divided his goods into twelve parts and "fited out twelv larg canoes for differant parts of the Mississippy river. Each cannew was mad of birch bark and white seader thay would carry seven thousand wate."[30–1] "In Sept. I had my small fleat readey to cross lake Mishegan."[33]

Pond had engaged nine clerks to handle the separate outfits to different parts and with this large contingent he left for Green Bay. He reached the mouth of the bay in three or four days and crossed over to the southwest side in the lea of some islands. On this side they followed the shore to the mouth of the river and to the small French farming village a short distance up. The people raised corn and "sum artikles for fammaley youse in thare gardens"[33] and they had "fine black cattal and horses with sum swine." [33–4 (note that Innis omits a description of the trading habits of these people between the two quotes)] They traded to a certain extent with the Indians going by this route. Pond also mentions the Menominee village on the north side of the Bay, the people of which were chiefly hunters although they depended also on wild rice which they gathered in September.

After two days in the French village they ascended to the Puan village at the east end of a lake Winnebago.[2] The women raised corn, beans and pumpkins and they lived on rabbits, partridges and some venison but there was little fish in the lake. Pond was not impressed with these Indians and "we made but a small stay."[35] He was not conversant with their language. "They speake a hard un couth langwidge scarst to be learnt by eney people."[34] He narrates with great zest the story of the visit of a chief and a small band of this nation to Capt. Turnbull at Michilimackinac. "He held a counsel with them but he couldn't get an intarpetar in the plase that understood them. At length the Capt. said that he had a mind to send for an old Highland solge that spoke little but the harsh langwege – perhaps he mite understand for it sounded much like it."[35] They were not a sociable tribe – "Thay will not a sosheat with or convars with the other tribes nor inter-marey among them – They live in a close connection among themselves."[34 (1st half of quote); 35 (2nd half of quote)] Pond's curiosity was aroused by these people as he later enquired at Detroit "of the oldest and most entelagant Frenchman"[34] regarding them. He was told that they formerly lived west of the Missouri, that they were very quarrelsome and that they were driven by other tribes across the Missouri and the Mississippi to their present location. The Fox tribe it was thought lived near them, fitting neighbours, since this tribe was driven from Detroit for misbehaviour. Whether this reputation was deserved or whether Pond had tried to carry on trade with them without success or whether he had traded with them and lost, it would be difficult to determine but the chief objection to them was given forcibly. "They are insolent to this day and inclineing cheaterey thay will if thay can get creadit from the trader in the fall of ye year to pay in the spring after thay have made thare hunt but when you mete them in Spring as know them personeley ask for your pay and thay will speake in thare one language if thay speake at all which is not to be understood or other ways thay will look sullky and make you no answer and you loes your debt,"[34] which sounds like the voice of sad experience.

Later acquaintance did not improve early impressions. Pond continued up the river to the Grand Butte des Morts where this tribe "yous to entar thare dead when thay lived in that part."[35] He describes the ceremony of some of the natives gathered to pay their respects to one of the departed. "Thay had a small cag of rum and sat around the grave. Thay fild thar callemeat [calumet] and began thar saremony by pinting the stem of the pipe upward – then giving it a turn in thare and then toward ye head of the grav – then east and west, north and south after which thay smoked it out and filf it agane and lade [it] by – then thay took sum rum out of the cag in a small bark vessel and pourd it on the head of the grave by way of giving it to thar departed brother – then thay all drank themselves – lit the pipe and seamed to enjoi themselves verey well. Thay repeated this till the sperit began to operate and thare harts began to soffen. Then thay began to sing a song or two but at the end of every song thay soffened the clay. After sumtime had relapst the cag had bin blead often. Thay began to repete the satisfaction thay had with that friend while he was with them and how fond he was of his frends while he could git a cag of rum and how thay youst to injoy it togather. They amused themselves in this manner til they all fell a crying and a woful nois they made for a while til thay thought wisely that thay could not bring them back and it would not due to greeve two much – that an application to the cag was the best way to dround sorrow and wash away greefe for the moshun was soon put in execution and all began to be marey as a party could bee. Thay continued til near nite. Rite wen thay ware more than half drunk the men began to aproach the females and chat frelay and apearantley friendly. At lengh thay began to lean on each other, kis and apeared verey amaras. – I could observe clearley this bisiness was first pusht on by the women who made thare visit to the dead a verey pleasing one in thare way. One of them was quit drunk as I was by self seating on the ground observing thare saremones, cam to me and askt me to take a share in her bountey – But I thought it was time to quit and went about half a mile up the river to my canoes whare my men was incampt but the Indians never came nigh us. The men then, shun [mentioned] that three of the women had bin at the camp in the night in quest of imploy."[35–6] With these observations Pond left this tribe of Indians.

His trip over the portage from the St. Lawrence drainage basin to the Mississippi drainage basin by the Fox river into the Wisconsin river was the next object of concern. The whole river was easily navigated as far as the lake of the Puans and except for one or two small rapids from the lake as far as the portage. Above the rapids the channel became narrow and very winding and the water less swift. "In maney parts in going three miles you due not advans one. The bank is almost leavel with the water and the medoes on each sid are clear of wood to a grate distans and clothd with a good sort of grass the openings of this river are cald lakes but thay are no more than larg openings. In these plases the water is about four or five feet deap. With a soft bottom these plases produce the gratest quantaties of wild rise of which the natives geather grat quantities and eat what thay have ocation for and dispose of the remainder to people that pass and repass on thare trade. This grane looks in its groth and stock and ears like ry and the grane is of the same culler but longer and slimer. When it is cleaned fit for youse thay boile it as we due rise and eat it with bairs greas and sugar but the greas thay ad as it is bileing which helps to soffen it and make it brake in the same maner as rise. When thay take it out of thare cettels for yous thay ad a little sugar and is eaten with fresh vensen or fowls, we yoused it in the room of rise and it did very well as a substatute for that grane as it busts it turns out perfeckly white as rise."[37] Wild rice and ducks were of appreciable value in conserving the food supply. The ducks had fattened on the wild rice and "when thay ris made a nois like thunder. We got as meney as we chose fat and good. – You can purchis them verey cheape at the rate of two pens per pese. If you parfer shuting them yourself you may kill what you plese."[38]

After Pond's escape from the Indian women, he and his party proceeded up the winding river to a shallow lake with an abundance of wild rice and ducks. They encamped here for the night and spent "the most of ye next day to get about three miles – with our large cannoes the track was so narrow. Near nite we got to warm ground whare we incampt and regaled well after the fateages of the day."[37 (Innis substitutes "regaled" for "rest[?]")] On the next day more slack water and a winding stream "we have to go two miles without geating fiftey yards ahead so winding"[37] but at night they came within sight of the portage and arrived there at noon next day. They unloaded the canoes and "toock them out of the water to dry that thay mite be liter on the caring plase."[37]

He describes the portage as very level for two-thirds of a mile and consequently bad in wet weather. In the centre the ground rises to a considerable height and is covered with a fine open wood similar to that located back from the banks of the river. The land was described as excellent and covered with good timber, – the fires having destroyed the small wood. The height of land located in the centre extended for about one quarter of the whole distance. "The south end is low flat and subject to weat."[38] "After two days hard labor we gits our canoes at the carring plase with all our goods and incampt on the bank of the river Wisconstan and gumd our canoes fit to descend that river. About midday we imbarkt."[39 (note that Innis omits a story that Pond relays about a French soldier that deserted the army and was burned in effigy by the courts when he could not be captured)]

Pond's journal represents with full force his reactions to the variety of travel. Writing from memory, the physical reactions had left a strong impression. He notes with feeling "the warm ground"[37] on which to camp after a hard day in marshy country, "the fat and good"[36] wild ducks. After crossing the portage he describes the river in two places as "a gentel glideing stream."[39] "As we desended it we saw maney rattel snakes swimming across it and kild them."[39]

In about a day's travel they reached the village of the Sauks on the north side of the river. At this village he stayed two days. "This beaing the last part of Sept. there people had eavery artickel of eating in thare way in abundans."[39] They were of interest to Pond. "Thay are of a good sise and well disposed – les inclind to tricks and bad manners than thare nighbers. Thay will take of the traders goods on creadit in the fall for thare youse. In winter and except for axedant thay pay the deat [debt] verey well for Indians I mite have sade inlitend or sivelised indans which are in general made worse by the operation."[40]

To the anthropologist the Wisconsin portage route had the greatest interest and the fur trader was always an anthropologist. On this route a number of tribes had settled, partly because of its importance to trade and the incidental wars which had swept the area in the French period and partly because of its position – marginal to the plains Indians, the southern woods Indians, and the northern Indians. Pond noted the cultural traits of the Sauks. In the first place "thare villeag is bilt cheafely with plank thay hugh out of wood – that is ye uprite – the top is larch [arched] over with strong sapplins sufficient to suport the roof and covered with barks which makes them a tile roof. Sum of thare huts are sixtey feet long and contanes several fammalayes. Thay rase a platform on each side of thare huts about two feet high and about five feet broad on which thay seat and sleap. Thay have no flores but bild thare fire on the ground in the midel of the hut and have a hole threw the ruf for the smoke to pas."[40 (added paragraph break)]

The total population was about one hundred. "The women rase grate crops of corn, been, punkens, potatoes, millans and artikels." They had a comparatively large cleared space with excellent land. Fishing was very poor, "wild foul thay have but few."[41] "Thare woods afford partrageis, a few rabeat, bairs and deear are plenty in thare seasons."[41] In the fall "thay leave thare huts and go into the woods in quest of game and return in the spring – before planting time."[40] "The men often join war parties with other nations and go aganst the Indans on the Miseure and west of that. Sometimes thay go near St. Fee in New Mexico and bring with them Spanish Horseis."[41 (note that Innis shuffles the order of information from the original text so that it is easier to comprehend)]

"Thare amusements are singing, dancing, smokeing, matcheis, gameing, feasting, drinking, playing the slite of hand, hunting, and thay are famas in Mageack. Thar religion is like most of the tribes. Thay alow thare is two sperits – one good who dweles a bove the clouds superintends over all and

Peter Pond: Fur Trader and Adventurer

helps to all the good things we have and can bring sickness on us if he pleases – and another bad one who dweles in the fire and air, eavery whare among men and sumtimes dose mischief to mankind"[40–1 (note that Innis rearranges Pond's account here so that amusements and religion are together in the account rather than separated by other information)] – in other words they had come under the influence of French missionaries.

Like most traders Pond was interested in their courtship and marriages. "At night when these people are seating round thare fires the elderly one will be teling what thay have sean and heard or perhaps thay may be on sum interesting subject. The family are lisning. If thare be aney young garl in this lodg or hut that aney man of a differant hut has a likeing for he will seat among them. The parson of his arrant [errand] being prasent hea will watch an opertunity and through a small stick at hair [her]. If she looks up with a smile it is a good omen. He repets a second time perhaps ye garle will return the stick. The Semtam [symptoms] are still groing stronger and when thay think proper to ly down to slape each parson raps himself up in his one blanket. He taks notes whar the garl seats for thare she slepes. When all the famaley are quiet a[nd] perhaps a sleap he slips soffely into that and seat himself down by her side. Presantlay he will begin to lift her blanket in a soft maner. Perhaps she may twich it out of his hand with a sort of a sie and snore to gather but this is no kiling matter. He seats awhile and makes a second atempt. She may perhaps hold the blankead down slitely. At lengh she turns over with a sith [sigh?] and quits the hold of the blanket. – This meatherd is practest a short time and ye young Indan will go ahunting and [if] he is luckey to git meat he cum and informs the famaley of it and where it is he brings the lung and hart with him and thay seat of after the meat and bring it home this plesis and he begins to gro bold in the famerley. The garl after that will not refuse him. – He will then perhaps stay about the famarley a year and hunt for the old father but in this instans he gives his conseant that thay may sleap togather and when thay begin to have children thay save what thay can git for thare one youse and perhaps live in a hut apart."[41–2 (added paragraph break)]

As in most visits described by traders, the voyageurs lost little time in making the acquaintance of the women. Pond remarks of this tribe "Thay are not verey gellas of thare women."[40 (note that this information is provided in a different order from the original)]

"After I had given them a number of cradeat to receve payment the next spring I desended to the fox villeag – about fiftey miles distans."[42 (slightly edited by Innis)] Again like most traders Pond attributes the maliciousness of this tribe (Foxes) to the influence of the missionaries. "Hear I meat a differant sort of people who was bread at Detroit under the french government and clarge [clergy] till thay by chrisanising grew so bad thay ware oblige to go to war aganst them."[42] He heard echoes of the Fox wars[3] of the French regime in which the Fox Indians were driven from Detroit and forced to flee to the Fox river, and in which the French again carried on war against them to break up their monopoly over the Fox river portage, and he attributed their misfortunes in part to these wars. But the Foxes were also suffering from disease. "As I aprocht the banks of the villeag I perseaved a number of long Painted poles on which hung a number of artickels, sum panted dogs and also a grate number of wampum belts with a number of silver braslets and other artickels in the Indan way. I inquired the cause. Thay told me thay had a shorte time before had a sweapeing sickness among them which had caread of grate numbers of inhabitans and thay had offered up these sacrafisces to apease that being who was angrey with them and sent the sickness – that it was much abated tho thar was sum sick. Still I told them thay had dun right and to take cair that thay did not ofend him agane for fear a grater eavel myte befall them."[42–3] The produce of their fields was reduced as a result of the sickness[4] and Pond stayed only one day. He got the articles he needed and which they could spare and "gave them sum creadeat and desended the river to the mouth which emteys into the Masseippey and cros that river and incampt."[43]

There follows no rhapsody on the mighty Mississippi. "Just at night as we ware incampt we perseaved large fish cuming on the sarfes of the water."[43] After leaving the Fox village Pond was apparently joined by another trader with several men – in any case he camped with another trader. Hooks and lines were put out in the river and in the morning they hauled in the catch. "They came heavey. At lengh we hald one ashore that wade a hundered and four pounds – a seacond that was one hundered wate – a third of seventy five pounds. – The fish was what was cald the cat fish. It had a large flat head sixteen inches between the eise. – The men was glad to sea this for thay had not eat mete for sum days nor fish for a long time. We asked our men how meney men the largest would give a meale. Sum

Peter Pond: Fur Trader and Adventurer

71

of the largest eaters sade twelve men would eat it at a meal. We agreed to give ye fish if thay would find twelve men that would undertake it. Thay began to dres it. – They skind it – cut it up in three larg coppers such as we have for the youse of our men. After it was well boild thay sawd it up and all got round it. Thay began and eat the hole without the least thing with it but salt and sum of them drank of the licker it was boild in. The other two was sarved out to the remainder of the people who finished them in a short time. Thay all declard thay felt the beater of thare meale nor did I perseave that eney of them ware sick or complaind."[43–4 (note that Innis reorders the information so that it makes more sense and provides an explanation of weights)]

The following morning they crossed the river and ascended about three miles "to the Planes of the dogs [Prairie du Chien]."[44] The plain was a large level stretch of land on the east side of the river at the junction of the Wisconsin and the Mississippi. Prairie du Chien was the rendezvous of traders and Indians from New Orleans, from Michilimackinac, and the tributaries of the Mississippi. When Pond arrived he "meat a larg number of french and Indans makeing out thare arrangements for the insewing winter and sending of thare cannoes to differant parts – likewise giving creadets to the Indans who ware all to Rondoveuse thare in spring. I stayed ten days sending of my men to different parts."[44] His nine clerks were dispatched to various tributaries.

After completing the business at Prairie du Chien, Pond and two other traders left in October for St. Peters river. They proceeded very slowly lest they should overtake the Nottawaseas who had preceded them and in order that "we mite not be trubeld with them for creadit as thay are bad pay masters"[44] – "We had plenty of fat gease and ducks with venson – bares meat in abundans – so that we lived as well as hart could wish on such food – plentey of flower, tea, coffee, sugar and buter, sperits and wine, that we faird well as voigers. The banks of ye river aforded us plenty of crab apels which was verey good when the frost had tuchd them at a sutabel tim."[44 (Innis edits "a Bantans [abundance]" in the Gates version to "abundans")] Eventually they reached St. Peters river and Pond claims they found about fourteen miles from the mouth Carver's old hut in which he had wintered in 1766–7. "It was a log house about sixteen feet long covered with bark – with a fireplase but one room and no flore."[45]

72   Innis's Writings on Pond and the Fur Trade

Finally they decided to build their houses for the winter. "We incampt on a high bank of the river that we mite not be overflone in the spring at the brakeing up of the ice, and bilt us comfortbel houseis for the winter and trade during the winter and got our goods under cover. – In Desember the Indans sent sum young men from the planes a long the river to look for traders and thay found us. After staying a few days to rest them thay departed with the information to thare frends. In Jany. thay began to aproach us and brot with them drid and grean meat, bever, otter, dear, fox, woolf, raccone and other skins to trade. They ware welcom and we did our bisness to advantage."[44–5 (note that Innis separates the above anecdote about Carver's cabin and rearranges information to make this section easier to comprehend)] Pond had a French competitor "for my nighber who had wintered among the Nottawase several winters in this river well knone by the differant bands. I perseaved that he seamed to have a prefrans and got more trade than myself. We ware good frends. I told him he got more than his share of trade but obsarved at ye same time it was not to be wondered at as he had bin long a quanted. He sade I had not hit on ye rite eidea. He sade that the Indans of that quorter was given to stealing and aspachely the women. In order to draw custom he left a few brass things for the finger on the counter – sum needles and awls which cost but a trifel, leattel small knives – bell and such trifels. For the sake of stealing these trifels thay com to sea him and what thay had for trade he got. I beleaved what he sade and tried the expereament – found it to prove well after which I kept up sides. – We proseaded eastward with ease and profet till spring."[45–6]

The ice finally broke up in the spring and according to Pond the water rose 26 feet washing away a large part of the banks. With the fall of the water they loaded their canoes and drifted down stream to Prairie du Chien – "whare we saw a large colection from eavery part of the Misseppey who had arived before us – even from Orleans eight hundred leagues belowe us."[46] – The boats from New Orleans "are navagated by thirty-six men who row as maney oarse. Thay bring in a boate sixtey hogseats of wine on one – besides ham, cheese etc. – all to trad with the french and Indans."[45] Fall and spring Prairie du Chien was the scene of great activities in the fur trade. "The Indians camp exeaded a mile and a half in length. Hear was sport of all sorts."[46] "The gratest games are plaid both by

Peter Pond: Fur Trader and Adventurer

french and Indians. The french practis billiards – ye latter ball."[45] But Pond was a trader. "We went to collecting furs and skins – by the differant tribes with sucsess."[46] Competition was apparently keen with numerous French traders. He estimated not less than 130 canoes from Michilimackinac each carrying sixty to eighty hundredweight as well as numerous boats from New Orleans, Illinois and other parts, and that 1500 hundred pound packs went to Mackinac. "All my outfits had dun well. I had grate share for my part as I furnish much the largest cargo on the river. After all the bisness was dun and people began to groe tirde of sport, thay began to draw of for thare differant departments and prepare for the insewing winter. In July I arived at Mackenaw whare I found my partner Mr. Graham from New York with a large cargo. I had dun so well that I proposed to bye him out of ye cosarn and take it on myself. He excepted and I paid of the first cargo and well on towards the one he had brot me."[46–7] Here ended the first venture.

From a pecuniary point of view Pond had learned the lessons of the fur trade to advantage. He knew men and was able to judge men to superintend his outfits. Success in the trade was dependent on judgment of character since the men were far removed from direct supervision throughout the winter.

He knew how to get along with competing traders and his old genius for making friends stood him in good stead. For a competitor to give information enabling him to get a larger share of trade is no slight testimony to the man's character. To be able to gather information as to the reputations of various Indians in repaying their debts required a genial disposition as well as shrewd judgment. He had camped, travelled and traded with competitors and with pronounced success. He also knew how to handle his voyageurs. "I had with me one who was adicted to theaving – he took from me in silver trinkets to the amount of ten pound but I got them agane to a trifle."[31] And he emerged with sufficient profit to warrant a venture on his own account.

B. The Peacemaker (1774–1775)

Pond had arrived at Michilimackinac, had disposed of his cargo and was immediately engaged in acquiring a new outfit. "I apleyd myself closely to ward fiting out a cargo for the same part of the country."[47] With the coming of the traders Michilimackinac was similar to Prairie du Chien. "Hear was a grate concors of people from all quorters sum preparing to take thair furs to Cannadey – others to Albaney and New York – other for thare intended wintering grounds – others trade in with the Indans that come from different parts with thare furs, skins, sugar, grease, taller etc. – while others ware amuseing themselves in good company at billiards, drinking fresh french wine and eney thing thay please to call for while the more vulgar ware fiteing each other. Feasting was much atended to – dancing at nite with respectabel parsons. Notwithstanding the feateages of the industress the time past of agreabley for two months when the grater part ware ready to leave the plase for thare differant wintering ground."[47]

The cargo and canoes had to be purchased and the men to be hired. It would be difficult to state the number of Pond's men who rehired with him but he probably had little difficulty in securing a complement. The young man Baptiste who had committed the theft during the winter almost certainly rehired. At Michilimackinac one of the visiting priests was hearing confessions and "the young man heard from his comrads who had bin to confess"[31] of the priest "who was doing wonders among the people."[31] "His consans smit him and he seat of to confess but could not get absolution. He went a seacond time without sucksess but was informed by his bennadict that something was wanting. He came to me desireing me to leat him have two otter skins promising that he would be beatter in future and sarve well. I leat him have them. He went of. In a few minets after or a short time he returned. I askt him what sucksess. O sade he the father sais my case is a bad one but if I bring two otter more he will take my case on himself and discharge me. I let him have them and in a short time he returned as full of thanks as he could expres and sarved me well after."[31] Pond had acquired a full complement and he writes "I had now a large and rich cargo."[47]

At this point trouble appeared. About the first of August a trader coming from Lake Superior brought news that war had broken out between the Sioux and the Chippewas, "and made it dangres for the trader to go in to the country."[47] The only prospect of peace lay in the hands of the commander of the garrison. "A counsel was cald of all the traders and the commander laid his information befoar the counsel and told them it was out of his power to bring the government into eney expens in sending to these

Peter Pond: Fur Trader and Adventurer 75

but desird that we would fall on wase and means among ourselves and he would indeaver to youse his influens as commanding offeser. We heard and thanked him we then proseaded to contrebute towards making six large belts of wampum – three for the Notawaysease and thre for the Ochpwase. Thay ware compleated under the Gidans of the comander and speacheis rote to both nations. I was bound to the senter of the Notawaseas contrey up St. Peters river. The counsel with ye commander thought proper to give me ye charge of thre belt with the speacheis and the traders to Lake Superer ware charged with the others. The import of the bisness was that I should send out carrears into the planes and – all the chefes to repare to my tradeing house on the banks of St. Peters river in the spring and thare to hear and obsarve the contents of the offesers speache and look at the belts and understand thare meaning – likewise to imbark and acompany me to Mackenac."[47–8] Pond assumed the role of peace-maker as well as trader and the lives of many as well as of the traders depended on his success.

We are told nothing of his second journey from Michilimackinac to Prairie du Chien, but it probably did not differ from his first. At Prairie du Chien he found the Indians disturbed but not about the war. On inquiring "thay gave me to understand thare was a parson at that plase that had an eevel sperit. He did things beond thare conseption. I wished to sea him and being informed who he was I askd him meney questions. I found him to be a french man who had bin long among the nations on the Misura that came that spring from the Ilenoas"[50–1] to Prairie du Chien. "He had the slite of hand cumpleately and had such a swa[y] over the tribes with whom he was aquanted that thay consented to moste of his requests. Thay gave him the name of Minneto [Manitou] which is a sperit. – As he was standing among sum people thare came an Indan up to them with a stone pipe or callemeat carelessly rought and which he seat grate store by – It was three times larger than minnetos mouth"[51 (note that Innis rearranges information from Gates to make it easier to understand)] – and "made of the read stone of St. Peters river so much asteamed among the eastern and southern nations."[51 (once again the text is rearranged)] – "Minneto askd ye Indian to leat him look at it and he did so. He wished to purchis it from the Indan but he would not part with it. Minneto then put it into his mouth as the Indan supposed and swallod it. The poor Indan stood astonished. Minneto told him not to trubel himself about it – he should have his pipe agane in two or three days – it must first pass threw him. At the time seat the pipe was presented to the Indan. He looked upon it as if he could not bair to part with it but would not put his hand upon it. Minneto kept the pipe for nothing."[51 (once again the text is rearranged)]

After enjoying this episode he left Prairie du Chien and reached his old house on St. Peters river on the thirteenth day. Pond was now actively interested in prosecuting the trade and he knew the country and the people. He learned from other Indians of a large band about 200 miles farther up "which wanted to sea a trader. I conkluded ameatley to put a small asortment of goods into a cannoe and go up to them – a thing that never was atempted before by the oldest of the traders on acount of the rudeness of those people who ware Nottawaseas by nation but the band was called Yantonoes – the cheafe of the band allwase lead them on the plaines."[51–2] Pond writes that the Sioux were formerly one nation but they had broken up because of internal disputes into "six different bands each band lead by chefes of thare one chois."[56–7] These bands were "1. the Yantonose [Yankton branch of the Dakotas or Sioux] 2. the band of the leaves [the Wapeton branch] 3. the band of the wes [the Leaf buds, one of the divisions of the Santee] 4. the band of the stone house [the Sisseton division of the Dakota] the other two bands are north one cald Assonebones [Assiniboines] the others dogs ribs. These speke the same langwege at this day."[57]

The anxiety with which the Yanktons awaited the arrival of a trader was shown by the arrival of the chief to invite him to go up and trade just as he was preparing to leave. They both set off together, the chief going by land and Pond by water. The chief arrived before him since he was able to take a more direct route "across the plaines."[52] "I was nine days giting up to thare camp."[52] By this time it was getting late in the season. Coming to a "larg sand flat by the river side"[52] – "about three miles from the Indians camp and it beaing weat wether and cold I incampt and turned up my canoe which made us a grand shelter. At night it began to snow and frease and blowe hard. – Earley in the morning the wind took the canew up in the air – leat hir fall on the frozen flat and broke hir in pecis."[52 (note that Innis shuffles the order of the writing to make it easier to understand)] Fortunately a number of the Indians came down on the opposite side of the river about noon, crossed over and "offerd me thare asistans to take my goods to thare camp. I was glad and excepted thare offer."[52]

Peter Pond: Fur Trader and Adventurer 77

The horses were loaded and the party marched to the camp. This was Pond's first experience in meeting Indians who were strangers to white traders. "Thay never saw a trader before on thare one ground at least saw a bale of goods opend. Sum traders long before sent thare goods into the planes with thare men to trade with these people – thay often would have them cheaper than they french men could sell them. These people would fall on them and take ye goods from them at thair one price til thay could not git eney. I was the first that atempted to go thare with a bale of goods."[54]

His reception by them involved numerous ceremonies. "Cuming near the camp made a stop and seat down on the ground. I preseaved five parsons from the camp aproching – four was imployd in caring a beaver blanket finely panted – the other held in his hand a callemeat or pipe of pece – verey finely drest with different feathers with panted haire. They all seat by me except the one who held the pipe. Thay ordered the pipe lit with a grate dele of sarremoney. After smoeking a fue whifs the stem was pinted east and west – then north and south – then upward toward the skies – then to ye earth after which we all smoked in turn and apeard verey frendlye. I could not understand one word thay said but from thare actions I supposed it to be all frendship. After smoking thay toock of my shoes and put on me a pair of fine Mockasans or leather shoes of thare one make raught in a cureas manner – then thay lade me down on the blanket – one hold of each corner and cared me to the camp in a lodg among a verey vennarable asembly of old men. I was plased at the bottom or back part which is asteamed the highest plase. After smoekeing an old man ros up on his feet with as much greaveaty as can be conseaved of he came to me – laid his hands on my head and grond out – I – I – I three times – then drawed his rite hand down on my armes faneing a sort of a crey as if he shead tears – then sit down – the hole follode the same exampel which was twelve in number. Thare was in the midel of the lodg a rased pece of ground about five inches in hight five feet long two and a half brod on which was a fire and over that hung three brass kettles fild with meete boiling for a feast. – At length an old man toock up some of the vittels out of one of ye kittles which apeared to be a sort of soope thick and with pounded corn mele. He fead me with three sponfuls first and then gave me the dish which was bark and the spoon made out of a buffeloes horn to fead myself. As I had got a good apatite from the fateages of the day I eat hartey. – While we ware imployd in this saremony thare was wateing at the dore four men to take me up and care me to another feast."[52–3] – As soon as he had finished the first feast "The people in wateing then toock me and laid me on another skin and carred me to another lodg whare I went threw the same sarremony. There was not a woman among them – then to a third after which I was taken to a large [lodge] prepaird for me in which they had put my people and goods with a large pile of wood and six of thare men with spears to gard it from the croud." [53–4]

Pond had been advised by the chief who had come down the river to invite him to come up to trade with the Indians that the trade "was to begin at sundown,"[54] and he had warned him that "if I was to contend with them thay mite take all that I had."[54] Unfortunately the chief was absent and "thay compeld me to begin befoar the time – At four o'clock I cummenced a trade with them but ye croud was so grate that the chefe was obliged to dubel this gard [of six] and I went on with my trade in safety – seventy five loges at least ten parsons in each will make seven hundred and fifty. My people ware by-standers – not a word to say or acte."[54 (Innis rearranges information so that it makes more sense)] – "I was in a bad sittuation but at sundown the chefe arived and seeing the crowd grate he put to the gard six men more and took the charge on himself. He was as well obade and kept up as smart disapline as I ever saw. One of ye band was more than commonly dairing – he ordered one of the gard to throw his lans threw him in case he persisted in his impedens – the fellow came again – the sentanal threw his lans and it went threw his close and drew a leattel blod but he neaver atempted agane. I continued my trade till near morning. By that time thare furs ware gon."[54 (Innis adds a paragraph break)]

"Thay prepared to March of as thay had lane on the spot sum time befour my arival thay had got out of Provishon. I was not in a situation to asist them beaing destatute myself."[54] But Pond had still to fulfil his mission as peace-maker. "I informd the chefe of the belts I had with me and ye commanding offisers speach and desird him to make a speach befour thay decampt. This chefes name was Arechea. The chefe that came to me first had a smattran of the Ochipway tung – so much so that we understood each other at least suffisantly to convarse or convae our idease. He made a long speach. By the yousel sine of a shout threw the camp thay ware willing to

Peter Pond: Fur Trader and Adventurer 79

cumply."[56] They began to move off. "By day lite I could not sea one but the chefe who cept close by me to the last to prevent aney insult which mite arise as thay ware going of. – These people are in thare sentaments verey averishas but in this instans thay made not the least demand for all thare sarvis. Late in the morning the chefe left me."[54–5]

In spite of the shortness of the time Pond had seen this band of Yankton Indians he had learned much about their life and customs. Undoubtedly his knowledge was supplemented by information gained from other tribes but he was a keen observer. He notes that they "are faroshas and rude in thare maners perhaps being in sum masher to thare leadg an obsger [obscure] life in the planes. Thay are not convarsant with evrey other tribe. Thay seldom sea thare nighbers. They leade a wandering life in that extensive plane betwene the Miseura and Missicippey."[57] "The planes where these people wander is about four hundred miles brod east and west three hundred north and south."[59] "Thay dwell in leather tents cut sumthing in form of a Spanish cloke and spread out by thirteen in the shape of a bell – the poles meet at the top but the base is forten in dimerter – thay go into it by a hole cut in the side and a skin hung befour it by way of a dore – thay bild thare fire in the middel and do all thare cookery over it – at night thay lie down all around the lodg with thare feat to the fire – Thay make youse of Buffeloes dung for fuel as there is but little or no wood upon the planes."[57–8] – "Thay have a grate number of horses and dogs which carres there bageag when thay move from plase to plase."[57–8] – "When thay are marching or riding over the planes thay put on a garment like an outside vest with sleves that cum down to thare elboes made of soft skins and several thicknesses that will turn an arrow at a distans – and a target two and a half feet in diameter of the same matearel and thickness hung over thare sholders that gards thare backs. When there is a number of them to gather going in front of thare band thay make a war like apearans. – Thay are continuely on the watch for feare of beaing sarprised by thare enemise who are all round them. Thare war implements are sum fire armes, boses and arroes and spear which thay have continuely in thare hands. When on the march at nite thay keep out parteas on the lookout."[57–9] (Innis rearranges information)]

These Indians had cultural traits of peoples living on the plains and dependent on the buffalo. "Thay run down the buffelow with thare horses and kill as much meat as thay please. In order to have thare horseis long winded thay slit thair noses up to the grissel of thare head which makes them breath verey freely. I have sean them run with those of natrall nostrals and cum in apearantley not the least out of breath."[58]

From the standpoint of the higher priced furs the country was not promising. "Thay make all thare close of differant skins. These parts produce a number of otters which keep in ponds and riveleats on these planes and sum beavers but the land anamels are the mane object [of] the natives."[59]

As to other traits Pond is not less observant. "Thay are verey gellas of thare women. – Thay genaley get thare wife by contract with the parans. – It sumtimes happens that a man will take his nighbers wife from him but both are oblige to quit the tribe thay belong to but it is seldum you can hear of murders cummitted among them. They have punnishment for thefts among themselves. They sumtimes retelate by taking as much property from the ofender if thay can find it but I seldum hurd of thefts among themselves whatever thay mite due to others. – Thay beleve in two sperits – one good and one bad. – When a parson dies among them in winter thay carrea the boddey with them til thay cum to sum spot of wood and thay put it up on a scaffel till when the frost is out of the ground thay intare it."[58 (Innis rearranges information)]

Meanwhile the Yanktons had departed. "I went to work bundling or packing my furs which I got from them. I was now destatute of frends or assistans except my one men and thay could not aford me aney asistans in the provishon line of which I was much in want. Nighther could thay assist me in the transportation of my furs. I then concluded to leave a boy to take care of them until we could return with sum provishon. The poor fellow seamd willing to stay by himself and all we could aford him was three handfulls of corn. In case of want I left him two bever skins which had sum meat on them and wone bever skin which he could singe the haire of and roste in the fire that he mite live in cas we ware gon longer than we calkalated. The furs ware in a good lodg that he mite keep himself warm. We left him in that sittuation and got back to the house whare we had left the goods by crossing the plaines. I found all safe and the clark had colected a leattel provishon but the provishons could not be sent to the boy on acount of the wather seating in so bad that the men would not under take to go across the plane. Sum days after it grew more modrat and thay seat of five in num-

Peter Pond: Fur Trader and Adventurer

ber and reacht him in fifteen days from the time we left him. Thay found him well but feeble. Thay gave him to eat moderately at first and he ganed strength. Thay went to work and put the furs on a scaffle out of the way of woods [wolves] or eney varment and all seat of for home. The day befour thay arived thay ware overtaken by a snow storm on the planes and could not sea thare way near night. Thay seat down on the plane thare beaing no wood nigh and leat the snow cover them over. Thay had thare blankets about them. In the morning – it was clear with ye wind norwest and freasing hard. Thay dug out of the snow and beaing weat in sum of thare feet thy was badley frosted tho not more than ten miles to walk. The boy ascaped as well as eney of them – I beleve the best. I had a long job to heal them but without the loss of a limb."[55–6]

During the winter as in the previous year the Indians "found out whare we ware and came in with meet and furs to trade"[56]. With the approach of spring arrangements were made to bring the furs down from the cache to the post. "In the Spring I sent my people after the furs thay had put on a scaffel in the winter. Thay had an Indan hunter with them who kild them sum buffeloes. The men cut down small saplens and made the frames of two boates – sowed the skins togather and made bottoms to thare frames – rub'd them over with tallow which made tite anuf to bring the furs down to me whare I had canoes to receve them."[56]

"The Spring is now advancing fast. The chefes cuming with a number of the natives to go with me to Mackenac to sea and hear what thare farther had to say."[59] Pond was successful in his mission and "asembled eleven chefes who went with me besides a number of conscripted men. By the intarpretar I had the speach expland and the intenshun of the belts – and after we had got ready for saleing we all imbarkt and went down the River to its mouth."[48]

Pond had left the St. Peter's river forever. Throughout his journal he constantly refers to the character of the country. "The intervale of the river St. Peter is exsalant and sum good timber – the intervels are high and the soile thin and lite. The river is destatute of fish but the wood and meadows abundans of annamels. Sum turkeas, buffeloes are verey plenty, the common dear are plentey, and larg, the read and moose deare are plentey hear, espesaley the former. I have seen fortey kild in one day by surrounding a drove on a low spot by the river side in the winter season. Raccoons are verey large. No snakes but small ones which are not pisenes. Wolves are plentey – thay follow the buffeloes and often destroy thare young and olde ones, – The natives near the mouth of the river rase plenty of corn for thare one concumtion."[56]

Arriving at the junction of St. Peter's River with the Mississippi "we found sum traders who com from near the head of the Misseppey with sum Chippewa chefes with them. I was much surprised to sea them so ventersum among the people I had with me for the blod was scairs cold – the wound was yet fresh – but while we stade thare a young smart looking chef continued singing the death song, as if he dispised thare threats or torments. After we had made a short stay hear we imbarkt for the Planes of the Dogs [Prairie du Chien]."[48]

Arriving at Prairie du Chien "we joined a vast number of people of all descripsions wateing for me to cum down and go to Macanac to counsel for these people had never bin thare or out of thare countrey except on a war party. It excited the cureosatay of everay nation south of the Lake of the woods and from that [place] was a number chefes which was more than two thousand miles. Indead the matter was intresting all parties espechaley to the trading party for the following reson – each of these nations are as much larger than eney of thare nighbering nations as the Inhabitans of a sittey are to a villeag and when thay are at varans property is not safe even traveling threw thare countrey."[48–9] It was imperative for the safety of the trade on the Mississippi, which was of the greatest importance, that the difficulties should be settled.

Leaving Prairie du Chien "everay canoe made the best of thare way up [the Wisconsin] to the Portage and got over as fast as thay could."[49] Pond apparently had special obligations to the Indians from St. Peter's river. "While we ware on the Portage one of my men informed me that thare was an Indan from St. Peter's River that was in Morneing for his departed friend and wished me to take of the morneing for he had worn it long anuf. I desired he mite cum to me which was dun. He was blacked with cole from the fire – hand and face. His haire was hanging over his eyes. I askd what I should due for him. He desird that his haire mite be pluckd out to the crown of his head, his face and hands washed and a white shirt put on him. I complied with the request and seat him on the ground – seat a cupel of men to work and with the asistans of a leattel asheis to prevent thare fingers

Peter Pond: Fur Trader and Adventurer

slipping thay soon had his head as smooth as a bottle. He washt up and I put a shirt on him which made the fellow so thankfull to think that he could apear in a deasant manner that he could scairs contain himself. We desended the Fox river to the botam of Greane Bay so cald and thare joind the hole of ye canoes bound to Macenac. The way ther was fair and plesant we all proseaded together across Lake Misheagan at the end of two days we all apeard on the lake about five miles from Macenac and aprocht in order. We had flags on the masts of our canoes – eavery chefe his flock. My canoes beaing the largest in that part of the cuntrey and haveing a large Youon [Union] flage I histed it and when within a mile and a half I took ye lead and the Indans followed close behind. The flag in the fort was histed – ye cannon of the garreson began to play smartley – the shores was lind with people of all sorts who seat up such a crey and hooping which seat the tribes in the fleat a going to that degrea that you could not hear a parson speak. At lengh we reacht ye shore and the cannon seasd. I then toock my partey to the commander [Capt. de Peyster] who treated us verey well. I seat with them an our and related the afare and what I had dun and what past dureing the winter. After interreduseing the chefe I went to my one house where I found a number of old frends with whom I spent the remainder of the day."[49–50]

Pond's work on the Mississippi as a peace maker was over but the final arrangements had still to be made. "The people from Lake Supereor had arivd befour us and that day and next day the grand counsel was held before comander in the grate chamber befour a vast number of spectators whare the artickels of pece ware concluded and grate promises ware mad on both sides for abideing and adhearing closely to the artickels to prevent further blodshed the prinsapel of which was that the Nottaweses should not cross the Missacepey to the East side to hunt on thare nighbers ground – to hunt nor bread eney distarbans on the Chipewan ground. Thay should live by the side of each other as frinds and nighbers. The Chipewase likewise promis on thare part strickly to obsareve the same reagulations on thare part toward ye Nottawasis – that thay will not cross the river to hunt on the west side – after all the artickels ware drown up thay all sind them. The Commander then made a presant of a cag of rum to each nation and thay left the fort and went to thare camp whare thay seat round and ingoied thare present – sung a fue songs and went to rest in a verey sivel manner.

The next day thare was a larg fat ox kild and coked by the solgers. All of the nations were biden to the feast. Thay dined to geather in harmoney and finished the day in drinking moderately, smokeing to gather, singing and britening the chane of frindship in a veray deasant way. This was kept up for four days when the offeser mad them each a present and thay all imbark for thare one part of thare cuntrey."[50]

With the return of Peter Pond from the second and last venture in the Mississippi country, this journal comes to an end. He was at this time a trader and an explorer and thoroughly experienced in dealing with the Indians. [Pond's journal comes to an abrupt end at this point and is not referenced throughout the rest of Innis's account.]

IV. The Northwest Company

A. *The Explorer (1775–1778)*
In the summer of 1775 after his arrival at Mackinac, Pond decided to leave the Mississippi and to venture to Lake Superior, Grand Portage and the Northwest. It is probable that a number of considerations led him to take this step. He had doubtless paid the remainder of his debt to Mr. Graham,[5] and was now independent, able to purchase his own cargo, and to go where trade seemed most profitable. The furs on the Mississippi were becoming less important, especially with competition, and trade with the Plains Indians brought small supplies of such fine furs as otter and beaver. Proof of the finer quality of furs obtained in the north was shown in the profitable character of ventures which were being made to the Northwest. Finlay had wintered on the Saskatchewan in 1768. Three years later in 1771 Thomas Curry had wintered at Cedar Lake and taken down a large number of furs in 1772. Trade to the Northwest was profitable and competition with the Hudson's Bay Company could be carried out with great effectiveness. Alexander Henry as well as Peter Pond decided in the same year that he could greatly increase his returns by going to the Northwest. It is possible that Pond decided that the peace between the Sioux and the Ojibway was not of a stable character and with Henry he may have heard of the rumblings of war in the colonies which promised further disturbances. Moreover competition was keen on the Mississippi and he had found it necessary

Peter Pond: Fur Trader and Adventurer 85

to go far up the St. Peter to find new tribes of Indians. Pond had many friends among the traders and these in turn may have prevailed upon him to try the Northwest. Indeed it would not be difficult to accept a theory that Pond, Alexander Henry and Cadotte, the Frobishers, James Finlay, McGill and Patterson, and Holmes and Grant had decided upon the formation of an association for carrying on trade to the Saskatchewan in the spring of 1775. Probably the combination of considerations led him to decide for new territory; and more important than all was Pond's inherent restlessness which urged him to see new country. From the Mississippi it was customary to spend at least two months at Mackinac and this to Pond was wasted time. The Mississippi had little more to offer the trader.

In any case he bought a new cargo at Mackinac, hired his men and started for Sault Ste. Marie, the north shore of Lake Superior and Grand Portage. Taking his goods across the portage he followed the well known route to Lake Winnipeg; and Alexander Henry on August 18 shortly after he had left the Cree village at the mouth of the Winnipeg river notes that he was joined "by Mr. Pond, a trader of some celebrity in the northwest." Alexander Henry and Cadotte left the Sault with a large outfit on June 10, 1775. It is probable that Pond with a smaller outfit left much later and travelled much more rapidly. Together they proceeded along the east side of Lake Winnipeg. The following day the party was overtaken by a severe gale and forced to take refuge on "the island called the Buffalo's Head" but only after they had lost a canoe and four men. As far as possible they secured their provisions in the country and Henry writes that they took catfish of six pounds weight. On the twenty-first they crossed over to the south shore to Oak point where they spent some time in fishing. "The pelicans which we every where saw appeared to be impatient of the long stay." On September first they passed Jack-head river and on the seventh of September were overtaken by Messrs Joseph and Thomas Frobisher and Mr Patterson increasing the size of the party to thirty canoes and a hundred and thirty men. Henry writes "On the twentieth we crossed the bay together – on the twenty-first it blew hard and snow began to fall. The storm continued till the twenty-fifth by which time the small lakes were frozen over, and two feet of snow lay on level ground in the woods. This early severity of the season filled us with serious alarms for the country was uninhabited for two hundred miles on every side of us and if detained by winter, our destruction was certain. In this state of peril, we continued our voyage day and night. The fears of our men were a sufficient motive for their exertions." They reached the mouth of the Saskatchewan on the first of October.[6] Two miles up the river they came to the Grand Rapids "up which the canoes are dragged with ropes. At the end of this is a carrying-place of two miles." They reached Cedar Lake on October third and crossed that lake on the fourth. The following day was apparently spent in catching sturgeon using a seine of which the meshes were large enough to admit the fish's head and which was fastened to two canoes. On the sixth they started up the Saskatchewan. Two days later they began the "voyage before daylight making all speed to reach a fishing place, since winter was very fast approaching. Meeting two canoes of Indians we engaged them to accompany us as hunters. The number of ducks and geese which they killed was absolutely prodigious." At the Pas they found an Indian village of thirty families with a chief named Chatique, who succeeded in forcing them to give presents to the extent of "three casks of gunpowder, four bags of shot and ball, two bales of tobacco, three kegs of rum and three guns together with knives, flints, and some smaller articles." Moreover he followed them up and levied another keg of rum. "Every day we were on the water before dawn and paddled along till dark. The nights were frosty and no provisions excepting a few wild fowl, were to be procured. We were in daily fear that our progress would be arrested by the ice." On the twenty-sixth "we reached Cumberland House" which had been built the previous year for the Hudson's Bay Company by Samuel Hearne and which was now under the charge of Matthew Cocking, "by whom though unwelcome guests, we were treated with much civility."

At Cumberland House the party broke up and Pond went to Fort Dauphin on the northwest corner of Lake Dauphin. He turned his canoes down stream to Cedar Lake, crossed over a portage to Lake Winnipegosis and went along its full length to Mossy river and to Lake Dauphin. Alexander Henry reached Beaver Lake on November first and the following day it had frozen over. Pond was doubtless forced to travel constantly to reach Lake Dauphin before the Mossy river had frozen. Unfortunately it is only known that Pond wintered on Lake Dauphin. As to why he should have

Peter Pond: Fur Trader and Adventurer

gone to this district, as to whether he evaded Chatique successfully on his way down, and as to the time he arrived, conjectures can alone be made. Bain in his edition of the *Travels and Adventures of Alexander Henry* (p. 266) suggests that the Canadian traders stationed themselves on the three lines of communication, from the north, east and south, forestalling the Hudson's Bay Company at Cumberland House by meeting the Indians on their way to trade. Alexander Henry and the Frobishers wintered in the north, Peter Pond in the south and the remainder to the west on the Saskatchewan. Henry refers to his stock with that of the Frobishers and to the amalgamation of four interests on the Saskatchewan in 1775 but it is doubtful whether Pond was a party to the arrangements. He was probably an independent trader with two canoes and the probable complement of four men each. The other interests represented the great bulk of the canoes and they were in a position to take first choice and to control the best fields north to the Churchill and along the Saskatchewan. In the fleet of thirty canoes, Pond had two, Henry and Cadotte eight, the Frobishers six, and Patterson the remaining fourteen for Fort des Prairies. The twelve canoes of the Frobisher license in Montreal became twenty small canoes in the Northwest. To Pond with his smaller outfit, if he had not already become a member of the Saskatchewan group, was left the alternative of joining, or of co-operating with them by seeking a strategic wintering place. To the south on Lake Dauphin he was in a position to secure a supply of food from the buffalo as he was on the edge of the plains and to trade with the Assiniboines with whose language and customs he had become acquainted among the Yanktons on the Mississippi. Moreover as Bain suggests it was a point at which he could trade with the Assiniboines and other Indians going to Cumberland House or to Hudson Bay. It appeared to Pond or to the group as the most promising locality for a small outfit, but we know nothing about this venture other than that the letters P P 1775–6 are marked on Lake Dauphin on Pond's map of 1785.

Pond probably returned to Grand Portage or to Michilimackinac to dispose of his furs and to acquire another outfit. He was within striking distance of his old base at Michilimackinac and it is possible that he returned to that point. This may have been a deciding factor in his determination to winter at Lake Dauphin. In any case he would have learned as Alexander

Henry did of the troubles which had broken out in the colonies and of the capitulation of Montreal and he would have found that the old source of supplies at New York and Albany was effectively cut off.

Again we are forced to rely upon meagre information as to his second venture. The map of 1785 shows the letters P P 1776–7 on a post at the junction of the Sturgeon river and the North Saskatchewan a short distance above the forks. The rough map copied by Ezra Stiles shows at this point the inscription *Capt. Pond wintered 2 y with 160 men.* Other inaccuracies on this map lead one to conjecture that he wintered at this point in 1776–7 and 1777–8 with 4 canoes and 16 men. Pond, or the group, had decided that Fort Dauphin was not a profitable post at least for four canoes or a larger outfit and that the Saskatchewan offered the largest returns. This decision implied probable rearrangements in his plans. The longer upstream journey on the Saskatchewan almost certainly meant a shift from the base at Michilimackinac to Grand Portage. This would necessitate reliance on some connection at the latter point which would bring up an outfit from Montreal to Grand Portage and take down his furs to be sent to England. He would find a partnership or an arrangement with Montreal firms essential after the beginning of war with the colonies.

Again we can only conjecture as to the arrangements. Pond as has been suggested may have proceeded to the Northwest on his first voyage in 1775 with the support of George McBeath and Simon McTavish. The latter was engaged in forwarding rum from Albany to Detroit in 1774, and in 1775 he owned in partnership with George McBeath a boat of thirty tons on Lakes Erie and Huron. He apparently left the Albany trade after the outbreak in the colonies and made his headquarters at Montreal. With Bannerman he owned a small boat (periauger) on Lake Superior which wintered at Grand Portage in 1775–6. Pond's supplies may have been taken up on this boat on his first venture. In 1776 McTavish took to England about £15,000 worth of furs presumably from Grand Portage and possibly including Pond's returns. McBeath however appears to have acted as agent for the house with which Alexander Ellice was connected. The firm of Phyn and Ellice had been forced to leave Albany and some members of the firm moved to Montreal. James Ellice died in Montreal in October 1787. James Phyn merchant on Old Broad Street, London was a correspondent of Alexander Henry's in 1781. In any case George McBeath took out a license for the first time in 1777 to take five canoes to Grand Portage and Alexander Ellice acted as guarantor. It is probable that Pond knew George McBeath since the latter had been at Michilimackinac at least as early as 1768. It is also probable that Pond was not averse to forming a connection with the old Albany firm of Phyn and Ellice with the new Montreal headquarters. The conjecture is submitted that in 1776 Pond at Michilimackinac arranged to have the next season's goods brought to Grand Portage and that the license secured by George McBeath in 1777 included goods which were for his outfit. Pond and McBeath later became partners who were supplied by Phyn and Ellice and it is quite possible that the arrangements began at this early date. With these plans Pond proceeded to the post on the North Saskatchewan after his trip down from Fort Dauphin confident that in the following year McBeath would meet him at Grand Portage with a new outfit and prepared to take his furs. And according to expectations Pond probably met McBeath in 1777 at Grand Portage and returned for his second winter at the post on the North Saskatchewan.

It is impossible to state how far Pond was still an independent trader and as to whether the arrangements with other traders on the Saskatchewan became more definite and tangible. But Pond had apparently established his post above the other Canadian posts and if he was still an independent trader, as seems to be the case, he was acting with his usual superb skill as a trader in reaching the Indians farthest up the Saskatchewan. In the same year (1776–7) that Pond had decided to winter on the North Saskatchewan in the hope of securing a larger return than he had secured at Fort Dauphin, the Hudson's Bay Company had also decided on a similar move. Cumberland House had not been adequate to check the Canadians. As Bain has shown the Canadian traders had made a successful countermove by forestalling the Indians in the more important routes. As a further move in the struggle the Hudson's Bay Company decided to establish a post farther up the Saskatchewan than that of any of the Canadian posts. Consequently while Pond was establishing his post above the Forks the Hudson's Bay Company under Turnor's direction was building a post still farther up the North Saskatchewan at Hudson's House not far from the present site of

Prince Albert. Pond was doubtless successful the first year 1776–7 since both posts were newly established, but in the second year 1777–8 competition apparently led him to think of fresh fields of larger profits. He may have found himself in possession of a large stock of goods at the end of the winter and a relatively small supply of furs.

An alternative field was suggested in the successful expeditions which had been made by Henry and the Frobishers on the Churchill in 1775–6 and of Thomas Frobisher who had wintered at Isle à la Crosse Lake in 1776–7. The best furs were to be obtained in the north and the profits from the trade with the Indians on the Churchill River were large. The Hudson's Bay Company had advantages on the Saskatchewan with direct access to the Bay but on the Churchill where the skill of canoe-men was at a premium it was difficult to follow. The Canadians had a more promising field. It was this area which Pond had decided to attack.

On the other hand the area had decided difficulties. From the standpoint of trade the canoe had definite limits. These limits were primarily those of food supply. The canoe could not carry a large quantity of food in addition to the trading goods and men. To penetrate to the Churchill river and beyond meant dependence on the food supply of the country and especially on fish. It was extremely difficult with the relatively large complement of men for a canoe to travel rapidly and to secure an adequate supply of fish. The experience of Pond, Henry and the Frobishers on Lake Winnipeg in 1775 had shown this very clearly. Incidental to the problem of an adequate food supply was the shortness of the season in which to make the journey from Grand Portage to the interior. Alexander Henry and his party had secured liberal supplies of rice on the route to Lake Winnipeg and depended on fish for the remainder of the journey. Thomas Frobisher had solved the problem in part by continuing from the fort built on the Churchill river in 1776 with the goods left over from the trading of Henry and the Frobishers and wintering at Isle à la Crosse lake where an adequate supply of fish was available. Although Frobisher had planned to return with the Indians to Lake Athabaska apparently he was unable to carry it out. If in spite of the help of the Indians he had failed and had been obliged to stop at Isle à la Crosse lake, how far was it to be expected that Pond would succeed.

The account of the expedition available in Alexander Mackenzie's *A general history of the fur trade* (London, 1801) is probably accurate

Peter Pond: Fur Trader and Adventurer

since Mackenzie doubtless gained this information during the winter of 1777–8 with Pond in Athabaska. The paragraphs may be quoted in full. "The success of this gentleman [Thomas Frobisher in 1777 at Isle à la Crosse] induced others to follow his example and in the spring of the year 1778 some of the traders on the Saskatchiwine river finding they had a quantity of goods to spare agreed to put them into a joint stock, and gave the charge and management of them to Peter Pond, who, in four canoes, was directed to enter the English river, so called by Mr. Frobisher, to follow his track, and proceed still further; if possible to Athabaska, a country hitherto unknown but from an Indian report. In this enterprise he at length succeeded, and pitched his tent on the banks of the Elk River by him erroneously called the Athabaska river about forty miles from the lake of the Hills into which it empties itself."

"Here he passed the winter of 1778–9; saw a vast concourse of the Knisteneaux and Chepewyan tribes, who used to carry their furs annually to Churchill the latter by the barren grounds, where they suffered innumerable hardships and were sometimes even starved to death. The former followed the course of the lakes and rivers, through a country that abounded in animals, and where there was plenty of fish; but though they did not suffer from want of food, the intolerable fatigue of such a journey could not be easily repaid to an Indian, they were therefore highly gratified by seeing people come to their country to relieve them from such long toilsome and dangerous journies; and were immediately reconciled to give an advanced price for the article necessary to their comfort and convenience. Mr. Pond's reception and success was accordingly beyond his expectation, and he procured twice as many furs as his canoes would carry. They also supplied him with as much provision as he required during his residence among them and sufficient for his homeward voyage. Such of the furs as he could not embark, he secured in one of his winter huts and they were found the following season, in the same state in which he left them" (pp. xii–xiii).

No direct record of his first expedition to Athabaska has been made available but a letter from Alexander Henry to Joseph Banks dated Montreal, Oct. 18, 1781 enclosing a memorandum on an overland route to the Pacific printed in L.J. Burpee, *Search for the Western Sea* (Toronto, 1908) pp. 578–87, throws some light on the excursion. Henry does not mention his informant but undoubtedly it was Pond with whom he probably had numerous conversations in the winter of 1779–80 and he may have seen Pond in the summer of 1781 after his second visit to Athabaska. Henry had not penetrated beyond Isle à la Crosse lake and the account of the route beyond that point was almost certainly based on Pond's information. Henry recommends securing guides at Churchill river "as the natives inhabiting these parts, seems sepparated, and unconnected with the Southern Indians theire language differing but little from the kristinay the passages very difficult to find in the river on acco't of its breadth and number of islands – and great lakes, here the canoes must be refitted and when ready, proceed up this river, in the streights of which, are great rappids and dangerous places from the great body of watters, coming down from the melting of the snow in this season and proceed to Orrabuscaw carrying place, two hundred and fifty leagues, from where you fall on the Great River, course, near west, supposed to be in sixty degrees lattitude, day nineteen hours long the twenty second of June, the north side of this river appears a barren mountaneous country mostly bare rocks great quantity of fish in this river, the natives appear, as you proceed to the Westward, to increase in number." With this section Henry was familiar. Pond probably gave him a description of the portage which Henry or Pond locates at 60 N. Lat. 140 W. Long. "at this carrying place, provisions must be procured from the natives dry'd mouse and rein deer to subsist the people while carrying over this carrying place which is twelve miles long, and as far as Orabuscaw Lake, it will take six days to carry over, at the other end of which you fall on the river Kiutchinini which runs to the westward, takes its rise to the northward of this place, current, gentle, the land low and marshy great plenty of wild fowl in the fall – the season by this time will be advanced, it will be necessary to prepare for winter, build houses etc. the frost very severe, imploy the natives to hunt, for the subsistance of the men – which is mostly flesh, dry'd buffaloes meat, and mouse deer, it is not only the provisions for the winter season, but, for the course of next summer must be provided which is dry'd meat, pounded to a powder and mixed up with buffeloes greese, which preserves it in the warm seasons here every information must be procured from the savages, relating to the course of this river, the inhabitants of the lower parts the Orabuscaws, makes war on the Kitchininie therefore, it will be necessary to procure a

Peter Pond: Fur Trader and Adventurer

peace between the two nations which would be no difficult matter for the natives, from all parts, hearing of Europeans being here, will come in the winter season to bring provisions on acco't of European trinkets, by which means, intelligence may be procured, and conveyed to any distant parts, it is common for these wandering tribes to remove two hundred leagues in the winter season, and carry their tents, family's and everything belong to them, when every thing is ready and provisions procured for the summer, as no dependance can be put, on what you are to receive in an unknown part. Every precaution should be taken, but very often, must expect to be dessappointed. A new sett of interpretors and guides must be procured, which can always be had, from the difft nations and proceed down this great river, untill, you come to the sea, which cant be any very great distance. Suppose it should be thirty, or forty degrees of longitude unless some accidents should entervene, it can be done in thirty days which will be in July,[7] here an establishment may be made in some convenient bay or harbour, where, shipping, may come to. In the meantime a small vessel may be built, for coasting and exploaring the coast which can be no great distance from the streight which seperates the two contenants." Henry continued the memorandum showing the advantages of an establishment to exploration and trade, the probable cost of the expedition and the distances to be covered. Based as this memorandum must have been on Pond's observations it illustrates clearly the organization of the food supply in the Athabaska district and the conception which had been gained at this date of the possibilities of what is at present the Western Arctic department of the Hudson's Bay Company.

Pond had succeeded in overcoming the difficulties by proceeding inward from Cumberland House with the surplus goods of the winter trade early in the season and not delaying by a trip to Grand Portage, and by securing an ample supply of provisions at his post on the Athabaska river. It was a remarkable tribute to Pond's ability that he should have been chosen by the other interests to represent them and that he should have been entrusted with four canoes of goods. He undoubtedly impressed his colleagues as a man of sterling character, of courage, aggressiveness and ability. To Pond must be given the credit of being the first white man to cross the Portage La Loche and of discovering the Athabaska river and Lake Athabaska. He had succeeded where Thomas Frobisher had failed. This success was in part the result of organization. He was probably supplied with dried meat as a supply of food and which in conjunction with the excellent fishing of the Churchill river waters and the short distance from Cumberland House made it possible to reach the district whereas Frobisher was dependent on fish. After reaching the Athabaska he became dependent on the pemmican and meat supplied by the Indians of that area. Pond was an explorer as well as a trader and as he had been first on St. Peters river, had gone farther than the Canadian traders in the North Saskatchewan, he was first into Athabaska. He traded successfully with large numbers of new tribes of Indians as in the days of 1774–5 on the Mississippi.

Success in the Athabaska district required an organization in the neighbourhood of Cumberland House and an organization of provision supplies in the Athabaska district for the return journey. It involved further the development of provision supplies in the Red River district adjacent to the southern end of Lake Winnipeg. It was not possible to cover the long distances and depend on the supplies obtained along the way. The use of pemmican[8] which may have been a contribution of the Athabaska Indians facilitated the development of this organization. Later improvements followed with the establishment of an advanced depot at Lac la Pluie. This wide organization necessitated extensive co-operation between a variety of interests located in separate territories. The Athabaska district was important to the development of the Northwest Company and the work of Peter Pond was of fundamental importance.

B. The Organizer (1778–1790)

Pond had been unusually successful in his trip to Athabaska in 1778. He came out the following summer (1779) and went down to Montreal. He had left Montreal in 1773 – six years of expeditions to the Mississippi and to Athabaska – and in 1779 he was 39 years of age. In the fur trade of the Northwest he was an old man. It was primarily conducted by young men. Alexander Mackenzie left the Northwest at the age of 30, David Thompson left at 40, and Alexander Henry, Pond's contemporary at 37. It was a hard life which demanded much and the profitable character of the trade in the early period enabled men to retire at an early age and at the same time gave

Peter Pond: Fur Trader and Adventurer

the organization the full advantage of youth and energy. According to the standards of the trade Pond should have left the Northwest after he had discovered Athabaska in 1779. But for him the mystery of the Mackenzie river drainage basin had not been solved.

When he came out in 1779 presumably the arrangement with his supporters did not end as there remained in Athabaska a large supply of his furs in cache. This arrangement was apparently continued through the appointment of Waden to take his place during his absence to Montreal. According to Mackenzie, Waden wintered in 1779 at Lac La Ronge. The agreement of 1779 which provided for his selection was a formal arrangement in which each of the traders was given a definite share. McBeath and Co. which probably included Peter Pond held two shares. In 1780 McBeath's name does not appear among the grantees since Pond was in Montreal. In that year the latter held two licenses, nos. 11 and 19, each permitting to take to Grand Portage 2 canoes, 250 gallons of rum, 20 rifles, 600 lbs. gunpowder, 8 cwt. ball and shot, and valued at £750. With these goods he probably went in to Athabaska wintering there again in 1780–1 and bringing out the furs which had been cached in 1779. He probably came out to Grand Portage in 1781 and secured the goods which included 4 canoes, with 33 men, 600 gallons of rum, 50 gallons wine, 50 rifles, 600 lbs. powder and 20 cwt. of shot valued at £3000 which had been brought up under a license granted to McBeath, Pond, and Graves with McBeath and R. Ellice as guarantors. In the same year Mr. Waden's "partners and others engaged in an opposite interest, when at the Grand Portage agreed to send a quantity of their goods on their joint account, which was accepted and Mr. Pond was proposed by them to be their representative to act in conjunction with Mr. Waden."

The quotation from Sir Alexander Mackenzie's *voyages* is confused as to dates. According to his statement Waden was killed in 1781 but according to the sworn statement of "Joseph Fagniant de Berthier ordinairement voyageur dans le Pays en hault" he died in the month of March 1782 "dans le pays en hault du lac de la Riviere aux Rapids dans la Riviere des Anglois – dans un petit Fort avec Peter Pond et Jean Etienne Waden commercants." According to Mackenzie "Mr. Waden, a Swiss gentleman, of strict probity and known sobriety, had gone there [Lac la Ronge] the year 1779 and remained during the summer of 1780." In this year Pond is alleged to have wintered with Waden, the latter meeting his death about the end of the year 1780 or the beginning of 1781.

Waden's position in the fur trade of the Northwest warrants consideration. The licenses issued in his name throw some light on his importance. In 1772 a license permitted him to take a canoe and 8 men to Grand Portage giving his own name as security; in 1773, 2 canoes with 16 men; in 1775, 2 canoes with 15 men, Mme Waden as guarantor; in 1777, 3 canoes and 17 men, J.E. Waden as guarantor; in 1778, 3 canoes and 23 men, with Richard Dobie and J. McKindlay as guarantors. In 1779 his name does not appear but that of V. St. Germain appears in two licenses both having J. McKindlay as guarantor and one license reading for 1 canoe and 10 men the other for 2 canoes and 18 men. The general agreement of that year in which Waden and Co. held two shares and which was represented by Waden at Lac la Ronge found the firm represented in Montreal by St. Germain. In 1780 the firm of Waden and St. Germain secured two licenses, one for 4 canoes and the other for one canoe. In 1781 the firm of Waden and St. Germain with St. Germain and Dobie as guarantors secured a license for 4 canoes and 38 men.

The problems of the fur trade from 1778 to 1783 are extremely complex.[9] The sources of information are meagre and in many cases biassed. Conjectures based on this information will be subject to revision but an attempt to reconstruct the history may be made. The evidence points very directly to the formation of a large organization probably as early as 1775. This organization was apparently built directly around the Frobishers, the McGills, the Ellices, and McTavish or the larger houses of Montreal. In the agreement of 1779 this general vague organization possibly included Todd and McGill, B. and J. Frobisher, McGill and Patterson, McTavish and Co. and McBeath and Co. a total of ten shares of the sixteen. Pond was probably despatched by these interests to Athabaska in 1778, the two larger houses that of McTavish and the Frobishers joining to support the venture. Pond was well known to Todd and McGill as he came up from Montreal to Michilimackinac with them in 1773 and to the other traders including the Frobishers and Henry and he was trusted as a thoroughly competent trader. McBeath, and the firm of Phyn and Ellice were probably his direct supporters and in turn he would be connected with McTavish.

Peter Pond: Fur Trader and Adventurer

He had gone in to the Northwest in 1775 with the Frobishers and Alexander Henry and was the first to penetrate the Athabaska department in 1778. He was the logical choice of these interests to push the trade into Athabaska. The difficulties of the fur trade were the result of the struggle which developed between this large group and the number of small traders who had no such allegiance. In the small group Waden, later Waden and St. Germain, was a typical representative, and also Oakes and Co. a firm which had been supported by Lawrence Ermatinger, Ross and Co. and probably Holmes and Grant, although this firm had early affiliations with the larger group. It was possibly as a concession to this group that Waden "of strict probity and known sobriety" was chosen to take Pond's place in the trade with the Athabaska Indians in 1779. Pond as already shown probably returned to Athabaska in 1780 and came out to Grand Portage in 1781. Waden possibly came out to Grand Portage in 1780 but in view of Pond's visit it would not be necessary for him to come out in 1781 and he is reported as summering in the district.

In 1781 the problem arose as to the appointment of representatives which would satisfy all the interests. Waden was in the interior and the small traders were probably insistent that he should remain as their representative. But Pond had been the representative of the larger group. He was familiar with the trade and the Indians of Athabaska and was, through his long experience as a trader, very successful. A compromise was apparently reached in which Pond was chosen to represent the larger interests and to trade a joint stock with Waden at Lac la Ronge. It is not difficult to imagine the causes of contention which would arise between Pond and Waden, the one chosen to carry out the policies of the larger group and anxious to develop the Athabaska department, the other interested in the policies of the smaller group anxious to keep down expenses and content to wait at Lac la Ronge for the Indians to bring out the furs from Athabaska in the spring. Pond was selected by the larger group because its members were confident in his ability to carry out their policy and Waden was probably chosen by the members of the smaller group for a similar reason. Moreover Alexander Mackenzie wrote "two men of more opposite characters could not perhaps have been found. In short from various causes their situations became very uncomfortable to each other and mutual ill-will was the natural consequence." The sworn testimony of Joseph Faignant de Berthier is probably all the evidence that is available as to these natural consequences. "Au commencement du dit mois de mars [after a winter living in close proximity in a small fort] vers le neuf heures du soir, le deposant s'etant retiré dans sa maison qui etoit à côte et touché la maison du dit sieur Waden, de chez qui le deposant revenoit et etoit après se dechosé le deposant en dix minutes ou environ après avoir arrivé, ayant quitté le dit Waden sur son lit avoit entendu tirer deux coups du Fuzils, l'un après l'autre subitement dans la maison du dit Waden, sur quel le deposant envoyoit un homme pour voir ce que c'etoit qui alloit et revenoit et rapportoit a ces deposant que Mons. Waden etoit a terre ayant recu un coup du Fuzil sur quel le deposant se levat et courut immediatement au dit Waden et lui trouvat a terre a coté de son lit ou le deposant lui a quitté le peu de tems au paravant, et trouvat son jambe gauche cassé de son genu, jusqu'en bas; qu'en aprochant le dit Waden lui disoit. *Ah mon amis je suis mort* sur quel le deposant a assayé de dechirer ses culots a metapes pour l'examiner, et trouvat la marque de poudre sur son genu, et de trois ou deux balles avoitent entré et trouvat la jambe casse jusqu'en bas ou les deux balles ont sortis a derier, les ayant trouvé sur la place; que le dit sieur Waden disoit au deposant de trouver la Boam Turleton et d'arretter le sang; qu'ayant lui demandé ce qui lui a fait cela; il a repondu je vous le dirai; mais ayant perdu bien du sang alors, il n'etoit pas capable de lui dire plus; Que le deposant en entrant chez le dit Waden sur cette occasion a percu le dit Peter Pond et Tousaint Sieur, sortant de chez le dit Waden et entrant chez eux et trouvat, un fuzil vide et un autre cassé dans la ditte maison de Waden, et apercu que cel qui etoit vide etoit dernierement tiré mais que l'autre etoit emporté. Que le deposant en entrant chez M. Waden apres le coup a vu le dit Peter Pond et Toussaint Sieur á la porte et le dit Sieur demanda du dit Waden si c'etoit lui le Sieur qui l'avoit tire. Que le dit Waden a reponder *allez vous en tous les deux que je ne vous voyez plus*. Que la dessus deux nommes amenerent le dit Tousaint Sieur pour coucher et Peter Pond entra chez lui, qu'environ un mois devant le dit Peter Pond et le dit Waden se batterent ensemble et le meme soir que le dit Waden a ét tué. Environ une heure devant soupé Peter Pond se quarrelloit et disputoit avec le dit Waden. Que le deposant a grande raison a croire que c'etoient les dits Peter Pond et Toussaint Sieur ou un de eux qui ont tué le Sieur Waden et pour le present n'a rien plus a dire. Affirmé pardevant moi a Montreal le 19 May 1783 [signe] Neveu Sevestre C.C." [a true copy of the original].

Peter Pond: Fur Trader and Adventurer

This differs from Mackenzie's account which states "Mr. Waden had received Mr. Pond and one of his clerks to dinner; and in the course of the night, the former was shot through the lower part of the thigh, when it was said that he expired from the loss of blood, and was buried next morning at eight o'clock." And this in the hard frozen ground of Northern Saskatchewan in March! Alexander Mackenzie was not partial to Pond but he states that "Mr. Pond and the clerk were tried for this murder at Montreal and acquitted." No record has been found of the trial at Montreal but presumably all the available evidence was taken including the above testimony and Pond was acquitted. It is not customary to go behind the verdict of the courts but Mackenzie in his work published in 1801 probably knowing that Pond was at that time impoverished and that he had severed his connection with the Northwest Company and Canada, apparently felt that he was safe in writing "nevertheless their innocence was not so apparent as to extinguish the original suspicion." This was doubtless the view taken by the small group of traders whose interests Mackenzie had always represented but the verdict of the courts cannot be disregarded.

Despite the unsatisfactory character of Mackenzie's account it is the only one available. It is necessary as far as possible to make corrections for the bias and to assume that the remainder is accurate. According to this account Pond despatched Toussaint Sieur (the above mentioned clerk) "to meet the Indians from the Northward who used to go annually to Hudson's Bay; when he easily persuaded them to trade with him, and return back that they might not take the contagion which had depopulated the country to the eastward of them; but most unfortunately they caught it here and carried it with them, to the destruction of themselves and the neighbouring tribes." It is not possible to determine whether Pond came down to Grand Portage in 1782 or whether his clerk was sent but it is probable that Pond went down. The news of Waden's death doubtless precipitated a disruption of the agreement and again divided the trade between the small group and the large group. Both groups therefore "began seriously to think of making permanent establishments on the Missinippi river and at Athabaska for which purpose in 1781–2 [probably 1782–3] they selected their best canoe-men being ignorant that the small-pox penetrated that way. The most expeditious party got only in time to the Portage La Loche, or Methy-Ouinigam, which divides the waters of the Missinippi from those that fall into the Elk river, to despatch one canoe strong-handed, and light loaded to that country; but on their arrival there, they found, in every direction, the ravages of the small-pox, so that from the great diminution of the natives, they returned in the spring with no more than seven packages of beaver. The strong woods and mountainous countries afforded a refuge to those who fled from the contagion of the plains; but they were so alarmed at the surrounding destruction, that they avoided the traders and were dispirited from hunting, except for their subsistence." No intimation is given in this account as to whether Pond was in command of the party to Athabaska but there is reason to believe that the traders successful in reaching Athabaska belonged to the small group. Their lack of knowledge of the country as well as the desolation of the small pox would account for the small returns in furs. Moreover Pond's map of 1785 shows that he wintered on Isle à la Crosse lake in 1783. He probably represented the interests of the larger group and was unsuccessful in getting into the Athabaska. His trip to Grand Portage and return would place him at a disadvantage with the other interests who were able to start off directly news was received of Waden's death. It is not known whether he went down to Grand Portage in 1783 but the scarcity of furs may have warranted the abandonment of the trip and let him proceed to Athabaska from Isle à la Crosse lake. Madame Waden had asked for his apprehension at Grand Portage in 1783 but he did not come out to Montreal until 1784. Probably he went direct from Isle à la Crosse lake to the Athabaska department in the spring of 1783.

In any case he went into Athabaska in 1783 and came down to Grand Portage and Montreal in 1784. The memoir which accompanies his map of 1785 is dated Arabosca 15 Mars 1784. From the map and the memoir it is possible to reconstruct in part the activities of the winter. If the foregoing analysis is correct this was Pond's third winter in Athabaska. In the two earlier visits he probably had little time for exploration because of the shortness of the season but if he went in early in 1783 from Isle à la Crosse lake he may have had time to carry out a more adequate survey. Certainly he gained from the Indians a vast amount of accurate information. He probably explored Lake Athabaska in part but it is extremely doubtful whether he went below it. Peace river is shown as running directly

Peter Pond: Fur Trader and Adventurer

101

into Slave Lake and although he might have descended the Slave river without noticing that the Peace came in near Lake Athabaska, it is extremely doubtful. He did however from the Indians learn the approximate location of Slave Lake and of Bear Lake and the entrance of the river into the Arctic Ocean. The map is not accurate but from the standpoint of the fur trader it gives all the necessary information. He was fortunate in meeting Indians who had accompanied Hearne on his expedition to the mouth of the Coppermine and to elicit from them information gained on that visit. This information should be noted. "J'ai tenu conseil avec 40 des naturels qui vivent a une petite distance dela mer du N.O. Les autres tributs les appellent les gens du couteaux rouge. Ce nom leur vient de ce que presque tous leurs articles son faits de cuivre rouge dont leur pays est rempli (no. 6). Ils confirment le flux et reflux des eaux dans cette mer. Ils assurent qu'ils ne connoissent aucune terres nord, que les cotes courent vers l'ouest, que la navigation des rivieres qui tombent dans cette mer est ouverte dans le commencement de l'eté; qu'ils ont vu plusieurs foix des isles de glace, flottant sur ces (?) arages (no. 7) Ice herring [Hearne] pendant les annees 1773, 1774, et 1775 a entrepris un long et penible voyage avec les naturels font aller examiner les grandes mines de cuivre. On a etouffé les plus petite circonstances de son voyage et des ses decouvertes. Jai recu ces details des sauvages qui l'accompagnerent et aujourd'hui il est defendu a touts personnes d'aller vers l'ouest."

During his winters in Athabaska and especially in 1783–4 he had come in contact with a large number of the Indians of the Mackenzie river district. In 1782 Fort Churchill was destroyed by the French and Matonnabee, the trader of the northern Indians who had been influential in bringing trade to the Hudson's Bay Company, committed suicide. The organization by which trade was carried on from the Mackenzie river drainage basin to Fort Churchill was destroyed. The establishment of Pond's fort in Athabaska was a final blow to Hudson's Bay Company supremacy and it finally brought into the hands of the Canadian traders the trade of the large area drained by the Mackenzie river and its tributaries. Mackenzie[10] writes "Till the year 1782, the people of Athabaska sent or carried their furs regularly to Fort Churchill, Hudson's Bay. – At present, however, this traffic is in a great measure discontinued."

In 1784 Pond came out to Grand Portage and was among those interests which arranged for the formation of the Northwest Company. The organization of the Athabaska district demanded strong capital support and it was felt that the agreement which began during the previous decade and was broken through the disruption of the small traders should be renewed and made more permanent. Arrangements were made for signing the agreement but the small traders continued to show their hostility to the large group and they were especially hostile to any agreement which threatened their interests. These small interests had suffered through the loss of Waden but they were as yet unwilling to surrender. The sixteen share agreement which was finally decided upon by the larger interests probably included six shares divided evenly between the two large houses of McTavish and B. and J. Frobisher, two shares each, held by Small and Montour probably the direct representatives of those houses in the interior, two shares each, to McBeath and Grant, and one share each, to Holmes and Pond. No provision was made for the small individual traders including Peter Pangman and John Ross. The latter had sent 1 canoe and 9 men to Grand Portage in 1779 and in the following year the firm of Ross and Pangman sent 4 canoes. Ross was given one share in the agreement of 1779 but no mention is made of these individuals in the licenses of later years. On the evidence given by the licenses it is difficult to understand the basis on which they could expect to be included in the agreement of 1783–4. They entered the trade at a very late date, were probably included in 1779 through the force of circumstances since in that year licenses were given out very late and closely restricted but certainly their contribution in capital or experience could not be regarded as important. Since they were excluded they decided to arrange for the formation of a new company.

At the time they were supported very curiously by Peter Pond. Pond was dissatisfied and with some reason because only one share had been given to him whereas McBeath his old partner secured two shares. Pond had been in the front line and had served with great energy and success for the larger group of traders in the Northwest and in Athabaska. He consequently expected that he should be rewarded for having borne the heat of the day. So far as is known McBeath, his partner, had never been beyond Grand Portage. But capital and not skill was the determining factor and Pond was assigned one share. He refused to sign and came down to Montreal at first apparently determined to throw in his lot with the small traders Ross and Pangman for whose defeat he had earlier been so largely responsible.

Little is known of his activities in 1784–5 during his year at Montreal. It may be assumed that he reported for trial for the murder of Waden and was acquitted. There can be little doubt that he reported to his old friends in Montreal his discoveries in Athabaska and that he soon forgot his grievances against the Company. It was hardly to be expected that he would continue with the small traders since he had nothing in common with them. Taking advantage of his loyalty to his old friends the Frobishers probably had little difficulty in persuading him to take his share in the Company. He may have visited his home at Milford as he apparently on the first of March 1785 presented a map to Congress. In the introduction to the note for which no date is given there is written, "Il est reparti pour constater quelques observations importantes." On April 18, 1785 at Quebec he signed a memorial probably written by the Frobishers. The memorial gives some hint as to the means by which he had been prevailed upon to rejoin his friends. He writes "Your memorialist begs leave to assure your Honour that the persons connected in the Northwest Company are able and willing to accomplish the important discoveries proposed in their memorial to His Excellency General Haldimand; provided they meet with due encourage-ment from government, having men among them who have already given proof of their genius and unwearied industry, in exploring those unknown regions as far as the longitude of 128 degrees west of London; as will appear by a map with remarks upon the country therein laid down, which your memorialist had lately the Honour of laying before you for the informa-tion of government, and the Company will procure at its own expense such asistants as may be found necessary to pursue the work already begun, until the whole extent of that unknown country between the latitudes of fifty-four and sixty-seven to the North Pacific ocean is thoroughly explored, and during the progress of this enterprize the Company will engage to trans-mit from time to time to His Majesty's Governor of this province for the information of government, correct maps of those countries and exact ac-count of their nature and productions, with remarks upon everything else useful or curious that may be met with in the prosecution of this plan."

Pond was apparently promised a free hand in carrying out his explorations of the Mackenzie river drainage basin and of rounding out the information which he already acquired.

In 1785 Pond returned to Grand Portage and to Athabaska. But he was again to come in conflict with the small traders who were dissatisfied with the agreement of the Northwest Company. Ross and Pangman had been successful in enlisting the support of Gregory, McLeod and Co. of Montreal. These interests had been engaged with the Detroit and Michilimackinac trade but seeing the prospect of decline and loss of this trade through the success of the American Revolution were ready to listen to proposals for entering the Northwest trade. It was not a promising venture. Of the members of the new concern John Gregory had never as far as is known engaged in the trade of the Northwest, Peter Pangman and John Ross had been in the trade for a short time but were apparently not very successful traders, Alexander Mackenzie who had been in the counting house of Mr. Gregory for five years and had never been beyond Detroit, Normand McLeod, was a dormant partner, Duncan Pollock "had served his time in the post office of Quebec but had lately been engaged in the trade among the Indians of Michilimackinac and of course was understood to be learned in Indian affairs," of whom [Roderick Mackenzie writes "His conduct was often very unpleasant to me and at length brought on an explanation which placed us on a good footing for the rest of the voyage if not orever after"] Laurent Leroux apparently knew something of the trade, James Finlay, was a son of James Finlay the early trader, and a brother-in-law of Gregory, and Roderick Mackenzie came to Canada in 1784. "The guides, commis, men, and interpreters were few in number and not of the first quality." These men were expected to compete with the traders of the Northwest Company and their success was not great.

John Ross probably accompanied by Laurent Leroux was despatched to Athabaska to compete with Peter Pond. Nothing is known of the movements of Pond or of the success of Ross during the winter of 1785–6. Pond's map of 1790 has remarks on it to the effect that he made excursions from his post on the Athabaska during the summer of 1786 and 1787. Alexander Mackenzie notes that a post (probably two posts) were established on Slave Lake to the east of the entrance of the Slave River by Leroux and Grant. It is probable that Leroux established a post under Ross and the opposition

Peter Pond: Fur Trader and Adventurer 105

and Cuthbert Grant under Pond's direction, both erecting their buildings in the same locality. In the same year it is probable that a post was established on Peace river above Vermilion Falls referred to on Alexander Mackenzie's map as the old establishment. Pond's summer of 1786 was probably spent in organizing the district so that an ample supply of provisions could be obtained to enable the canoes to make the return journey to Grand Portage without difficulty and so that the trade and exploration could be developed to the largest possible extent. It was only through the establishment of an adequate base in the Athabaska district for provisions and furs that exploration could be carried on. During the winter of 1786–7 competition between Ross and Pond became more severe and news reached Roderick Mackenzie about the beginning of June that Mr. Ross "had been shot in a scuffle with Mr. Pond's men." The amalgamation of 1787 was arranged at Grand Portage between the small traders and the Northwest Company. Alexander Mackenzie received one share and was appointed to replace Pond who was apparently anxious to devote his final years exclusively to exploration. In the same summer Pond appears to have visited Slave Lake as he notes that in July 1787 there was a great deal of ice on that lake. It is not known whether he crossed over to the north side of the lake but he apparently learned that the Mackenzie river flowed from the western end and it is quite possible that he may have gone as far as the entrance of the Mackenzie. According to Ogden's report of a conversation with Pond the entrance of Mackenzie river was in Lat. 64.° Long. 135.° Alexander Mackenzie in 1789 was able to proceed directly to the entrance of the river.[11]

In 1787 Alexander Mackenzie arrived as his successor and Pond was obliged to leave Athabaska forever in 1788. During the winter however he apparently fired Alexander Mackenzie with the possibilities of discovery down the Mackenzie. There can be no doubt but that he gave Mackenzie all the necessary information and that Mackenzie's journey was the fulfilment of Pond's plans. Mackenzie was not at this time a successful trader or an explorer but he learned much from Peter Pond during the winter of 1787–8. He was given full instructions in the management of the new district. Alexander Mackenzie wrote in a letter dated Athabaska, Dec. 2, 1787 that McLeod and Boyer had been sent to the Beaver country on Peace river for provisions. Leroux had been ordered with Pond's concurrence to abandon Slave Lake. Masson suggests that in January 1788 Mackenzie had become convinced of the possibilities of the expedition to the Arctic. To his subordinate Roderick Mackenzie he wrote "I already mentioned to you some of my distant intentions. I beg you will not reveal them to any person as it might be prejudicial to me, though I may never have it in my power to put them in execution." The context however makes it difficult to decide that the "distant intentions" referred to the voyage down the Mackenzie river. From his superior Patrick Small, in a letter dated February 24, 1788, we learn of "the wild ideas Mr. Pond has of matters, which Mr. Mackenzie told me were incomprehensibly extravagant – He is preparing a fine map to lay before the Empress of Russia." Pond appears to have decided on the venture after a journey to Grand Portage in 1788. This may be inferred from a letter to Small dated December 3rd 1787. Small gave orders to him "to go with or after the packs, but represented to him that he required to be expeditious, if he intended returning after seeing the Grand Portage." Probably Pond decided to go down the Mackenzie in 1789 but arriving at Grand Portage in 1788 found it necessary to go to Montreal. It was at this point that he left instructions to "another man by the name of McKenzie – with orders to go down the river and from thence to Unalaska and so to Kamschatka and thence to England through Russia." Whether Pond left these instructions or not Alexander Mackenzie had reached the conclusion that Mr. Pond's ideas were not as wild as they had at first seemed and with Pond out of the country it was possible for Roderic Mackenzie to write in July 1788. "He [Alexander Mackenzie] then informed me, in confidence that he had determined on undertaking a voyage of discovery the ensuing spring by the water communications reported to lead from Slave Lake to the Northern Ocean." In a letter dated February 15th, 1789 he outlined to the partners of the Northwest Company plans for the voyage.

Pond came down to Montreal in 1788 and remained at Montreal and Quebec until March 1790 when he returned to Milford. He may have learned by the winter express by that time of the voyage of Alexander Mackenzie and realized that his conclusion formed during the past five years had been disproved. With Pond as with Alexander Mackenzie the Mackenzie River was the River Disappointment. Pond sold out his share in the Northwest Company in that year for £800 to Mr. William McGillivray and

Peter Pond: Fur Trader and Adventurer

severed his connection with the Company forever. He was fifty years of age at this time and an old man for the fur trade. It was left for a young man to reap the rewards of his work and his experience.

V. The Man and His Work

Peter Pond was one of the sons of Martha. His achievements considering the handicaps[12] under which he laboured were in many ways remarkable but they were not of a sensational character. He was the first to cross the Methye Portage into, and to outline the general character of, the Mackenzie river drainage basin but aside from a little known map nothing has remained to show the importance of his work. He apparently wrote a journal but only after he had reached the age of sixty; and because of its inaccurate spelling it was only published a century later, after a large part of it had been destroyed, and chiefly as an example of orthography. He apparently had little training in astronomy and mathematics and worked with his instruments under great handicaps but he produced a map of very great value – the first map of the Canadian Northwest. It was one of the misfortunes of Peter Pond that the fur trade was productive of bitter enmities and that the chief chronicler of his activities in the Northwest should have taken the opportunity not only to neglect the importance of his work but actually to malign him. The hostility of the small traders to the Northwest Company was never overcome. Alexander Mackenzie was probably never a member of the Northwest Company with the full support and loyalty of its chief shareholders. His work was written after he had broken from them and his account of the fur trade was written from the standpoint of that small band of traders who never surrendered. History has not been kind to Peter Pond. It has taken the word of the chief chronicler of his activities without question.

The intention of the foregoing sketch of Peter Pond's life is not to place him on a pedestal above the traders of his time. He had his faults. He was very proud and very sensitive. One needs only to read the remarks of his journal on Lahontan, and on Carver and of the making of a map to present to the Empress of Russia to realize his egoism but this egoism was partly the result of his age. He had achieved great things. It was unfortunate that he was unable to make people realize the extent of his achievements. He apparently died in poverty in 1807 without recognition when Sir Alexander Mackenzie was receiving the rewards of his own and of Pond's labours. His achievements have already been indicated. He was the first to penetrate to Athabaska and to suggest the lines of future exploration on the Mackenzie. He was the first to organize the trade as it was carried on to Athabaska. To him belongs the honour of having solved the problem of conducting trade over such long distances and of organizing the Athabaska department which was crucial to the development of the Northwest Company and to the prosecution of further exploration.

The task remains of indicating more specifically Pond's contributions to exploration. His map will probably remain an outstanding and permanent witness to his ability and energy. It is difficult to indicate the extent to which he had been trained in mathematics adequate to determining position but it is probable that a commission in the army may have required some training along these lines and that this may have been supplemented by information acquired on his two voyages to the West Indies. But an adequate training was not a substitute for accurate instruments. To gain an accurate knowledge of degrees of longitude it was necessary to have accurate chronometers and to maintain accuracy over long distances and for two or three years was extremely difficult. Pond had explored the St. Peters river beyond the limits previously reached by Carver or by any other white man but this exploration had no immediate importance. The penetration of the Athabaska district opened to explorers the possibilities of a new and large drainage basin. The results of Pond's first visit to the Athabaska country were given in Alexander Henry's letter dated Montreal, 18th October, 1781 to Joseph Banks. Pond probably had no instruments on his first expedition and the estimate of Alexander Henry based on Pond's information giving a location for Methye Portage of 60° N. latitude and 140° West longitude from London was very inaccurate. On the other hand Pond had acquired a fairly accurate conception of the character of the country. Henry suggested that a party should be sent down the river to explore the Arctic coast "which can be no great distance from the streight which seperates the two contenants." But he advised that the party should return "by the way of Hudsons Bay being much the shortest way back." This information based on Pond's work indicates that Pond believed at that date that the Mackenzie river drained to the Arctic Ocean. He returned to his old post in Athabaska

Peter Pond: Fur Trader and Adventurer

in the summer of 1779, but came out to Grand Portage in 1780. He may have had instruments on this expedition but the results make this improbable. He was not able to return to Athabaska until 1783 and then was obliged to come out in the following year. He was compelled to acquire the necessary information on the district in these three intervals scattered over a period of four years. His chronometers,[13] if he were in possession of those instruments, would consequently be of slight value. According to Pond's map of 1785 Lake Athabaska is placed in longitude 130° whereas the Atlas of Canada for 1916 gives 112°. Lac La Ronge according to Pond is 105° longitude and according to the Atlas 116°. On the other hand his instruments for determining latitude did not suffer through the lapse of time and the Atlas of Canada gives for Lake Athabaska 58° and Pond's map 60°, and for Lac la Ronge 56° and Pond's map 55°. The problems of determining latitude and longitude are fundamentally different from the standpoint of obtaining accuracy over a long period of time. Although Pond's map was inaccurate it did show clearly the routes which were followed by the traders to Athabaska and the relative location of the important rivers, lakes and portages. It showed further the accuracy with which Pond was able to gather information from the Indians. "Il ne faut pas ecrire que les details que je mets sur cette carte ont aucune analogie précise avec l'endroit meme eloigne dans les bois avec peu de papier j'ecrivai mes reflexions et les placoir ou je pourais."

The comments which accompanied the map and which have been printed in Davidson should be given more than a casual notice. In the first place he comments on the area south of 49° and east of the great plains the greater part of which is ideal country for beaver. "Cette region peut veritablement etre appellie la region des castors." Secondly he estimates that the number of degrees from Churchill to Athabaska is 23° whereas his map shows approximately 35° and it is actually 17°. He concludes that it is 71° between Athabaska and Behring straits whereas it is actually 57°. "Je présume que la distance reelle ne peut pas être de plus de 60 dégrés." Above latitude 54° the country is thinly populated and the Indians live during the summer on reindeer, fish, and game. They trap the reindeer in nets and use the leather for clothing. In the winter they hunt beaver to trade with the English for rifles, powder and other necessaries. This applies particularly to the country above 58° and below that line the people depend on buffalo and moose.

He divides the Indians of North America roughly into two groups east and west of a line drawn from 40° lat. 95° long. to 60° lat. 13° long. or according to his map a line roughly following the edge of the Canadian Shield from the Mississippi to Lake Athabaska. All the tribes east of this line [the Algonquin family] speak a language similar to that of the Eskimo in the Labrador coast, are very adept in the construction and navigation of canoes and are friends and allies among themselves as far as 60° North. The tribes west of the line speak "un langage extraordinaire, que consiste dans un bruit de gosier qu'il est impossible d'aprendre." They are ignorant of the canoe, are allies and friends among themselves but constantly at war with the Indians of the first group. On the death of the parents the western Indians cut off one of their fingers while those of the east pinch the skin of the arms and legs and pierce them with the point of a knife to make them bleed. The tribes of the east are steadily gaining on those of the west although the latter attempt to break through but they are forced back because of the possession of fire-arms by those in the east. The contrast between the two peoples forced him to conclude that the Eastern part of the continent was settled from Europe and the Western from some part of Siberia. The constant warfare may have been due to these discrepancies. In any case the people of the west had been forced back a great distance during the past 40 years.

These comments appear to describe very accurately Pond's reflections on the Indians and on the country. They are taken from a memoir supposedly written by Pond which also contains much other information. With this memoir is included an extract covering much the same material but according to Davidson written in a different hand and using much better French. The second memoir has also rearranged much of the material confusing it and in some places making it clearer. From the two accounts it becomes apparent that Pond was interested in gaining information from all the natives he had met. The words "a Arabosca le 15 mars 1784" are given a different place in the memoirs. In the second memoir they refer definitely to the visit of the Copper Indians on that date. These "gens du couteau rouge" lived a short distance from the North sea and had a large number of copper knives. Pond purchased some of these and brought them down with him. They told him the sea "etoit sujette au flux et reflux que ses côtes couroient fort loin vers l'ouest, et qu'ils ne connoissent aucune

Peter Pond: Fur Trader and Adventurer

terre au nord: que les rivieres de leur pays couroient au Nord ouest et alloient de jetter dans cette mer; que toutes les rivieres etoient navigables des le commencement de l'été et qu'ils avoient vu plusieurs fois des isles de glace flotter sur leurs cotes: mais ce qu'ils ajoutoient qu'il n'y a point pendant l'été d'obscurite totale dans leur pays, mais toujours une espece de Crepuscule, me fit croire que cette nouvelle mer est sous le cercle Polaire Arctique." They apparently could not see the midnight sun and Pond concludes they were under the Arctic Circle. The meeting with Hearne's Indians is again described without change. The country north of Slave Lake he describes as an immense plain "dans lesquelles il n'y a ni bois, ni herbe; on y trouve seulement quelques buissons dont le grosseur n'excede pas celle de la jambe. Tous les sauvages du Nord sont gens fidels et honnetes." It was through this country that Pond expected they would find the Northwest Passage. Under the 60th degree of latitude and around the 125th degree of longitude or south of Lake Athabaska the rivers are full of ice, from the beginning of May whereas those which run into Hudson Bay are not open until the middle of June and this in spite of the more southerly location of York Fort and Churchill Fort. Under 60° "on trouve tous les fruits naturels a l'Amerique et au climat tels que les fraises, groseilles etc et une infinite d'autres pour lesquels je n'ai pas de noms. Ils croissent sur les bords des rivieres et des lacs qui abondent en poisson, et sont couverts d'une multitude infinie d'oyes et de Canards sauvages. Dans ce canton quand le vent est a l'ouest l'atmosphere est convert de nouages et de brouillards humides meme pendant l'hiver, mais au contraire quand le vent est sud-est tout est clair et serein." Pond later proved that the climate was adapted to agriculture by his garden. Alexander Mackenzie wrote that when he arrived at Athabaska in the fall of 1787 "Mr. Pond was settled on the banks of the Elk river where he remained for three years and had formed as fine a kitchen garden as I ever saw in Canada. – In the summer of 1788 a small spot was cleared at the old Establishment, which is situated on a bank thirty feet above the level of the river, and was sown with turnips, carrots and parsnips. The first grew to a large size and the others thrived very well. An experiment was also made with potatoes and cabbages the former of which were successful; but for want of care the latter failed."

These memoirs also include information acquired from Indians and elsewhere regarding the character of the country west of the Rocky Mountains.

Pond suggests that he had seen the mountains "J'ai aussi vu dans ces montagnes des pierres a fusil, pleines de veines d'un metal blancs; je ne sais si c'est de l'argent, ou ce que ce peut-etre." In this uncertain use of the French language this should probably be interpreted as meaning that he had seen gun flints brought from these mountains full of veins with a white metal. There is no other indication of his having been as far west as the Rocky Mountains. He had met Frenchmen who had lived among the western Indians as in the case of old Pinnashon at the Wisconsin Portage, a Frenchman who "impose upon Carver respecting the Indans haveing a rattel snake at his call which the Indans could order into a box for that purpos as a feat. This frenchman was a solder in the troops that ware stasioned at the Elenoas. He was a Sentanel. At the Magasean of powder he deserted his post and toock his boate up the Miseura among the Indans and spent many years among them. He larnt maney langwedgeis and from steap to steap he got among the Mandans whare he found sum french traders who belonged to the french factorey at fort Lorain on the Reed River. This factorey belonged to the french traders of Cannaday. These people toock Pinneshon to the factorey with them and the consarn toock him into thare sarvis til the hole cuntrey was given up to the English and he then came into thare sarvis. The french strove to take him up for his desarson but fald. However they ordered him to be hung in efagea which was dun. This is the acount he gives of himself. I have heard it from his one lips as he has bin relateing his adventures to others." Pond's attitude toward "Pinneshon" explains the accuracy of the information which he obtained from Indians and others. He was a shrewd judge of human nature. He complains that this man "found Carver on this spot going without understanding either french or Indan and full of enquirey threw his man who sarved him as an interptar and thought it a proper opertunity to ad sumthing more to his adventers and make his bost of it after which I have haird meney times it hurt Carver much hearing such things and putting confadens in them while he is guvner." His appraisal of Carver is worth noting. "He gave a good a count of the small part of the western countrey he saw but when he a Leudes to hearsase he flies from facts in two maney instances." Pond took no stock in stories of pet rattlesnakes.

His account of the country west of the Rocky Mountains could not be accurate but it illustrates again Pond's ability to secure information. These mountains were called by the Indians the Rocky Mountains and "en plusieurs endroits elle est taillée a pic." They extend the full length of the plains and at places are as wide as 150 leagues. Along the mountains there were "sources d'eau bouillante, d'autres d'une chaleur plus modérée et un nombre infini de froides." The Indians apparently explained in detail the character of Peace river. "Les naturels disent encore qu'il un chasme ou passage souterrain à travers cette montagne par ou coule la riviere qui vient du Lac Arabosca, que les rochers au dessus sont perpendiculaires et d'une hauteur immense et qu'ils ont osé pénétrer à une petite distance dans leur canots, sous ces voutes terribles." The description probably applies to the Peace river below the junction of the Finlay and the Parsnip. "Ce qu'il y a certain c'est que le long des bords de cette riviere et du Lac Arabosca on trouve des sources de bitume qui coulent sur la terre." There could be no doubt as to the reports of coal and tar.

On the other side of the mountains "toutes les rivieres courent vers l'ouest et vont se jetter dans la mer du sud suivant ce que m'ont dit les sauvages." On that side there are many plains which leaving 45 degrees of latitude "et allant vers de midi, sont fort chaudes dans l'été." The tribes of these plains have nothing in common with those on the other side of the mountains "avec lesquelles sont toujours en guerre. Toutes ces tributs de l'ouest sont tres unies entr'elles et en general tres simples et de moeurs fort douces." These tribes did not use canoes and having no knowledge of fire-arms were very much at a disadvantage in war with the Indians east of them. Their language differs from those on the plains although they cut off a finger on the death of the parents. These tribes extend to the Pacific Ocean where the eastern tribes pursue them and take them prisoners. "J'ai meme vu plusieurs chevelures de negres qui avoient été tués dans ces rencontres" a statement for which one can find no explanation. The animals are different from those of the plains and resemble those of "l'Amerique meridionale" especially the lama with its beautiful wool. The Indians situated near the 48th degrees raise "un excellent tabac dont le saveur est toute particuliere." They have also horses, some mules, and asses, and great troops of buffalo from 54° to 63°.

Pond had gained as shown in these comments a surprising knowledge of the general topography of the North American continent. He had during his experience as a trader visited the Mississippi, Lake Dauphin, the North

Saskatchewan and the Athabaska and from these rivers of three drainage basins he had obtained a thorough grasp of the character of the country and of its inhabitants. On his visit to Montreal in 1785 he had come in contact with the volumes of Cook's voyages, possibly W. Ellis, *An authentic narrative of a voyage performed by Captain Cook and Captain Clarke* (London, 1782). Cook's inlet is shown on his map and also Prince William sound and King George's sound. The references in his memoir to Cook's voyages are few and were probably added to the notes he had made in the interior. He notes that the Indians west of the Rocky Mountains cut off a finger on the death of their parents similar to those inhabitants of Middlebourg in the Friendly Islands of the Southern Pacific mentioned by Capt. Cook. The location of Behring Strait, of Cook's inlet and other points on his map were borrowed directly from the volumes on Cook's voyages. The map of 1785 is the most enduring testimony of Pond's contribution to the geography of North America.

He returned to Athabaska with a detailed knowledge of Cook's voyages and with plans to bridge the gap of territory to the Northwest which was still unknown and also to verify the information he had obtained from the Indians. Prior to his departure the Montreal merchants had become thoroughly aroused as to the possibilities of the fur trade on the Pacific coast and especially in the territory served by Cook's river. In Pond's memorial to the Hon. Henry Hamilton dated Quebec, April 18, 1785 he writes that "he has had positive information from the natives who have been on the coast of the North Pacific ocean, that there is a trading post already established by the Russians; and your memorialist is credibly informed that ships are now fitting out from the United States of America, under the command of experienced seamen [who accompanied Captain Cook on his last voyage] in order to establish a fur trade upon the Northwest coast of North America, at or near to Prince Williams Sound and if the late treaty of peace is adhered to respecting the cession of the upper posts, the United States will also have an easy access into the Northwest by way of Grand Portage. From these circumstances your memorialist is humbly of opinion that this branch of trade will very soon fall a prey to the enterprizes of other nations, to the great prejudice of His Majesty's subjects, unless some means are speedily used to prevent it. It therefore becomes necessary for government to protect and encourage the Northwest Company in the earliest prosecution of the

Peter Pond: Fur Trader and Adventurer

proposed plan; in order that trading posts may be settled and connections formed with the natives all over that country even to the sea coast; by which means so firm a footing may be established as will preserve that valuable trade from falling into the hands of the other powers; and under proper management it may certainly in a short time be so extended as to become an object of great importance to the British nation and highly advantageous to this mutilated Province." Alexander Henry, who had probably been in frequent consultation with Pond wrote to his friend William Edgar, who at that time lived in New York, having made substantial profits in the forwarding trade from Montreal to Detroit during the American Revolution, on Sept. 1st., 1785 regarding the trade on the Northwest Coast. "By yours [of the 15th, July] I find you intend to become an adventurer in Chinna trade. I think it will answer until overdone, which will soon be the case were the last adventurers are fortunate, my scheme for the North coast of America I think will soon take place as I am told they are fitting Albany sloops for Chinna, they may as well send them to Cook's river where I am persuaded they will receive more profits than from all the upper posts." In a later letter of March 5, 1786, Henry makes his plans more specific. "Montreal, 5th March 1786. Dear Edgar, I find you are largely adventuring in the East India business, I am not the least doubtful of its proving beneficial I also observe you have some idea of putting my favourite plan into execution, of carrying the trade to the North west coast of America, it is a shame for America to let slip such a valuable trade and extensive territory which nature has given them the best title to, the world in general sees it at present what I acquainted you of two years ago, and I doubt not but the Empress of Russia will make settlements from Kamschatka soon, there is a long extent of country from Cape Blanco to Cook's river, extensive Bays, and large rivers empty or fall in the sea, establishments should be made at the enterance of each as far up as shipping could go, and a small fort built at each for the protection of those remaining which could be done at a very moderate expense, as we are obliged always in the North to build Stockade forts, such establishments if proper persons conduct the business in a short time would bring numerous tribes of Inland Indians with the finest furs in America and in great quantities exclusive of the sea beaver and sea otter skins sells at such great prices in China, whose numbers would be increased by their having other means of destroying them than what they have at present, as for provision they would be easily procured from the abundance of fish and wild fowl with which all Northern countrys abound but more particularly the rivers Cook entered, I make no doubt but Cook's River [called also Sandwich Sound] has a communication with those parts of the Northwest I was at, by which a road would be opened across the Continent and in the end might produce great discoverys which would prove beneficial to the world and society in general were I without a family which must stay with and provide for I would set off immediately for there is no one I could recommend so well as myself, nor no voyage could please me so well, but should you be serious in your intentions (a better scheme, I am sure you could not undertake) let me know and I will perhaps find some person which may be of service to you." In the postscript of a letter Oct. 22, 1787, Henry writes "I am informed there is an expedition to the South Seas from Boston. I hope you will have the honour of being concerned as it will redound much to those who are the first undertakers, let me know particularly about this matter."

The discovery of a large river by Cook emptying into the Pacific [Cook's Inlet] was the occasion for much speculation. Alexander Henry was convinced that the Athabaska river eventually found its way to Cook's Inlet. Pond also became convinced that the Mackenzie river emptied into the Northern Pacific. Whether he arrived at this conclusion before he left for the Northwest as a result of conversations with Henry and others or whether he arrived at it during the later years in Athabaska cannot be determined. It represented a reversal from the opinion set down in the map of 1785.

On his arrival in 1788 he was the object of much interest. There can be no doubt that he had persuaded himself, possibly after his visit to the entrance of the Mackenzie in 1787, and Alexander Mackenzie that the river flowing from Slave Lake was that which emptied into Cook's Inlet. Mackenzie wrote to Lord Dorchester on November 17th, 1794 that he had followed "the course of the waters which had been reported by Mr. Pond to fall into Cook's river, they led me to the Northern ocean." A part of Mackenzie's journal cited in Davidson from the Stowe MS notes "It was in the summer of 1789 that I went this expedition in hopes of getting into Cook's River, tho' I was disappointed in this it proved without a doubt that there is not a North west passage below this latitude." In a letter to Roderick Mackenzie

Peter Pond: Fur Trader and Adventurer

at Fort Chipewyan, March 2, 1791, he refers to the "river Disappointment." In a tirade against the English chief on his return journey he writes "I stated to him that I had come a great way, and at a very considerable expense, without having obtained the object of my wishes." But he did learn of the Yukon river on the other side of the mountains and from constant inquiry of the Indians concluded that the fort which had been described as at the mouth of the river was "Unalaska Fort and consequently the river to the west to be Cook's River. I made an advantageous proposition to this man to accompany me across the mountains to the other river but he refused it." He realized that the voyage was a failure and in a letter to Roderick Mackenzie dated Grand Portage 16th July 1790 he wrote "my expedition was hardly spoken of but that is what I expected."

Pond's actual report on the river has not been found and information regarding his views must be obtained at second hand from a letter written by Isaac Ogden at Quebec dated 7th November, 1789 to David Ogden in London describing conversations on the subject. The report is extremely difficult to follow but its comments are suggestive as to Ogden's confusion. He describes Grand Portage which leads to the waters of the Northwest, and the Mississippi which is reached by another portage from the head of Lake Superior, and the navigation down the Mississippi to the mouth with no interruption except St. Anthony's Falls. It is difficult to understand what is meant by the sentence "the traders go on this course westward leaving the Mississippi to the eastward one thousand miles" but presumably he means west one thousand miles from Grand Portage. "The furs in this district are much inferior to those from the Northwest posts." From the end of the portage at the head of Lake Superior all the lakes and waters as high up as Lat. 58° and long. 124° [probably Methye Portage] set first to the Northwest and North and then take a south easterly and south course and empty into York [Hudson's Bay] probably meaning that the Red river flows to the north and the Saskatchewan to the south although this is difficult to imagine. The Canadian traders pass one of the Hudson's Bay Company's post at lat. 57° long. 110° [Cumberland House?] and proceed to Methye Portage and Athabaska in which the rivers drain to the north into Slave Lake and the Northern ocean. The lakes emptying into Slave Lake include the Arabaska, the Lake of the Hills (which is the same) and Lake Pelican which is difficult to identify. The Slave river carries the waters of these lakes to Slave Lake. It runs northwest and is several hundred miles long. A very large river leaves Slave Lake at 64° lat. and 135° long (out nearly 20° on long. and probably 3° on lat.) and it has one of the largest falls in the world at 141° long. It is possible that Pond may have visited the entrance of the Mackenzie river and taken observations and learned from the Indians of the falls on the Hay River which empties into Slave Lake near this point. The Mackenzie River leaves the lake in a south westerly direction. Ogden pointed out that the Rocky Mountains terminated in 62-1/2° lat. and 136° long. and that the Slave River running to the westward of them emptied into the Pacific in lat. 59° or at the mouth of Cook's river. From Cook's voyages he concluded that the river emptied in 59° 40 lat. and 154° long. W. Since Cook had explored the river for 70 leagues it was concluded that there remained a very short stretch to be explored. The amount of drift wood found in Cook's river could only have accumulated on the Slave river. Two Indians had brought a blanket to Slave Lake from the mouth of the river in 1787 and there could be no doubt that the Northwest Passage had been found. On July 15, 1787 there was a great quantity of ice on Slave Lake and the Indians penetrated to the Arctic in that year and killed some of the Eskimos. Cook had gone as far as 72° and was stopped by ice therefore Ogden believed and rightly that the coast extended to the south from this northern point to 68-1/2°. Ogden summarizes his conclusions and reaches the significant results "that an easy communication with, and an advantageous commerce may be carried on by posts established on Lakes Slave, Arabaska, Pelican, etc., etc. and to deliver the fruits of their commerce at the mouth of Cook's river to be then carried to China, etc. and that as Cook's river and the lands on Slave Lake, Arabaska, etc. are very fine, some advantageous settlements may be made there which may be beneficial to government." Mackenzie had been left by Pond to go down the river to make a report.

These were Ogden's observations on Pond's conversations. In the main they were probably accurate although Pond appears to have reported to Captain Holland that the Slave river took its course from Slave Lake to the Northwest and to Prince Williams Sound. On his arrival at Montreal and Quebec in 1788, Pond and other members of the Northwest Company appear to have thrown their energies into the project of securing government aid for a discovery of the river. To the traders of the Northwest Com-

Peter Pond: Fur Trader and Adventurer 119

pany at Montreal, Pond's information raised hopes of a Northwest Passage, of access to the profitable Pacific trade and of a short route to the important Chinese market for the furs of the Northwest – all of these under their control. The competition on the Pacific coast which followed the publication of Cook's voyages from the Russian and the American and other foreign vessels was an additional incentive to government exploration. Captain George Dixon who had just returned from a very profitable voyage on the Pacific coast wrote to Evan Nepean on July 14, 1789: "if something is not done and that immediately this valuable branch of commerce will be lost to this country and in consequence of that loss the traders both from Hudson's Bay and Canada will find themselves in a bad neighborhood."

The Hudson's Bay Company was also alert to the possibilities of this new route falling into the hands of the Canadian traders. Ogden's letter to his father was forwarded to Evan Nepean on Jan. 23, 1790. Alexander Dalrymple, later (1795) the hydrographer of the Admiralty, presented a memorandum on Feb. 2nd, 1790, discrediting Pond's observations but preferring the despatch of two vessels, one "round Cape Horn without delay and another to Hudson's Bay and the Hudson's Bay Company have expressed their readiness to cooperate with government." Dalyrymple reported on Feb. 11th, 1790 that "My Friend Mr. Wegg, the governor of the Hudson's Bay Company, desires me to say that the Directors of that Company have unanimously determined to send their sloop of about 90 tons at the Company's expense if government will send a proper person in her to examine if any outlet can be found from Hudson's Bay to facilitate the communication with the West Coast. They are particularly solicitous that government would send a proper person in her that the publick may be assured of everything being done to effect the desired purpose. They also wish that two proper persons may be sent by government to travel inland to ascertain the shortest communication by the lakes and rivers and the Hudson's Bay Company will defray any reasonable expense of that undertaking." Indeed the Company despatched Philip Turner[14] to Athabaska in 1791 to determine the locations on the new route. The Company had already received Hearne's report and probably expected little from the journey but they were anxious to get all the information possible. Nevertheless the Canadians were not to be thwarted and Captain Holland worked out a plan with considerable detail for the exploration of the land lying between "Lake

120   Innis's Writings on Pond and the Fur Trade

Aurabusquie – and the line of coast discovered by Cook." As late as July 25th, 1790 Captain Holland in a letter to Evan Nepean suggested plans for the prosecution of exploration in the following year. The news of Alexander Mackenzie's journey to the Arctic brought these plans to a sudden end. A map of T. Conder published in London on Jan. 1st, 1794 included for the first time the route followed by Alexander Mackenzie down the Mackenzie to the Arctic and gave the first outline of the Arctic coast from the mouth of the Coppermine to Icy Cape.

Pond had retired to Milford. On Monday, March 8, 1790 he made a first visit to Ezra Stiles the President of Yale University and from items in Stiles' diary additional information may be gained as to Pond's views although again these are by no means clear. He estimated that his house and settlement (presumably the old establishment on the Athabaska River) was located thirty days west of Hudson's Bay and in the 60th degree North latitude. He claimed to have been "within six days travel of the Grand Pacific Ocean or the western side of N. America," or possibly the entrance of the Mackenzie River. On March 24th the diary notes that Pond had resided three years – in 64th deg. of N. Lat. (at the right of the entrance of Slave River in Slave Lake) [as] verified on Ezra Stiles' copy of Pond's map. He described the various traits of the Indians stressing the general similarity of Indian culture throughout northern North America. According to his account there were over twenty trading posts beyond Lake Superior. He expressed the opinion that Lord Dorchester, the Governor of Quebec, was anxious to conceal all the discoveries in the Northwest and to monopolize the fur trade. Finally Pond contributed geological specimens to the museum of Yale College. He apparently left a copy of a "large map of his own construction" since the copy found among the Stiles papers is dated March 25th. But Stiles was engaged in copying the map at least until April 7th. On Sept. 15 President Stiles paid a return visit to Pond at Milford. The map copied by Stiles as already suggested provides an excellent basis for a study of the posts and the trade routes but has serious limitations as to latitude and longitude. On the left hand corner Nootka is located at 130° longitude and 49° latitude but Pond does not include a map of the prospective outlet of Slave Lake through a river to the Pacific Ocean. After learning of Mackenzie's failure he probably destroyed the large map which he had shown to Ogden and submitted a rough revised map to Stiles. His reversal

Peter Pond: Fur Trader and Adventurer

of opinion after the map of 1785 which was the occasion for numerous projects to prove the existence of a direct line of communication from Athabaska river to Cook's inlet and which Alexander Mackenzie disproved had a sad ending. He left Canada with all his later conclusions disproved. Had his conjecture proved correct he would have been accorded a place among the great discoverers of Canadian history. But it was proved wrong and his former friends and supporters probably regarded him as a traitor. Alexander Mackenzie found that he was also mistaken but youth was on his side and he lived to make the journey to the Pacific by the Peace River. The latter achievement offset the disappointment incidental to the voyage down the Mackenzie river.

He apparently spent the remainder of his days reading the works available on the Northwest including Lahontan and Carver. Later accounts attribute to Pond considerable bitterness which resulted from the lack of recognition for the great services which he had rendered. There are suggestions that he was disappointed with the Northwest Company and that he gave information to the United States government in the settlement of boundary disputes but there appears little to substantiate these charges. One would not have been surprised to find this bitterness but his journal which was apparently written after 1800 is the most direct evidence to the contrary. Peter Pond had a full life and he had much to think of in the last days of poverty. One cannot forget the old man noting down his story, becoming confused as to the sequence of events, with so much to write and such difficulty in writing it, remembering the campaigns of the Conquest, the ginger bread and "small bear," the cold tents, the fighting at Ticonderoga under Abercrombie, his old comrades in arms, his trips to the West Indies, the duel, the trade, on the Mississippi and in the Northwest, chuckling to himself as he remembered the stories of the trade, the Indians, and the *voyageurs*, remembering with the detail which always comes with physical effort, the good and fat ducks, the warm ground, his garden at Athabaska, the pull upstream of the canoes, the portages, the gentle gliding stream "as we desended it we saw maney rattel snakes swimming across it and kild them."

Canadians must ever remain grateful to Pond for his pioneer work in organizing the fur trade to Athabaska, and for his active part in the development of the Northwest Company which was the precursor of the present Confederation. Above all, the most experienced fur trader and in that an

122   Innis's Writings on Pond and the Fur Trade

explorer and an organizer, he laid the basis for the later exploration for Northwestern Canada. Like the other traders from the colonies Alexander Henry, Simon McTavish and the Ellices he felt no strong allegiance to any government but allegiance to Great Britain was a prerequisite to a supply of manufactured goods essential to the fur trade. Capital, skill, and connections with English supply houses were brought from Albany to Montreal to eventually establish the Northwest Company which became one of the important influences in the establishment of Canadian unity from the Atlantic to the Pacific and in the maintenance of Canadian allegiance to Great Britain. Peter Pond did important work in organizing the Athabaska department which became the raison d'être of the Northwest Company and the keystone by which it was able to extend its operations from the Atlantic to the Pacific. If lessons were to be drawn from his life, nothing would be more obvious than the fruitlessness of sentimental lamentations over the weakening of the ties of the British Empire. The Empire has grown and been maintained on stronger bonds than political bonds and it has grown in spite of its builders as well as because of them.

Bibliography

The works dealing with the activities of Peter Pond are extremely scanty and in most cases very unreliable. The only record from Pond's own hand is a manuscript of a journal, a large part of which has been destroyed and the remainder of which is in the hands of Mrs. Nathan Gillett Pond. This remnant was printed in the *Connecticut Magazine*, Vol. X, pp. 239–59 and reprinted in the *Wisconsin Historical Collections*, Vol. XVIII, pp. 314–54. A reprint of a small part of the journal was given in the *Journal of American History*, Vol. I, pp. 358–65. The manuscript was written probably after 1800 but the details which have been checked by the editor, the late R.G. Thwaites leave no doubt as to its accuracy and authenticity. I have included a large portion of this journal, rearranging it to give proper sequence and omitting less important details, because of its very great importance to a study of Peter Pond as well as of the fur trade. The extent to which I have been indebted to the Wisconsin Historical Collections will be evident to any student in the field. A memoir written in French and accompanying a map presented to Congress in 1785 published in G.C. Davidson, *The*

Peter Pond: Fur Trader and Adventurer

Northwest Company (Berkeley, 1918) pp. 259–66, affords some light on his later activities but otherwise we are dependent for information on data supplied by his contemporaries. A memorial dated Quebec, April 18th, 1785 was presented to the Honourable Henry Hamilton by Peter Pond on behalf of the Northwest Company but the voice is the voice and indeed the hand is the hand of B. and J. Frobisher. The information which he gave to contemporaries was most unsatisfactory and it is not difficult to imagine the old trader recounting his experiences, becoming confused as to dates and events and leaving his hearers in a veritable maze.

The first of these accounts is given in a letter from Alexander Henry to Joseph Banks, Montreal, October 18, 1781 printed in L.J. Burpee, *Search for the Western Sea* (Toronto, 1908) appendix. Sir Alexander Mackenzie who wintered with him in Athabaska was unable to straighten out the sequence of events as is shown in his account *A general history of the Fur trade from Canada to the Northwest* printed with the voyages (London, 1801). Isaac Ogden "after several conversations with the map before me" wrote a description of the northern interior as given by Pond, in a letter dated Quebec, November 7th, 1789, to David Ogden, London which was published in the *Report on the Canadian Archives* 1889, pp. 29–32, but the account leaves much to be desired.

His reports to President Stiles are given in a sketchy manner in the *Literary Diary of Ezra Stiles, D.D., LL.D. President of Yale College*, ed. by F.B. Dexter (New York, 1901) Vol. III, pp. 383, 385–6, 388, 402. A map was presented to the Hon. Henry Hamilton, Lieutenant-Governor of the Province of Quebec dated April 18th, 1785 and printed in the *Report on the Canadian Archives*, 1890, p. 52. Mr. L.J. Burpee has kindly shown me a letter dated Jan. 8, 1907 from P. Lee Phillips of the Library of Congress, Washington, D.C., expressing the opinion that this map or "the lithographed reproduction" is a copy of the original and that the Kohl copy preserved in the Archives of the Hudson's Bay Company in London and printed in L.J. Burpee, *Search for the Western Sea* (Toronto, 1908) p. 102 and in G.C. Davidson, *The Northwest Company* (Berkeley, 1918) p. 32 is a copy of a map by Crèvecoeur which in turn was a copy, with various changes and omissions, of the original. A report of the Coast and Geodetic Survey Office, Jan. 16, 1907, disputes this however and suggests that the lithograph map is a later edition of the Kohl map. Davidson located two copies in the British Museum, one of which he printed (p. 37). There appears little doubt but that the map which he was supposed to have been preparing in Athabaska to show to the Empress of Russia was the map which he showed to Ogden. With the news of Mackenzie's failure this map was doubtless destroyed and a revised map was made. A copy of the revised map was made by Stiles, President of Yale University, March 25, 1790, and is now in the possession of Yale University library. It again illustrates the confusion in which interviewers of Peter Pond were left. Notes were written on the map which obviously conveyed wrong information. Pond is said to have prepared another map of the Northwest at this period but no copies appear to be extant. An interesting controversy as to the date of the 1785 map will be found in L.J. Burpee, *Search for the Western Sea* (Toronto, 1908) ch. VII, and G.C. Davidson, *The Northwest Company* (Berkeley, 1918), pp. 36ff. and especially the notes on pp. 37–8.

There are numerous later works which deal with Pond but most of them are unsatisfactory and based on the material cited generally without a critical appreciation. It would be possible to go through account after account and point out the errors which have persisted. One cannot afford to depart from the primary material and even this must be used with great caution in a study of the life of Peter Pond.[15] *The report of the Canadian Archives* 1889, pp. 29ff. has reprinted some valuable documents on later history. *David Thompson's Narrative* ed. J.B. Tyrrell (Toronto, The Champlain Society, 1916) may be cited as a work which should be used with caution in the reference to Pond. Thompson joined the Northwest Company some time after Pond had left it and he can scarcely be regarded as a primary source. Stiles *Itinerary* vol. 6, 1791, pp. 49, 406–7 gives additional information as shown in the following extracts.

"Rev. Mr. Prudden of Enfd. was born at Milfd. & well acquainted with the Pond Famy. there. The Boys were all enterprizing, bold & adventurous. When the last Fr. War begun wc. was 1754 & 1755, they would list one after another in the Army. Peter Pond might be then 17 or 18 AEt. & so born about 1737 or 1736. He rose to an Ensigncy by the Peace 1763. In the war he & his Brothers had become acquainted with the Wildness & Indian & Fur Trade. And after Peace 3 or 4 Brs. were concerned in Fur trade among Indians. Peter went a Voyage to W. Ind. About 1766 he went into the Ind. Country & tradg in furrs was absent from his Wife & family

Peter Pond: Fur Trader and Adventurer

seven years. In connexion with Brs. a Trade thus: – They sent down Furrs in Hudson R. to N. York – sold them for goods in Fall – came & traded out the Goods at Milfd. in the Winter & made remitta. to N.Y. In Spring took up Goods suitable for Ind. Trade & spent the Summer in Ind. Countries. Thus circuitously till Br. Zecha. was cut off by Indians. After Absence of y. Peter visited his Famy. at Milfd. – then 1773 went off again to the Sources of Mississippi & spent there & on the N.W. Waters to 64th. deg. Lat. seventeen years – employed in a System of a Fur Trade Compa. at Quebec which kept up 21 Tradg. Houses guarded by 800 West of L. Superior almost over to Western Ocean. In March 1790 Capt. Peter Pond returned again to his country & Famy, at Milford." (pp. 406–7)

"Major Sheshan acquainted with Sir Peter Pond in Montreal 1784 or 1785. – Knew him a sailor in Mr. Morgans Vessel at Killingwth – Saw Capt. Charles Pond at N.Y. 1785 or after – Charles told him his brother Peter killed Gen. Arroldy. Mate quarreled with him, kept another rifle, fought another duel with the Captain – fled to Canada by a Vessel bound from W. Ind. up St. Lawrence – that the Family at Milfd afterwards recd a Lett. fr. Canada informing that Peter was killed by the Indians." (p. 49)

A further reference is found in *Saint John de Crèvecoêur sa vie et ses ouvrages* (Paris, 1883), pp. 108–9. "Crèvecoeur fit aussi, en 1785, parvenir en France la carte manuscrite d'un voyage dans l'intérieur du continent jusqu'à Arabosca (63° de latitude)."

Since this volume went to press the Detroit Public library has discovered and drawn to my attention various accounts and memoranda in the Williams Papers relating to Peter Pond. Mr. R.H. Fleming has also copied for me one or two documents in the Phyn Ellice papers in the Buffalo Historical Society library. In a letter dated November 17, 1771, in the latter papers, we find the statement "enclosed you have also Graham and Pond's draft on Felix Graham from Phyn Ellice and Porteous for £50.15, – Graham and Williams, draft on Felix Graham £6.6.8. Graham and Pond's note on demand £38. Graham and Pond for freight of 235 gallons rum and 25 bu. corn." It is certain from this that Pond was in partnership with Graham in 1771 and that the partnership of 1773 was simply a renewal (p. 20). The goods belonging to this partnership are described in detail in "An invoice of sundries received from Felix Graham on account of the partnership of Graham and Pond, Michilimackinac 30th. June, 1773," valued at

£1244.13.11½ (p. 22). A document headed "Goods Left with Mr. Boban" [Beaubien] in Pond's handwriting and apparently dated December 20th, 1773, includes three bales of goods. Beaubien may have been his French competitor but was more probably a clerk. The returns for this venture (1773–4) are indicated in an "Invoice of peltreys delivered to Felix Graham by Peter Pond to be sold on ye act of Graham and Pond marked and numbered as pr margen Michlemekenac 3 July, 1774," including 31 packs (p. 45). The partnership with Graham was brought to an end, and an account beginning July 28th, 1774, is headed "Leidger Pond and Williams 1774–5" (p. 47). The new firm sold a small quantity of furs to Graham in 1774. A partial list of the goods bales Nos. 11 and 16 and additional pieces probably belonging to the outfit for 1774–5 and valued at £778.14½ is included among the documents (p. 47). Another document dated Le Bay, 22 May, 1775, "Memorandum of goods received from Mr. Shaney" [Chenier] valued at £1008.12.6 and signed by P. Pond provides an indication of the extent of the trade in the Mississippi. The furs acquired in the venture of 1774–5 are shown in the ledger under date June 22, 1775 (p. 67). The "Leidger Pond and Williams 1774–5" shows Peter Pond Dr. June 22 and July 3rd. for the outfit probably taken to the Northwest (p. 69). It includes a beaver hat bought on June 14, 1775, and a small red trunk. Alexander Henry writes that he left the Sault June 10th, but according to the Askin papers 202 lbs. of grease were delivered to him June 15th (p. 69). In the Porteous papers in the Buffalo Historical Society library an account is headed "Adventure to the N.W. per Messrs. Pond and Greves" dated Grand Portage 22nd July, 1775, and includes 6 new canoes – probably 2 large ones brought to the Portage and 4 small ones taken to the North. The firm Pond and Greves was apparently a subsidiary of Pond and Williams. A document entitled "An account of goods debts and notes in the hands of Thomas Williams belonging to Pond and Williams dated Michilimackinac, 16th. July, 1775," gives an inventory of the latter's possessions (p. 69). The partnership of Pond and Williams dissolved in 1777 and was replaced by that of Pond and McBeath, apparently on April 17, 1777 (p. 36). These documents serve to render more certain and accurate the discussion of the events in the period 1775 to 1778. Other documents show that Pond probably returned to Athabaska in 1779 for the furs left in cache and that he came out in 1780 (H.A. Innis, "Peter Pond in 1780," *Canadian Historical*

Peter Pond: Fur Trader and Adventurer

Review, Dec., 1928). The firm of McBeath, Pond, and Greves was granted a license to Grand Portage in 1781. The discussion following p. 82 should probably be corrected accordingly. Photostat copies of the above documents may be consulted in the University of Toronto library.

Regarding the murders of Waden and Ross of which Pond has been accused, the evidence against him is extremely slight. In "A report of the special privy council to consider its powers to try cases of murder in the Indian territory and a number of cases so tried including that of Francois Nadeau and Eustache Le Comte for the murder of John Ross at Arabaska" Q. 36, -1, 276–310, there is no mention of Pond. The report dated June 9, 1788 includes minutes of proceedings from May 20th, 1788 to May 29th, 1788 and represents a first inquiry into the whole question of the right to try cases of murder in the Indian territory. There is no mention of the murder trial of Waden as establishing a precedent and while this is not conclusive evidence of Pond's innocence it does show that evidence of his guilt was not sufficient to even raise the question of jurisdiction of the judical machinery of the province of Quebec.

[ed] *End of* Peter Pond: Fur Trader and Adventurer *by Harold A. Innis*

NOTES

1 Sir William Johnson Papers (Albany, 1927), Vol. V., p. 830. His headquarters probably continued at Detroit as a sale of 120 acres of land on Gros Point by Beaubien, a trader, for £200. 18s. 2d. N.Y. currency to "Peter Pond of Detroit, Merchant" is recorded on Aug. 13, 1770. Registrar des Notaries, Detroit, Vol. V., p. 105.

2 L.P. Kellogg, *The French Regime in Wisconsin and the Northwest* (Madison, 1925) p. 314 a map dated 1730.

3 See L.P. Kellogg, *op. cit.*, chs. XIII, XV.

4 Carver notes an epidemical disorder among this tribe in 1766. *Travels* (London, 1781) p. 48. His journal should be compared with that of Pond 8 years later.

5 A document dated 1778 protested on behalf of three houses, Alex. Ellice and Co., Felix Graham, and Todd and McGill against the unsatisfactory conditions of the Niagara Portage under the control of Mr. Stedman, and

it is possible that Mr. Graham may have joined the exodus from Albany and New York to Montreal. He had apparently been engaged in the trade for two previous years 1776 and 1777 and it is possible that his connection with Pond continued. On the other hand the licenses give no reference to Mr. Graham and probably Pond sought new alliances. There is evidence to suggest that Pond was supplied by George McBeath and in turn by Simon McTavish in 1775 and that he may have been persuaded by these men to undertake at this date the voyage to the Northwest.

6 Henry writes elsewhere that he was twenty-eight days crossing the lake.

7 Alexander Mackenzie began the return journey from the mouth of the Mackenzie on July 16.

8 Alexander Henry mentions dried meat but not pemmican in his journal. He describes pemmican in detail in his letter of 1781 which was dependent on Pond's observations. "It is not only the provisions for the winter season, but, for the course of next summer, must be provided which is dry'd meat, pounded to a powder and mixed up with Buffeloes greese which preserves it in the warm seasons here." It is quite possible that Pond solved the problem of the Athabaska trade by discovering the use of pemmican rather than dried meat. Alexander Mackenzie refers especially to the Chipewyans in his description of the method of making pemmican.

9 See H.A. Innis, *The Northwest Company*, Canadian Historical Review, Dec., 1927.

10 Hearne wrote from Churchill in 1780, "The Canadians have found means to intercept some of my best Northern Traders. However, I still live in hopes of getting a few [furs] from that quarter [Athabaska]." *David Thompson's Narrative, op. cit.* p. XXIII.

11 He was guided by one of the Indians but he was never in doubt as to his direction.

12 Even David Thompson writes, "He was a person of industrious habits, a good common education, but of a violent temper and unprincipled character," *op. cit.* p. 172.

13 David Thompson held that Pond used a compass "and for the distance adopted those of the Canadian canoe men in leagues." Thompson claimed that Pond reckoned the league as three miles whereas it should have been two miles and that this error occasioned most of the difficulty as to longitude. *David Thompson's Narrative, op. cit.* p. 72.

Peter Pond: Fur Trader and Adventurer

14 See *David Thompson's Narrative*, *op. cit.*, pp. 173–4.

15 Roderick Mackenzie wrote in his notebook "Peter Pond, became rather ancient in the N.W. He retired in 1788. He thought himself a philosopher and was odd in his manners. I understood he published something of the Northwest. He died poor."

H.A. Innis, "Some Further Material on Peter Pond," *Canadian Historical Review* 16 (1935): 61-4

Since the publication of my *Peter Pond: Fur Trader and Adventurer* (Toronto, 1930), additional material has been made available from a variety of sources which warrants brief discussion. Mrs. LeGrand Cannon of New Haven, Connecticut, a descendant of Peter Pond, has confirmed minor points and has been good enough to arrange for photostats to be made of the journal in the possession of Mr. LeGrand Cannon, Jr. These are now in the possession of the University of Toronto library. Pond's Beaver Club medal in the possession of Mr. Winthrop Pond of New Rochelle, New York carries "Peter Pond Fortitude in Distress 1769" on one side and "Beaver Club Instituted Montreal, Industry and Perseverance 1785" on the other. The Beaver Club minutes, on the other hand, state that he went west in 1770. It is probable that he first wintered at, or west of, Mackinac in 1769–70.

As to his later activities there is much evidence to suggest that he stayed in the country on his first trip in 1778 two years and not one, and that he came out in 1780 and wintered at Mackinac in 1780–1.[1] He went in from Grand Portage to winter with Waden in 1781–2.

The scepticism expressed by various reviews of my book, including that by Professor A. S. Morton in the *Review* of June, 1932, as to Pond's probable innocence in the murders of John Ross in 1787 and Étienne Waden in 1782, warrants a brief review of the evidence, particularly as additional material has come to light since the publication of the volume. In reply to the question "whether upon the examination before the committee of

François Nadeau for the murder of John Ross, the committee of Privy Council does think the said François to be vehemently suspected of the said murder?," Mr. Grant replied for the affirmative and Mr. Baby, Mr. de St. Ours, Judge Mabane, Judge Dunn, and Mr. Finlay for the negative. The same question, substituting the name Eustache le Compte, brought a reply in the negative from all the members.[2] Having cleared the names of these men we may turn to that of Peche, a name suggested by J.J. Bigsby in his narrative on Peter Pond.[3] According to Bigsby, Pond "persuaded his men to rob Mr. Ross of a load of furs in open day. In the course of the altercation Mr. Ross was shot, really by accident, from a gun in the hand of a voyageur named Peche." The publication of the *Journals of Samuel Hearne and Philip Turnor*, edited by Mr. J.B. Tyrrell (Toronto, The Champlain Society, 1934), throws light on this and other problems. Peter Fidler in his journal of 1791 writes: "Mr. Ross was shot by one Peshe a Canadian by orders of Pond" (p. 394 n.) and again Peche was apparently in charge of the North West Company post at the mouth of the Slave River as "The Canadian master ... absconded with the Chepewyans and remained with them 3 winters and 3 summers, before he could venture back ... frightened of the gallows." In 1800 at Fort Chipewyan James McKenzie wrote of Peche as "a little crack brained and as variable as the wind" (p. 417 n.). It would appear that Professor Morton's interpretation of Roderick Mackenzie's statements to the effect that "Pond so far from restraining his men, had encouraged them to go to extremes in case of a clash with the men of the rival fort, but there again they [the statements] may mean much more" should be modified at least by omission of the part beginning "but there...." It is obvious that we cannot accuse Pond of the murder of Ross.

The case against him in the charge of the murder of Waden is based on the affidavit of Joseph Fagniant. Mr. F.J. Audet has sent a copy of the sworn statement which has been collated since the copy in *Peter Pond: Fur Trader and Adventurer* (pp. 94–6) was made. Minor changes now make possible the more adequate translation given below.[4] The petition of Josette Waden, dated May 29, 1783, was based on the affidavit: "That from the affidavit here annexed your petitioner hath a great cause to believe that the said murder was committed by one Peter Pond and one Toussaint le Sieur the deceased's [Waden's] clerk."

The examination and report of Joseph Fagniant of Berthier, voyageur to the upper country, who having sworn on the Bible, declared that having wintered in the upper country at the Lake de la Rivière aux Rapides in the English River, he was, in the month of March 1782 in a small post with Peter Pond and Jean Etienne Waden traders. On a day early in March about 9 o'clock in the evening he retired to his house which was at the side and touched the house of Sieur Waden, which he had just left, and after taking off his shoes or about ten minutes after his return, having left Waden on his bed, he heard two gun shots, one after the other, suddenly, in Waden's house on which he sent a man to see what it was. The man went and returned saying that Mons. Waden was on the ground having received a gun shot, at which he got up and ran immediately to Waden and found him on the ground beside his bed on which he had left him a short time before, with his left leg shattered from the knee down. On approaching Waden the latter said to him *Ah mon amis je suis mort*, at which he attempted to tear his trousers [dechirer ses culots et metasses] to examine the leg and found the mark of powder on his knee and holes where two balls had entered and the leg shattered below the knee where the two balls had left from behind, having found them [the balls] on the spot. Sieur Waden asked him to find the Turlington Balsam and stop the blood. Having asked him who had done this to him he replied *I will tell you*, but having lost very much blood by that time he was not able to say more. On entering Waden's house on this occasion, he saw Peter Pond and Toussaint Sieur leaving it and entering their own. He found an empty gun and another broken in the house and saw that the one which was empty had been recently fired but that the other had been carried away [mais que l'autre etoit emporté]. On entering Waden's house after the shots he saw Peter Pond and Toussaint Sieur at the door. Sieur asked Waden if it was he Sieur who had killed him. Waden replied *Go away both of you that I may not see you*. Thereupon two men led Toussaint Sieur to bed and Peter Pond entered his own house. About a month before Peter Pond and Waden had fought and again on the same evening that Waden was killed. About an hour before supper Peter Pond quarrelled and argued with Waden. That he has good reason to believe that it was Peter Pond and Toussaint Sieur or one of them who killed Sieur Waden and for the present has nothing more to say.

"Some Further Material on Peter Pond" 133

Such is the evidence. Sieur's question and Waden's answer lead one to suggest that a scuffle had occurred and that Sieur had been implicated in the fatal shots.

The volume edited by Dr. Tyrrell makes his activities more definite on other minor points. In 1775, contrary to Alexander Henry's account, Pond did not go to Cumberland House before proceeding south to Lake Dauphin. He passed Cumberland House on October 7, 1777, on his way up the Saskatchewan in that year, and he arrived with five canoes on May 26, 1778 at Cumberland House on his way to Athabasca. Fresh evidence of a generous disposition is available in the following citation from the Cumberland House journal of the Hudson's Bay Company, dated May 26, 1778:

> [Pond] brought Isaac Batt with two bundles of furs from the Upper Settlement, he not having a canoe to come down in. I could not but in civility ask him to come in for his kindness, I also returned him thanks for the supply of provisions he gave to William Walker when he arrived at the Upper Settlement, which Wm. Walker informs me was of great service to him, there being no Indians there to trade provisions with. (p. 55)

A final item of interest, touching Pond's activities as an explorer rather than as a trader, has been made available through the discovery by Miss Grace Lee Nute in one of the copies of the *Gentleman's Magazine* for March, 1790, of a map accompanying the well-known letter in that issue. The map[5] brings out clearly the general belief in a river from Slave Lake to Cook's Inlet and supports the letter written at Quebec on November 7, 1784, by Isaac Ogden to David Ogden in London and forwarded on January 28, 1798, to Evan Nepean. It is possible that the map was drawn in London and based on the contents of the letter but it is quite probably a copy of the map referred to by Ogden as in Pond's possession. It should be consulted with the copy of Pond's map made by Ezra Stiles, president of Yale University, and at present in the possession of the library of Yale.[6] This map shows no outlet either by the Mackenzie or by Cook's Inlet. It is difficult to believe that Pond had learned of Mackenzie's failure in 1789 by March, 1790. The latter returned from the mouth of the Mackenzie to

Chipewyan on September 12 and there is no evidence of a winter express which would enable the news to reach Montreal by March, 1790. Prospects of success would certainly have deterred Pond's departure from Montreal. That he left Montreal by that date and that the Stiles map shows no reference to Cook's Inlet would seem to indicate that by March, 1790, he had lost faith in the possibilities of the route. The map published for the first time in that month is definite evidence that he believed in the route in early November of the preceding year, and that the map submitted to Stiles had been redrawn to conform to his doubts.

H.A. INNIS

NOTES

1 See *Canadian Historical Review*, December 1928, 33.

2 Public Archives of Canada, *Series Q*, vol. 26-1, pp. 276–310.

3 J.J. Bigsby, *The Shoe and Canoe* (London, 1850), I, 117.

4 In making this translation I have had the assistance of Miss Doris Shiell of the University of Toronto library. The original is in the Public Archives of Canada, *Series B* (Haldimand), vol. 219.

5 Reproduced in *Minnesota History*, March, 1933, 81–4.

6 Reprinted in G.C. Davidson's *The North West Company* (Berkeley, Cal., 1919), 42.

H.A. Innis, "A Note on Recent Publications on the Fur Trade," *Canadian Review of Economics and Political Science / Revue canadienne d'Économique et de Science politique* 2 (4) (November 1936): 562–73

The volumes of the Champlain Society edited by Mr. Tyrrell and Mr. Wallace include the final evidence which makes it possible to present a fairly adequate account of the business organization which preceded the North West Company. We are now able to link the earlier contributions of Mr. Wallace, Mr. R. H. Fleming, and others[1] with material from the Hudson's Bay Company Archives, and to unravel the threads which formed the warp and woof of the North West Company. Problems of continental organization have become conspicuous during the present depression, on the one hand in the emergence of regionalism, and on the other in the emphasis on centralization: for example, the agitation for amalgamation of the railways. These problems have been to a large extent a result of the difficulties of the Prairie Provinces and it is suggestive that they appear in the fur trade in the same regions and in territory far distant from the St. Lawrence.

The French provided the basis for expansion to the North-west, and Blondeau, according to the licences issued in 1767 – the first year in which traders were allowed to trade beyond the posts – sent two canoes to the Red River district, and François (?) six canoes to the Red River and the Saskatchewan. From Pink's Journal of 1767,[2] and evidence at York Fort, it is apparent that Canadian traders with four large canoes, with four people in each canoe, came into the Saskatchewan district in 1767. Pink found Shash (François?) in the spring of 1768, with a total of twelve French, in a post on the Saskatchewan. Two more canoes were expected in that year, and Pink actually met a large canoe with eleven men. A Canadian house was reported in the Red River district in 1767–8. "Large quantities of furs" were taken down to Canada by at least three French masters, including François, and more traders were expected in 1768. James Finlay had been interested in the trade at an earlier date and he was found by Pink in the spring of 1769 with twelve Frenchmen and three canoes. Lower down the river a canoe with one Englishman and five Frenchmen was located, and again at two different places still farther down two canoes were placed. The one Englishman apparently stayed over the summer of 1769. Unfortunately an early season overtook the canoes before they reached the Saskatchewan and they were robbed by the Indians. B. and J. Frobisher had made their first venture in that year and were among those who suffered. It was not until the spring of 1770 that the French arrived to take out the young Englishman. The Frenchman Sarschew was expected in the fall of 1770. Finlay returned in 1769 and went to England, apparently dealing with Hunter and Bailey. The French who were supporting the young Englishman probably included Blondeau, who had sent in goods under a licence in 1769 and again in 1770. Lawrence Ermatinger sent in two canoes in 1769, and Dobie and Benjamin Frobisher three canoes in 1770. Joseph Frobisher apparently wintered in the Red River district in 1770–1. Four licences for one canoe each were issued to French traders in 1770 to go to Grand Portage.

Advance to the Saskatchewan followed the occupation of the Assiniboine district, but it was less sustained until sufficiently strong support was available. The Indians were being weaned from the Hudson's Bay Company, and apparently in 1770 Wappenassew left the Company's service to assist the Canadians and possibly to recoup losses of the preceding year. In 1771 he assisted Thomas Corry in obtaining seven large canoes loaded with beavers on the Saskatchewan. Corry planned to return to London in the fall of 1772 and to be replaced by Askin. The activities of Corry were based on an extended organization: goods were sent by Thomas Walker in Quebec to Blondeau in Montreal and by him to Michilimackinac and to Rainy Lake, where "Francis and Mishel Buoy two brothers reside who are old standing traders to the southward and have great command over the Indians," and to Lake Winnipeg and the Saskatchewan. A company had emerged consisting of "Blondeau at Montreal and his brother Keshew, George McBeath Tod and Thomas Corry at Michilimackina, John Erskine [Askin] at Emis-

"Recent Publications on the Fur Trade" 137

sions nine miles above that Fort and another French Gentm., name unknown."[3] This information, obtained from John Cole who deserted Corry for the Hudson's Bay Company in 1772, indicated the co-operation which was essential to the penetration of the North-west. Askin brought rum from New England, and with other traders provided supplies and provisions for the interior. In 1772 four licences were granted to French traders for one canoe each to go to Grand Portage, one licence to Blondeau for three canoes, and one to B. and J. Frobisher for three canoes. The evidence that Corry wintered on the Saskatchewan in 1772–3 is not conclusive, and it appears probable that his place was taken by François who had twenty men at Nipowin and two men at Pasquia and a partner, possibly Bartheleme Blondeau (five canoes), at Red Deer River below. William Bruce from the Mississippi had four men at the Pasquia, but had sent two canoes to Grand Portage. The Frobishers probably sent the "four canoes more ... lying in the track of the natives who are more to the southward and who paddled down the Chuckitanaw [Hill] River in their voyage to York Fort."[4]

In 1773, Blondeau secured a licence for three canoes, Waden for two canoes, and Ermatinger for three canoes; and Cocking reported that forty-five canoes came up (Blondeau ten: two at Jack River, two at Red Deer River, and six up the Saskatchewan). François brought eleven canoes and wintered with Blondeau. Thomas Frobisher with six canoes "wintered on the south side of the lesser sea lake," and probably Joseph Frobisher and Primeau (with seventeen others) wintered on the Saskatchewan at Pine Island Lake. Bruce wintered at Red Deer River. Frobisher was guided by Primeau in the spring to intercept the Churchill Indians. Joseph Hansom wintered with Frobisher and reported that twenty canoes came up in 1774 of which nine belonged to Benjamin Frobisher, Isaac Todd, and John McGill (Joseph Frobisher and Franceway being present with three canoes, and Bruce with six canoes near the easternmost settlements at a place called Bloody River); five more to George MacBeath, with George Graham and Captain James Tute present with the canoes; three to Blondeau, present with his canoes; and three to Solomon, a Jew who employed "an old Canadian to go in with the canoes who had been upwards of these thirty years amongst the Indians."[5]

In the following year (1774) James McGill and Charles Paterson took out a licence for five canoes, Blondeau and Adhemar for four canoes, B.

138 Innis's Writings on Pond and the Fur Trade

Frobisher for four canoes, Ermatinger for four canoes, and Waden for two canoes. Hearne reported the arrival at Cumberland House on October 9, 1774, of six canoes belonging to the Frobisher brothers, with Joseph Frobisher in charge, and their departure to a house on the Churchill which Primeau and three men had been sent to build in the spring. Paterson, Holmes, and Franceway with eight canoes, and apparently Pangman with four canoes, wintered up the Saskatchewan in the more favourable buffalo country, but they also had two canoes near Pasquia. "Mr. Paterson in partnership with many others all of which except Homes and Franceway went differant ways when a little above the great lake or Wenipegg. The reason of their separating so wide from each other is on account of getting the furs cheaper and at the same time enables them to provide provision for the men at less expense and with greater sertinty than they possibly could do if in greater bodies."[6] Whether Bruce, Blondeau, Tute, and others, – who went to the south (Lake Winnipegosis) and made up the thirty to forty canoes of a total of sixty from Grand Portage which interfered with the trade of the Hudson's Bay Company – belonged to the same group, would be difficult to determine, but it is quite probable that Blondeau's interests were concerned with the more southerly group. He apparently wintered at Rocky Shore River on Lake Winnipegosis. Co-operation between these interests was evident in the despatch of five men from the impoverished camp of the Frobishers on the Churchill to winter with Paterson's settlement on the Saskatchewan.

In 1775, McGill, Frobisher, and Blondeau[7] secured a licence for twelve canoes; Lawrence Ermatinger for six canoes; Waden for two canoes; and three separate French interests, two for two canoes and one for three canoes. Frobisher apparently sent Primeau with two canoes to establish a post at Primeau Lake in the summer of 1775. Primeau arrived with six canoes at Cumberland House along with Alexander Henry, "a new adventurer this way," and four canoes, *en route* to winter at Beaver Lake.[8] Henry paid a visit to the settlement up the Saskatchewan. He had been a trader on Lake Superior and had already acquired a competency, but as he had several men in his debt he made the trip with Frobisher "to trade as well as to clear his debtors." Three canoes belonging to two Frenchmen, new adventurers, went to Swan River and were apparently plundered. Bruce wintered below Lake Winnipeg, allegedly as a result of his reputation – dating from his

"Recent Publications on the Fur Trade"

trade on the Mississippi – for cruelty to the Indians, which made it necessary for him to move about to new territory. Pond, possibly with Isaac Batt, went with two canoes to Lake Winnipegosis. By October 14, 1775, according to Cocking, eighteen canoes had gone up the Saskatchewan past Cumberland House and a total of twenty-three canoes were to winter in the district. These included Paterson, with Blondeau as interpreter.

> That at present the traders, most of them carry on the business separately being supplied with men and goods from Montreal but being so numerous several of them are obliged often to reside in one place, when to prevent confusion the goods are laid in one common stock for the time and one person takes the direction of the whole, each trader receiving his proportion, of furs according to his stock ... this year no less than sixty canoes with goods came from the Grand carrying place: by this means the profits considering the great adventures in coming here to trade are reduced to near as low an ebb as the Mississippi trade and the minds of the natives are continually corrupted by the separate interest of the traders who use very ungenerous methods with each other.[9]

According to Alexander Henry (and his volume is shown to be extremely unreliable), four different interests were struggling for the Saskatchewan trade, but by 1775–6 they had pooled their stock. Apparently the arrangement was unsatisfactory, as Cocking noted on May 17, "that the master pedlers up above are at present at variance and have some of them parted stocks, one in particular [Pangman] is tenting and trades without the stockades."[10] The interests, in addition to Paterson, probably included Greaves (Graves) and Holmes. McTavish reported on July 26, 1776, at Grand Portage, that Pond made only ten packs out of two canoes and that Bruce had arrived but had done very little trade. Possibly Greaves was supported by McTavish and apparently he was fairly successful, for McTavish reported a successful season on August 15, 1776, in spite of earlier news of misfortune from Pond and Bruce: "Our bad success at Detroit has been in some measure made up by my jaunt to the carrying place [Grand Portage]. We can say with a heart felt satisfaction, that this fall we can pay every one their own."[11]

The firm of Pond and Graves had six large canoes at Grand Portage in 1775 and probably Graves took four canoes and Pond two canoes. Apparently this firm was a subsidiary to Pond and Williams and may have been supported by Bannerman and McTavish. In a letter to Wm. Edgar, James Bannerman writes: "Try if possible to get money to pay Thos. Williams and Fleming. I would not like to give them dfts."[12]

The decline of the Mississippi and of the Detroit trade, and the embargo on trade with Great Britain enforced by the Continental Association on October 20, 1774, contributed to the decline of the Albany route and the migration of traders to Grand Portage and the North-west. Apparently McTavish secured his goods from Blackburn by the Quebec route in 1775. The general movement was evident in a letter from Phyn and Ellice, dated February 9, 1776: "I am confident that upwards of £30,000 value in skins was shipped from Montreal last fall by traders who (for most part) used to send their property to this place [Albany]." In 1776, McTavish took furs valued at £15,000 for sale in England. "I am very sensible of the treatment we have met with last year from our London friends – but I shall put it out of their power to use me so for time to come." With Todd, agent for Phyn and Ellice at Montreal, he apparently had few dealings: "Todd and I bids bon jour to one another when we meet and thats all. I have purchased the few things I send up from Mr. Kay who was concerned with Paterson" (September 22, 1776). McTavish was apparently among the first to realize the handicaps of the Albany route for the old organizations and to concentrate on the Ottawa route and the North-west. In 1776 goods were scarce. James Bannerman, writing on June 23, 1776, stated: "Mr. Henry and others from Albany bought to the amount of £15,000 stg in merchandise which they sent from Montreal in sleds to Albany. So that Indian goods are very scarce in Canada." "We are to have no goods this year (tant mieux) our friend Alexander the coppersmith is at the bottom of this disappointment." Licences do not appear to be extant for 1776, but according to Cocking's journal differences between the traders on the Saskatchewan, which broke out in the spring, continued in the fall of that year. However, severe competition forced them to join in one stock, with the exception of one master (probably Pond as Isaac Batt was again with him) with a few goods at the lower settlement. Late in 1777 the pool again broke up into two different interests. Cocking reported that Cole left Cumberland House on July 6, with nine Canadians, to build further up the Saskatchewan. On October 4, two canoes with five masters (including Frobisher) were on their way up. On October 9, Captain Tute, possibly under Frobisher, came with two canoes on his way to Frobisher's old place on Beaver Lake. Primeau had moved farther up the Churchill to Isle à la Crosse Lake and Frobisher planned to come down early in 1777 with two canoes to go north to Churchill. Primeau established communications during the winter from Isle à la Crosse to Frobisher on the Saskatchewan. Blondeau was on the Saskatchewan as interpreter and trader. Frobisher and Primeau apparently had made sufficient from the trade since Primeau declared in 1777 that "last year being the fifth his gains were in the whole increased to £9,000 and upwards and this is seemingly not to be discredited when the large quantities of furs carried down by him are considered," and since both left the North-west in that year.[13] Pond was at the settlement on the Saskatchewan, presumably supported by Williams, although a new partnership was formed on April 17, 1777, with McBeath; Holmes was also at the upper settlement and probably in 1776–7 occupied a house for Frobisher – at that time the highest up the river – but we are uncertain as to the movements of the other traders.

In 1777 apparently goods were not as scarce as they had been in 1776. Licences for Grand Portage were issued to St. Germain and to Charles Paterson for one canoe each, to Waden and Chaboillez for three canoes each, to McBeath for five canoes, to Oakes for seven canoes, to Kay for seven canoes, and to Adhemar for ten canoes. On October 1, Captain Tute arrived at Cumberland House with four canoes to winter with St. Germain at Beaver Lake where he had wintered the preceding year; they were possibly supported by Waden, and on October 7, Pond and Bruce arrived on their way up the Saskatchewan. They were associated with Graves and possibly had left John Ross as a clerk at Pasquia with two canoes, and were probably supported by McBeath. Blondeau and his associate Nicholas Montour may have been supported by Chaboillez. Pangman was also at the Canadian settlement, and Charles McCormick apparently came up for the first time. On November 3 it was reported that all the masters had joined one general concern at the Canadian settlement. This concern involved at least thirty-nine canoes. The increased number of traders on the Saskatchewan, and the withdrawal of Frobisher, probably facilitated the possibility of union and of concentration on the occupation of the Churchill and Athabaska country. Pond arrived at Cumberland House on May 26 with five large canoes loaded with goods. "He is going to penetrate into the Athopuskow country as far as he can possibly go and there to stay this next winter."[14] For the first time apparently a general concern had been maintained throughout the winter and had been sufficient to support Pond's expedition to Athabaska. The North West Company in the interior may be said to have been established in 1777–8.

The situation was by no means stabilized. Licences for Grand Portage were issued to Charles Chaboillez and to W. and J. Kay and D. Rankin, for two canoes each (four canoes), to Waden for four canoes, to McBeath and Wright for six canoes, to Forest Oakes for six canoes, to McTavish and Bannerman for eight canoes, and to John McGill[15] and Thomas Frobisher for twelve canoes. The return of Frobisher interests in the North-west is evident in the arrival at Cumberland House on September 6 of "six canoes of Canadian traders ... the masters of which are Monsieurs St. Germain and Primo, the former wintered last year in the Beaver Lake, the latter is come from Montreal this summer; they intend to proceed nigh hard to the Athopuskow country where Primo wintered two years ago. They are in the employ of Mr. Frobisher and partners."[16] Later a canoe of traders arrived on their way to Beaver Lake. It was estimated that ten canoes had gone to the Northwest to Churchill. Blondeau and Pangman wintered up the Saskatchewan as did also Holmes and Graves who took ten canoes up the river. Philip Turnor found Blondeau at the old Sturgeon River settlement with Robert Grant in opposition. Farther up the river the Hudson's Bay Company occupied a house belonging to Blondeau, and near trading establishments of Gibosh in trust for Waden, of Holmes and Graves, and of Nicholas Montour in trust for Blondeau. In the fall of the year Blondeau and Pangman were partners; and Graves, Holmes, and Grant were partners. Later, all the Canadian traders in the river were in a general partnership, except Blondeau, "and they expected he would likewise join them." This partnership included a settlement at Montagne d'Aigle Fort, nine miles below the Battle River, first settled by Pangman, McCormick, and Gibosh. Graves followed and forced a general partnership. This general partnership implied ownership in the upper settlement of Pangman, Blondeau, Holmes, Grant, and Graves, McCormick and Gibosh. "They found they should have ruined each other

"Recent Publications on the Fur Trade" 143

had they not entered into a general partnership."[17] Difficulties with the Indians in which John Cole (earlier associated with Graves) was killed, led to the abandonment of the post in the spring and probably accentuated interest in the Athabaska. Graves brought down two canoes of goods to go to the north and to follow in the path of Pond. Blondeau planned to leave Tute as his representative on the Saskatchewan and to proceed up the Churchill in the fall of 1779. Small is said to have wintered on the Churchill in 1779, almost certainly with the support of McTavish.

Turnor reported the following returns for 1778–9 of the Canadians on the Saskatchewan:[18]

Blondeau	6 canoes	63 packs
McCormick	6	46
Gibosh	3	31
Pangman	5	36
Graves	5	118
Holmes & Grant	5	——
		294

The Montreal merchants shared in the general interest of 1779 in the Saskatchewan.

Last year the passes for the Indian goods were given out so late that it was impossible to forward goods to the places of destination especially in the Northwest. For that reason those concerned in that quarter joined their stock together and made one common interest of the whole as it continues at present in the hands of the different persons or companies at foot of this. Quebec 24th, April 1780, Todd and McGill, two shares, Ben and Jos. Frobisher two, McGill and Patterson two, McTavish and Co. two, Holmes and Grant, two, Waden and Co. two, McBeath and Co. two, Ross and Co. one, Oakes and Co. one.

Licences for that year were issued to George McBeath for two canoes, to St. Germain for three canoes, to W. and J. Kay for two canoes, to McTavish and Bannerman for four canoes, to Porteous, Sutherland, and Company for two canoes, to J. Ross for one canoe, to B. and J. Frobisher

144   Innis's Writings on Pond and the Fur Trade

for six canoes, to F. Oakes for two canoes, and to Paterson and Frobisher for four canoes.

The organization in the North-west and in Montreal had a strong tendency toward unification. Pond's return on July 2, 1779, with a small quantity of furs (but leaving a large quantity in the Athabaska) made an addition to the returns of the general concern of 1777–8 and of 1778–9. The general concern enabled him to bring out the supply in 1779–80. The agreement for 1779–80 may have been renewed in 1780 to support Waden who probably wintered at Lac la Ronge in 1780–1 (to replace Pond who came out that winter) and summered in 1781. In 1780 licences were issued to Frobisher and Paterson for eight canoes, to Holmes and Grant for five canoes, to Waden and St. Germain for five canoes, to Peter Pond for four canoes, to Ross and Pangman for four canoes, to F. Oakes for three canoes, to S. McTavish for five canoes, to W. and J. Kay for two canoes, and to B. and J. Frobisher for two canoes. According to MacKenzie's account (allowing for an error of one year), Pond went in to carry on a joint trade with Waden in 1781–2 for a general concern decided upon at Grand Portage. In that year a licence for twelve canoes was issued to Todd and McGill, B. and J. Frobisher, and McGill and Paterson; for four canoes to S. McTavish; for four canoes to McBeath, Pond, and Graves; for four canoes to Holmes and Grant; for four canoes to Waden and St. Germain; for two canoes to F. Oakes; and for one canoe to B. and J. Frobisher. The death of Waden in the spring of 1782, the rush of two interests to the Athabaska in the summer of that year, the threatened danger of a prospective treaty in connection with choosing a boundary line at Grand Portage (thereby destroying the route), the losses through the spread of smallpox, and the reduction of interests to twelve in number in 1782, led to the agreement of 1783 which was to run for five years, which appointed Messrs. Joseph and Benjamin Frobisher as directors, and which is generally regarded as the basis of the North West Company. The twelve interests reported in 1782 include so far as the licences were concerned: S. McTavish (six canoes), Waden and St. Germain (four canoes), Holmes and Grant (two canoes), B. and J. Frobisher (ten canoes), and George McBeath and Company (four canoes). In 1783 B. and J. Frobisher sent five canoes, S. McTavish six canoes, and Holmes and Grant three canoes. The agreement of that year probably included McBeath (two shares), Pond (one share), Grant (two shares), Holmes (one

"Recent Publications on the Fur Trade"

145

share), McTavish (three shares), Small (two shares), Frobisher (three shares), and Montour (two shares).

In the period preceding the emergence of the North West Company, and indeed throughout the history of the Company, the difficulties of achieving unity are striking and significant. A competitive organization, which characterized the Albany trade, the trade as carried on by English firms, and the Montreal trade, was adapted to the demands of the internal trade only with extreme difficulty. Throughout the history of the numerous organizations described as the North West Company, competition was a continuous threat and unity was achieved in nearly every case after blood had been shed and the fear of governmental jurisdiction became evident. The intensity of competition and the drive toward unity were greatest in the frontier regions of the trade. The central core of unity was provided by the Frobishers in their extension of trade to the Churchill. Among the Saskatchewan traders unity was impelled and welded in the extension to Athabaska. The dominant role of the Frobishers in the North West Company was a result of their primary interest in the Churchill and Athabaska. The enormity of the task of organizing and prosecuting trade on a continental scale forced an intensely competitive organization into unity. The pressure became most acute in the interior and was passed back to the Montreal organization and finally to the British trade organization. The trend toward centralization, dependent on a continental task, was strengthened by the blows rained upon it from the south. Disappearance of the Albany route enhanced the centralizing influences of the St. Lawrence. Boundaries established in 1783 through Grand Portage necessitated a common front on the part of the trading interests to the North-west. Migration of traders from the south during the American Revolution, and after the Jay Treaty, brought new problems which were solved by amalgamations. Far less conspicuous but more powerful were the demands of the trade incidental to extension in the interior. The intractability of the material from the standpoint of centralization left its stamp on the history of the North West Company in the length and character of the agreements as well as in the periods of competition, from 1785 to 1787, with the X Y Company, and with the Hudson's Bay Company. The final achievement of centralization facilitated amalgamation with the Hudson's Bay Company in 1821. Anglo-American competitive commercialism was hammered into a Canadian structure.

The problems of maturity in the North West Company were obscured by the intensity of the competitive struggle with the Hudson's Bay Company. Recent documents suggest that the confusion of the later financial history of the North West Company was a result of more fundamental causes. As a first transcontinental organization it was faced with problems not dissimilar to those of the present Dominion. Exhaustion of virgin fur-bearing regions necessitated the adjustment of transportation rates to avoid undue burdens on the more distant areas. Decline in the rate of expansion and disappearance of new territory were basic problems for the North West Company and the Dominion. The rates established in 1804 represent a first attempt to allocate the burden of increasing transportation costs. The failure of the North West Company to solve the problem is shown in withdrawal from the Mackenzie River in 1815, and probably in the consequent breakdown of morale. With amalgamation the problem was solved temporarily by the narrowing of the size of the region and the bringing in of goods from Hudson Bay. On the other hand, flexibility characterized trade from the St. Lawrence and with the disappearance of the St. Lawrence the less flexible structure of the Hudson's Bay Company became more important.

With a central organization in London and the dominance of the governor, Sir George Simpson, in the amalgamated company, signs of strain, as Mr. Montgomery's volume shows, were never entirely absent. Increasing centralization was destined to involve too heavy a burden for the structure. John McLoughlin, as the representative of the wintering partners of the Montreal company in the negotiations leading to amalgamation, was given a prominent position as chief factor of the western department on the Pacific coast region. The loss of Oregon was in part a result of the struggle between centralization and decentralization, between the Hudson's Bay Company and the North West Company, between Scottish Canadians and English, and between Catholic and Protestant. Evidences of strain became most conspicuous on the marginal geographical area.

The problems of adjustment between centralization and decentralization, and the dangers of centralization, became acute not only in the marginal areas such as the Columbia, the Yukon, and the Labrador, but also in central policy. Donald Smith, like his predecessor, John McLoughlin, insisted upon the rights of the wintering partners in the reorganization of the Hudson's Bay Company in 1863 and in the transfer of Rupert's Land to Canada in 1869. Again, even under Donald A. Smith, as Lord Strathcona, the trend toward centralization led to the breakdown of morale described by Mr. Godsell. Improved transportation accentuated competition in the more accessible territory and compelled the reorganization essential to survival. The success with which the Company met the problems arising from far-reaching disturbances of the War, the intensity of competition which arose with the high prices of furs in the American market – so vividly described by Mr. Godsell and the depletion of furs – was a tribute to the effectiveness of reorganization. In the Hudson's Bay Company as in the Dominion, the inevitability of unity is accompanied by inevitable problems of organization.

H.A. INNIS
The University of Toronto

NOTES

Journals of Samuel Hearne and Philip Turnor. Edited with introduction notes by J.B. TYRRELL (Publications of the Champlain Society, XXI). Toronto: The Champlain Society, 1934. Pp. xviii, 611.

Documents relating to the North West Company. Edited with introduction, notes, and appendices by W.S. WALLACE (Publications of the Champlain Society, XXII). Toronto: The Champlain Society, 1934. Pp. xiii, 527, xii.

The White-Headed Eagle: John McLoughlin, Builder of an Empire. By RICHARD G. MONTGOMERY. New York: The Mcmillan Company [Toronto: The Macmillan Company of Canada], 1935. Pp. xiii, 358. ($4.00)

Arctic Trader: The Account of Twenty Years with the Hudson's Bay Company. By PHILIP H. GODSELL. New York: G.P. Putnam's Sons, [1934]. Pp viii, 329. ($3.50)

1 R.H. Fleming, "Phyn Ellice and Company of Schenectady" (*Contributions to Canadian Economics*, vol. IV, pp. 7–41); W.S. Wallace "The Pedlars from Quebec" (*Canadian Historical Review*, Dec., 1932, pp. 387–402); The

148   Innis's Writings on Pond and the Fur Trade

Ermatinger Papers in the Public Archives of Canada; *The Askin Papers* (Detroit, 1928); and the Williams Papers (see H.A. Innis, *Peter Pond, Trader and Adventurer*, Toronto, 1930, pp. 151–3; this volume 126–9).

2 Tyrrell (ed.), *Journals of Hearne and Turnor*, pp. 7–8.

3 Wallace (ed.), *Documents relating to the North West Company*, pp. 39–44.

4 Tyrrell (ed.), *Journals of Hearne and Turnor*, p. 17.

5 *Ibid.*, p. 241.

6 *Ibid.*, p. 122.

7 Probably this group with or without other traders was responsible for the reference in 1776 in the extract of a letter: "The Northwest Company are not better than they ought to be, their conduct in sending an embassy to Congress in '76 may be traced now to matters more detrimental." Also in a letter of Lawrence Ermatinger, Nov. 28, 1776.

8 Tyrrell (ed.), *Journals of Hearne and Turnor*, pp. 37–40.

9 *Ibid.*

10 *Ibid.*, pp. 41–2.

11 Wallace (ed.), *Documents relating to the North West Company*, p. 56.

12 *Ibid.*, pp. 54 *ff.*

13 Tyrrell (ed.), *Journals of Hearne and Turner*, p. 51.

14 *Ibid.*, p. 55.

15 John Askin wrote on June 13, 1778, to these men, "As I'm informed that you have to transact the business of the N.W. Co. this season," and on June 14 to Todd and McGill, "As to the supplying of others with rum, corn etc. after I have made sure of what will be wanted to the great Co. (as we must now term them for distinction sake)."

16 Tyrrell (ed.), *Journals of Hearne and Turnor*, p. 57.

17 *Ibid.*, pp. 221–2.

18 *Ibid.*, p. 253.

H.A. Innis, "Alexander Mackenzie, Peter Pond, David Thompson," in *Les explorateurs célèbres*, ed. André Leroi-Gourhan, 154–9. Paris: Éditions d'art Lucien Mazenod, 1947

MACKENZIE

1764-1820

ALEXANDER MACKENZIE naquit en 1764 près de Stornoway, dans l'ile de Lewis. En 1774, son père se rendit à New-York et s'enrôla dans l'armée britannique. Alexander fit ses études à Montréal. A l'âge de quinze ans, il entra au service de la compagnie Gregory McLeod, firme de Montréal qui était intéressée au commerce des fourrures dans la région de Detroit. Devant l'intensité croissante de la concurrence qui se produisit dans ce secteur après le triomphe de la Révolution américaine, la compagnie, acceptant la proposition de Peter Pangman, s'établit à Grand Portage afin de participer activement au commerce du Nord-Ouest. Pangman n'était pas entre dans la Compagnie du Nord-Ouest. Suivant la procédure habituelle, il opérait contre celle-ci pour son compte personnel. En 1785, Alexander Mackenzie fut envoyé au lac d'Isle a la Crosse. La violente concurrence qui y mettait aux prises la Compagnie du Nord-Ouest et les organismes rivaux entraina la mort dans l'Athabaska, en 1787, de John Ross, l'un des associes de la petite compagnie de Peter Pangman. Mais, au cours de la même année, cette rivalité aboutit finalement à la fusion des deux sociétés. Alexander Mackenzie, devenu un des partenaires du nouvel organisme, se rendit dans l'Athabaska. Après le départ de Peter Pond, il reprit les projets conçus par ce dernier, et il entreprit de descendre le grand fleuve auquel il a laissé son nom. Mackenzie, profondément déçu de constater que la rivière s'écoulait dans l'océan Arctique, et non dans le Pacifique comme il l'avait espéré, la baptisa « rivière du désappointement » (Disappointment River). En 1791, il regagna Montréal. Puis il se rendit en Angleterre ou il acheta des livres et des instruments et s'appliqua à l'étude de l'astronomie et de la navigation. Il revint au Canada en 1792. L'année suivante, il entreprit l'expédition qui le conduisit aux sources de la rivière la Paix (Peace River) et de la rivière Parsnip, puis, par la faite de partage des eaux, à la Bad river, affluent du Fraser. Il descendit le cours du Fraser jusqu'au site actuel de la ville d'Alexandrie. De là il retourna à la rivière Blackwater, tributaire du Fraser, qu'il suivit en direction de l'ouest; franchissant la rivière Bella-Coola, il atteignit enfin le Pacifique. Il reprit ensuite en sens inverse le chemin de la Peace River et du Grand-Portage, et, de Montréal, il se rendit à Londres en 1794. Pendant les cinq années suivantes, il fut l'agent de la Compagnie McTavish-Frobisher. Il l'abandonna alors pour entrer dans une nouvelle compagnie rivale, connue sous le nom de Compagnie XY ou Nouvelle Compagnie du Nord-Ouest, ou il joua un rôle prépondérant. A l'automne de 1799, il se rendit en Angleterre et il écrivit avec William Comte, « écrivain fantôme », ses *Voyages from Montreal through the Continent of North America to the Frozen and Pacific Oceans* (Londres, 1801) – (« Voyages de Montréal à travers le continent nord-américain vers l'océan Glacial et le Pacifique »). Après une période de grandes difficultes, la Compagnie XY fusionna à son tour avec la Compagnie du Nord-Ouest en 1804. En 1805, Mackenzie se retira en Grande-Bretagne. Il y déploya une vive activité pour tenter de s'assurer le contrôle de la Compagnie de la Baie d'Hudson et pour amplifier le commerce avec l'océan Pacifique. Il fut essentiellement un élément de trouble dans le commerce des fourrures. L'énergie qu'il y déploya lui permit d'accomplir une œuvre du plus haut intérêt en matière d'exploration. En 1797, il recommanda à la Compagnie du Nord-Ouest d'admettre dans son personnel David Thompson, et il engagea celui-ci dans la réalisation de son grand projet, c'est-à-dire dans l'établissement d'une carte précise de la moitie septentrionale du continent nord-américain. Alexander Mackenzie mourut en 1820, et, l'année suivante, la Compagnie du Nord-Ouest fut absorbée par la Compagnie de la Baie d'Hudson.

La contribution de Mackenzie a la connaissance géographique de l'Amérique du Nord a été décrite en détail dans ses publications. Le caractère spectaculaire de ses découvertes a éveillé l'attention du public en raison de la

"Mackenzie, Pond, Thompson" 151

très large diffusion de ses ouvrages et du fait qu'un fleuve important porte son nom. Pour ces raisons, il est difficile d'en apprécier la véritable portée. Il avait une vaste conception de la stratégie du commerce des fourrures, et il se proposait, pares publications, d'améliorer sa position entre les compagnies rivales. Ses récits n'amoindrissent pas son rôle personnel, mais n'exagèrent pas non plus les services rendus par les autres. L'énergie avec laquelle il s'effana de découvrir en territoire britannique la route du Pacifique fut aidée par le solide travail que ses concurrents avaient realisé. Il consacra relativement peu de temps au commerce des fourrures dans le Nord-Ouest, préférant s'occuper à Montréal et à Londres de problèmes d'organisation afin de s'assurer une plus grande part de bénéfices. Il s'attira ainsi l'hostilité des traitants, et il termina sa carrière active en dehors de l'Amérique du Nord. Il est possible qu'il ait surestime la valeur de ses services, mais il convient de mettre en balance la dépréciation injuste dont ils ont été l'objet. Certainement, il eut peu d'influence sur la part que la Compagnie du Nord-Ouest prit à l'exploration après son départ de l'Amérique du Nord. Il serait difficile de dire, cependant, à quel point se fut là le résultat des antagonismes qu'il avait Crées dans la compagnie elle-même. L'oeuvre qu'il accomplit dans le domaine de !'exploration lui donnait le droit de demander que ses services fussent reconnus. Et l'importance de son œuvre se mesure au fait qu'il précisa le vrai caractère du fleuve Mackenzie, qu'il établit l'impossibilité de l'utiliser comme voie d'accès au Pacifique, et la difficulté de faire usage de la voie, relativement impraticable, du Fraser.

HAROLD-A. INNIS
Professeur à l' Université Toronto (Canada)

POND

1740-fin XVIIIe

PETER POND naquit à Milford, dans le Connecticut, le 18 janvier 1740. D'après un journal curieusement orthographie, qui constitue la principale source d'information pour sa biographie, il débuta comme apprenti cordonnier; a seize ans il s'enrôla dans l'armée coloniale et, en 1756, il se trouvait au fort George. En 1758, il participa à l'attaque du fort Ticonderoga.

En 1759 il était à la prise de Niagara et, en 1760, il assistait à la prise de Montréal avec une commission d'officier. En 1761, il accomplit un voyage dans les Indes occidentales. En 1765, adoptant la carrière de son père, il participa pendant six ans au commerce des fourrures dans la région de Detroit. Revenu à Milford en 1771 il effectua l'année suivante un nouveau voyage dans les Indes occidentales. En 1773, il s'associa avec Felix Graham, dont les opérations commerciales s'étendaient de Michilimackinac a Green Bay et au Mississipi. Il se rendit au poste qui lui fut assigne par Montréal et la route de l'Ottawa. Pendant les années 1773 et 1774, il fit la traite des fourrures sur le fleuve Saint-Pierre (St Peter's River), affluent du Mississipi, et, après un voyage à Mackinac, il reprit ses affaires en 1774 et 1775.

Les difficultés qu'il rencontra parmi les Indiens des Plaines, la concurrence qui ne cessait de s'accroître dans le commerce des fourrures et les troubles qui éclatèrent dans les colonies anglaises éloignèrent Pond du Mississipi. Avec d'autres traitants, il se rendit alors au nord-ouest du lac Supérieur. Lorsque, en 1775, un important commerce de fourrures, axe sur la voie du Grand Portage, se développa dans le territoire que la Compagnie de la Baie d'Hudson dominait grâce au poste de Cumberland fonde par Samuel Hearne en 1774, un plan de campagne fut soigneusement établi : l'exécution de ce plan explique la présence de Peter Pond au lac Dauphin pendant l'hiver 1775-1776. Au cours des deux hivers suivants, il fit du commerce au confluent de la rivière Sturgeon et de la Saskatchewan du Nord. La révolte des colonies américaines obligea Pond et les autres trafiquants à faire de Montréal centre principal de leurs opérations. En 1778, soutenu financièrement par des négociants canadiens, il entreprit de suivre les expéditions d'Alexander Henry et de Thomas Frobisher sur la rivière Churchill et de pénétrer, par le Methy Portage (Portage la Loche), jusqu'à la rivière Clearwater êta l'Athabaska. Apparemment, il quitta l'Athabaska en 1780, mais il retourna avec Waden au lac la Range, ou il passa l'hiver 1781-1782. Il hiverna au lac d'Isle a la Crosse en 1782-1783, et probablement dans l'Athabaska en 1783. Il partit pour Montréal en 1784, après avoir organisé le commerce des fourrures pour le compte des négociants canadiens dans l'Athabaska et le Mackenzie. Ayant dresse une carte sommaire de la partie nord-ouest du continent, il conclut des explorations du capitaine Cook que le Mackenzie débouchait dans le golfe de Cook

"Mackenzie, Pond, Thompson"

(Alaska). Il retourna dans la région en 1785 pour vérifier ses conclusions, et, deux ans plus tard, il découvrit probablement l'embouchure du Mackenzie dans le lac des Esclaves. Il regagna Montréal en 1788, laissant à Alexander Mackenzie le soin de découvrir l'embouchure réelle du fleuve dans l'océan Arctique.

L'œuvre essentielle de Peter Pond consista à franchir le Methy Portage et à commencer !'exploration du bassin du Mackenzie. En outre, il organisa, dans la région de la rivière la Paix (Peace River), un service d'approvisionnements qui permit le fonctionnement du commerce des fourrures entre le Nord-Ouest et Montréal, et il jeta les bases nécessaires à la réalisation des voyages de Mackenzie en 1789 et 1793.

La contribution de Pond a la connaissance géographique l'Amérique du Nora a été longtemps méconnue du fait de son manque d'instruction. La relation écrite qu'il nous a laissée a été publiée longtemps après sa mort et sans subir de révision. Elle ne couvre d'ailleurs que le début de sa biographie, qui en est la partie la moins significative. Son œuvre dans le Nord-Ouest canadien est surtout connue par les récits d'autres explorateurs, et ceux de ces récits qui ont été publiés, en particulier le Journal d'Alexander Mackenzie, sont, pour des raisons faciles à comprendre, charges de préjuges à son égard. Sa carte est nécessairement inexacte puisqu'il n'avait ni les instruments ni les connaissances qu'eut exigés un pareil travail. Elle n'en indique pas moins dans leurs grandes lignes les bassins de drainage de l'océan Arctique et de la baie d'Hudson. Pond fut avant tout un traitant de fourrures qui exploita les ressources du Mississipi à partir du lac Michigan, celles de la Saskatchewan, de la rivière la Paix et de la rivière des Esclaves. Sa connaissance des langues et du commerce indigène, les capacités qu'il manifesta dans l'exploitation et l'organisation des régions inexplorées lui permirent déjouer un rôle de premier ordre en effectuant un travail préliminaire dont l'honneur et les bénéfices revinrent à ses successeurs plus qu'à lui-même. Il fut incapable de contrecarrer les manœuvres d'ambitieux qui eurent tôt fait de profiter de sa faiblesse et de déprécier son œuvre. En fait, il se trouva entraine dans les difficultés d'une âpre concurrence commerciale et il dut en subir les pénalités. Non seulement sa position s'en trouva affaiblie, mais les jalousies qu'il suscita lui firent attribuer la responsabilité des complications relatives à la détermination de la frontière entre les États-Unis et le territoire britannique. On ne saurait cependant lui contester l'honneur d'avoir réalisé l'organisation économique du bassin du Mackenzie, sans laquelle l'œuvre de ses successeurs n'eut pas été possible.

HAROLD-A. INNIS
Professeur à l'Université Toronto (Canada)

THOMPSON

1770-1857

DAVID THOMPSON naquit en Angleterre en 1770. A l'âge de quatorze ans, il entra au service de la Compagnie de la Baie d'Hudson en qualité d'apprenti et fut envoyé au fort Churchill sur la baie d'Hudson. Il fut affecté l'année suivante au poste d'York (York Factory). Jusqu'à 1791, date où se termina sa période d'apprentissage, il séjourna dans différents postes, dans la région des Grandes Plaines. A Cumberland-House, pendant les hivers de 1789-1790 et de 1790-1791, il apprit sous la direction de Philip Turner l'art de faire et de noter des observations. Les années d'apprentissage terminées, il fut affecté à différents postes plus proches de la baie d'Hudson. Mais ce ne fut qu'en 1796 qu'il fut capable d'entreprendre un voyage du Reindeer lake (lac Caribou) par le lac Wollaston jusqu'au lac Athabaska. En 1797, il décida de se joindre à la Compagnie du Nord-Ouest et fut nommé astronome et topographe. Pendant la première année, il s'occupa d'établir un relevé des différents forts situes près de la Swan river et le long du quarante-neuvième parallèle afin de déterminer s'ils se trouvaient en territoire américain ou britannique. Cette même année, il effectua un voyage des sources du Mississipi à Fond-du-Lac, d'où il gagna la coté méridionale du lac Supérieur. En 1798, il passa l'hiver au bord du lac La Biche, dans le nord de l'Alberta, et, en 1799, il fit un vaste relevé de la région comprise entre la rivière Saskatchewan et la rivière la Paix (Peace River). On l'encouragea alors à tenter la traversée des Montagnes-Rocheuses par le cours supérieur de la Saskatchewan, mais des difficultés survenues avec les Indiens vouèrent la tentative a l'échec. En 1805-1806, il se trouvait de nouveau dans la région limitrophe de la baie d'Hudson. En 1807, il traversa les montagnes, du cours supérieur de la Saskatchewan a la rivière Columbia, et il établit un poste près du lac Windermere. Il explora minutieusement le système fluvial complique du bassin de la Columbia. En 1811, il poussa jusqu'à l'embouchure de la rivière, ou il trouva les Américains déjà en possession du pays (fort Astoria). En 1812, il quitta Grand Portage pour Montréal. Durant les années 1813-1814, il acheva sa grande carte géographique. De 1816 à 1826, il fut nommé représentant de l'Angleterre dans la commission qui établissait la frontière internationale du Saint-Laurent au lac des Bois. Thompson avait relevé le cours de la plupart des rivières du continent nord-américain jusqu'à leurs sources. Ses observations détaillées constituèrent de précieuses indications pour la connaissance de la topographie générale de l'Amérique du Nord. Il mourut en 1857.

Cette contribution de David Thompson a la connaissance géographique de l'Amérique du Nord resta, exception faite de sa carte, complètement ignorée jusqu'à notre siècle. Un manuscrit considérable fut alors découvert, et il fut enfin possible d'estimer la valeur de son œuvre. Tant qu'il était reste au service de la Compagnie de la Baie d'Hudson, ses initiatives et ses efforts avaient été paralyses. Au contraire, la Compagnie du Nord-Ouest lui permit de réaliser des plans qui fortifièrent la position de cette société dans sa lutte incertaine avec la compagnie britannique. La technique qu'il avait acquise, sa patience et la valeur de ses instruments lui permirent de faire des relevés précis et de réunir les données nécessaires à l'établissement d'une carte exacte. A cote du travail ardu consistant à déterminer des positions à travers de vastes étendues, il démêla la topographie extrêmement complexe des cours d'eau qui formaient le bassin de drainage de la rivière Columbia, et il fut pout beaucoup dans l'ouverture d'une route de la Prairie a la cote du Pacifique.

L'intérêt qu'il portait aux problèmes techniques de la géographie explique peut-être la lenteur qu'il mit à atteindre la Pacifique et la faiblesse des prétentions qu'il lègue à l'Angleterre sur la région de la Columbia. Mais ces préoccupations scientifiques permirent de résoudre de nombreux problèmes avec une précision jusque-là sans exemple.

Obsède de questions géographiques, Thompson négligea peut-être, en conséquence, le côté commercial de ses entreprises. Faut-il conclure à l'échec total de celui-ci? C'est ce que parait suggérer son départ des pays de l'ouest, aussitôt après l'occupation de la Columbia par les Américains. Son activité n'en fut pas moins efficace en fructueuse. Grace à David Thompson, la connaissance des bassins fluviaux de l'Amérique du Nord fut mise au point. Sur le plan des réalisations plus immédiates, il ouvrit à la Compagnie du Nord-Ouest la voie de son expansion vers l'océan Pacifique.

HAROLD-A. INNIS
Professeur à la Université Toronto (Canada)

2

Cannon-Innis Correspondence

Introduction

Eight letters between Harold Innis and Florence Atherton Pond LeGrand Cannon from the 1930s have been located: three from Cannon to Innis (found in the Innis Papers at the University of Toronto), three from Innis to Cannon (found among a collection of Cannon's letters in the possession of her niece, Laura Burns), and two (from Cannon to Innis) found at the Thomas Fisher Rare Book Room at the University of Toronto. The last two letters, along with some other documents, accompanied an annotated version of Innis's biography of Peter Pond (Innis and Pond 1930) (a presentation copy to his wife, Mary Quayle Innis), formed an accession to the library from Innis's daughter-in-law, Wendy Innis, in 1991.

The letters from Cannon to Innis were dated 1932 (no specific day given, but between 11 September and 18 October 1932), 11 September, 18 October 1932, and November and 28 April 1935. The letters from Innis to Cannon were dated 15 September 1932, 21 October 1932, and 21 May 1935. Innis's letters to Cannon were accompanied by two of his offprints (referred to as "pamphlets" in the correspondence).[1] On the basis of their contents and timing, the letters can be organized into a 1932 cluster and a briefer 1935 exchange. Mrs Cannon initiated the correspondence with Innis because she had become aware of his biography of Peter Pond (Pond and Innis 1930), which was generally available by early 1932 (Innis and Pond 1930).

By virtue of his intersecting interests in biography, genealogy, and Peter Pond, Innis was probably intrigued with having made contact with one of

Pond's descendants. In the case of Mrs. Cannon, the maintenance of the lineage was closely bound up with her ongoing efforts to preserve Pond's memoir with a view to making copies of it available.

Mrs Cannon (née Florence Atherton Pond) (1868–?) was married to LeGrand Cannon, president of Stoddard, Gilbert & Company, Inc., wholesale grocers. Born in Milford, Mrs Cannon lived with her husband in New Haven, Connecticut. She was the niece of Dr Nathan Gillette Pond (1832–1894), son of Charles Hobby Pond (1781–1861)[2] and Martha Gillette (1810–1831). She was the daughter of Charles Hobby Pond Jr (1833–1881) and had seven brothers and sisters (one of whom, Winthrop (1865–?) eventually inherited Pond's Beaver Club medallion.

The key figures in maintaining Peter Pond's legacy were likely Dr Nathan Pond and his wife, Sophia. Born in New York, Dr Pond was the great-nephew of Peter Pond (and the great-grandson of Charles Pond [Peter's brother]). He had married Sophia Matilda Mooney (1836–1920) in 1856. Both were avid amateur historians and were very interested in the Pond family's history. Sophia is credited with having rescued Pond's manuscript from destruction. According to her account, the "ancient manuscripts were found by me in 1868, about to be destroyed with waste paper in the kitchen of the home of Hon. Charles Hobby Pond" (Chapin 2014, 310). Around four decades later, after her husband had passed away, she arranged for the publication of the memoir in the *Connecticut* magazine (Mrs. N.G. Pond and McLachlan 1906).[3] The original manuscript, in turn, was passed from the son of Sophia and Nathan Pond (Harold Gillette Pond) to Florence's son, Le Grand "Lee" Cannon Jr, a well-known author.[4] He had two sisters, one of whom (Laura Tuttle Cannon, BA, Vassar 1918) had been enrolled in the Graduate School at Yale in 1919–1920. Evidently, Florence Cannon not only arranged to have a photostat copy[5] of the original memoir made (and sent to Innis) but took it upon herself to have the entire memoir copied into more legible handwriting. It was her daughter Laura (Tuttle Cannon) Burns who completed this task. Laura Burns also was the recipient of Florence Cannon's letters, which in turn were passed on to her daughter-in-law, Catherine Burns. Among these letters were three from Harold Innis, which Ms Burns has kindly sent to me. I brought them to the University of Toronto Archives where they are being added to the

Harold Innis papers, filed with the letters from Cannon to him. The original of the memoir was donated to Yale University in 1947. The whereabouts of Ms Burns's transcription is not known.

Mrs LeGrand Cannon to Harold Innis, 11 September 1932

Your recent book *Peter Pond: Fur Trader and Adventurer* [Innis and Pond 1930] was called to my attention a few weeks ago, and I have read it with much interest. I am enclosing a sketch of the obverse & reverse sides of a gold medal which is now the property of my brother, Winthrop Pond [1865–?] of New Rochelle, New York. The family legend as told me by my father, Charles Hobby Pond of Milford, Conn., was as follows:

The Beaver Club of Montreal[6] occasionally presented one or more of its members with a gold medal, in recognition of some special act of heroism or merit – one side of the medal bearing an illocution of the deed for which the medal was awarded, the other side the insignia of the Beaver Club. Peter Pond was so honored for having carried the King's messengers thru the wilderness, a journey which included a dangerous descent of some falls – a service to the Crown for which he is said to have been knighted.

Whether this story has some basis in fact, or whether it is a myth told to amuse children, I do not know. My aunt, Mrs. Nathan Gillette Pond, died some years ago, and Peter Pond's original diary was given by her son, Harold Gillette Pond, to my son, Le Grand Cannon Jr. It is too frail to handle at all, & we have considered having a photostat copy made but have not yet done so. Your book, as you can easily understand, is of much interest to my family, in as much as both diary and medal were in my home from my childhood. In our dining room windows were colored glass medallion illustrations copied from the medal. All these things made "Uncle Peter" a very real personality and quite like a member of the immediate family. With this explanation I trust you will not regard this letter as an intrusion.

Yours truly,

Florence Atherton Pond Cannon

Harold Innis to Mrs Le Grand Cannon, 15 September 1932[7]

As you may suspect I was immensely interested in your letter on Peter Pond. I have never heard of the medal before and I believe it throws new light on the Beaver Club and on Peter Pond's earlier life. The date 1769 suggests that he was in the Mississippi area at that time and enables us to fill in another difficult period of his biography.[8] I would like very much to get further details on the story you have given of his being rewarded for taking the King's messages. This may have been confused with the story he gives in his diary of bringing the Indians to Michilimackinac[9] to act as a peacemaker.[10] I hope to write a short article[11] bringing together new information which has come to hand since the publication of the book (1930) and I wonder whether it would be possible to get a photostat copy of the diary with a view to rechecking with the published material. Needless to say I would be glad to bear any expense involved. One of my students is planning to publish documents relating to Pond's business in the December number of Minnesota History.[12] I shall try to get a reprint for you when it appears. I am very grateful to you for your letter and for any information which throws light on one of the most energetic and forceful figures in North American exploration. Again many thanks.

Yours sincerely,

Harold A. Innis

Mrs LeGrand Cannon to Harold Innis, 25 September 1932[13]

This reply to your recent letter has been a bit delayed, to enable me to report on the success of a photostat copy of Peter Pond's diary. Taking into consideration the condition of the manuscript, I think we have an excellent negative. I am sending you in a mailing tube a sample page. If you care to order one, I will be very glad to attend to it. There are thirty-two pages and the cost is twenty-five cents per page. I am very glad to have been of any assistance to you in gathering information. In your book you quote Ezra Stiles's diary [Pond and Innis 1930, 146].[14] I am told by a friend, Mrs. Sydney Knox Mitchell,[15] who was searching thru the diary for material concerning New Haven county, that it contains many references to Peter Pond. You may be familiar with all of them but I will enclose two or three which she copied for me. In the New Haven Colony Historical Society[16] are some papers, which formerly belonged to my uncle Nathan G. Pond of Milford. I hope soon to look thru them and if I find there, or among papers now belonging to Sebastian Pond of Milford,[17] anything concerning Peter Pond, I will be glad to inform you. When your article and that of your pupil are published, I shall be much interested in reading them.

Florence A.P. Cannon

[references on Pond from Stiles diary copied by Mrs. Sydney Knox Mitchell]

(1)
Ezra Stiles Literary Diary III, 383
March 10, 1790
"On Monday last visited me Capt. Peter Pond of Milford who has been 17 y. on his travels in the indian countries ..."

(2)
p. 384, March 24
"Capt. Peter Pond of Milford spent the aft & eve with me ..."

(3)
p. 386 [March 24]
"Capt. Pond doubts not there is a passage by water round the n. of Africa ... brot & presented to the Museum of Yale College above a Peck of Petrafactions of shells & other natural mineral & fossil Curiosities"

(Ezra Stiles Literary Diary III 402)
Sept. 15, 1790
"Rode to Milford & visited Mr. Pond & had much Light & Information from him respecting the N.W. of America"

Mrs LeGrand Cannon to Harold Innis, 18 October 1932[18]

Yesterday I mailed to you the photstat copy of Peter Pond's diary, – or more correctly, autobiography – by first-class registered mail, for which I paid the bill per enclosed receipt. I am told that Ezra Stiles' diary contains a "mass of manuscript." Whether there is more than one edition published or not I do not know. – but imagine not. Doubtless the one you have contains the same explanation in the preface that appears in the copy which I consulted in the library here. Omissions in Ezra Stiles diary. 3 Classes:

1. Repetitions and material easily available in other books & magazines
2. Accounts of Journeys
3. Treatise for Scriptural subjects and passages.

As to Peter Pond's gift to the Yale Museum,[19] I fear there is little chance of locating any specimens presented so long ago, & which were simply a "p [ac] k of petrafactions"[20] so far as we know. However, I will endeavor through personal acquaintances at the Peabody Museum to get some information concerning them. I am quite sure that all Yale collections of this sort are now housed in the Peabody Museum.[21] I expect to be out of town next week but will be glad to attend to the matter. – and also to look thru the papers at the [New Haven Colony] Historical Society which belonged to my uncle, Mr. Nathan Pond. I shall be very glad to have any further data which you might receive from London.

Cordially yours
Florence A.P. Cannon

Harold Innis to Mrs Le Grand Cannon, 21 October 1932[22]

My dear Mrs. LeGrand Cannon–,
The photostat copy arrived safely and is obviously an excellent copy. I am sending herewith payment for the bill and the bill. I would be grateful if you would note receipt on the bill and return it so that I can present it for final payment to the university. It would be interesting to learn which Stiles diary contains material relating to Peter Pond which has not been published. I am afraid that what you say about the "pack of petrefactions" is all too true and that there is little possibility of locating any evidence concerning them. Needless to say I shall be glad to get any further material you may discover. I have not heard from London as yet but will send you any material of common interest when it arrives. I send by separate post a pamphlet[23] which contains nothing new or which has not been published in the book

Cannon-Innis Correspondence

[Innis and Pond] but it occurred to me you might wish to have it. Very many thanks for all the trouble you have taken in arranging for the photostated material.

Mrs LeGrand Cannon to Harold Innis, 1 November 1932[24]

Mr Dear Prof. Innis,

Please pardon the delay in acknowledging the pamphlet you so kindly sent me [Innis 1928a] and your prompt remittance. Thank you for both. The receipted bill is enclosed as you request. A few days ago, I had a conversation with Prof. [Carl Owen] Dunbar, Curator of the Peabody Museum.[25] He tells me that at the time Peter Pond presented the "pk of petrafacations," the college museum consisted of one or two cabinets. The specimens were probably put in these, unlabelled and uncatalogued, used at will by the faculty for teaching purposes & their return to the cabinets often neglected. There may at present be a few of the specimens in the museum but Prof. Dunbar, who has personally gone over that section of the collections, feels sure that it is now impossible to identify them. I have also made a partial search thru the papers now at the New Haven Colony Historical Society and which formerly belonged to my Aunt & Uncle, Dr. Nathan and Mrs. Pond. Tho I have found nothing of value concerning Peter Pond, the two enclosed extracts may interest you.[26] I have lent my copy of your book to my nephew, Charles H. Pond of Hartford so at the moment cannot consult it to know whether you have used the Antiquarian Society at Montreal[27] or [Robert Wallace] McLachlan's records to secure data.[28] I hope by further searching to discover further correspondence between McLachlan and my aunt concerning Peter Pond.[29] I have consulted several people who would be likely to be informed, and the general opinion is that there is but one publication of Ezra Stiles' diary so I judge that you have at hand all the information which (4) can be secured from that source.

If I am fortunate enough to find anything further among the papers of the historical society I will certainly let you know.

Yours cordially,

Florence A.P. Cannon

Mrs LeGrand Cannon to Harold Innis, 28 April 1935[30]

Many thanks for the pamphlets concerning Peter Pond and your courteous acknowledgements of the slight aid which I have been able to render. Certainly upon this evidence it hardly seems probable that he fired the fatal shot which killed Waden.[31] It is obvious that the life these men led made them ever ready to quarrel and quarreling meant shooting – yet frequently without deliberate intent to murder. It may interest you to know of two circumstances which are the result of your "Peter Pond Fur Trader and Adventurer." Q memorial bridges I am told to be built in Milford, Connecticut – and dedicated in 1939 to commemorate the three hundredth anniversary of the settlement of the town.[32] One stone is to be placed to the memory of Peter Pond. Also Peter Pond has a namesake ... two year old son[33] of Joseph Lawrence Pond[34] of Milford.

Cordially yours,

Florence A.P. Cannon

Harold Innis to Mrs Le Grand Cannon, 21 May 1935[35]

My dear Mrs. LeGrand Cannon–,

Many thanks for your letter and for your comments. I was tremendously pleased to learn of the memorial that has been planned to commemorate Peter Pond. He has of course left important memorials to his work in Canada but they are of a more intangible form. I hope that the tribute which has been planned will pay adequate respect to his international contributions. We have had requests from the Minnesota Historical Society for a mimeograph copy of the journal which you were good enough to send us.[36] I gather Mr. Wallace,[37] our librarian, has arranged that a copy would be made and sent to them. The interest in Canadian history and especially the history of Western Canada[38] renders recognition of his work more and more certain as time goes on. It is nice to hear that his name is being perpetuated in the family.[39]

Yours cordially,

Harold A. Innis

NOTES

1 These were Innis (1928a, 1935f). The first was sent by separate post around the same time as his letter of 21 October 1932. The second was sent in 1935 (perhaps accompanying his letter to Mrs Cannon of that year).

2 Charles Hobby Pond (1781–26 April 1861), born in Milford, Connecticut, nephew of Peter Pond. An 1802 law graduate of Yale, he held positions of judge and sheriff in New Haven. He then moved into politics and was elected lieutenant governor of Connecticut in 1850, 1852, and 1853, serving as Connecticut's seventh governor in 1852–3. He did not seek re-election at the end of his final term, retiring from public service.

3 The narrative was also published in two other early versions: as part of a section on "the British Regime in Wisconsin – 1760–1800," within a historical series volume (Thwaites and State Historical Society of Wisconsin 1908) and in a fragmentary form in the *Journal of American History* 1 (1907): 357–65 (Gough 2014, 211).

4 That the memoir was passed on to Cannon from his mother reflects the extent to which the memory of Peter Pond spanned generations of the Pond family. It is not clear what Cannon thought of the memoir and why it was eventually placed in the Yale University library.

5 See introduction, lxxxix n. 30.

6 The members of the Beaver Club of Montreal (established in 1785) were merchants involved in the Canadian fur trade. The main criterion for membership was the experience of having wintered in "Indian country." Originally, the number of members was limited to nineteen, but this was later expanded to fifty-five, with ten honorary members. "The object of the meetings" (as set forth in the rules) was "to bring together, at stated periods, during the winter season, a set of men highly respectable in society, who had passed their best days in a savage country and had encountered the difficulties and dangers incident to a pursuit of the fur trade of Canada" (Beaver Club n.d.)

7 Catherine Burns, private (now in University of Toronto Archives).

8 1769 is engraved on his medal. The requirement for membership in the Club was having spent a winter "in the interior", i.e., the western and northern territories. Pond had spent the winter of 1769 in Michilimackinac, his first experience of this kind (Chapin 2014, 64). Pond was a charter member of the Club, having been elected in February, 1785 (Gough 2014, 119).

9 This was Fort Michilimackinac, a major British trading post located just south of the straits of Mackinac separating Lake Huron from Lake Michigan. As described by Alexander Henry, it had come to play the duel role as "the place of deposit, and the point of departure, between the upper countries and the lower." Quoted in (Gough 2014, 56). In 1773, Michilimackinac served as the staging ground for Pond's trading expedition to Wisconsin and Minnesota (Gough 2014, 58).

10 He is likely referring to his efforts to mediate between the Ojibwas and the Dakotas in 1774 (Chapin 2014, 114–15).

11 Likely Innis (1935f).

12 This was R. Harvey Fleming. While the article was never published, a number of drafts of it, in different stages of copy editing – accompanied by transcripts of Pond's provisions accounts held by the Burton Historical Collection, Detroit (Michigan) Public Library and the Porteous papers of the Buffalo Historical Society – can be found in the archive of the Minnesota Historical Society. The material is listed as "PETER POND: An Inventory of His Papers at the Minnesota Historical Society," p. 851, Fur trade accounts, 1773–1775. 3 folders. A positive and a negative photostatic copy, with a typed transcript and an explanatory narrative and notes by R. Harvey Fleming (accession no. 3551). The originals are in the John R. Williams Papers in the Burton Historical Collection, Detroit (Michigan) Public Library. Some of the copies were given to the Society by Fleming; they were his personal copies, which he made from the Burton Collection originals. The accounts list quantities and value of trade goods articles received from Graham and others, and of peltries delivered to him. (See appendix B, this collection.)

13 File 13, box 4, A76-0025, Harold Innis Papers, University of Toronto Archives.

14 Ezra Stiles (1727–1795) graduated with a degree in theology from Yale in 1746. After a brief career in law, he returned to religious work, serving as minister and pastor to various congregations. He helped to draft the charter for the college that became Brown University, and served as the seventh president of Yale College from 1778 until his death. He kept a diary from 1782 to 1795 that was eventually published (Stiles and Dexter 1901). It records a meeting he had with Peter Pond during which he made a copy of one of the latter's maps.

15 Mary Mitchell (1876–?) was the wife of Sydney Scott Mitchell (1876–?) a Yale historian from 1920 to 1943. He was best known for his writings on British constitutional history and taxation in medieval England.

16 Founded in 1862, the New Haven Colony Historical Society was made up of local civic leaders. Its aim was to assemble and preserve documents and artifacts related to the community's history going back over two hundred years to the colony's establishment. It moved into a new building in 1930 and today is known as the New Haven Museum.

17 Sebastian Pond amassed a large fortune that enabled him to leave a considerable bequest to his niece Nadine Lawrence Pond (1869–1950), who became a prominent benefactor in Milford.

18 File 13, box 4, A76-0025, University of Toronto Archives.

19 Pond's donation would have fit well with Yale's museum collection of the day, which was akin to a "cabinet of curiosities," consisting of an assortment of items from around the world. It was only after the appointment of Benjamin Silliman as professor of chemistry and natural history in 1802 that a more systematic collecting of specimens began.

20 Petrifaction or petrification is the process by which organic material becomes a fossil through the replacement of the original material and the filling of the original pore spaces with minerals.

In his literary diary, Yale president Ezra Stiles, in describing the meeting that he had had with Peter Pond on 24 March 1790, noted that his visitor "brot & presented to the Museum of Yale College above a Peck of Petrefactions of shells & other natural mineral & fossil Curiosities."

Florence Cannon's friend, Mrs Sydney Mitchell, had copied this sentence from Stiles's diary and passed it on to Mrs Cannon indicating its date and origin (Ezra Stiles Literary Diary III, 386). Cannon, in turn, attached her transcription of Mitchell's notes –including the "Petrefactions" reference – to her letter to Innis of 25 September 1932. Stiles was an enthusiastic amateur scientist, which perhaps accounts for his somewhat pretentious phraseology.

21 Built in 1876, the first Peabody museum soon lacked the capacity to house its growing paleontological collections and was demolished in 1917. A new larger facility was constructed, opening in 1924.

22 Laura Burn, private (now in University of Toronto Archives).

23 This was likely Innis (1928a).

24 Thomas Fisher Rare Book Room, University of Toronto.

25 A native of Kansas, Carl Owen Dunbar (1891–1979) received a BA from the University of Kansas in 1913 and a PhD in geology from Yale University in 1917. He taught at Yale from 1920 to 1959 and also served as the curator of invertebrate palaeontology at the Yale Peabody Museum as well as its director from 1942 until his retirement. Over the course of his career, he published more than 200 scientific articles and monographs on invertebrate palaeontology.

26 These were not found with the letter in the Fisher Library.

27 Founded in 1862, the Montreal Numismatic and Antiquarian Society was one of the oldest Montreal institutions to be involved in heritage protection and presentation. It housed an extensive collection of documents relating to eighteenth-century fur merchants and published the *Canadian Antiquarian and Numismatic Journal* beginning in 1872. Its collections can now be found in Library and Archives Canada.

28 A native of Montreal, Robert Wallace McLachlan (1845–1926) was an official in the archives department of the Montreal Court House. He was a leading figure in the Antiquarian and Numismatic Society of Montreal and member of the editorial board of its journal. Recognized as an authority on Canadian numismatics, he published extensively in the area and had one of the largest collections of coins, tokens, and medallions in the country. In his correspondence with Sophia Pond, he shared information about Peter Pond's Beaver Club medallion.

29 Some of these can still be found in the Pond Collection of the New Haven Museum.

31 File 13, box 4, A76-0025, Harold Innis Papers, University of Toronto Archives.

31 Jean Étienne Waddens (also Vuadens, Wadins, Waden, Wadin), baptized 1738, died 1782.

Born in Switzerland, he served with the French colonial troops in New France before becoming an independent fur trader. He was a member of the "nine parties agreement" in the Saskatchewan Valley, which many consider to have been the forerunner of the Northwest Company. He subsequently moved to the Athabasca region and died in an incident involving Peter Pond, for which the latter was accused of murder.

32 This may have been the Sikorsky Bridge, completed in 1939. It was demolished in 2004, replaced by the Igor I. Sikorsky Bridge, built in 2003. Bill McDonald, editor of the Peter Pond newsletter, believes that the memorial stone for Pond on the bridge never materialized.

33 Peter L. Pond (1933–2000) grew up in Milford and graduated from Yale University in 1954 with a degree in American studies. He subsequently attended Yale Divinity School and was ordained in the First Congregational Church, Milford. He became heavily involved in the 1980s Khmer Rouge terror in Cambodia to the point that he adopted sixteen Cambodian children to add to the eight he already had. He was badly wounded by Khmer Rouge soldiers in 1989 but continued working until his death in 2000 (e-mail, Bill McDonald, 27 December 2017).

34 He was a descendant of Peter Pond, for whom he named his son.

35 Laura Burns, private (now University of Toronto Archives).

36 These formed the basis for *Five Fur Traders of the Northwest*, edited by Charles Gates (Gates 1933).

37 William Stewart Wallace (1884–1970) was educated at the University of Toronto (BA 1906) and Oxford University (BA 1909, MA 1912). He joined the faculty at McMaster University in 1909 and then the staff at the University of Toronto in 1920. While at McMaster he was a lecturer in history and assistant in Greek. During World War I he served as a major in the Canadian Expeditionary Force, battalion adjutant, and commanding officer of Khaki College at Shorncliffe. In his capacity as librarian at the University of Toronto, he worked closely with Innis. He was also a notable historian in his own right, authoring numerous books and articles, including some related to the fur trade.

38 Innis may have been gesturing to the massive history of Western Canada written by Arthur S. Morton for which he had served as a consultant (Morton 1938).

39 In 1955 the young Peter Pond mentioned by Florence Cannon in her 1935 letter to Harold Innis (now a grown man) came to Prince Albert, Saskatchewan, to unveil the plaque at Fort Sturgeon commemorating his namesake ancestor (*Prince Albert Herald* 1955).

3

R. Harvey Fleming Material

Harold Innis, R. Harvey Fleming, and the North American Fur Trade

In a letter from Harold Innis to Florence Atherton Pond Cannon of 15 September 1932[1] he noted that one of his students (R. Harvey Fleming) was "planning to publish documents relating to Pond's business in the December [1932] number of *Minnesota History*."[2] While the publication did not appear as planned, a number of drafts of an article by Fleming entitled "Trading Ventures of Peter Pond in Minnesota" can be found among the Peter Pond papers at the Minnesota Historical Society (Minnesota Historical Society 1996). They were accompanied by transcripts that Fleming made of various business records related to Pond that he had found in the Williams Papers at the Burton Historical Collection of the Detroit Public Library and at the Porteous Papers at the Buffalo Historical Society.[3] The article seems to be as an overview of the material in the transcripts, which he had carefully annotated. As evident in some of the marginalia, the material had gone through considerable copy-editing by the journal's editor, Bertha Lion Heilbron (1895–1972), with some assistance from Grace Lee Nute (1895–1990), an authority on the history of the colonial fur trade, a staff member of the Minnesota Historical Society, and a frequent contributor to *Minnesota History*.[4] It appears that the article was nearing completion, as Fleming had responded to numerous suggestions for revising it; few queries remained to be addressed.[5] For whatever reason, the article never saw the light of day, but the various drafts found their way into the archives of the Minnesota Historical Society, along with other material related to Peter Pond.[6]

It is noteworthy that Innis described the author, Fleming, as his student, even though the latter had completed his B.Comm. degree at the University of Toronto in 1925. This indicates that although Fleming was no longer a University of Toronto student, Innis continued to be his mentor, even though not in any official capacity. That Innis continued to take a close interest in Fleming's academic fortunes is evident in his correspondence regarding Fleming's deliberations about doing graduate work at Harvard and the University of Chicago in 1928.[7] For whatever reason, Fleming did not pursue graduate studies at either university that year. While it is not clear if he worked or studied in the subsequent period, he maintained his contact with Innis, accompanying him on a research visit to Newfoundland and Labrador by way of eastern Ontario, Quebec, and the Maritimes in 1930.[8] Innis obviously thought highly of Fleming's scholarship, as evident in his sending of one of his articles to a University of Toronto colleague.[9] Fleming finally entered graduate studies in the fall of 1932, enrolling in the Department of Economics at the University of Chicago, working with Innis's former mentor, Chester Wright.[10]

This close mentor–student relationship can be traced back to Fleming's stint in the Commerce and Finance program at the University of Toronto, which formed one of the three courses of undergraduate study (along with political science and economics) in the Department of Political Economy. Those who successfully completed this program would be awarded the Degree of Bachelor of Commerce (B.Comm.) within the Faculty of Arts at the University of Toronto.[11] The intent of the course, as described in the catalogue, was to "provide a training for business and commercial life in general and at the same time to prepare applicants for the consular service, trade commissionerships abroad, for the foreign representation of Canadian firms, for employment service etc., as well as for the statistical and employment departments of large business houses."[12]

However, judging by his graduation entry in the University of Toronto yearbook (*Torontoensis*) for 1924–25, Fleming was decidedly ill-suited to have a life as an erstwhile captain of industry, trade commissioner, or personnel maven. Rather than framing his entry in terms of his anticipated ascent in the world of business, he deployed the metaphor of a book's history to capture his emergent biography. Following the self-description – "I love to browse in a library" – he noted that his "Introduction" was

"Barrie," "Published" in "MDCCCXCIX" [1899]. His "Educational Preface" had been "Grimsby, Owen Sound" with his "First important chapter" – "Signaller C.E.F. '17–'19." Subsequently, he reported that he had "turned a new leaf and 'bound' for Varsity '21." In terms of "Circulation" he referred to "C.P.R.'s western lines" and "The Great Open Spaces." Included in his "Index of kindred subjects" were "billiards, musicales, debates, dances." The "Dedication" he provided was "Any Hudson Bay post." His "Bibliography" was made up of "Sessional papers; *Encyclopedia Britannica*." Finally, he enigmatically stated that his "Copyright" was "'Reserved.'"

Innis had likely come to know Fleming in his capacity as faculty sponsor of the Commerce Club and through his involvement in the student-run *Commerce Journal*. He also offered a fourth-year seminar course that was required by Commerce and Finance students – 4i. Special Subject: "The study of the fur trade on the North American continent and its effects on civilization." As described in the catalogue entry, "Attention will be given to the causes, extent, and character of its development. Special consideration will be given to technical demands of the fur trade, its organization and marketing peculiar to the various stages of its history. Further, an attempt will be made to estimate the effects of the trade on the development of economic institutions. The course will be conducted in such a way as to require independent work on the part of each student as a contribution to suggested problems."

However, the seminar represented much more than just another course to be taken by commerce and political science students to meet their requirements to graduate. Rather, it was seen as "the first of a series of studies dealing with the chief industries of Canada to be produced under the auspices of the Department of Political Science, Toronto University (*Times Literary Supplement* 1927). It was viewed of potential interest not only to the general public but to leaders of industry and to policymakers. To this end, Innis organized the seminar in such a way that the members of the seminar could collectively produce a coherent and wide-ranging body of work that could be made available to a wider audience. The class was "conducted largely as an experiment ... carried out by fourth-year men including all those in The Commerce course and three in the Political Science course." At the first class, Innis presented the seminar members with a list of subjects "divided chronologically and topically" from which they were to choose, undertaking "a separate and distinct piece of research." Underpinned by a stress on the "idea of unity" for the research projects in the seminar, "each reported the general conclusions of his study and out of the whole series of discussions certain broad conclusions emerged." At the end of the course, Innis submitted revised versions of the papers to the University of Toronto Department of Extension, which in turn produced "a memorandum on the contents of the course [which was] sent out to a selected mailing list including most of the trade journals, [making them] available to be borrowed for a two-week period free of charge." While he makes mention of a number of the partnership agreementin the examination determinism, "o the fur trade incific Coast. T[13] Their availability was not only announced in local media, but both Innis and the Department of Extension contacted parties that potentially would have an interest in the material.[14] As the director of Extension, W.J. Dunlop, noted to Innis, "The demand for loan of the theses is so great that we cannot begin to keep pace with it. All the theses, except the historical ones, are out all the time on loan and we have a waiting list of considerable proportions."[15] Since the response to the theses was quite enthusiastic, copies of the most popular of the theses were made and circulated. As Innis described the success of the venture to MacIver: "Several of the more important fur trade reviews and journals have published the conclusions of these theses [giving them] much wider publicity than would otherwise have been possible … [D]ue recognition has been given to the student and the University. Large numbers of government departments and private firms have made copies of their own for further references."[16]

Given the "success of the experiment," it was the hope of MacIver that "the investigation into the Fur Trade of Canada" as conducted in the department would signal "the beginning of a series of studies of Canadian industries." Specifically, he proposed that "every two years a member of the staff be assigned to make an investigation of a selected industry … [R]esearch material should be worked up with the assistance of Fourth year students in Commerce and possibly some graduates … put in the form of a convenient bulletin which shall be available to those interested." Pointing out that Innis had "expended at least three hundred dollars on his own account," and that "two copies each of the series of eight bulletins … were provided by the students at their own expense" with a "long waiting list," MacIver suggested that "a sum of a thousand dollars be allocated to this work."[17]

Promising as this "experiment" appeared to have been, neither the funding nor the series as a departmental initiative ever materialized. Shortly thereafter, MacIver, who had provided unstinting advocacy for the venture, left the department (and his chairmanship of it), to accept a position at Barnard College. The burgeoning Commerce and Finance course, which would have served as the principal source of the fourth-year students who were to conduct the research, was shifting its orientation away from teaching research skills towards an emphasis on applied training for success in the business world, a tendency strenuously resisted by Innis (Watson 2006, 140–3). Adding to Innis's growing dissatisfaction with the department was his chagrin at having a colleague promoted ahead of him (129–32).[18]

Hence, while the venture was initially grounded in the research efforts of the fourth-year students, it culminated in a publication that was largely based on Innis's research and analysis (Innis 1927b). All the same, by virtue of the seminar, the fourth-year students were able to engage in topic-based research projects that in some cases were circulated in published form,[19] and with others, provided the foundations for future research endeavours.

R. Harvey Fleming belonged to the latter category. He was among those who wrote his paper on a historical subject, namely the North American fur trade, 1763–1821. It is noteworthy that all eight historical theses had North America as their primary focus.[20] This suggests that his early interest in Canadian staples industries notwithstanding, Innis's frame of reference for the fur trade from the outset was very much a continental one. Fleming's thesis also provides some clues about the approach taken to the historical study of the fur trade in the seminar. While temporally he examined various periods within the 1763–1821 time frame, spatially he examined the fur trade in terms of four drainage basins, namely the St Lawrence/Mackenzie, Hudson Bay, Mississippi, and Pacific Coast. This corresponded closely to the framework that initially informed Innis's history of the Canadian Pacific Railway (1923) and later drawn upon in his second volume made up of selected documents in Canadian economic history (Innis and Lower 1933).

Yet in contrast to Innis's accounts, which did not include the Mississippi drainage system and only briefly addressed the Pacific Coast drainage system, that of Fleming was quite comprehensive, examining four drainage systems (albeit with different degrees of emphasis). The final examination question to be answered by "those working on Historical material" provides further insights into the historiographical position that informed the course (and that likely affected Fleming's perspective): "How far and why do you accept the hypothesis that the technical demands of an industry determines the institutions of the people engaged? Support your conclusion with references to the history of the fur trade in North America in general, giving detailed evidence from your study of a particular period."[21] Assuming that the examination-writer did not subscribe to a form of technological determinism, this question would allow him or her to explore to what extent the institutions and practices of the fur trade were based on the initiatives of particular individuals.

In Fleming's first published article (1928), which appeared in the "Notes and Comments" section of the *Canadian Historical Review*,[22] he examined the extent to which individual initiative played a role in the organization of the early fur trade. In this case, the institution in question was the co-partnership arrangement agreed to by various leading figures of the fur trade in 1803 "in opposition to the North West Company" (137). While he makes mention of a number of the partners involved in the agreement (including William Parker, Samuel Gerrard, and John Ogilvie), he felt it was "essential to recognize in Sir Alexander Mackenzie the central personality throughout the whole development" (137). In effect, Fleming sought to go beyond "three recent publications" on him, which had focused primarily on Mackenzie, the explorer.[23] Fleming, rather, wished to focus on Mackenzie as a fur trader, with particular reference to his "widespread duties as agent" (140). To this end, he addressed the strategies used by Mackenzie to improve the efficacy of the emerging partnership, which included "sound organization, active leadership, and the use of considerable capital" (140). He gave particular attention to the role played by Mackenzie in drafting and putting in place the 1803 partnership agreement. His primary point of reference was "the three known agreements of the North West Company," including the one of 1790 discussed by Innis (1927c).[24] Fleming found the spatial-temporal aspects of the agreement to be particular striking, as it allowed for the coordination of activities with widely dispersed individuals over sustained periods: "The men intimately associated with, and thoroughly experienced in, the various branches of the fur trade, could be widely distributed, and could be held responsible for their particular share of the activities of the whole" (1928, 137). Fleming was very impressed by how Mackenzie was able to help Forsyth, Richardson to avoid oblivion, because he "was experienced in all phases of the fur trade ... knew the secret of the success of the North West Company [and] was competent to build, upon similar principles, an organization in co-partnership form which would link together the two widely separated but vital points of the trade, the contact with the Indians, and the combination of interests centred at Montreal" (141). Eventually, "because of his special knowledge of the Athabaska region, and of the affairs of the North West Company in general," Mackenzie was to play a leading role in building "a coalition of the two North West Companies" (Fleming 1928, 146–7). He was also intrigued by how Mackenzie was able to unite the opposing factions while still reorganizing "the quarter interest obtained in the North West Company into a more compact unit under the name of 'Sir Alexander Mackenzie and Company' – a company which continued to function until the union of the North West Company with the Hudson's Bay Company in 1821" (147).

Fleming's second article, which appeared the following year in the *Canadian Historical Review* (again in the Notes and Comments section), examined a different fur-trade partnership, namely that of McTavish and Frobisher. This entity formed in 1787 within the North West Company as an agent taking care of some of the organization's major operations. Rather than exploring the agency of a particular individual (such as Mackenzie), Fleming explored the other side of the equation in Innis's examination question – the extent to which the institutions of the fur trade were determined. Of particular interest to him was the how the North West Company emerged as "an association of the various partnerships which had developed between the Montreal merchants and the traders at Grand Portage, the rendezvous on Lake Superior" (1929, 136). He gave particular attention to the formation of the partnership between McTavish and Frobisher following the death of Benjamin Frobisher in 1787.

While Fleming traced how McTavish and Frobisher were able to work out an arrangement, his account emphasized the degree to which the exigencies of conducting the fur trade constrained their activities. These included "importing goods and liquors, arranging credit, preparing the goods for shipment in the canoes or bateaux, superintending the shipment to Grand Portage, attending the annual meeting, transporting the furs and other returns to Montreal, sorting, packing, beating and storing the furs there, and, finally, shipping the furs to London for the annual sales." Moreover, "the firm ... was responsible for the accounts of each yearly outfit ... and also acted as bankers for the surplus funds of the share holders on which they paid 5 per cent interest" (Fleming 1929, 140). In order to cope with mounting structural problems, including "keen competition in buying supplies and in trading with the Indian," increasing transportation costs, the financing of credit, and the creation of a "steadier market for the sale of furs," Fleming stressed how the organization moved towards "greater central control." This also involved "keeping a controlling number of shares" and limiting membership "to fur-traders experienced in the trade of the North-west" (141). "The co-partnership of McTavish, Frobisher and Company ... expired on November 30, 1806," superseded by a new company bearing the name "McTavish, McGillivrays and Company." However, the earlier firm had left its imprint: "There continued to function an organization which had been developing both a technique and institutions capable of meeting the peculiar difficulties of marketing furs – a commodity which was continually being exhausted in old areas and which continually required new sources of supply" (Fleming 1929, 144).

Fleming's next article (1932) departed from the Notes and Commentary format of his first two. While it had a brief appendix, the sources he used were for the most part woven into body of the text. Focusing on the Schenectady-based firm of Phyn and Ellice, it appeared in the University of Toronto–based *Contributions to Canadian Economics*, receiving a glowing introduction in the introductory notes to the issue:

We are fortunate in being able to publish ... a very suggestive article by Mr. R.H. Fleming on Phyn Ellice and Company of Schenectady. The latter traces the history of the Northwest Company back to one of its main roots, and, along with other articles by the same author, contributes much to the solution of the difficult problem of unravelling the history of this important and complex organization. It is particularly important in showing the place of the St. Lawrence in the development of business organization in North America, the significance of London as a trade centre, and the conditions that gave rise to the peculiar elastic structure of Northwest Company organization. Only by work of this nature can we hope to build up our knowledge of the peculiarities of Canadian business structure. (1932a, 5–6)[25]

In contrast to his previous two articles, Fleming's discussion of Phyn and Ellice examined institutions and agency in more or less equal measure. Moreover, rather than offering a close reading of a specific document as a prelude to the material in question, he was now painting on a much broader canvas, examining how the middleman firm mediated between suppliers, financiers, and administrators located in Montreal, New York, and London in relation to the far-flung fur-trade empire of the North West Company. Unlike his previous two articles that largely examined the institutions and practices in positive terms, his discussion of Phyn and Ellice and its successors explored both the peaks and valleys of their operations. This involved an intricate analysis of how the business practices of Phyn and Ellice evolved in relation to the shifting geopolitical circumstances. He saw the firm as typical of the "small commercial middleman" operating simultaneously on two fronts. On the one hand, it supplied goods in the Northwest through various modes of operation, including direct trading with aboriginal peoples, selling to middlemen, or furnishing the government – centred in the military posts – with strategic materials. With the lifting of restrictions and the opening up of trade, this business was becoming quite lucrative. On the other hand, it was dependent on mercantile interests in New York and London for its trade supplies, as well as marketing and credit. These relationships were fraught with difficulties, particularly those stemming from the efforts made by the firm to have their earlier debts liquidated. These challenges were compounded by an increasingly unfavourable business environment. The American colonies had begun to revolt, putting measures in place to restrict British trading practices through non-importation rules. In addition, Montreal was emerging as a major centre for the conduct of the fur trade, aided in part because the St Lawrence–Ottawa River route to the rich trading area of the Northwest had decided advantages over the Hudson–Mohawk–Lake Ontario route emanating from Albany and Schenectady. Fleming deftly examines how and to what extent the firm's difficulties with New York– and London-based economic interests – along with the growing threat posed by Montreal-based traders – led it to explore a bewildering variety of initiatives, including bolstering its trading fleet, importing via Quebec, modifying the partnership in order to limit risk, entering into the grain business, and even cooperating with its rivals. Ultimately, however, as Fleming argues, because of the innumerable impediments, doing business from Schenectady proved to be untenable; Phyn and Ellice shifted its base of operations to Montreal.[26] However, there was more to Fleming's analysis than simply charting the rise, decline, and rebirth of Phyn and Ellice attendant upon its efforts to survive in a hostile and unpredictable business environment. He was also examining the extent to which the redoubtable Montreal-based North West Company actually had its origins in a firm based in the American colonies. What made this possible, as the note accompanying it suggests, was the "peculiar elastic structure" most evident in the shifting groupings of partnerships, which became a central characteristic of the North West Company.[27]

The manuscript that Fleming submitted to *Minnesota History* in the latter part of 1932 was based on a similar premise. In this case, he suggested that it was only by virtue of having honed his skills on the upper Mississippi region that Peter Pond was able to flourish as a fur trader and adventurer in the area northwest of the Great Lakes. He also demonstrated his continuing interest in the operations of various fur-trade enterprises (1928, 1929, 1932). However, rather than examining in detail the workings of particular partnerships, he turned his attention to Pond's day-to-day activities as a fur trader on the upper Mississippi. To some extent at least, following in Innis's footsteps, Fleming sought to demonstrate how Pond's work regime revealed his organizational skills and business acumen, thereby offsetting his rather unsavoury reputation, at least to some extent.

He indicated at the outset that he wished to clarify the "puzzle" or "enigma" of Pond as someone recognized by commentators for his contributions to exploration and mapmaking, yet dogged by accusations that he had committed murder on at least one occasion.[28] Echoing Innis's efforts to redeem Pond's reputation, Fleming appeared to believe that by underscoring Pond's accomplishments, he could counter the widespread biases that had pervaded accounts of his life and career. This involved presenting evidence of Pond's financial wherewithal, his ability to work collectively, his knowledge of trading goods, his ability to prepare, and the extent to which he was able to work effectively with both partners and his employees. He also gave attention to how Pond prepared for his journey with Booty Greves to the rich fur-trade territory north of the Great Lakes, based on an item that he believed to be "the first document after the Conquest of Canada by the British to give the details of an adventure to the Northwest" (Fleming, this volume). It is likely because of Fleming's insights into how Pond's upper-Mississippi experience set the stage for his eventual movement to the Canadian Northwest that Innis appeared to view the draft article as an extension of his own line of argument.

Fleming's manuscript, which combined an interpretive essay with a collection of annotated documents, was very much in line with the historians' craft of the day, as evident not only in Innis's work but that of many of his colleagues (Shortt 1925–6; Wallace 1934; Tyrrell 1934; Gates 1933; Nute 1933). It also mirrored the ongoing publication series of the Champlain Society (e.g., Wallace 1934). Fleming's submission represented something of a departure for him. His B.Comm. thesis at the University of Toronto examined the early North American fur trade in general. Two articles that he published in the "Notes" section of the *Canadian Historical Review* (1928, 1929) dealt primarily with the business arrangements of partnerships related to the North West Company. Hence his focus on Pond's activities in the fur trade from 1773 to 1775 took him in a new direction; the industry during this period was still quite inchoate and lacking in the organizational structure that would develop later.

By transcribing the fur-trade ledgers and accounts, Fleming was able to make this material much more accessible to researchers (even though the fruits of his labour have remained largely undetected in the Minnesota Historical Society Archives). His annotations, consisting of numerous notes, provide insights into what the documents tell us about the travels and activities of Pond and his partners, the division of labour in Pond's various ventures, as well as how he went about selecting items for his canoe brigades. His brief introduction, drawing on Innis's biographical work on Pond, outlines the extent to which the fur-trade ledgers and accounts shed light on some of the key issues that his mentor sought to address.

Moreover, as Fleming suggested, the spatial-temporal circumstances of the documents were crucial to a better understanding of the trajectory and timing of the continental fur trade – as explored by Harold Innis. Pond and his partners, while still operating in the upper Mississippi, were about to relocate to the Canadian Northwest, as part of an exodus of traders who saw great possibilities in doing business in what had become British-controlled territory. The particular period of the documents (1773–75) was just prior to Pond (in partnership with Booty Greves), undertaking what he described as the "adventure" to the Northwest (Fleming 1932b, 12). For Fleming, the transcripts – by virtue of their specific references to time, place, and organizational arrangements – made it possible to determine with greater precision not only the movements of Pond and his partners during the period in question, but also the nature of the shifting and intersecting alliances. In doing so, he was finding another piece in the puzzle that Innis had been working on for the previous five years, namely the overall arc of Pond's travels as he slowly made his way from the Michigan/Wisconsin and upper Mississippi regions to the Athabasca territory (1928b).[29] Drawing on all documents he could find, as well as on-site research, Innis had already begun to chart Pond's movement from Fort Dauphin (near Lake Winnipeg) to Fort Sturgeon (on the North Saskatchewan), through to the fort he established on the Athabasca River. The material unearthed and transcribed by Fleming filled in the picture by shedding light on Pond's movements and activities before he embarked on his adventure to the Northwest.[30] In doing so, he was able to confirm and amplify many of Innis's observations. It was not surprising that Innis promised to provide Mrs Cannon with an offprint of Fleming's article that was scheduled to be published in *Minnesota History*.

It is not clear to what extent Innis had encouraged Fleming to do work with the American archival documents, annotating them as part of an article on Pond's fur-trading activities in the Great Lakes and upper Mississippi valley regions. Fleming was aware that Innis had discovered and partially made use of the documents, as evident in the latter's discussion of them in the bibliography to his Pond biography (Fleming, n3, this volume). As Innis noted, this commentary was written after the main text had gone to press (in the fall of 1930). He also revealed that "Mr. R.H. Fleming has ... copied for me one or two documents in the Phyn Ellice papers in the Buffalo Historical Society Library" (Innis and Pond 1930, 150). Innis referred to one of these, "a letter dated November 17, 1771," which included a statement about various transactions involving Pond, Felix

Graham, and Thomas Williams. Innis was able to conclude from this document that "Pond was in partnership with Graham in 1771 and that the partnership of 1773 was simply a renewal" (150).[31] Innis gave considerably more attention to "various accounts and memoranda in the Williams Papers related to Peter Pond," discovered by the Detroit Public Library, which had drawn Innis's attention to these items. Innis made a link between this material and the documents in the Buffalo Museum Library, referring to a number of the documents discussed by Fleming. The invoice of 30 June 1773 revealed in detail "the goods belonging to the [Innis-Graham] partnership." According to Innis, the document dated 20 December 1773 (describing goods left with "Mr. Boban"), which included "three bales of goods," possibly referred to "his French competitor but was more probably his clerk" (150–1).[32] Innis noted that a related document (the invoice of 3 July 1774) described "the returns for this venture [1773–4] ... including 31 packs" (151). As Innis attested, this information corroborated Pond's remarks included by him in his biography: "'I had dun so well that I proposed to bye him out and take it on myself. He excepted and I paid of the first cargo'" (45).

Innis was interested in what the ledger entries said about the trajectory of Pond's fur-trade ventures in the Michigan/Wisconsin and upper Mississippi regions. He observed that "the partnership with Graham was brought to an end," and an account beginning 28 July 1774 is headed "Leidger [sic] Pond and Williams 1774–75."[33] Innis called attention to a document within this collection – Dr Peter Pond – which Fleming had copied, transcribed, and partially annotated. He observed that the document showed "Peter Pond Dr. June 22 and July 3rd for the outfit probably taken to the Northwest," connecting this bit of information to the narrative of Pond's movements that he had described in his Pond biography.[34] Anticipating Fleming's reading of the document, he noted that Pond's outfit for the journey included "a beaver hat bought on June 14, 1775, and a small red trunk" (Innis and Pond 1930, 152). Innis also examined the memorandum of the goods received from Jacques Chénier (noting the amount and Pond's signature), judging that it provided "an indication of the extent of the trade in the Mississippi" (151). Along the same lines, he called attention to the "furs acquired in the venture of 1774–5 ... in the ledger under date June 22, 1775" (151).[35] He found further clarification in a document of 16 July 1775 itemizing "goods debts and notes" for Pond and Williams, which provided "an inventory of the latter's possessions" (152).[36] Like Fleming, Innis made reference to the amount of grease that had been delivered to Alexander Henry prior to his voyage north as recorded in the Askin papers.[37]

Innis gave a good deal of attention to the document "dated Grand Portage 22nd July, 1775" itemizing the "adventure to the Northwest" of Pond and Graves (found in the Porteous papers in the Buffalo Historical Society Library).[38] He was struck by the fact that it included "6 new canoes – probably 2 large ones brought to the Portage and 4 small ones taken to the North" (Innis and Pond 1930, 152). Overall, Innis was of the view that "these documents serve to render more certain and accurate the discussion of the events in the period 1775 to 1778" (152). He added that with the revelation that the "firm of McBeath, Pond, and Greves was granted a license to Grand Portage in 1781" (covered in his account in the pages following p. 82 of his biography) "should probably be corrected accordingly" (152–3).[39]

Given that the Pond material in the Minnesota Historical Society was still in a draft state when it was discovered, we were obliged to distill its various parts to create a more coherent document. The text for the initial interpretive section of the draft essay was largely retained in its original form. However, for the material that he cited, notations consistent with the format of the rest of the volume was added (author and date within the text), with the full source included in the references at the end of the entire collection. In addition, since Fleming used the Thwaites volume as his source for the Pond memoir, we have provided the page numbers where all the citations can be found in Innis's Pond biography (Innis and Pond 1930, pp. 47–129 in this volume). This will allow readers to situate Fleming's citations from the archival documents in relation to Innis's biographical narrative of Pond's life. For each of the endnotes that serve exclusively to annotate the archival documents (nn6–29), we have included an excerpt of Fleming's transcribed rendition of it, in which form and spelling have been corrected. Fleming's own annotative notes have largely been retained, albeit with the addition of an occasional elaboration or clarification. For the most part, we have not reproduced entire documents, but rather excerpts from them pertinent to the endnote in question.

The exceptions are a reproduction of "Memorandum of Goods Rec[ei]ved from M[r] Shaney [Jacques Chénier]," La Baye, 22 May 1775 (written and signed by Pond), and a transcription of "Adventure to the N. W p Mess[rs] Pond & Greves," Grand Portage, 22 July 1775. The former was included because it is a rare example of Pond's writing and because it reveals insights into Pond's relationships with his clerks. The latter is of interest for its detailed portrayal of how Pond and Greves prepared for their "adventure" to the Northwest. While the invoices vary a great deal in format, they can be seen as variations of a general template, with similar elements present in different degrees. The core was a list of items, indicating the number of them in question. This was followed by a column providing the unit value for each. The next three columns showed the total value of each item in pounds, shillings, and pence. The more extensive lists included the dates for the transaction in the first column and the summation of costs in a final column (or three columns).[40]

It is beyond the scope of this introduction to analyze the form of the documents in any detail. But in examining them one should keep in mind that they not only provided an extensive record of a particular organization's financial transactions, but also were likely intended to be circulated among partners as well as business associates.[41] As such, each document served the dual function of depicting the organization's business activities with clarity and detail while conveying to its readers a positive and flattering image of the association in question. This perhaps accounts for the tendency to feature the names of the partners in large florid script at the top of the first page followed by a chronological listing of the organization's transactions in neat columns, often containing cross-referenced material. In some instances, as with the document outlining the items accompanying the "adventure" of Pond and Greves to the Northwest, the phrasing of the document's heading could be quite hyperbolic.

As Fleming suggested in his annotations, the lists in the ledgers and accounts went well beyond simply describing the provisions for trading furs and the kinds of furs that were acquired during trading ventures. What is particularly notable about Fleming's manuscript is the attention that he gave to the details of the provisions that were assembled for the various expeditions and activities undertaken by Pond and his partners. Provisions go well beyond the goods that were exchanged for furs, which have been so evocatively chronicled by commentators (e.g., Ray and Freeman 1978); they refer to the whole array of objects that were crammed into canoes prior to an expedition. They included not only items for trade, but also foodstuffs, tools for hunting and fishing, cooking utensils, equipment for repair and maintenance, various "notes" to be conveyed to particular parties, as well as items for personal health, hygiene, and apparel.[42] For the most part, provisions were anticipatory, drawing on one's knowledge and experience in order to prepare for long and demanding journeys into what was more often than not unfamiliar territory.

In the case of Pond, the provisions he decided upon for his various fur-trade ventures speaks to the skills he had acquired in negotiating wilderness travel under a broader range of circumstances. Each trip, however, had its own particularity as rooted in the number of canoes that were to be outfitted, the anticipated length of the journey, its destination, the season, and its broader purposes. In this regard, the preparations he made for his "adventure" to the Northwest with Booty Greves is particularly revealing, particularly for what it said about his personal tastes and preoccupations. Fleming noted that the purchases listed in the ledger account for "Dr. Peter Pond" in 1775 were of interest because at this point he was "preparing for his journey to the Northwest." While Fleming did not elaborate on what purchases he had in mind, what seems to distinguish this ledger from the others is the presence of a number of items that fell in the category of personal apparel, including a pair of trousers, a calico waistcoat, a blanket coat, a beaver hat, a small red trunk, as well as the cost for deploying a "wash woman" and a barber. The fact that the objects were primarily singular suggests that they were not intended for trade but rather for Pond's personal use. This is borne out by Fleming's judgment that the inclusion of the beaver hat was reflective of Pond's desire to have a good appearance.[43] The inclusion of the costs for a "wash woman"[44] and a barber indicated that Pond was preparing for a sustained encounter with what he considered to be civilization, which would involve being appropriately groomed and attired. All of these items (with the exception of the beaver hat) were listed in the inventory of goods that accompanied Pond and Greves on their journey to the Northwest in 1775. Additional clothing items for personal use (or perhaps trade) included two pairs of shoes, three pairs of trousers, a

Innis, Fleming, and the North American Fur Trade

spotted jacket, a calico jacket, a dozen red night caps, and forty-eight linen shirts. One can reasonably conclude that Pond had a certain flair for style and fashion, belying the usual claims that he was a rather rough-hewn frontiersman who was uncomfortable in civilized urban settings.[45] The "small red trunk" mentioned in the earlier document might have been listed as "Mr. Pond's chest," which contained mostly medicinal[46] and culinary objects.[47] It is not clear to what extent these items were to be used only by Pond or if they were available to other members of the brigade. If the latter were the case, this would suggest that two of Pond's major duties were to administer to the health needs of his employees and to stockpile material for the preparation of meals. In any event, they do suggest that Pond had a strong interest in both the arts of healing and nutrition, adding to the list of his organizational and administrative capacities identified by Harold Innis. By transcribing and annotating the largely overlooked fur-trade documents pertaining to Peter Pond – shedding further light on his character, taste, and activities – Fleming has made the "elusive Mr. Pond" somewhat less chimerical.

NOTES

1 Harold A. Innis to Florence A. Cannon, 15 September 1932. Florence Cannon correspondence, formerly in private collection of Catherine Burns (now in the Harold Innis Papers, University of Toronto Archives). See appendix A, this collection, p. oo.

2 Born in 1899 in Barrie, Ontario, Robert Harvey Fleming grew up in Owen Sound and Grimsby. After serving as a signaller in the Canadian Overseas Expeditionary Force from 1917 to 1919, he enrolled in the Commerce and Finance course at the University of Toronto, graduating with a B.Comm. degree in 1925. Little detail about his subsequent biography is available. He enrolled at the University of Chicago as a postgraduate student in 1932, but there is no evidence that he graduated with a degree. He is listed as a member of the staff at the University of Toronto for 1936, and for 1937–38 he appeared to have been employed as an assistant in that university's Department of Political Economy. From 1938 to at least 1940 he resided in London, U.K., where he served as an assistant to Professor E.E. Rich,

who had been appointed to edit the newly created Hudson's Bay Record Society series, which had been mandated to publish material from the Hudson's Bay Company archives (Schooling 1920; Rich 1938; Clark 1938; Davenport and Rylance 1980; Simmons 1996, 2007). After having served as assistant editor on the first two volumes of the series (Simpson, Rich, and Martin 1938; Robertson, Fleming, and Rich 1939), he was appointed editor of the third volume (Rich, Fleming, and Innis 1940), for which Innis wrote the introduction (1940a). This text was highly regarded by reviewers (e.g. *Free Press* 1940; Barker 1941; Nute 1941; Fay 1942; Sage 1942; W.P.M. 1942), as were the first two volumes, to which Fleming had contributed his considerable expertise on the history of the fur trade (e.g., Sage 1939; Innis 1940b). Later in the decade he returned to the University of Toronto, serving as a lecturer in the Department of Political Economy from 1946–47 through to 1951–52, and as a special lecturer in the same department in 1952–53. He died in 1983 and was buried alongside his father, Robert Harvey Fleming (1859–1940), his mother, Ada Sitzer Fleming (1866–1935), and sister (Eva Fleming (1893–1980) in the Pine Hills Cemetery, Scarborough, Ontario.

3 Fleming may have come across this material while preparing his article on Phyn and Ellice (1932a), which appeared in the same year as he submitted the Pond manuscript.

4 There is evidence that Ms Nute had some familiarity with ongoing research in Canada. See, for instance, #42, Grace Lee Nute, *Report of Field Trip to the Public Archives of Canada and the State Historical Society of Wisconsin, September 26, 1932,* 10 pp., typed. Grace Lee Nute Papers, Manuscripts Collection, Minnesota Historical Society.

5 According to a note following the first draft of the manuscript, Fleming had corresponded with "Miss Heilbron" on 14 July, 7 December, and 12 December 1932.

6 These include a copy of Peter Pond's narrative (accession no. 4007, negative photostat, 34 pages), which "was received in 1935, made from a photostatic copy held by the University of Toronto (Ontario, Canada) Library." Innis originally had arranged to have the photostat of the original made by Mrs Cannon. He then deposited it in the University of Toronto Library. Subsequently, the Minnesota Historical Society requested that a further copy be made of it.

Innis, Fleming, and the North American Fur Trade 193

7 Chester Wright to Harold Innis, 1 March 1928. UTA, DPE, A76-0025, box 4, file 1. Wright had been in touch with Fleming about applying. He informed Innis that "if Fleming wants to carry on his study of the fur trade ... the Newberry Library has a lot of material. I believe nearly 3000 transcripts from the library of the Hudson's Bay Company." Harold Innis to N.S.B. Gras, professor of business history, Graduate School of Business Administration, Harvard University, 23 March 1928. UTA, DPE, A76-0025, box 4, file 1. In this case Innis was responding to a letter from Gras in which the latter had made suggestions about Fleming's possibly enrolling as a graduate student at Harvard.

8 The initial part of the trip (to Sydney, Nova Scotia) was by automobile, with Fleming driving (Innis was unable to drive). The trip was not without its contretemps. Innis noted that both of them had been intermittently ill, and "after running the car into a ditch and being pulled out by a bootlegger we slept beside an old deserted house." Harold Innis, Metapedia [Matapedia] Valley, to Mary Quayle Innis, 14 June 1930, HUA, DPE, B72-0003, box 4, file 17. In his preface to *The Cod Fisheries*, Innis expressed his gratitude to "Mr. R. H. Fleming [who] at much personal sacrifice accompanied me on trips along the North Shore of the St. Lawrence, through the Gaspé Peninsula, and from St. John's to the Labrador" (1940b, xv). Fleming also read the entire manuscript for the volume.

9 De Glazebrooke to Innis, 14 June 1931. UTA, DPE, A76-0025, box 4, file 2. Fleming brought Innis up to date about his activities in the early days of the fall quarter at the University of Chicago (9 October 1932, UTA, DPE, A76-0025, box 4, file 13). On 7 December 1932 he wrote to Innis again, describing his project on "the wholesale history of Chicago" and "his paper for [John] Nef on the felt hat trade in the 16th and 17th centuries" (UTA, DPE, A76-0025, box 4, file 13).

10 That Fleming was having some difficulties in his program is evident in the remarks that Wright made about him in a letter to Innis the following year: As regards Fleming I am still somewhat uncertain. In his classes his work seems to have been about average. He took hold of his research with interest and much energy and I think devoted more time to it than the contract called for. Yet despite my emphasis upon having the results written up by the close of the year I have not received them yet, so that text is lacking. As he frequently complained of feeling bewildered or lost in the

problem (and it is a very difficult one) I was especially anxious to get his results. I suspect part of the delay is due to his being over conscientious and thorough though he says writing is difficult for him. (Wright to Innis, 6 September 1933, UTA, DPE, A76-0025, box 5, file 2)

11 *University of Toronto Catalogue, 1924–25*, 321.

12 *University of Toronto Catalogue, 1924–25*, 321.

13 Harold Innis, "Memorandum on the Fur Trade for Professor MacIver," ca 1 September 1925, UTA, DPE, A76-0025, box 2, file 6.

14 Innis notified both domestic statistician Robert Coats and James H. Prichard, secretary, Canadian Silver Fox Breeders' Association, about the theses, suggesting that each organization provide material to be included with the theses in order to take advantage of the mailings. Harold Innis to James H. Prichard, 27 October 1925; Innis to Robert Coats, 17 November 1925, UTA, DPE, A76-0025, box 2, file 6.

15 W.J. Dunlop to Harold Innis, 16 July 1925, UTA, DPE, A76-0025, box 2, file 12.

16 Innis, "Memorandum on the Fur Trade for Professor MacIver."

17 Robert MacIver to Robert Falconer, 5 October 1925, UTA, DPE, A76-0025, box 2, file 6.

18 This led to his resignation (which he withdrew) in 1929, and his efforts to seek employment elsewhere, in both academia and the private sector.

19 These were Dougall (1925) and Keast (1925).

20 The other time periods covered were 1492–1627, 1627–63, 1663–1713, 1713–63, 1821–69, 1869–1900, 1901 to the present time. A number of these dates came to define the beginnings and ends of the periods covered by Innis in his history of the Canadian fur trade ([1930] 1956, 1), namely 1663, 1713, 1763, 1821, and 1869. It is instructive that Innis largely periodized the histories of the North American and the Canadian fur trade in the same way. This suggests that, even at the outset of his historical work on the fur trade, he viewed its development in Canada as inseparable from its broader North American context.

21 University of Toronto, Faculty of Arts, annual examinations, 1925, fourth year – honours.

22 It consisted of an interpretive essay, along with the entire text of "Articles of Agreement and Copartnership between Sir Alexander Mackenzie, William Parker, Samuel Gerrard, John Ogilvy, Thomas Yeoward, George

Innis, Fleming, and the North American Fur Trade 195

Gillespie, John Gillespie and John Mure," dated 24 October 1803. The original was "preserved in the archives of Montreal, notarial records, by M. Montarville B. de la Bruère" (Fleming 1928, 147).

23 These likely included Mackenzie (1927) reviewed by Innis (1927b).

24 See pp. 3–17 this volume.

25 Since the name of the journal's editor does not appear in the masthead, one cannot decisively state the author of this note. However, since Innis founded the journal in 1928, remained closely involved with it, and was familiar with Fleming's writings and the issues he was addressing, that he wrote the note was a strong possibility.

26 Fleming noted that "the business was continued under the firm of Forsyth, Richardson and Company, an organization which was to play a prominent part in the fur trade of Canada" (1932, 37). Innis ([1930] 1956) makes frequent mention of the key role played by the new company in the early days of the North West Company.

27 Further evidence that it was Innis who was responsible for the introductory note accompanying Fleming's article is evident in the following sentence that he wrote about the North West Company in *Fur Trade of Canada*: "The evolution of the Northwest Company after the amalgamation of 1787 illustrated the importance of an *elastic organization*" (Innis [1930] 1956, 249; emphasis mine).

28 While Fleming initially assumed that Pond was responsible for the death of Ross (1925, 50), he may have been swayed by Innis's claim that solid evidence for this was lacking (Pond and Innis 1930).

29 This explains why Innis was so excited to learn that Pond's Beaver Club medallion bore the date 1769, the year that he first wintered in the wilderness (at Michilimackinac). As he noted in a letter to Florence Cannon, "I have never heard of the medal before and I believe it throws new light on the Beaver Club and on Peter Pond's earlier life. The date 1769 suggests that he was in the Mississippi area at that time and enables us to fill in another difficult period of his biography." See Harold Innis to Florence Cannon, 15 September 1932 (appendix A, p. 162 this volume).

30 This involved two round-trip journeys between Michilimackinac and the upper Mississippi region, traversing the portage between the Mississippi and St Lawrence watersheds four times. This provided him with great familiarity with both the rich St Peter's river trading area and the bustling

straits of Mackinac region, as well as points in between Michilimackinac – most notably Prairie du Chien (on the Wisconsin river) – and La Baye (on the Fox River) (see Chapin 2004, 90–103; Gough 2014, 52–74).

31 Fleming did not address this material in his article.

32 Innis was able to recognize that the document had been written by Pond (Innis and Pond 1930, 150–1). The fur trader in question may have been Eustache Trottier Beaubien (1726–1799).

33 He related this document to what he had written in his Pond biography: "Pond had arrived at Michilimacinac, had disposed of his cargo and was immediately engaged in acquiring a new outfit: 'I apleyd myself closely to ward fiting out a cargo for the same part of the country'" (Innis and Pond 1930, 47; p. 73 this volume).

34 Innis remarked that because of his "inherent restlessness" Pond wished to "see new country." Since "the Mississippi had little more to offer the trader … he bought a new cargo at Mackinac, hired his men, and started for Sault Ste Marie, the north shore of Lake Superior and Grand Portage" (Pond and Innis 1930, 69).

35 While Fleming had Photostated and transcribed this document, he did not provide any annotations for it. Innis appeared to believe that this account confirmed his view that "trade with the Plains Indians brought small supplies of such fine furs as otter and beaver," which compared unfavourably with "the finer quality of furs obtained in the north" (Pond and Innis 1930, 67; p. 84 this volume).

36 While Fleming had the document Photostated and made a transcription of it, he did not refer to it in his article.

37 He called attention to the fact that Henry had "left the Sault June 10th but according to the Askin papers 202 lbs. of grease were delivered to him June 15th" (Pond and Innis 1930, 152). Innis compared the timing of the Pond and the Henry expeditions in his Pond biography (69). Fleming also addressed the amount of grease delivered to Henry, comparing this to that used by Frobisher (Fleming 1932b, n28).

38 Consistent with his interest in the details of fur-trading ventures, he observed that "the firm of Pond and Greves was apparently a subsidiary of Pond and Williams" (Pond and Innis 1930, 152; p. 126 this volume).

39 Reflecting his concern to contribute to future fur-trade scholarship, Innis

noted that "the photostated documents may be consulted in the University of Toronto library" (Pond and Innis 1930, 152–3; pp. 127–8 this volume).

40 I am grateful to Professor Arthur Ray for his assistance in helping me understand the format of the invoices and ledgers.

41 Of particular importance to all concerned was the cost for each item. This was expressed in the British currency of the day in three consecutive numbers representing pounds, shillings, and pennies. The conversion table for them is as follows:

12 pennies (d.) = 1 shilling (s.)

20 shillings = 1 pound

42 Fleming was rounding out the detailed and nuanced accounts of provisions that Innis had written in his magisterial history of the Canadian fur trade ([1930] 1956). Innis, for the most part, simply listed the provisions that were carried in the canoes of particular brigades with little commentary about how they were selected or what they signified. His examples were largely taken from the post-1785 period, a time when the fur trade was becoming increasingly institutionalized. Hence, he tended to dwell more upon broader economies of transport rather than the more specific decisions made about the mix of goods that should be transported (219).

43 See Fleming, "Trading Ventures of Peter Pond in Minnesota," n25.

44 Most likely equivalent to a "washerwoman" or laundress.

45 Pond's evident concern with appearance and style is in line with Chapin's judgment that in his later years Pond was "something of a dandy ... dressed in what his granddaughter thought was the garb of a prince" (Chapin 2014, 311).

46 These included eighteenth-century medical staples such as brimstone (sulphur), purges, vomits, salves, Turlington's, peppermint water, Hungary water, Spanish flies, Diachytum, healing salves, allum, vitriol, and sassafras.

47 These included cinnamon, cloves, white sugar, beef, and shrub (a beverage made from fruit juice, sugar, and a liquor).

R. Harvey Fleming, "Trading Ventures of Peter Pond in Minnesota"

Fresh evidence is required in the attempt to reconcile differing viewpoints of history. Studies of Peter Pond, the geographer and explorer, have resulted in a "Peter Pond puzzle" or a description of him as "mapmaker and murderer ... the most enigmatical of all the fur adventurers of the West."[1] A study of Peter Pond as fur-trader and adventurer reveals that "to him belongs the honour of having solved the problem of conducting trade over such long distances and of organizing the Athabasca department which was crucial to the development of the Northwest Company and to the prosecution of further exploration." "Indeed without his organization of the trade of Athabasca, the later voyages of Mackenzie would not have been accomplished at such an early date." The above estimate of Peter Pond places emphasis on his trading proclivities; the importance of his discoveries to the extension of geographic knowledge are revealed in the statement that "the map of 1785 is the most enduring testimony of Pond's contribution to the geography of North America."[2]

In order to confirm the value of this economic approach to historical research, part of the accounting records for the years 1773–75 of Pond's trading ventures from Michilimackinac to the St. Peter's or Minnesota River are submitted herewith.* These documents parallel and corroborate

---

"Fur Trade Accounts, 1773–1775," Peter Pond Papers, accession no. 3551, Minnesota Historical Society. Originals in John R. Williams Papers, Burton Historical Collection, Detroit (Michigan) Public Library.

* Editor's note: a few from later dates (e.g., 1777) were included as well.

"Trading Ventures of Peter Pond in Minnesota" 199

Pond's well-known narrative journal, which was preserved at first as only a curious example of orthography and later carefully edited by Rueben G. Thwaites for its information concerning trade routes in Wisconsin.[3] The merging of the accounting records and the descriptive journal makes more real the details of Pond's expeditions into the Minnesota country. The wide variety of the trading goods, their origins and prices are concisely stated; the names of the clerks and the dates of the arrival and the departure of the canoes are to be found in the documents. The kinds of furs obtained from the Indians, the number of packs, and the final selling prices are all set forth. Finally, the accounts record the commercial relationships that were gradually evolving and making possible continued penetration inland, until the commerce in furs covered the continent. The progress of national development has been the dominating theme of history; geographic environment has received elaborate attention; but the institutions of commerce remain obscure. It is from a study of business records that an insight may be gained into their evolution.

By the extension of the trade into the upper Mississippi Valley, Peter Pond was adding to the commercial organization existing in the fur trade. In 1773 he formed a partnership with Felix Graham, with whom he had already been in business at Detroit in 1771.[4] Graham furnished the capital for this partnership in the form of the equipment and the trade goods that were taken by him from Albany to Michilimackinac. He received in return the packs of furs to be sold in the various fur markets of New York or London. Pond, as always, furnished his experience in trading with the Indians and his organizing ability. The following year the partnership of Pond and Thomas Williams was formed, indicating another step in organization by which the high risks of trade were diminished. Williams, who provided only part of the capital, became the middleman in a restricted territory. He made his headquarters in Detroit and bought trade goods from merchants such as Graham. He also made arrangements for expeditions, kept the accounts, and transacted all business, making it possible for the trader to remain in contact with the actual Indian trade. The returns in furs were sold and profits divided.

In 1775 Pond made the most momentous decision of his fur-trading career when he determined to go to the Northwest. He was influenced by the accumulating evidence of the high profits to be gained from the finer quality of furs in that area. Definite information about the successful ventures of Finlay,* Curry,† and the Frobishers‡ was widely circulated, with the result that both Alexander Henry and Pond decided in the same year to penetrate into the Northwest. A partnership was formed by Pond and [Booty] Greves [or Graves] and from existing documents the fact is established that on July 22, 1775, Peter Pond's canoes and goods were over the Grand Portage and ready to advance into the territory that was to hold his interest for fourteen years.[5]

The partnerships of this early period were of a particularly transitory character, being arranged usually for each separate venture. In form they resembled a contract in which each party must fulfill certain obligations for a definite period. Pond continued this form of organization in the Northwest by a partnership with George McBeath, son-in-law of Felix Graham, in 1777, as indicated in the accounting records; and another of McBeath, Pond, and Greves was formed in 1781. The continued penetration inland until Pond reached the Athabasca brought a need for increased capital and consolidation of interests. It was only a step, but a very difficult one, to bring the competing partnerships within the scope of one organization. The most successful attempt in this direction was the formation of the Northwest Company in which Peter Pond was one of the early partners.

R. HARVEY FLEMING
University of Toronto
Toronto, Canada

---

* James Finlay (d. 1797).

† Thomas Curry, sometimes referred to as "Thomas Corry." (See Gough 2014, 79).

‡ Benjamin Frobisher (1742–1787), Joseph Frobisher (1740–1810), and Thomas Frobisher (1744–1788).

Documents 201

Documents

I(a) Invoice of Sundries received from Felix Graham, on account of the partnership of Graham and Pond, Michilimackenac, 30th June 1773[6]

			[£ s d] [pounds, shillings, pence]
1 pˢ Blue Strowds	N 63	23 ½ yards	13 3 3

I(b)

... amount of Patterson & Kayˢ bill parcill [parcel]
dated the 8th May Qubeck [Québec] Curʸ £32 14 3 }
advance a 25 p Cent 7 18 6 ¾ 40 12 9 ¾[7]

I(c)

... Sundries received of Charles Patterson 19 15 1
2700 white wampum[8] 14/ 2 2

I(d)

... To Rapers ... To Cords ... To *Baling*[9] 1

I(e)

... To [freight] of 2½ [bateau] load from Schenectady @ £70 &
all [expenses].[10]

I(f)

... To 18 Gallons High wines	@ 3/11	3 11 6
To half the Barrel		2 6
To 6 Gallons rum	@ 8/ 6	2 11
To 8 Tongs	1/ 9	15 0
		8 11 11

£1244 13 11½[11]

John R. Williams Papers, Burton Historical Collection, Detroit Public Library, Felix Graham and Peter Pond fur trade accounts, 1773–75, showing quantities and qualities of goods Pond received from Graham and others, also peltries delivered.

II(a) Goods left with Mr Boban [Beaubien][12]
... N° 7 1 pes Blue Strouds

II(b)
... Decr 1773.[13]
By one [Keg] Rum [given] to Rock.
By 11150 [wampum] ...

III(a) Memorandum of Goods Rec[ei]ved from Mr Shaney [Jacques Chénier][14]

	[£ s d]	
Lea bay [La Baye]* 22 May 1775		
19 lb brass kettles	2	38
6 half axes	2 10	15
2 traps (one of them broken)	6	12
2 cotton shirts	5 10	11
white ditto mens	4 10	18
marten coats	7 10	15
blankets 3 points	6	30
ditto 2 ½ ditto	5	35
12 ½ ells strouds		60
7 ditto *calama*nco		10
2 bridles	3	6
11 long knives		4 5
peltries		
55 *martens*	30	82 10
3 otters	6	18

---

* In 1634, the French explorer Jean Nicolet gave the name *La Baie des Puants* (French for "the Bay of Stinking Waters") to the large arm of water on the west coast of Lake Michigan (in today's Wisconsin). A small settlement near the southern extremity of the bay became known as "La Baye" (or La Bey). By 1655 a fur-trading post had been established nearby. Later, however, British fur traders referred to the town as "Green Bay," because of the green tints in the bay's water during early spring. This name gradually replaced the old French title. However, at the time of Pond's visit, this settlement still went by the name "La Baye" (Chapin 2014, 92–3). Innis rendered it as "Le Bay" in his Pond biography (Innis and Pond 1930, 151).

Documents 203

182 doe skins	40	364
3 cats		
2 ditto }	30	7 10
25 raccoon	15	18 15
34 lbs good beaver	50	85
10½ bad ditto two for one		13 2 6
13½ *fishers*	40	27
30 *buckskins* 102		102
1 panther		12
1 raccoon		15
11 rats		2 15
7 bear		21
		1008 12 6

The above is a [true account] of all I could find as you have [in] accounts with you/ Be so good to [settle] with him. [He] has [also] a [north canoe] which you will be so good as to take on your [arrival] as he waits for you.

Wish [you] a good [passing] over [the lake].

[yours] &cc

[P.] Pond[15]

III(c)

...

34	
34	55
17	27.10
— —	
85	82.10
	182
182	
—	
	364[16]

Lea bay 22 may 1775

Memorandum of Goods Reaved from M.r Shaney —

19.a Brass Kettels	2 —	38
6 half axes	2.10.	15
2 Traps one of them Broke	6 —	12
2 Cotton Shirts	5.10	11
4 White do Mens	4.10	18
Macklon Cotes	7.10	15
Blankets 3 pts	6	30
ditto 2½ do	5	35
12½ Ells Strouds		60
7 do Collemince		10
2 Bridels 3		6
11 Longs Knives		4 " 5

Peltrye —

55 Martains	30	82.10
3 Otters	6	18
182 Doe Skins	40	364
3 Cots	30	7.10
2 Do	30	
25 Raccoons	15	18 .15
34.a Good Bever	50	85
10.a Bad do two for one		13 — 2 — 6
13½ Fishers	40	27
30 Bucks Skins 10½		10½
1 Panter		15
1 Raccoon		
11 Rats		2 " 15
7 Baires		21
		1008 "12 "6

The above is a Trew act of all I Could find as you have
...cts with you be so good to Seattel with him he
has Allso a North Connew which you will be so good
as to take on your arivel as he waits for you —
                With you a good Passag over ye
                        Lake ———
                                yors &cc
                                        P. Pond

33	
35	55
17	27.10
85	82.10

182
182
364

Donné a St paul Laprise pour Mr Guillon

60 peaux Rouges	40	120
47 peaux Passes	20	47
27 Chats	20	27
22 peaux Deux pour une	20	22
		216

257
216
41
23
64

255
216
39

206   R. Harvey Fleming Material

IV(a) Invoice of [peltries delivered] to Mr. Felix Graham by Peter Pond to be [sold] on [the account] of Graham and Pond marked & [numbered] as [per margin].
[Michilimackinac] 3rd July 1774 ...[17]

IV(b)
...
29 Red Skins   118 lb
N° 30 Mixt [mixed] Pack   ⎡   76 Otters
                             ⎨   25 fishers
                             ⎣   15 Cats
31 Otter   100 in Number[18]

V(a) "Accounts for the Adventure of 1774–75"
              Continewed [continued][19]   [£ s d]
N° 11 1 pes Blue Strouds   250/   £12 10...
... brought forward £214 1 3

V(b)
Turlington & *Bitters*   £ 12
10 lb Cokalat [chocolate][20]   @2/   1
1 pr Troussis   8
3 lb twine   3/   9
2 " Cord   2/   4   20 16
Wine *Shrub* & Sperrits [*spirits*]

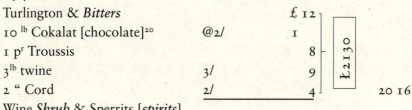

V(c)
...
Red Trunks[21]   1 16
2 Nests Tin Kettels [kettles]   40/   4
Cag [keg] of Salt   2
14 Gallons *High Wines*   10/   7   26   1
                                                         £574 19 2

V(d)

Wortap [*watap?*]		6
Covering Bark	16	
1 p^r Pistils [pistols][22]		

VI(a) Various Ledger Accounts of Pond and Williams
– Dr. Felix Graham

1774

July 28th	To 1 pack 121 lb Drest [dressed] Leather
	To 42 lb Beaver …

1775

June 22	To 1 Quart Rum				
	"617 Red Skins	2/6	77	2	6
	"2356 1/4 Beaver		12/	1413	15
	"466 lb Scraped Skins	2/6	58	5	
	"160 Gray Skins	5/4	42	13	4
	"96 Wolves	12/	57	12	
	"677 Otters	28/	947	16	
	"96 Fishers	4/4	20	16	
	"20 Catts [cats]	4/4	4	6	8
	"4 Foxes	5/	1		
	"225 Minks & Martins [*marten*]	5/4	60		
	"100 Elks	15/	75		
	"64 Bears	16/	51	4	
	"37 Buffaloes	20/	37		
	"680 Raccoons	2/8	90	13	4
	"17 Soft Elks	12/	10	4[23]	

VI(b)
– Dr. Peter Pond

1775	[£ s d]		
June 22			
To McNamara & Co	2		
To Mr Gulpin	2	14	9

To 1 pair Trowsers [trousers] from Mr Kane   13
July 3^d24

VI(c)

July 3^d To McTavish & Bannerman   29   17   10
To 1 Beaver Hatt [hat] from Jon [John]   3   4
  Martin[25]

VI(d)

... 1777
Ap^r 17 To Geo McBeath pr order[26]   141   17   8 ¼

VII(a) Accounts of Dr. John Askins [Askin][27]

1774

June 23	To 12 Copper Kettles	7/6	4	10
July 11	To 1 Butlap [burlap?]	Settled	1	12
1775				
June 14	To 43 Grease	2/6	5	7
15	To 202 Mr Henry	2/6	25	

VII(b)

...

June 14. Grease ... Frobisher 2/6   5   7   6
June 15. Grease ... Alexander Henry 2/6   25   5[8]

Papers of John Porteous

I(a) Adventure to the N. W p Messrs Pond & Greves[29]
Grand Portage 22^d July 1775

24 pieces *strouds*	2 coats, 5 *ells*	15½ "box "
96 blankets 2½ p^t	5 " 4½ "	4 "horn "
48 " 1 & 1½ p^t	5 " 4 "	3 " razors
27 chiefs' coats	7 " 3½ "	2 pipes tomahawks

M-65-1, Buffalo and Erie County Historical Society, Buffalo, New York

Documents

27 " hats

8 1/12 gross large knives

7¾ "small "

25 7/12 "brass rings

4" buck handed knives (?)

7 " yawls

7 1/2 " iron boxes

4 doz. large japan'd boxes

(?)

24 bunches beads assort'd

4 ᵇ thread " "

12 " net "

14 rolls large brass wire

45 "small "

102 pʳ large sleeves

36 do "2ᵈ size "

19 dᵒ small "

6 *quire paper*

100 pʳ legins [*leggings?*]

l ᵇ nerdigrass?

6 pʳ small wusted [*worsted?*] Hose

1000 needles

1 *calico* jacket

6 *calumets*

In Mʳ Pond's chest are

1 ᵇ *brimstone*

12 *purges*

12 *vomits*

1½ pieces *salves*

11 " 3 "

9 " 2½ "

28 " 2 "

6 " 1½ "

30 " 1 "

50 pˢ gartering (garters?)

48 linen shirts

3 feathers

8 small basins

68 ᵇ *vermillion*

3½ gross *gun worms*

12 *burning glass* boxes

2 bags *flints* no. 28 & 30

12 pocket compasses

10 dozˢ cased *looking*

glasses

21 small robes

1½ pine holland *gimp*

9 dozˢ ivory combs

4 sticks *sassifrass*

8 pictures

12 pˢ Indian *riband*

1 paper cinnamon

l "cloves

10 medals

6 large pictures

2 loaves white sugar

2 cases Qʳʸ?

2 *truncheons*

tomahawks

21 doz. *fire steels*

2 " *snuff boxes*

4 "*box looking* glasses

33 Natichanee belts?

34 packs cards

24 *worsted* belts

8 pʳ beaded garters

4 1/12 Gross *hawk bells*

1 "*none-so-pretty*

12 pictures

24 pʳ scissors

10 doz. small cross-handed knives?

3 gross thimbles

1 doz red *night caps*

2 pʳ shoes

3 "trousers

2 cod lines

1 spotted jacket

3 " Prawleen [*praline?*]

15 bags lead

49 kegs rum

64 bags corn

5 "flour

3 kegs sugar

1 "salt

3 "grease

1 "beef

2 " shrub

3 bales kettles

10 bottles *Turlington's*	6 *canoe awls*	3 cases guns 8 in a case
3 " *peppermint water*	12 files	1 keg natichanee?
4 *Hungary water*	1 *tap borer*	9 metre du rea?
1 paper *Spanish flies*	3 auguers?	7 white fish nets
3 Sticks *diachylum*	1 drawing knife	7 cod lines
1 paper healing salves	20 half axes	7 sponges
1 "*alɪum* ·	10 tomahawks	7 sails
¼ lb white *vitriol*	1 padlock	7 kettles
2 papers Grand River	21 bales tobacco	6 new canoes
Medicine?	19 kegs powder	1 old D°

Advanced the men before they left the other End of the Carrying place ... 3 men's equipment delivered them here.

NOTES

1 Lawrence J. Burpee, *The Search for the Western Sea*, 322–349 (Toronto, 1908) [Burpee 1908, 322–49]; Arthur S. Morton, ed., *The Journal of Duncan M'Gillivray*, xxxi (Toronto, 1929) [M'Gillivray and Morton 1929, xxxi].

2 Harold A. Innis, *Peter Pond, Fur Trader and Adventurer*, 115, 127 (Toronto, 1930) [Innis and Pond 1930, 115, 127]; "Peter Pond," in Royal Society of Canada, *Transactions*, 192, vol. 22, p. 139 (third series, section 2) [Innis 1928a].

3 The "Journal of 'Sir' Peter Pond" appears in the *Connecticut Magazine,* 10: 235–259 (April–June, 1906); it is reprinted in Thwaites "The British Regime in Wisconsin," in *Wisconsin Historical Collections*, 18: 314–354 (1908) [Innis and Pond 1930, 1–66] . The latter work is cited in the present footnotes. For an account of the discovery and partial use of the documents published herewith, see Innis, *Peter Pond*, 150–153 [Innis and Pond 1930, 150–3].

4 Innis, *Peter Pond*, 150 [Innis and Pond 1930, 150].

5 The available information concerning Greves or Graves is very meagre. It is probable that, in addition to capital, he brought into the partnership a knowledge of transportation on the Great Lakes, a technique that was becoming of great necessity for the longer water routes to Grand Portage. In

"Trading Ventures of Peter Pond in Minnesota" 211

an account of "The King's Shipyard," published as a *Burton Historical Collection Leaflet*, 2: 25 (January, 1924), the following statement appears: "Two of the King's vessels are to remain at Fort Erie till the 10th regiment goes up. Binnerman [*Bannerman*] and Graves command these." Since James Bannerman entered the fur trade as a partner of Simon McTavish, who became the head of the Northwest Company, it is probable that Graves pursued a similar commercial development to that of Bannerman. At a later note he was known to be an Indian trader. In a letter written to [Frederick] Haldimand on October 5, 1779, [Arent Schuyler] De Peyster refers to some people who were murdered by Indians in the Northwest, and adds: "I understand that the mischief was brought on thro' the imprudence of two of the killed ... and by the misconduct of Messrs. Homes [William Holmes?], McCormick, and Graves." See *Wisconsin Historical Collections*, 18: 403 (Thwaites and State Historical Society of Wisconsin 1908, 403). For an example of the spread of information about the early fur trade of the Northwest see *The Papers of Sir William Johnson*, 7: 953 (Albany, 1931). The document relating to the partnership between Pond and Graves is cited and reproduced in endnote #29.

6 This document confirms Pond's account of his first venture from Michilimackinac, as described in *Wisconsin Historical Collections*, 18: 324–341. (Thwaites and State Historical Society of Wisconsin 1908, 324–41) [Innis and Pond 1930, 20–44].

7 This corroborates Pond's statement that he reached Michilimackinac by the way of the Ottawa River after making purchases of trade goods in Montreal. *Wisconsin Historical Collections*, 18: 326 (Thwaites and State Historical Society of Wisconsin 1908, 326) [Innis and Pond 1930, 24–5].

8 The large amount of wampum included in the invoice points to a destination among certain tribes of southern Indians, as contrasted with those of the Northwest, who were unfamiliar with its use.

9 The item enclosed in brackets is crossed out in the original accounts.

10 This entry shows the route over the Great Lakes by which the bulky trade goods reached Michilimackinac. See *Wisconsin Historical Collections*, 18: 325 (Thwaites and State Historical Society of Wisconsin 1908, 325) [Innis and Pond 1930, 28].

11 The large amount of money involved and the amazing variety of goods listed are evidences of the responsibility placed upon Pond.

12 This document illustrates Pond's method of conducting the fur trade. He hired subordinate clerks and left with each of them an amount of goods to be traded for furs with the Indians on their own responsibility. (Thwaites and State Historical Society of Wisconsin 1908, 329) [Innis and Pond 1930, 28; p. 64 in this volume].

13 The items listed under this date are on the credit side of the ledger. They probably were goods given to a neighbouring clerk for which no return was made. The credit accounts with the Indians would be kept separately.

14 Although this memorandum is for the trading venture of 1774–75, it supplements the preceding document for it shows how goods that remained in the hands of the clerks in the spring were returned to the trader when the peltries gained in trade were delivered. A clue to Pond's arrival at Michilimacinac in the spring of 1775 is found in the date of this document. In his journal the trader describes a voyage of two days from Green Bay to Michilimacinac. See *Wisconsin Historical Collections*, 18: 345. (Thwaites and State Historical Society of Wisconsin 1908, 345) [Innis and Pond 1930, 28; p. 64 in this volume].

15 Pond's signature is very rare.

16 These figures illustrate Pond's system of rapid calculation.

17 This date corresponds with that of Pond's journal, in *Wisconsin Historical Collections*, 18: 341. (Thwaites and State Historical Society of Wisconsin 1908, 341) [Innis and Pond 1930, 63; p. 82 in this volume].

18 The total number of packs for the expedition must have been much greater. At the values listed for 1775 [as listed in document IIIa above], these peltries would be worth less than a thousand.

19 Although this document is without a title or a date, and can be identified only by the handwriting, it is almost certainly part of the outfit for 1774–75, when Pond was in partnership with Williams. The goods listed probably are those selected for Pond's own canoes, which were going to the St. Peter's or Minnesota River.

20 Pond invariably included in his supplies a few bottles of Turlington, a kind of patent medicine, and a quantity of chocolate.

21 This is one of the few means of identifying this document. A nest of red trunks, fitting inside of one another, remained unsold, and they are listed in "An account of Goods, debts, & notes in the hands of Thomas Williams, belonging to Pond & Williams," dated July 16, 1775, in the Williams pa-

"Trading Ventures of Peter Pond in Minnesota" 213

pers. Pond bought one, which he probably took with him to the Northwest. [A "small red trunk" is listed has having been sold for £8 in a document that Fleming did not annotate: "Dr. Pond and Williams."]

22 Although Pond went among the Indians as an envoy of peace during a period of intertribal war, he seems to have believed in being prepared with a new pair of "pistils." See *Wisconsin Historical Collections*, 18: 342–345 (Thwaites and State Historical Society of Wisconsin 1908, 342–45) [Innis and Pond 1930, 62–6; pp. 81–4 in this volume].

23 Pond's adventure for 1774–75 to the St. Peter's River must have been highly successful, for the value of the furs according to the prices given, amounts to £3904.2.9.

24 At this late date Pond was preparing for his journey to the Northwest. The purchases he made are of interest.

25 Pond seems to have believed in the advice:
"Have a good hat; the secret of your looks
Lives with the beaver in Canadian brooks."
[Editor's note. This is the source of Fleming's quote:
Oliver Wendell Holmes, *Urania: A Rhymed Lesson*
Have a good hat; the secret of your looks
Lives with the beaver in Canadian brooks;
Virtue may flourish in an old cravat,
But man and nature scorn the shocking hat.
Does beauty slight you from her gay abodes?
Like bright Apollo, you must take to Rhodes –
Mount the new castor, – ice itself will melt;
Boots, gloves, may fail; the hat is always felt.
(Holmes 1846)]

26 This probably formed part of the capital for the partnership of Pond and George McBeath.

27 See "Diary of John Askin at Mackinac, 1774–5," Milo M. Quaife, ed., *The John Askin Papers*, I: 50–8 (Detroit, 1928) [Askin and Quaife 1928].

28 Compare the amounts of grease taken to the Northwest by these two expeditions with that listed by Pond (This was 3 kegs). Frobisher must have [had] other sources of supply.

29 This is the first document after the conquest of Canada by the British to give the details of an adventure to the Northwest. The wide assortment of

goods may be compared with that taken by Pond to the Mississippi. Note the large quantities of provisions included in the list, as well as equipment for obtaining food along the way. The seven canoes would be north canoes, which were smaller than those used on lakes. The number does not agree with the account given by Alexander Henry, in his Travels & Adventures in Canada and the Indian Territories, 251 (Bain ed., Boston, 1901) [Henry, Maverick, and Bain 1901].

Glossary

Selected items from "Felix Graham and Peter Pond Fur Trade Accounts, 1773–75," John R. Williams, Burton Historical Collection, Detroit Public Library; and "Adventure to the NW of Messrs Pond and Greves," Papers of John Porteous, Buffalo and Erie County Historical Society, Buffalo, NY.

alum – Possibly potassium alum, which has been used since antiquity as a flocculent to clarify turbid liquids, and as an astringent (or styptic) as well as an antiseptic. It has also been used to facilitate the dyeing process.

baling – Large bundle or package prepared for transport, tightly compressed and secured by materials such as wires, hoops, or cords.

bedgown (bed gown, short gown) – Article of women's clothing for the upper body, usually thigh-length, of lightweight printed cotton fabric – fashionable in the 18th century as at-home morning wear.

bitters – Alcohol flavoured with bitter plant extracts, used as an additive in cocktails or as a medicinal substance to promote appetite or digestion.

blanket coat – Made from blankets or blanketing and attached with a sash – adapted by voyageurs – can be traced back to "Capots," originally a kind of a hooded coat or gown worn by French sailors in wet or bad weather.

brimstone (sulfur) – Used (mainly in creams) to alleviate such conditions as scabies, ringworm, psoriasis, eczema, and acne.

216   Glossary

buckskin – Soft, pliable, porous preserved leather made of buck (i.e., deer) hide.

burning glass (burning lens) – Converging lens that focuses the sun's rays onto a small area, producing intense heat, igniting the exposed surface.

calamanco (callimanco, calimanco, kalamink) – Thin fabric of worsted wool yarn with a glazed or calendared surface.

calico – Plain-woven textile made from unbleached and often not fully processed cotton. Name derives from Calicut, India, where the fabric originated.

calumet – A long-stemmed, highly ornamented pipe of North American Indians used on ceremonial occasions, especially in tokens of peace.

canoe awl (crooked awl) – Tool used for making holes in birch bark.

chints (chintz) – Printed multicoloured cotton fabric with a glazed finish often having floral patterns.

cooperage – Wooden barrel.

covering bark – Spare birch bark used to repair canoes.

cutlass – Short sword with a slightly curved blade, formerly used by sailors, and later adapted by agricultural workers as a harvesting tool (e.g., machete).

diachylon (diachylum, diaculum) – Originally a kind of medicament made of the juices of several plants used to form a type of adhesive plaster, often also containing lead oxide and glycerin.

ell – Former measure of length (originally a cubit, equivalent to 6 hand breadths or about 18 inches [457 mm]) used mainly for textiles.

fire-steel (strike-a-light, steel fire-striker) – Tool used in fire-making. Sparks are produced when the sharp edge of a hard, glassy stone such as quartz, jasper, agate or similar rock strikes a piece of carbon steel.

fisher – small, carnivorous mammal closely related to the marten.

flint – Very hard form of the mineral quartz, consisting of nearly pure silica (chert), occurring chiefly as nodules in chalk. Used primarily in fire-starting tools (see fire-steel) or in flintlock firearms.

gartering – Band, usually of elastic, worn round the arm or leg to hold up a shirtsleeve, sock, or stocking.

gimblet – Small screw-tipped tool for boring holes.

Glossary

gimp – Thread (often of silk) reinforced with wire, used as a fishing leader.

gun worm – Corkscrew-like device (consisting of one or two twisted tines) used to remove solid residues (produced by burning black powder) from the barrel of a musket.

hawk bells (Indian brass hawk bells) – Small ringing ornaments often made of brass originally used for falconry, became a trade-good staple used for decorative purposes by indigenous people.

high wine – Twice-distilled rum imported from the West Indies, with a very high alcohol content of roughly 80 per cent or 160 proof.

Hungary water (Queen of Hungary water) – One of the first alcohol-based perfumes in Europe, primarily made with rosemary.

Jew's harp – A small lyre-shaped musical instrument held between the teeth and played by hitting a metal strip with the finger.

looking glass – A mirror made of glass on which has been placed a backing of some reflecting substance, such as quicksilver.

madeira – Fortified wine from the Portuguese island of the same name in the Atlantic.

marten – Small predator, member of the weasel family.

night cap – Warm soft cloth cap worn while sleeping.

none-so-pretty – Decorative braid or tape used in the late 18th century for dress-making and furnishing.

parchment – Beaver pelts sun-dried immediately after skinning (*castor sec*).

peltry – Animal pelt.

peppermint water – Derived from peppermint oil (made from peppermint leaves), a traditional herbal medicine used to relieve discomfort in the gut, such as indigestion, flatulence and stomach cramps.

praline – Form of confection containing at a minimum nuts and sugar.

purge – Something that purges by removing impurities, acting as a laxative.

quire – Measure of paper quantity; collection of 24 or sometimes 25 sheets of paper of the same size and quality.

ratteen – a coarse, heavy, twilled woolen cloth, popular in 18th-century Britain.

riband – A ribbon, especially one used as a decoration.

218   Glossary

sassafras – Genus of deciduous trees native to eastern North America and eastern Asia, the roots, stems, twig leaves, bark, flowers, and fruit of which have been used for culinary, medicinal, and aromatic purposes.

scalping (butcher) knife – While "scalping knife" appeared frequently in popular American and European writings, for indigenous North American people it was just a simple and effective multi-purpose utility tool.

shrub – Sweetened vinegar-based syrup also known as drinking vinegar. Drinking vinegar was often infused with fruit juice, herbs and spices.

snuff – Smokeless tobacco made from ground or pulverized tobacco leaves, inhaled or "snuffed" into the nasal cavity.

snuff box – Small, usually ornamented, box for holding snuff.

Spanish fly – Toxic preparation made from the dried bodies of Spanish fly beetles, formerly used in medicine as a counterirritant and sometimes taken as an aphrodisiac.

spirit – Alcoholic beverage made by distilling grains, fruit, or vegetables that have already gone through the fermentation process.

stock buckle – Made of cut steel, silver, or even gold, and embellished with gemstones or paste jewels, this important piece of male jewelry sat on the back of a gentleman's neck and buckled a band of white linen wrapped around the lower neck.

stroud – Coarse woolen fabric, formerly used in the manufacture of blankets for sale to North American Indians.

tap borer – Tool for boring holes.

tomahawk – Single-handed axe used by North American indigenous people as a general-purpose tool including as a hand-to-hand or a thrown weapon. Metal tomahawk heads were used as a trade good in the early fur industry.

truncheon (billy club, nightstick) – A thick, heavy stick used mainly by police officers as a weapon.

Turlington's Balsam of Life – English merchant Robert Turlington obtained a royal patent for this mixture from King George II in 1744. It quickly gained popularity in both Britain and the colonies, and was used to treat a broad variety of ailments.

vermilion (vermillion) – A brilliant red or scarlet pigment, originally made from the powdered mineral cinnabar.

Glossary

vitriol – A sulfate of any of various metals (such as copper, iron, or zinc) thought to have medicinal properties.

vomit – An agent that induces vomiting; an emetic.

waistcoat – Close-fitting waist-length sleeveless garment with buttons in front, worn especially by men over a shirt and under a jacket.

wampum – Small cylindrical beads made from shells, strung together and worn as decoration or used as money by some North American indigenous peoples.

watap – Stringy thread made by North American indigenous people from conifer roots used for weaving and sewing.

worsted – a fine smooth yarn spun from combed wool.

References

Anderson, Fred. 1984. *A People's Army: Massachusetts Soldiers and Society in the Seven Years' War.* Chapel Hill: University of North Carolina Press.

Askin, John, and Milo M. Quaife. 1928. *The John Askin Papers.* Detroit: Library Commission.

Audet, Francis-J. 1927. "Discours du président. Progrès du Canada français depuis la Confédération." In *Transactions of the Royal Society of Canada, Section II*, 3rd ser., vol. 21, s. 2:1–7. Ottawa: la Société Royale du Canada.

Audette-Longo, Patricia H., and William J. Buxton. 2014. "Compiling Knowledge, Enacting Space, Binding Time: Innis's Canadian North (1928–1944)." TOPIA: *Canadian Journal of Cultural Studies* 32:229–52.

Baker, J. Percy. 1927. "Sir Alexander Mackenzie." *Musical Quarterly* 13 (1): 14–28.

Barbeau, Marius. 1927. *The Native Races of Canada.* Ottawa: Royal Society of Canada.

Barker, Burt Brown. 1941. Review of *Minutes of Council Northern Department of Rupert Land, 1821–31*, by R. Harvey Fleming and E.E. Rich. *Oregon Historical Quarterly* 42 (3): 263–4.

Beaver Club. n.d. "The Beaver Club." http://www.quebecgenweb.com/~qcmtl-w/BeaverClub.html.

Bélanger, Damien-Claude. 2011. *Prejudice and Pride: Canadian Intellectuals Confront the United States, 1891–1945.* Toronto: University of Toronto Press.

Belcourt, Napoléon-Antoine. 1927. "French Canada under Confederation." *Canadian Historical Association, Report of the Annual Meeting* 6 (1): 29–38.

Berdoulay, Vincent, and R. Louis Chapman. 1987. "Le Possibilisme de Harold Innis." *Canadian Geographer / Le Géographe canadien* 31 (1): 2–11.

Berger, Carl. 1996a. *Honour and the Search for Influence: A History of the Royal Society of Canada*. Toronto: University of Toronto Press.

– 1986b. *Writing of Canadian History: Aspects of English Canadian Historical Writing since 1900*. Toronto: University of Toronto Press.

Bigsby, John J. 1850. *The Shoe and Canoe*. London: Chapman and Hall.

Blondheim, Menahem. 2004. "Discovering 'The Significance of Communication': Harold Adams Innis as Social Constructivist." *Canadian Journal of Communication* 29 (2): 119–43.

Bolton, Herbert E. 1926. *The History of the Americas: History 8A–8B*. Berkeley: University of California.

– 1935. Review of *The Explorers of North America*, by John Bartlet Brebner. *American Historical Review* 40 (3): 517–19.

Bolton, Herbert E., and T.M. Marshall. 1920. *Colonization of North America*. New York: Macmillan.

Bothwell, Robert, Ian Drummond, and John English. 1990. *Canada 1900–1945*. Toronto: University of Toronto Press.

Brebner, John B. 1930. Review of *Select Documents in Canadian Economic History, 1497–1783*, by Harold A. Innis. *American Historical Review* 35 (4): 882–3.

– 1931. "Canadian and North American History." *Report of the Annual Meeting (101) Canadian Historical Association* 10 (1): 37–48.

– 1933. *Explorers of North America, 1490–1806*. London: A. & C. Black.

– 1937. *The Neutral Yankees of Nova Scotia: A Marginal Colony during the Revolutionary Years*. New York: Columbia University Press.

– 1945. *North Atlantic Triangle: The Interplay of Canada, the United States and Great Britain*. New Haven, CT: Yale University Press.

– 1960. *Canada: A Modern History*. Ann Arbor: University of Michigan Press.

– 1973. *New England's Outpost: Acadia before the Conquest of Canada*. New York: Burt Franklin.

Britnell, George E. 1939. *The Wheat Economy*. With a foreword by Harold A. Innis. Toronto: University of Toronto Press.

References

Brown, George W. 1942. "Have the Americans a Common History? A Canadian View." *Canadian Historical Review* 23 (2): 132–9.

Brunet, Pierre. 1948. Review of *Les explorateurs célèbres*. *Revue d'histoire des Sciences* 1 (4): 374.

Bryant, George Clarke, Nathan G. Pond, and Sophia Pond. n.d. *Old Milford Families Collection*. New Haven Museum. "Old Milford Families," Pond Collection box 9, folder e., coll. 96-B.

Buckingham, William, and George W. Ross. 1892. *The Hon. Alexander Mackenzie, His Life and Times*. Toronto: Rose.

Buffalo Bill Museum and Grave. 2010. "Did Buffalo Bill Visit Your Town?" http://www.buffalobill.org/pdfs/buffalo_bill_visits.pdf.

Bulletin of the Business Historical Society. 1935. "The Hudson's Bay Company Archives," 9 (4): 54–6.

Burpee, Lawrence J. 1908. *The Search for the Western Sea: The Story of the Exploration of North-Western America*. Toronto: Musson.

– 1910. "A Chapter in the Literature of the Fur Trade." *Papers (Bibliographical Society of America)* 5:45–60.

– 1926. *The Oxford Encyclopaedia of Canadian History*. Toronto: Oxford University Press.

– 1927a. *Journals and Letters of Pierre Gaultier de Varennes de La Vérendrye and His Sons: With Correspondence between the Governors of Canada & the French Court*. Toronto: Champlain Society.

– 1927b. "Report of the Management Committee." *Canadian Historical Association, Report of Annual Meeting* 6 (1): 8.

– 1927c. Review of *Mackenzie of Canada* by M.S. Wade, *Mackenzie and His Voyageurs* by Arthur P. Woollacott, and *Sir Alexander Mackenzie, Explorer and Fur Trader*, by Hume Wrong. *Canadian Historical Review* 8 (4): 335–7.

– 1929. *Two Western Adventurers: Alexander Henry and Peter Pond*. Toronto: Ryerson.

Buxton, William J. 1998. "Harold Innis' Excavation of Modernity: The Newspaper Industry, Communications, and the Decline of Public Life." *Canadian Journal of Communication* 23 (3): 321–39.

– 2004. "Harold Innis' 'French Inflection': Origins, Themes, and Implications of His 1951 Address at Le Collège de France." *Canadian Journal of Communication* 29 (2): 171–86.

– 2013. "Bringing Nordicity to the South City: Harold Innis as Reviewer of

Books on the North, 1928–1944." In *Harold Innis and the North Appraisals and Contestations*, edited by William J. Buxton, 186–210. Montreal and Kingston: McGill-Queen's University Press.

– n.d. "The Archival Practice of Harold Adams Innis: A Time-Binding Corrective to Monopolies of Knowledge." Library and Archives Canada. https://www.collectionscanada.gc.ca/innis-mcluhan/030003-4020-e.html.

Buxton, William J., and Risa Dickens. 2006. "Harold Innis' 'Crisis in Public Opinion': Performance, Retrieval, and the Politics of Knowledge." *Canadian Journal of Communication* 31 (2): 325–40.

Campbell, Sandra. 1995. "From Romantic History to Communications Theory: Lorne Pierce as Publisher of C.W. Jefferys and Harold Innis." *Journal of Canadian Studies* 30 (3): 91–116.

– 2013. *Both Hands: A Life of Lorne Pierce of Ryerson Press*. Montreal and Kingston: McGill-Queen's University Press.

Canada, National Committee for the Celebration of the Diamond Jubilee of Confederation and Jean-Baptiste Lagacé. 1927. *Diamond Jubilee of Confederation: Suggestions for Historical Pagents, Floats and Tableaux (with Illustrations in Colour) for the Guidance of Local Committees in Charge of Diamond Jubilee Celebrations; General Sketch of Canadian History with Special Reference to the Confederation Period; Bibliography of Canadian History*. Ottawa: Executive Committee of the National Committee for the Celebration of the Diamond Jubilee of Confederation.

Canada's Historic Places. n.d. "First Crossing of North America National Historic Site of Canada. https://www.historicplaces.ca/en/rep-reg/place-lieu.aspx?id=14662.

Canadian Baptist. 1931. Review of *Peter Pond: Fur Trader and Adventurer*, by Harold A. Innis, 10 December.

Canadian Historical Review. 1927. "Notes and Comments" 8 (2): 93–4.

Canadian National Parks Branch. 1928. "Some Historic and Pre-historic Sites of Canada." *Canadian Historical Association, Report of Annual Meeting* 6 (1): 113–18.

Canadian Pacific Limited and Prince of Wales, Edward. 1927. *Canadian Scenes July–August 1927. Diamond Jubilee of Confederation, Souvenir of a Visit to Canada by H.R.H. the Prince of Wales, H.R.H. Prince George, the Rt Hon. Stanley Baldwin and Party*. Montreal: Canadian Pacific.

Canadian Public Health Leader. 1961. "Medical Health Officer for the City of

Regina." http://resources.cpha.ca/CPHA/ThisIsPublicHealth/profiles/item.
php?i=1315&l=E.

Cannon, Le Grand. 1942. *Look to the Mountain*. New York: Holt, Rinehart,
and Winston.

Careless, J.M.S. 1954. "Frontierism, Metropolitanism, and Canadian History."
Canadian Historical Review 35 (1): 1–21.

– 1970. "The Review Reviewed or Fifty Years with the Beaver Patrol."
Canadian Historical Review 51 (1): 48–71.

Carlyle, Thomas, and Archibald MacMechan. 1904. *Carlyle on Heroes,
Hero-Worship, and the Heroic in History*. London: Chapman and Hall.

Chalmers, John W. 2003. *The Land of Peter Pond*. Vancouver: CCI.

Chapin, David. 2014. *Freshwater Passages: The Trade and Travels of Peter
Pond*. http://site.ebrary.com/id/10874972.

Cinefocus. n.d. "CW Jefferys: Picturing Canada." http://www.cinefocus.com/
public/CWJOnePage.pdf.

Clancy, Dorothy. 1978. "In the Land of Peter Pond." Unpublished manuscript.

Clark, Robert Carlton. 1938. "The Archives of the Hudson's Bay Company."
Pacific Northwest Quarterly 29 (1): 3–15.

Clayton, Daniel. 1999. *Islands of Truth: The Imperial Fashioning of Vancouver Island*. Vancouver: UBC Press.

Cochrane, Charles N. 1926. Canadian Historical Association. "Reports of the
Secretary-Treasurer." *Report of the Annual Meeting* 5 (1): 17–20.

Cochrane, Charles N., and Arthur G. Doughty. 1927. "Report of the Secretary-
Treasurer." *Report of the Annual Meeting* 6 (1): 17–19.

Colpitts, George. 2014. *Pemmican Empire: Food, Trade, and the Last Bison
Hunts in the North American Plains, 1780–1882*. New York: Cambridge
University Press.

Connecticut Circle: The Magazine of the Nutmeg State. 1939. "Milford
Tercentenary Scenes." November 1939.

Conrad, Margaret. 2007. "2007 Presidential Address of the Canadian Historical Association: Public History and Its Discontents or History in the Age of
Wikipedia." *Journal of the Canadian Historical Association* 18 (1): 1–26.

Contributions to Canadian Economics. 1932. Notes and Comment 4: 5.

Coo Boutique. n.d. "Hartford Ct Parks Antique Carousels Ct Monuments
War Memorials in Ct." http://www.cooboutique.com/connecticut/hartford-
ct-parks-antique-carousels-ct-monuments-war-memorials-in-ct.

Cooke, Edgar D. 1974. Peter Pond: Forgotten Developer of the North West. *Alberta Historical Review* 22 (1): 18–27.

Creighton, Donald G. 1957. *Harold Adams Innis: Portrait of a Scholar.* Toronto: University of Toronto Press.

– 1966. "Introduction to the Carleton Library Edition." In J.B. Brebner, *North Atlantic Triangle: The Interplay of Canada, the United States and Great Britain*, xiii–xxiii. Carleton Library 30. Toronto: McClelland and Stewart.

Crouse, Nellis M. 1928. "The Location of Fort Maurepas." *Canadian Historical Review* 9 (3): 206–22.

Cupido, Robert. 1998. "Appropriating the Past: Pageants, Politics, and the Diamond Jubilee of Confederation." *Journal of the Canadian Historical Association* 9 (1): 155–86.

– 2010. "Public Commemoration and Ethnocultural Assertion: Winnipeg Celebrates the Diamond Jubilee of Confederation." *Urban History Review* 38 (2): 64–74.

Davenport, J.B., and D. Rylance. 1980. "Archival Note. Sources of Business History: The Archives of the Hudson's Bay Company." *Business History Review* 54 (3): 387–93. http://www.jstor.org/stable/3114245.

Davidson, Gordon C. 1918. *The North West Company*. Berkeley: University of California Press.

David Spencer Ltd. 1927. *Tableaux of Canadian History and Industry, Commemorating Canada's Diamond Jubilee of Confederating Canada's Diamond Jubilee of Confederation*. Vancouver: Wrigley Print.

"David Thompson Monument." 1927. *Canadian Historical Association, Report of Annual Meeting* 6 (1): 9–16.

Davis, Bruce Pettit, and Carroll L. Davis. 1934. *The Davis Family and the Leather Industry, 1834–1934*: Toronto: Ryerson.

Dick, Lyle. 2009. "Public History in Canada: An Introduction." *Public Historian* 31 (1): 7–14.

Dillon, Richard H., and J. Mervin Nooth. 1951. "Peter Pond and the Overland Route to Cook's Inlet." *Pacific Northwest Quarterly* 42 (4): 324–9.

Dougall, H.E. 1925. "Government Regulation of the Fur Trade." BA thesis, University of Toronto.

Doughty, Arthur G., and Adam Shortt. 1907. *Documents Relating to the Constitutional History of Canada 1759–1791*. Ottawa: Public Archives of Canada.

References

Drummond, Ian M. 1983. *Political Economy at the University of Toronto: A History of the Department, 1888–1982*. Toronto: Faculty of Arts and Science, University of Toronto.

Duckworth, Harry W., and Northwest Company. 1990. *The English River Book: A North West Company Journal and Account Book of 1786*. Montreal and Kingston: McGill-Queen's University Press.

Edgar, Pelham. 1927. "Presidential Address: Are Our Writers in the Modern Stream?" In *Transactions of the Royal Society of Canada Section II*, 1–6.

Elliott, T.C. 1933. Review of *Peter Pond: Fur Trader and Explorer*, by Harold A. Innis. *Oregon Historical Quarterly* 34 (1): 84–6.

Ells, Sidney C. 1938. *Northland Trails*. Toronto: Garden City.

Ermatinger, James. 1833. *James Ermatinger Papers, 1883–1887*. Minneapolis: Minnesota Historical Society Library.

Evenden, Matthew. 2013. "The Northern Vision of Harold Innis." In *Harold Innis and the North: Appraisals and Contestations*, edited by William J. Buxton, 3–99. Montreal and Kingston: McGill-Queen's University Press.

Falconer, Robert. 1927. *Scottish Influence in the Higher Education of Canada*. Ottawa: Royal Society of Canada.

Fay, C.R. 1942. Review of *Minutes of Council, Northern Department of Rupert Land, 1821–31*, by R. Harvey Fleming, H.A. Innis, and E.E. Rich. *Economic Journal* 52 (205): 82–4.

Fedirchuk, Gloria. 1990. "Peter Pond: Map Maker of the Northwest (1740–1807)." *Arctic / Journal of the Arctic Institute of North America* 43 (2): 184–6.

Find a Grave. 2001. "David Thompson." https://www.findagrave.com/memorial/2662.

Fleming, R. Harvey. 1925. "The Fur Trade of North America from 1763–1821." BA thesis, University of Toronto.

– 1928. "The Origin of 'Sir Alexander Mackenzie and Company.'" *Canadian Historical Review* 9 (2): 137–55.

– 1929. "McTavish, Frobisher and Company of Montreal." *Canadian Historical Review* 10 (2): 136–52.

– 1932a. "Phyn, Ellice and Company of Schenectady." *Contributions to Canadian Economics* 4:7–41.

– 1932b. "Trading Ventures of Peter Pond in Minnesota." Fur Trade Accounts, 1773–5, accession no. 3551, Peter Pond Papers, Minnesota Historical

Society. Originals are in the John R. Williams Papers, Burton Historical Collection, Detroit (Michigan) Public Library (pp. oo this volume).

Forest, John William De, and Felix Octavius Carr Darley. 1851. *History of the Indians of Connecticut from the Earliest Known Period to 1850*. Hartford, CT: Wm Jas Hamersley.

Free Press. 1940. Review of *Minutes of Council Northern Department Rupert's Land, 1821–1831*, edited by R. Harvey Fleming. 19 July.

Garnett, David. 1949. *Two Memoirs: Dr Melchior: A Defeated Enemy and My Early Beliefs*. London: Rupert Hart-Davis.

Garvin, John W., and Alexander Mackenzie. 1927. *Master-Works of Canadian Authors*, vol. 3. Toronto: Radisson Society of Canada.

Gates, Charles M. 1932. Review of *Peter Pond: Fur Trader and Adventurer*, Harold A. Innis. *Minnesota History* 13 (2): 181–2.

– ed. 1933. *Five Fur Traders of the Northwest: Being the Narrative of Peter Pond and Diaries of John Macdonell, Archibald N. McLeod, Hugh Faries, and Thomas Conner*. Minneapolis: Published for the Minnesota Society of the Colonial Dames of America, University of Minnesota Press.

– 1965. *Five Fur Traders of the Northwest: Being the Narrative of Peter Pond and the Diaries of John Macdonell, Archibald N. McLeod, Hugh Faries, and Thomas Connor*. St Paul: Minnesota Historical Society.

Gibb, W.K. 1934. "Eight Hundred Miles on the Yukon." *Canadian Geographical Journal* 8 (3): 123–34.

Godsell, Philip H. 1934. *Arctic Trader: The Account of Twenty Years with the Hudson's Bay Company*. New York: G.P. Putnam's Sons.

Gordon, Alan. 2014. *The Hero and the Historians: Historiography and the Uses of Jacques Cartier*. Vancouver: UBC Press.

Gough, Barry M. 2004. "Peter Pond and Athabasca: Fur Trade, Discovery, and Empire." In B. Gough, *Britain, Canada and the North Pacific: Maritime Enterprise and Dominion, 1778–1914*, 1–18. Aldershot, UK: Ashgate.

– 2013. "Innis and Northern Canada: Fur Trade and Nation." In *Harold Innis and the North: Appraisals and Contestations*, edited by William J. Buxton, 51–64. Montreal and Kingston: McGill-Queen's University Press.

– 2014. *The Elusive Mr Pond: The Soldier, Fur Trader and Explorer Who Opened the Northwest*. Madeira Park, BC: Douglas & McIntyre.

– n.d. "Pond, Peter." Vol. 5 (1801–20) *Dictionary of Canadian Biography*. http://www.biographi.ca/en/bio/pond_peter_5E.html.

References

Grant, Hugh. 2017. *W.A. Mackintosh: The Life of a Canadian Economist.* Montreal and Kingston: McGill-Queen's University Press.

Grant, Ruth F. 1934. *The Canadian Atlantic Fishery, with an Editorial Preface by Harold A. Innis.* Toronto: Ryerson.

Greenfield, Bruce R. 2002. "Creating the Distance of Print: The Memoir of Peter Pond, Fur Trader." *Early American Literature* 37 (3): 415–38.

Hammond, Melvin O. 1917. *Canadian Confederation and Its Leaders.* Toronto: McClelland, Goodchild & Stewart.

Hanke, Lewis. 1968. *Do the Americas Have a Common History?: A Critique of the Bolton Theory.* New York: Knopf.

Harvey, D.C. 1927. "The Maritime Provinces and Confederation." *Canadian Historical Association, Report of the Annual Meeting* 6 (1): 39–45.

Hayes, D. 2002. "You Will Readily Conjecture: The Explorations and Maps of Peter Pond." *Mercator's World* 7:30–7.

Heaton, Herbert. 1930. Review of Harold Innis, *The Fur Trade of Canada. Journal of Political Economy* 38 (3): 22.

Heidenreich, Conrad E. 2006. *Champlain and the Champlain Society: An Early Expedition into Documentary Publishing.* Occasional Papers Number 3. Toronto: Champlain Society.

Henry, Alexander. 1901. *Travels & Adventures in Canada and the Indian Territories*, edited by James Bain. Boston: Little, Brown.

– 1908. Letter to Joseph Banks, 18 October 1781, reprinted in Lawrence J. Burpee, 1908. *The Search for the Western Sea: The Story of the Exploration of North-Western America.* Toronto: Musson.

– 2010. *Travels and Adventures in Canada and the Indian Territories: Between the Years 1760 and 1776.* Charleston: Nabu.

Henry, Alexander, and Barry M. Gough. 1992. *The Journal of Alexander Henry the Younger, 1799–1814.* Toronto: Champlain Society.

Heyer, Paul. 2003. *Harold Innis.* Lanham, MD: Rowman & Littlefield.

– 2004. "History from the Inside: Prolegomenon to the 'Memoir of Harold Adams Innis Covering the Years 1894–1922." *Canadian Journal of Communication* 29 (2): 159–70.

– 2013. "Harold Innis, Peter Pond, and the Fur Trade." In *Harold Innis and the North Appraisals and Contestations*, edited by William J. Buxton, 65–72. Montreal and Kingston: McGill-Queen's University Press.

Holland, Samuel, and D.C. Harvey. 1935. "*Holland's Description of Cape*

Breton Island and Other Documents. Halifax, N.S." Halifax: Archives of Nova Scotia.

Howay, Frederick W. 1925. "Judge Howay's Address (Unveiling of Memorial Tablet at Nootka Sound)." *Second Annual Report and Proceedings of the British Columbia Historical Association,* August, 22–5.

– 1927. "British Columbia's Entry into Confederation." Canadian Historical Association. *Report of the Annual Meeting* 6 (1): 67–73.

– 1928. *An Identification of Sir Alexander Mackenzie's for York.* Ottawa: Printed for the Royal Society of Canada.

Hudson's Bay Company: A Brief History. 1934. London, Hudson's Bay House.

Hutchins, Robert M. 1952. *Some Questions about Education in North America.* Toronto: University of Toronto Press.

Innis, Harold A. 1918a. "The Economic Problems of Army Life." *McMaster University Monthly,* December, 106–9.

– 1918b. "The Returned Soldier." MA thesis, McMaster University.

– 1923. *A History of the Canadian Pacific Railway.* London: P.S. King & Son.

– 1926. Review of *Lord Strathcona,* by John Macnaughton. *Canadian Historical Review* 7 (4): 348–9.

– 1927a. Review of *Documents Relating to Canadian Currency, Exchange and Finance During the French Period,* edited by Adam Shortt, *Canadian Historical Review* 8 (1): 62–5.

– 1927b. *The Fur-Trade of Canada.* Toronto: University Library.

– 1927c. "The North West Company." *Canadian Historical Review* 8 (1): 308–21.

– 1927d. Review of *Documents Relating to Canadian Currency, Exchange and Finance During the French Period,* by Adam Shortt. *Canadian Historical Review* 8 (1): 62–5.

– 1927e. Review of *Voyages from Montreal on the River St Laurence through the Continent of North America to the Frozen and Pacific Oceans in the Years 1789 and 1793 with a Preliminary Account of the Rise, Progress and Present State of the Fur Trade of That Country,* by Alexander Mackenzie. *Canadian Historical Review* 9 (1): 65.

– 1928a. "Peter Pond and the Influence of Capt James Cook on Exploration in the Interior of North America." *Transactions of the Royal Society of Canada,* 3rd ser., vol. 22, s. 2:131–41.

– 1928b. "Peter Pond in 1780." *Canadian Historical Review* 9 (4): 333.

References 231

- 1928c. Review of *The Askin Papers*, by John Askin, ed. Milo Quaife. *American Economic Review* 18 (4): 787.
- 1928d. Review of *Journals and Letters of la Vérendrye*, by J.L. Burpee. *American Economic Review* 18 (1): 96–106.
- 1929a. "A Bibliography of Thorstein Veblen." *Southwestern Political and Social Science Quarterly* 10 (1): 56–68.
- 1929b. *Select Documents in Canadian Economic History*. Toronto: University of Toronto Press.
- 1930a. "Allan, Hugh Bart (1810–82)." *Encyclopaedia of the Social Sciences* 6: 643.
- 1930b. "The Hudson Bay Railway." *Geographical Review* 20 (1): 1–30.
- (1930) 1956. *The Fur Trade in Canada: An Introduction to Canadian History*. Toronto: University of Toronto Press.
- 1931a. "Fur Trade and Industry." *Encyclopaedia of the Social Sciences*. New York: Macmillan, 30–6.
- 1931b. "An Introduction to the Economic History of the Maritimes (including Newfoundland and New England." Canadian Historical Association. *Report of the Annual Meeting* 10 (1): 85–96.
- 1931c. Review of *Historic Forts and Trading Posts of the French Régime and of the English Fur Trading Companies*, by Ernest Voorhis. *Canadian Historical Review* 12 (2): 211–12.
- 1932a. Review of *John Jacob Astor, Business Man*, by Kenneth Wiggins Porter, and *The Reflections of Inkyo on the Great Company*. *Canadian Historical Review* 13 (4): 440–3.
- 1932b. Review of "The Selkirk Purchases of the Red River Valley, 1811," by John Perry Pritchett. *North Dakota Historical Quarterly* 171–3.
- 1933a. "George Stephen, First Baron Mount Stephen (1829–1921)." *Encyclopaedia of the Social Science* 11:78–9.
- 1933b. "Interrelations between the Fur Trade of Canada and the United States." *Mississippi Valley Historical Review* 20 (3): 321–32.
- 1933c. *Problems of Staple Production in Canada*. Toronto: Ryerson.
- 1933d. "Sir William Mackenzie (1849–1823)." *Encyclopaedia of the Social Sciences* 10:28–9.
- 1934a. Review of *American Transportation System*, by H. Moulton, and *The Investor Pays* by Max Lowenthal. *Canadian Forum* January: 149–50.

232 References

– 1934b. Review of *Five Fur Traders of the Northwest*, ed. C.M. Gates. *Canadian Forum*, March, 28.

– 1934c. Review of *The Explorers of North America, 1492–1806*, ed. J.B. Brebner. *Canadian Historical Review* 15 (1): 71–2.

– 1935a. Review of *Canada's Eastern Arctic: Its History, Resources, Population and Administration*, by W.C. Bethune; *Sails over Ice*, by Captain "Bob" Bartlett; *Eskimo Year: A Naturalist's Adventures in the Far Nort*, by George Miksch Sutton; *To the Arctic with the Mounties*, by Douglas S. Robertson; *Trading into Hudson's Bay: A Narrative of the Visit of Patrick Ashley Cooper, Thirtieth Governor of the Hudson's Bay Company, to Labrador, Hudson Strait, and Hudson Bay in the Year 1934*, by R.H.H. Macaulay; *North to the Rime-Ringed Sun: Being the Record of an Alaskan-Canadian Journey Made in 1933–3*, by Isobel Wylie Hutchison; *La chasse des animaux à fourrure au Canada*, by Benoit Brouillette; *Arctic Trader: The Account of Twenty Years with the Hudson's Bay Company*, by Philip H. Godsell; *To Hudson's Bay by Paddle and Portage*, by J.A. Stern; *Pilgrims of the Wild*, by Wa-Sha-Quon-Asin (Grey Owl). *Canadian Historical Review* 16 (2): 196–200.

– 1935b. Review of *Documents Relating to the North West Company*, ed. W.S. Wallace. *Canadian Forum*, July.

– 1935c. Review of *Holland's Description of Cape Breton Island and Other Documents*, by Samuel Holland and D.C. Harvey. *Canadian Historical Review* 16 (4): 424–5.

– 1935d. Review of *Journals of Samuel Hearne and Philip Turnor*, ed. J.B. Tyrrell. *American Historical Review* 40 (3): 524–5.

– 1935e. Review of *The Journal of Duncan M'Gillivray of the North West Company at Fort George on the Saskatchewan, 1794*, by Arthur S. Morton. *Canadian Historical Review* 10 (2): 163–5.

– 1935f. "Some Further Material on Peter Pond." *Canadian Historical Review* 16 (1): 61–4.

– 1936. "A Note on Recent Publications on the Fur Trade." *Canadian Review of Economics and Political Science / Revue canadienne d'Économique et de*

– 1940a. Introduction to *Minutes of Council Northern Department of Rupert Land*, by Edwin E. Rich, R. Harvey Fleming, and Harold A. Innis. Toronto: Champlain Society.

– 1940b. Review of *Journal of Occurrences in the Athabasca Department,*

References

233

by George Simpson, 1820–1821, and Report, by George Simpson and E.E. Rich. *English Historical Review* 55 (217): 167–8.

– 1941a. Obituary, "Arthur James Glazebrook." *Canadian Journal of Economics and Political Science / Revue canadienne d'Économique et de Science politique* 7 (1): 92–4.

– 1941b. Review of *Colin Robertson's Correspondence Book, September 1817 to September 1822,* by Colin Robertson and E.E. Rich. *English Historical Review* 56 (222): 347.

– 1942. Review of *Henry de Tonty: Fur Trader of the Mississippi,* by Edmund Robert Murphy. *Journal of Political Economy* 50 (1): 154–5.

– 1943a. Editorial preface to *An Economic History of Canada,* by Mary Quayle Innis, v–vi. Toronto: Ryerson.

– 1943b. Foreword to *Fur: A Study in English Mercantilism, 1770–1775,* by Murray G. Lawson, vii–xx. Toronto: University of Toronto Press.

– 1944a. Obituary, "Stephen Butler Leacock (1869–1944)." *Canadian Journal of Economics and Political Science / Revue canadienne d'Economique et de Science politique* 10 (2): 216–30.

– 1944b. Review of *The Publications of the Champlain Society: Minutes of the Hudson's Bay Company, 1671–1674,* by E.E. Rich. *American Historical Review* 49 (2): 331–2.

– 1945. Obituary, "Edward Johns Urwick." *Canadian Journal of Economics and Political Science / Revue canadienne d'Economique et de Science politique* 11 (2): 265–8.

– 1946a. Obituary, "Charles Norris Cochrane, 1889–1945." *Canadian Journal of Economics and Political Science / Revue canadienne d'Economique et de Science politique* 12 (1): 95–7.

– 1946b. *Political Economy in the Modern State.* Toronto: University of Toronto Press.

– 1947a. "David Thompson 1770–1857." In *Les Explorateurs Célèbres,* edited by André Leroi-Gourhan, 158–60. Geneva: Mazenod.

– 1947b. "Mackenzie 1764–1820." In *Les Explorateurs Célèbres,* edited by André Leroi-Gourhan, 154–5. Geneva: Mazenod.

– 1947c. "Pond 1740 – End of the 18th Century." In *Les Explorateurs Célèbres,* edited by André Leroi-Gourhan, 156–7. Geneva: Mazenod.

– 1950a. Obituary, "William Burton Hurd (1894–1950)." *Canadian Journal of Economics and Political Science / Revue canadienne d'Economique et de Science politique* 16 (2): 143–5.

– 1950b. Review of *Two Memoirs – Dr. Melchior: A Defeated Enemy;* and *My Early Beliefs* by John Maynard Keynes. *Canadian Journal of Economics and Political Science / Revue canadienne d'Economique et de Science politique* 16 (1): 107–9.

– 1951a. Review of *Henry Wise Wood of Alberta,* by William Kirby Rolph. *Canadian Journal of Economics and Political Science / Revue canadienne d'Économique et de Science politique* 17 (4): 577–8.

– 1951b. "Sub Species Temporis." *Canadian Journal of Economics and Political Science / Revue canadienne d'Économique et de Science politique* 17 (4): 553–7.

– (1951) 1964. *The Bias of Communication.* Intro. by Marshall McLuhan. Toronto: University of Toronto Press.

– 1952a. *Changing Concepts of Time.* Toronto: University of Toronto Press.

– 1952b. Obituary, "William T. Jackman, 1871–1951." *Canadian Journal of Economics and Political Science / Revue canadienne d'Économique et de Science politique* 18 (2): 201–4.

– 1954. *The Cod Fisheries: The History of an International Economy.* Toronto: Ryerson.

– 1956. *Essays in Economic History,* edited by Mary Q. Innis. Toronto: University of Toronto Press.

– 2006. "The Crisis in Public Opinion: An Address by Dr Harold A. Innis," edited by William J. Buxton and Risa Dickens. *Canadian Journal of Communication* 31 (2): 307–25.

– 1995. *Staples, Markets, and Cultural Change: Selected Essays.* Edited by Daniel Drache. Montreal and Kingston: McGill-Queen's University Press.

– 2015. *Harold Innis's History of Communications. Paper and Printing from Antiquity to Early Modernity.* Edited by William J. Buxton, Michael R. Cheney, and Paul Heyer. Lanham, MD: Rowman and Littlefield.

– 2016. *Harold Innis Reflects: Memoir and WWI Writings/Correspondence.* Edited by William J. Buxton, Michael R. Cheney, and Paul Heyer. Lanham, MD: Rowman and Littlefield.

Innis, Harold A., and Morris L. Jacobson. 1936. *Agriculture and Canadian-American Trade.* Toronto: Ryerson.

References   235

Innis, Harold A., and Arthur R.M. Lower. 1933. *Select Documents in Canadian Economic History*. Toronto: University of Toronto Press.

Innis, Harold A., and Peter Pond. 1930. *Peter Pond: Fur Trader and Adventurer*. Toronto: Irwin & Gordon.

Innis, Harold A., Norman Ware, and Harold A. Logan. 1937. *Labor in Canadian-American Relations: The History of Labor Interaction*. Toronto: Ryerson.

Irving, Washington. 1836. *Astoria, or, Anecdotes of an Enterprise beyond the Rocky Mountains*. Philadelphia: Carey, Lea, & Blanchard.

Jackson, H.M. 1953. *Rogers' Rangers: A History*. Ottawa: n.p.

Jefferys, Charles W. 1927. *Collection of Pictures Illustrating the History of Canada: Pub. for the Diamond Jubilee of Confederation, 1927*. Toronto: *Star*.

Johnson, William, James Sullivan, and Alexander Clarence Flick. 1921. *The Papers of Sir William Johnson. Prepared for Publication by the Division of Archives and History*. Albany: University of the State of New York Press.

Keast, R.W. 1925. "Fur Trade Farming." BA thesis, University of University of Toronto.

Kelley, Geoffrey. 1984. "Developing a Canadian National Feeling: The Diamond Jubilee Celebrations of 1927." MA thesis, McGill University.

Kellogg, Louise Phelps. 1935. "Peter Pond." *Dictionary of American Biography* 15, 61.

Kelsey, Henry. 1929. *The Kelsey Papers [i.e. the Journals of Captain Henry Kelsey]*, edited by Arthur G. Doughty and Chester Martin. Ottawa: Public Archives of Canada and the Public Record Office of Northern Ireland.

Kennedy, W.P.M. 1922. *The Constitution of Canada. An Introduction to Its Development and Law*. London: Humphrey Milford.

Kevles, Daniel J. 1985. *In the Name of Eugenics: Genetics and the Uses of Human Heredity*. Cambridge, MA: Harvard University Press.

Klinck, Carl F., Alfred G. Bailey, Claude Bissell, Roy Daniells, Northrop Frye, and Desmond Pacey. 1976. *Literary History of Canada: Canadian Literature in English*. Vol. 1, 2nd ed. Toronto: University of Toronto Press.

Kupsch, W.O. 1977. "A Valley View in Verdant Prose: The Clearwater Valley from Portage La Loche." *Musk-Ox*, 28–50.

Lamb, W. Kaye. 1941. Review of *Colin Robertson's Correspondence Book, September 1817 to September 1822*, by E.E. Rich and R. Harvey Fleming. *Pacific Northwest Quarterly* 32 (1): 108–11.

Landon, Fred. 1927. "The American Civil War and Canadian Confederation." In *Transactions of the Royal Society of Canada, Section II*, 3rd ser., vol. 21, s. 2:55–62. Ottawa: Royal Society of Canada.

La Vérendrye, Pierre Gaultier de Varennes, Lawrence J. Burpee, and William D. Le Sueur. 1927. *Journals and Letters of Pierre Gaultier de Varennes de La Vérendrye and His Sons: With Correspondence between the Governors of Canada the French Court, Touching the Search for the Western Sea*. Toronto: Champlain Society.

Leroi-Gourhan, André, ed. 1947. *Les Explorateurs Célèbres*. Geneva: Mazenod.

Lindgren, Allana C. 2011. "Amy Sternberg's Historical Pageant (1927): The Performance of IODE Ideology during Canada's Diamond Jubilee." *Theatre Research in Canada / Recherches théâtrales au Canada* 32 (1): 1–29.

"List of Members and Affiliated Associations. 1927." *Canadian Historical Association, Report of the Annual Meeting* 6 (1): 110–16.

Lowenthal, Max. 1933. *The Investor Pays*. New York: A.A. Knopf.

Lower, Arthur R.M. 1938. *The North American Assault on the Canadian Forest: A History of the Lumber Trade between Canada and the United States*. Toronto: Ryerson.

Lower, Arthur R.M., and Harold A. Innis. 1936. *Settlement and the Forest Frontier in Eastern Canada*. Toronto: Macmillan.

Lower, Arthur R.M., and T.W. MacLean. 1946. *Colony to Nation: A History of Canada*. Toronto: Longmans, Green.

MacGillivray, Duncan, and Arthur S. Morton. 1929. *The Journal of Duncan McGillivray of the North West Company at Fort George on the Saskatchewan, 1794–5*. New York: Macmillan.

Mackenzie, Alexander. 1927. *Voyages from Montreal on the River St Laurence through the Continent of North America to the Frozen and Pacific Oceans: In the Years 1789 and 1793; with a Preliminary Account of the Rise, Progress, and Present State of the Fur Trade of That Country*. Toronto: Radisson Society of Canada.

Mackintosh, W.A. 1923. "Economic Factors in Canadian History." *Canadian Historical Review* 4 (1): 12–25.

MacMillan, Caleb. n.d. "The Untold History of Canadian Confederation – Mises Canada." Accessed 23 December 2017. https://www.mises.ca/the-untold-history-of-canadian-confederation/.

References 237

Macnaughton, John, and Walter Vaughan. 1926. *Lord Strathcona*. London: Oxford University Press.

Magnaghi, Russell M., and Herbert E. Bolton. 1998. *Herbert E. Bolton and the Historiography of the Americas*. Westport, CT: Greenwood.

Mail and Empire. 1931. Review of *Peter Pond, Fur Trader and Adventurer*, by Harold A. Innis, 5 December.

Manitoba Free Press. 1931. "Old-Time Fur-Trader's Story Is Naïve Record." 5 December.

Martin, Chester. 1927. "Confederation and the West." *Canadian Historical Association, Report of the Annual Meeting*, Canadian Historical Association, 6 (1): 20 28.

Martin, Ged. 1995. *Britain and the Origins of Canadian Confederation, 1837–67*. Vancouver: UBC Press.

– 2015. "Canada's 'Fathers of Confederation': Time to Retire an Outdated Concept?" http://www.csn-rec.ca/images/docs/todeleteonceperyearon January1/fathersofconfederation.pdf.

Masson, L.R. 1889. *Les Bourgeois de la Compagnie du Nord-Ouest: récits de voyages, lettres et rapports inédits relatifs au nord-ouest canadien: publié avec une esquisse historique et des annotations*. 2 vols. Quebec: Coté.

McArthur, Duncan. 1931. Review of *Peter Pond, Fur Trader and Adventurer*, by Harold A. Innis. *Queen's Quarterly*, Autumn, 770–1.

McDonald, William N. 2018. *The Rise and Fall of Peter Pond*. Manchester, MI: Wilderness Adventure Books.

McKinnon, C.S. 2008. "Some Logistics of Portage La Loche (Methy)." In *The Early Northwest*, edited by Gregory P. Marchildon, 105–23. Regina, SK: University of Regina Press.

McLachlan, Robert Wallace. 1906. "Connecticut Adventurer Was a Founder of Famous Fur Trust in 1783." *Connecticut Magazine* (New Haven) 10 (2): 236–7.

McPhail, Alexander J., and Harold A. Innis, eds. 1940. *The Diary of Alexander James McPhail*. Toronto: University of Toronto Press.

Meyrowitz, Joshua. 2014. *No Sense of Place: The Impact of Electronic Media on Social Behavior*. New York: Oxford University Press.

Milford Tercentenary Committee (Milford, Connecticut), and Federal Writers' Project. 1939. *History of Milford, Connecticut, 1639–1939*. Compiled and written by the Federal Writers' Project, Etc. Bridgeport, CT: Milford.

Minnesota Historical Society. 1996. "Peter Pond: An Inventory of His Papers at the Minnesota Historical Society Manuscripts Collection."

Montgomery, Richard G. 1934. *The White-Headed Eagle, John McLoughlin: Builder of an Empire*. New York: Macmillan.

Montreal Daily Star. 1932. Review of *Peter Pond, Fur Trader and Adventurer*, by Harold A. Innis.

Morgan, Cecilia. 2016. *Commemorating Canada: History, Heritage, and Memory, 1850s–1990s*. Toronto: University of Toronto Press.

Morse, Eric W. 1979. *Fur Trade Canoe Routes of Canada: Then and Now*. Toronto: University of Toronto Press.

Morton, Arthur S. 1932. Review of *Peter Pond: Fur Trader and Adventurer*, by Harold A. Innis. *Canadian Historical Review* 13 (2): 205–7.

Morton, Arthur S., and Chester Martin. 1938. *History of Prairie Settlement*. Canadian Frontiers of Settlement, vol. 2. Toronto: Macmillan.

Morton, W.L. 1966. "The North West Company: Pedlars Extraordinary." *Minnesota History* 46 (4): 157–65.

Murphy, Edmund Robert. 1941. *Henry de Tonty, Fur Trader of the Mississippi*. Baltimore: Johns Hopkins University Press.

Nelles, H.V. 2005. *The Politics of Development: Forests, Mines & Hydro-Electric Power in Ontario 1849–1941*. Montreal and Kingston: McGill-Queen's University Press.

Nettleton, De Witt Baldwin. 1939. "Peter Pond." Paper presented to the Daughters of the American Revolution, Milford, CT, 6 July 1939.

New Haven Register. 1953. "Milford Forgot Peter Pond But Canada Honors Him as Father of Fur Trade." 15 November.

Nova Scotia. 1934. *Report of Nova Scotia Royal Commission, Provincial Economic Enquiry*. Halifax: Provincial Secretary, King's Printer.

Nute, Grace L. 1932. Review of *Peter Pond: Fur Trader and Adventurer*, by Harold A. Innis. *Mississippi Valley Historical Review* 19 (1): 115–16.

– 1941. Review of *Minutes of Council, Northern Department of Rupert Land, 1821–31*, by R. Harvey Fleming. *Minnesota History* 22 (3): 309–11 .

Ogden, Isaac. 1889. Letter to David Ogden. *Report on the Canadian Archives 1889*, 29–32.

Oliphant, J. Orin. 1932. Review of *Fur Trade and Empire: George Simpson's Journal. Remarks Connected with the Fur Trade in the Course of a Voyage from York Factory to Fort George and Back to York Factory 1824–1825;*

together with Accompanying Documents, by Frederick Merk. [Harvard Historical Studies, vol. 31.] *Washington Historical Quarterly* 23 (2): 151–4.

Osborne, Brian. 2001. "Landscapes, Memory, Monuments, and Commemoration: Putting Identity in Its Place." Commissioned by the Department of Canadian Heritage for the Ethnocultural, Racial, Religious, and Linguistic Diversity and Identity Seminar Halifax, Nova Scotia. Provincial Secretary, King's Printer.

Pelletier, Yves Y.J. 2010. "The Old Chieftain's New Image: Shaping the Public Memory of Sir John A. Macdonald in Ontario and Quebec, 1891–1967." PhD diss., Queen's University.

Perkins, Simeon, and Harold A. Innis, eds. 1948. *The Diary of Simeon Perkins*. Toronto: Champlain Society.

Pond, Mrs Nathan G., and Robert Wallace McLachlan. 1906. "Introduction: Journal of 'Sir' Peter Pond – Born in Milford, Connecticut, in 1740: His Remarkable Experiences in Early Wars of New World and His Own Story of His Life as a Pioneer Fur Trader in the Savage lands of Northwest America." *Connecticut Magazine* 10 (2): 235–6.

Pond, Nathan G. 1889. *Inscriptions on Tombstones in Milford Conn, Erected Prior to 1800, Together with a Few of Aged Persons Who Died after That Date*. New Haven: Printed for the Society.

– 1906. "The Ponds of Milford Connecticut: Genealogy of a Distinguished American Family from the Time of Its settlement in the New World in 1630 to the Present Generation – From an Unfinished Manuscript left by Nathan Gillette Pond." *Connecticut Magazine* 10 (1): 161–76.

– 1987. *The Story of the Memorial in Honor of the Founders of the Town of Milford: Erected by Their Descendants and the Citizens of Milford, Dedicated August 28th, 1889, the Town's 250th Anniversary*. Ann Arbor, MI: University Microfilms.

Pond, Peter. 1906. "Journal of 'Sir' Peter Pond – Born in Milford, Connecticut, in 1740: His Remarkable Experiences in Early Wars of New World and His Own Story of His Life as a Pioneer Fur Trader in the Savage Lands of Northwest America." *Connecticut Magazine* 10 (2): 238–59.

Porter, Kenneth Wiggins. 1931. *John Jacob Astor, Business Man*. Vol. 1. Cambridge, MA: Harvard University Press.

Prince Albert Herald. 1955. "Cairn Unveiled at Historic Site. Pond's Fort Near Shell." 8 September.

240   References

Raddall, Thomas H. 1942. *His Majesty's Yankees*. Toronto: McClelland & Stewart.

Ray, Arthur J., and Donald B. Freeman. 1978. *"Give Us Good Measure": An Economic Analysis of Relations between the Indians and the Hudson's Bay Company before 1763*. Toronto: University of Toronto Press.

Rayburn, Alan. 2001. *Naming Canada: Stories about Canadian Place Names*. Toronto: University of Toronto Press.

Reimer, Chad. 2009. *Writing British Columbia History, 1784–1958*. Vancouver: UBC Press.

Rich, Edwin E. 1938. "The Hudson's Bay Company's Activities: Forthcoming Publication of Documents by Hudson's Bay Record Society Author(s)." *Pacific Historical Review* 7 (3): 267–73.

Rich, Edwin E., R. Harvey Fleming, and Harold A. Innis. 1940. *Minutes of Council Northern Department of Rupert Land*. Toronto: Champlain Society.

Riddell, William R. 1927. "Powers of a Colonial Legislature in Impeachment and Contempt." In *Transactions of the Royal Society of Canada, Section II*, 3rd ser., vol. 21, s. 2, 83–90: Ottawa: Royal Society of Canada.

Robertson, Colin, R. Harvey Fleming, and Edwin E. Rich. 1939. *Colin Robertson's Correspondence Book, September 1817 to September 1822*. Toronto: Champlain Society.

Robitaille, Georges. 1927. "La Confédération canadienne." *Canadian Historical Association, Report of the Annual Meeting* 6 (1): 62–6.

Rolph, William K. 1950. *Henry Wise Wood of Alberta*. Toronto: University of Toronto Press.

Ruddick, J.A., W.M. Drummond, R.E. English, and J.E. Lattimer. 1937. *The Dairy Industry in Canada*. Edited by Harold A. Innis. Toronto: Ryerson.

Sage, Walter N. 1925. "Unveiling of Memorial Tablet at Nootka Sound." *Second Annual Report and Proceedings of the British Columbia Historical Association*, August, 17–22.

– 1927. *Sir James Douglas and British Columbia*. Toronto: University of Toronto Library.

– 1933. Review of *New Spain and the Anglo-American West. Historical Contribution Presented to Herbert Eugene Bolton*. *Canadian Historical Review* 14 (3): 340–1.

– 1939. Review of *Journal of Occurrences in the Athabasca Department by*

George Simpson, 1820 and 1821, and Report, by George Simpson and E.E. Rich. *Oregon Historical Quarterly* 40 (1): 83–4.

– 1942. Review of *Minutes of Council, Northern Department of Rupert Land, 1821–31,* by R. Harvey Fleming and H.A. Innis. *Pacific Northwest Quarterly* 33 (2): 207–9.

Salter, Liora, and Cheryl Dahl, 1999. "The Public Role of the Intellectual." In *Harold Innis in the New Century: Reflections and Refractions,* edited by Charles R. Acland and William J. Buxton, 114–34. Montreal and Kingston: McGill-Queen's University Press.

Scholefield, Ethelbert O.S., and Frederick W. Howay. 1914. *British Columbia from the Earliest Times to the Present.* Vancouver: S.J. Clarke.

Schooling, William. 1920. *The Hudson's Bay Company 1670–1920.* London: Hudson's Bay Company.

Shortt, Adam. 1925–6. *Documents Relating to Canadian Currency, Exchange and Financing During the French Period.* 2 vols. Ottawa: Public Archives of Canada. Board of Historical Publications.

Simmons, Deidre. 1996. "The Archives of the Hudson's Bay Company." *Archivaria* 42. https://archivaria.ca/archivar/index.php/archivaria/issue/view/401.

– 2007. *Keepers of the Record: The History of the Hudson's Bay Company Archives.* Montreal and Kingston: McGill-Queen's University Press.

Simpson, George, E.E. Rich, and Chester Martin. 1938. *Journal of Occurrences in the Athabasca Department by George Simpson, 1820 and 1821, and Report.* Toronto: Champlain Society.

Skelton, O.D. 1923. Review of *A History of the Canadian Pacific Railway,* by Harold Innis. *Canadian Historical Review* 4 (3): 179.

Smith, Andrew. 2008. *British Businessmen and Canadian Confederation: Constitution-Making in an Era of Anglo-Globalization.* Montreal and Kingston: McGill-Queen's University Press.

Star Weekly. 1929. Review of *The Fur Trade of Canada,* by Harold Innis. 9 March.

Stiles, Ezra, and Franklin Bowditch Dexter. 1901. *The Literary Diary of Ezra Stiles.* New York: Charles Scribner's Sons.

Stevens, Wayne E. 1926. *The Northwest Fur Trade 1763–1800.* Urbana: University of Illinois Press.

Thomson, Robert Boyd, and Harold Boyd Sifton. 1922. *A Guide to the Poisonous Plants and Weed Seeds of Canada and the Northern United States.* Toronto: University of Toronto Press.

Thompson, David, and Joseph B. Tyrrell. 1916. *Narrative of His Explorations in Western America, 1784–1812.* Toronto: Champlain Society.

Thompson, John H., and Allen Seager. 1985. *Canada: 1922–1939: Decades of Discord.* Toronto: McClelland and Stewart.

Thwaites, Reuben Gold, and State Historical Society of Wisconsin. 1908. "The British Regime in Wisconsin." *Collections of the State Historical Society of Wisconsin.* 18:223–468.

Times Literary Supplement. 1927. Review of *The Fur Trade of Canada*, by Harold Innis, 29 September.

Toronto Globe. 1931. "A Pioneer Explorer," 5 December.

Toronto Star. 1926. "Theses on Fur Trade Are in Great Demand." ca 5 January.

– 1931. Review of *Peter Pond: Fur Trader and Adventurer*, by Harold A. Innis. 28 November.

Trotter, Reginald C. 1927. "British Finance and Confederation." *Canadian Historical Association, Report of the Annual Meeting* 6 (1): 89–96.

– 1939. "The Appalachian Barrier in Canadian History." *Canadian Historical Association, Report of the Annual Meeting* 18 (1): 5–21.

Tyrrell, Joseph B., ed. 1934. *Journals of Samuel Hearne and Philip Turnor. Edited with Introduction and Notes by J.B. Tyrrell (Journal of a Journey with the Chepawyans or Northern Indians, to the Slave Lake, & to the East & West of the Slave River, in 1791 & 2, by Peter Fidler).* Toronto: Champlain Society.

– 1944. *The Re-discovery of David Thompson.* Ottawa: Royal Society of Canada.

Underhill, Frank. 1927. "Some Aspects of Upper Canadian Radical Opinion in the Decade before Confederation." *Canadian Historical Association, Report of the Annual Meeting* 6 (1): 46–51.

Vipond, Mary. 1993. "Nationalism in the 20s." In *Interpreting Canada's Past*, edited by Jack M. Bumsted, 445–66. Toronto: Oxford University Press.

Voorhis, Ernest. 1930. *Historic Forts and Trading Posts of the French Regime and of the English Fur-Trading Companies.* Ottawa: Department of Interior.

W.P.M. 1942. Review of *Minutes of Council, Northern Department of*

References

243

Rupert's Land, 1821–1831, by R. Harvey Fleming. *English Historical Review* 57 (228): 534–5.

Wade, Mark S. 1927. *Mackenzie of Canada: The Life and Adventures of Alexander Mackenzie, Discoverer*. Edinburgh: W. Blackwood.

Wagner, Henry R. 1955. *Peter Pond: Fur Trader and Explorer*. New Haven, CT: Yale University Press.

Wallace, W.S. 1920. "The Growth of Canadian National Feeling." *Canadian Historical Review* 1 (2): 136–65.

– ed. 1926a. *The Dictionary of Canadian Biography*. Toronto: Macmillan Canada.

– 1926b. Review of *The Makers of Canada Series*, by W.L. Grant. *Canadian Historical Review* 7 (4): 325–6.

– 1927. *The Growth of Canadian National Feeling*. Toronto: Macmillan Canada.

– 1934. *Documents Relating to the North West Company*. Toronto: Champlain Society.

– 1954. *The Pedlars from Quebec*. Toronto: Ryerson.

Watson, A. John. 2006. *Marginal Man: The Dark Vision of Harold Innis*. Toronto: University of Toronto Press.

Waugh, William T. 1927. "The Development of Imperial Relations." *Canadian Historical Association, Report of the Annual Meeting* 6 (1): 82–8.

Webster, John C. 1927. "Canadian Cultural Development." *Canadian Historical Association, Report of the Annual Meeting* 6 (1): 74–81.

White, Richard. 2011. *The Middle Ground: Indians, Empires and Republics in the Great Lakes Region, 1650–1815*. Cambridge: Cambridge University Press.

Wintemberg, W.J. 1928. "Artifacts from Ancient Graves and Mounds in Ontario." *Transactions of the Royal Society of Canada*, 3rd ser., vol. 22, s. 2.

Winther, Oscar O. 1969. "A Dedication to the Memory of Robert Carlton Clark 1877–1939." *Arizona and the West* 11 (1): 1–4.

Woollacott, Arthur P. 1927. *Mackenzie and His Voyageurs: By Canoe to the Arctic and the Pacific, 1789–93*. London: J.M. Dent & Sons.

Wright, Donald A. 2005. *Professionalization of History in English Canada*. Toronto: University of Toronto Press.

– 2015. *Donald Creighton: A Life in History*. Toronto: University of Toronto Press.

Wrong, George M. 1927. "The Historian's Problem: President's Address." *Canadian Historical Association, Report of the Annual Meeting* 6 (1): 5–7.

Wrong, Humphrey H. 1927. *Sir Alexander Mackenzie, Explorer and Fur Trader*. Toronto: Macmillan Canada.

Yenckel, James T. 1987. "Hartford." *Washington Post*, 27 September. https://www.washingtonpost.com/archive/lifestyle/travel/1987/09/27/hartford/42b7d9e3-974c-4621-90d4-a9fc3abd2527/.

Young, Clarence R., John E. Dales, and Harold A. Innis. 1947. *Engineering and Society, with Special Reference to Canada*. Part I by Clarence R. Young. Part II by Harold A. Innis and John E. Dales. Toronto: University of Toronto Press.

Index

Abercrombie (Abercromby), General James (1706–1781), 21, 52, 55, 121
aboriginal peoples: 41, 84, 142; alliances with, 40; in Athabasca, 24–6, 67, 93–4, 96, 210n5; Canadian traders and, 89; cruel treatment of, 138; culture of, 109; in Great Lakes region, lxxviii, 58, 70–1, 67, 80–1, 84, 91, 151, 211n8; in Lake Winnipeg region, 86–7; plains, 23, 37, 67, 151, 211n5, 212n12; and Pond, lxxix, 28, 100, 104; representations of, xxi, lxxxix n. 24, lxxxix n. 25, lxxxix n. 26, lxxxix n. 27; in Saskatchewan, 23, 32, 35, 37, 45n8, 86, 135, 142, 154; trade with, 181, 199, 210n22
Adams, William, lxii
Adhémar, Jean-Baptiste (*dit* Saint-Martin Toussaint-Antoine) (1740–1804), canoes assigned, 5, 137, 141; and Pond, 33
Adventure of Pond & Greves [Graves], 1775, 31n3, 126, 185–6, 189–90, 200, 215
Albany, 6; and Montreal, xxviii, li, 7, 122, 127–8n5, 145; Pond and, 23, 51–2, 56, 89, 115, 127n1; traders of, 22–3, 60–1, 88–9, 199; trading route, 23–4, 140, 145, 183
Allen, Hugh Bart, lxxxvii n. 13
American colonies, li–lii, lxv, 4, 20, 52–3, 183–4
American Historical Association, Chicago meetings of in 1941, ciii n. 128; Toronto meetings of in 1932, lvi, ciii n. 128
American Revolutionary War, cvii n. 146, 4, 9, 37, 40 115, 145, 149, 183; impact of on Pond, 152; Pond in, xix; Revolutionary Navy of, lxxxvii n. 21; Simeon Perkins's diary and, cviii n. 146
Amherst, Field Marshall Jeffery (1st Baron Amherst) (1717–1797), 48, 57
Annesley, (F.C.), xcvi n. 85, xcvi n. 86
Arctic (northern ocean, sea), lxiii, 30, 106, 108, 111, 118, 120; Alexander Mackenzie and, 29, 6; Peter Pond and, cviii n. 156, 29, 101; Western, liv, 35, 93, 35

246   Index

Askin, John (1739–1815), 5, 86,
  136-7, 148n15; papers of, xxix,
  lxxxvi n. 11, cii n. 120, 18, 126,
  147, 188, 196, 208, 213n27
Assiniboine district, 136
Assiniboine people, 24, 76, 87
Astor, John Jacob (1763–1848), lii
Atcheson, Nathaniel, *History of
  Northwest Company*, 16n12
Athabasca (territory) (Arabosca,
  Arabaska), xxviii, 9–10, 26, 38, 39,
  94, 117–18, 141–2, 181; aboriginal
  people and, 7, 32–3, 45n8; Innis
  and, xli, xlvi; Pond and, xx, xxvi,
  xxxviii, xxxix, xlv–xlvi, lxxii, lxvi,
  lxxv–lxxviii, lxxx, 7, 18, 25–9,
  31n5, 33, 35–7, 90–5, 97, 99–100,
  102, 112; trade with, lxxv, 25, 30–
  1, 36, 38, 40, 44–5n4, 49, 170n31
Athabasca, Lake, xxxviii; Pond and,
  c n. 108, 26, 29, 33, 93, 100, 109–
  10; visits to, 36
Athabascan (Athapascan) people, 26
Athabasca River, xxxviii, lxxx, 33,
  40, 186
Audet, François (Francis) J., xxxiv,
  131
autobiography, lxvii–lxviii, xcvi n.
  88, 163

Baby, François, 16n16, 131
Bain, James, 214; on Canadian
  traders, 87, 89; on the Northwest
  Company (NWC), 4, 16n6
Baldwin, Captain David (1701–
  1784), 21, 51
Balfour Declaration, l, xciii n. 62
Bank of Montreal, xxxiii, 43; cente-
  nary of, 46n28
Banks, Sir Joseph, 1st Baronet, GCB,

PRS (1743–1840), lxxvii, lxxx–
  lxxxii, cviii n. 158, 108, 123
Bannerman, James, 33, 88, 140, 143,
  208, 210n5
Baptiste (young man), 74
Barbeau, Marius (1883–1969), xxxiv
Barrie (ON), 177, 191n2
Batt, Isaac (ca 1725–1791), 133,
  139–40
Bear Lake (AB), 29, 38, 101
Beaubien, Eustache Trottier Desri-
  vières (1726–1799), 126, 127n1,
  196n32, 202
beaver, li, lxxi, 27, 35, 42, 43–4n2,
  44n4, 77, 80, 84, 100, 109, 115,
  126, 136, 187, 190, 196n35, 203,
  207–8, 213n35
Beaver (people), lxxx
Beaver Club, 8, 161–2; description
  of, 167n6; medal, lxxxviii n. 23,
  130, 160–2, 170n28; Pond as mem-
  ber of, xxi, 161
Beaver Lake (SK), 5, 32, 86, 141–2
Belcourt, N.-A. (Napoléon Antoine)
  (1860–1932), xciv n. 66
Bentinck, Captain John (1737–1775),
  cviii n. 158
Berdoulay, Vincent, xiv, 222
Berger, Carl, xciii n. 61, cii n. 118
Bering, Vitus, cvi n. 145
Bigsby, J.J. (John Jeremiah) (1792–
  1881), ci n. 113, 131; *The Shoe and
  Canoe*, 134n3
biography, xiii, xiv; Canadian writing
  of, xxvii, xxxi–xxxii, xci n. 55;
  Innis and, xiii–xvi, xxv–xxvi, xxix–
  xxx, xxxix, xlii, xlvi, lxiv, lxvi–lxxi,
  lxxxvi n. 12, lcvi n. 88; and Pond,
  xvi, xxvi, xli, xlix, lxxi–lxxxiv,
  lxxxiv n. 2

Blondeau, Joseph-Barthélemy, 5, 135, 136; in Saskatchewan, 43–4n2, 44–5n4, 137–9, 141–3

Blondeau, Keshew, 136

Blondeau, Maurice-Regis (1734–1809), 5

Blondheim, Menahem, lxxxv n. 6

Boban (Beaubien?), Mr, 126, 187, 202

Bolton, Herbert Eugene (1870–1953), lv–lviii, lxvi, cii n. 122, civ n. 128, 222, 240; and Innis, lix, ciii n. 128

Braddock, General Edward (1695–1755), 51

Brebner, John Bartlet (1895–1957), lv–lviii, lxxii, cii n. 117, cii n. 125, cii n. 126, cvii n. 145, cvii n. 146; *Explorers of North America*, lxvi

Breckenridge, R.M., 46n27

British Columbia, lxiii, lxxiii, xciii n. 59, ciii n. 128, 42

British North America, xxx, lxv, lxxvi

Britnell, George Edwin (1903–1961), lxxiv n. 3

Brouillette O.C, M. Benoit, lxxxv n. 5, lxxxvi n. 12, cvii n. 145

Brown, George, cii n. 117, civ n. 128

Bruce, William, 43n2, 137–9, 141; death, 45n6

Brunhes, Jean (1869–1930), lxxxv n. 5

Bryant, George Clark (1873–1947), xviii

Buckingham, William, xxx, xci n. 50

buffalo, lxxxi–lxxxii, 25, 79, 87, 92, 109, 113; country, 24

Buffalo Bill Cody Wild West Show, lxxxix n. 27

Buffalo Historical Society, xlii, 126, 168n12, 186, 188; Phyn Ellice Pa-

pers in, 186; Porteous Papers in, 175, 188

Burns, Catherine, lxxxix n. 31, 159–60, 167n7, 171n35, 191n1

Burns, Laura, xxxiii, lxxxix n. 31, 159–60

Burpee, Lawrence Johnstone (1873–1946): and Innis, xxxv, xxxvi, xli, xcv n. 77, xcvii n. 9, 49; writings by, xxix, xxxiii, xxxvi, lxxii, lxxxv n. 11, xciv n. 68, 91, 123–4

Buxton, William J., xv

Cadotte (Cadot), Jean Baptiste (1723–1803), 4–5, 85, 87

Camp, Charles L.N., xx, xxxviii n. 22

Camps, Mr, 59, 63

Canada First, xxxiii

Canada: boundaries of, 21, 39; Britain and, xiii, 40, 58; Confederation of, xxix–xxxii, xxxiii, xxxiv, lxxi, lxxiii, xciii n. 59, xcvii n. 93, 20, 39, 42, 49, 121; Department of Railways and Canals of, xcvii n. 99; Diamond Jubilee of Confederation of, xxx–xxxvi, l, lx, lxxiii, xcii n. 54, xciii n. 60, xciv n. 66, xcv n. 73, xcvii–xcviii n. 93, xcix n. 100; fur trade companies of, 41, 73, 145–7; geography of, xxvi; Historic Sites and Monuments Board of, xxxiii, lxii, cv n. 137; Innis and, xv, xxv, xxvi, xxvii; Library and Archives Canada, 124, 170n27; and New France, 57, 111, 135; Pond and, xix, xxv; Public Archives of, xxvii, xxxvii, xciv n. 72, 134n2; Royal Society of, xxxiv, xxxvi, xxxvii, xxxix, xl, l, xli, xciii n. 61, xcv n. 77, xcvii n. 91, 20, 49, 210n2

248 Index

Canadian Antiquarian and Numismatic Society, lxxxviii n. 23, 28, 165, 170n27

Canadian Baptist, c n. 108, ci n. 110

Canadian Historical Association, x, xxxii, l, xciii n. 60, xciv n. 66, xciv n. 69, xciv n. 91, xcvii n. 93

Canadian Historical Review, xxxiii, xlviii, xci n. 52, xciii n. 60, civ n. 128, 18, 180–1

Canadian Overseas Expeditionary Force, xcviii n. 99, civ n. 129, 171n37, 191n2

Canadian Pacific Railway, xv, xxvi, xxxix, xl, 179

Canadian Shield, xcv n. 75, 42, 110

Cannon, Florence Pond Atherton (1868–?), xxii, xxiii, lxii, 192n6; and Harold Innis, xlix, lxi, lxxxix n. 30, ci n. 115, ci n. 116, cv n. 133, cv n. 134, cv n. 135, 130, 159–71, 186, 191n1, 192n6, 195n29

Cannon, LeGrand, 160

Cannon, LeGrand, Jr (1899–1979), xxii, xlix, l, 130, 161; biographical note on, lxxxix n. 29, 167n4; novel by, lxxxix n. 29

Cape Horn, 30, 119

Careless, J.M.S. (James Maurice Stockford) (1919–2009), xcii, ciii n. 127

Carlyle, Thomas (1795–1881), xv, xxix

Carnegie Endowment for International Peace, lvii, xlii, cvii n. 145; series on Canadian-American relations, lvii–lviii, cvii n. 145

Carver, Jonathan (1710–1780), xlvii, lxxiii, lxxiv, lxxix, 70; and Pond, 23, 71, 107–8, 112, 121, 127n4

Cedar Lake (MB), 23–4, 84, 86

centralization, xxxix, liii, 135, 145–7

Chaboillez, Charles Jean-Baptiste (1736–1808), 32–3, 141–2

Champlain Society, xxvii, xxxi, xxxv, 124, 135, 147, 185

Chapin, David, xx, lxxii, lxxiv–lxxviii, lxxx, lxxxii–lxxxiv, cviii n. 152, cvii n. 155, 195n30, 197n45

Chapman, Louis, xiv

Chateau de Ramezay Museum, lxxxviii n. 23

Chatique (Chief), 86–7

Chénier, Jacques (Shaney), xi, 126, 187, 189, 202

Chénier/Pond memorandum of 1775, xi, 189, 202

Chipewyan, Fort, 36–7, 117, 131

Chipewyan people, civ n. 131, 26, 128 n. 8, 131

Chippewa (Ojibwa): Pond and, 81–2, 84, 168n10; and Sioux, 23, 74–5, 168n10

Churchill (Fort) (MB), xcviii n. 99, 111, 128n10; destruction of, 101; on Pond's map, 109–10; trading visits to, 44n4, 91; Thompson at, 154

Churchill River, 86, 90, 131, 141; difficulties on, 24, 89; Frobishers and, 4, 145; guides for, 91; people of, 35, 136; settlements on, 93, 137

civic politics, xiv, lxix

Coats, Robert Hamilton (1874–1960), 194n14

Cochrane, Charles Norris (1889–1945), xxxiii, lxxxv n. 8

Cocking, Matthew (1743–1799), 86, 137–8, 140

cod fisheries, li, lxix, lxxi, 193

Colby, Charles W. (1867–1955), xxxv

Index

Cole, John (d. 1779), 44n4, 45n8, 137, 140, 143
Columbia River, lxv, 39, 146, 155
Columbus, Christopher, lxvi
Colpitts, George, civ n. 131
commemoration, xv, lxii, lxxiv, xciv n. 67, cv n. 132
Commercial Camera Company, lxxxix n. 30
Comte, William, 150
Conder, T., 120
Connecticut, xxv, xlvii, 21, 48, 50, 167n2
Connecticut Historical Society, lxxxix n. 28
Connecticut Magazine, xix, xxiii, xxiv, lxxxvii n. 19, lxxxviii n. 22, lxxxix n. 27, 122
Connecticut regiment, 21, 52
Constitutional Act of 1791, 41
Continental Association, 140
continentalism: Innis's shift to, xxvi, xlix, lii–lv, lviii, ciii n. 128, cv n. 132; and Pond, ci n. 117; views of, lv, ci n. 117, cii n. 118, ci n. 124, ciii n. 126, ciii n. 127
Contributions to Canadian Economics, 147n1, 182
Cook, Captain James FRS, 117, 119; Innis on, xxxvi–xxxviii, xcv n. 74, 20–31; Pond and, lxxxii, 114, 152; views on, 115–17, 119; voyages of, 116, 118
Cook's Inlet (River), 36; Pond's claims on, lxxxi–lxxxii, 29, 114, 117, 133; discussions of, 36, 115–16, 118, 120
Copper (aboriginal people), 36, 110
Coppermine River, 120
Corey, Albert, ci n. 117

Corey, T., 33
Corning Fountain, xxii, lxxxix n. 26
Corry, Thomas, 136–7, 200
Corry, Tod, 136
Cree people, lxxx, 85
Creighton, Donald Grant, xiii, xciv n. 67, ciii n. 126, ciii n. 127, 226; and Innis, lvii–lviii, lxxxiv n. 2
Crouse, Nellis Maynard, lxii
cultural memory: Canadian nationhood and, xiv, lxxiii; and Innis, xiv–xv, lxx, lxxiv, lxvii, lxxi; Pond's place in, xxv, lxi, lxxii, lxxiv
Cumberland House, 87, 94, 117; and aboriginal people, 87; and Canadian traders, liii, 5, 88–9, 142, 24, 25, 26, 45n4, 137–8, 140, 141, 142; establishment of, 23, 86, 152; Pond and, 23, 28, 85–6, 93–94, 117, 133, 152; Thompson at, 154
Cupido, Robert, xxxii, xcii n. 56, xcvii n. 93
Curry (Corry?), Thomas, 23, 84, 200

da Gama, Vasco (1460s–1524), lxvi
Dahl, Cheryl, xiv
Dakotas (people), 76, 168n10
Dalrymple, Alexander, cviii n. 158, 119
Darley, F.O.C. (Felix Octavius Carr), xxii
Dauphin, Fort (MB), 5, 87, 88–9, 186
Dauphin, Lake (MB), 24, 86–7, 113, 133, 152
Davidson, Gordon C., lvi, lviii, ci n. 117, cii; biographical note on, civ n. 129; history of NWC by, 29, 45n13, 123–4, 134; reproduction of Pond's material by, ci n. 114, 28–9, 43n1, 109, 110, 122, 134n6

Davis, Bruce, and Carroll Davis, lxxxv n. 9

Davis, Malcolm, xc n. 38

de Berthier, Joseph Fagniant, 95, 97, 132

decentralization, xxxix, 146

deckle, xl, xlv, xcvi n. 87

Deforest, John W., xxii

de la Blache, Paul Vidal (1845–1918), lxxxv n. 5

de la Bruère, Montarville Boucher, 194n22

de la Roche, Mazo (1879–1961), xciii n. 60

Demangeon, Albert (1872–1940), lxxxv n. 5

Dene people, lxxx, cviii n. 156

de Peyster, Colonel Arent Schuyler (1736–1822), xxiv, 83, 210n5

Depression (Great), liii, 135

Desjerlais (Joseph) and Plante (Baptiste), 34

de St Ours, Mr, 131

determinism, xiv, 178, 180, 194n20

de T. Glazebrook, Arthur James, lxxxv n. 8, xcv n. 79, 193n9

de Tonty, Henry, lviii

Detroit, 26, 38–9, 65, 149; Pond and, xxvii, xliv, lxxv, 22, 26, 58–62, 64, 70, 127n1, 152, 199; trade from, xxviii, 5, 6, 7, 9, 38, 39, 60, 88, 104, 115, 139, 140, 149

Detroit Public Library, xlii; Askin papers at, xxix, xxviii, 18, 147n1, 213n37, 221; Burton Historical collection of, xxviii, ci n. 117, cii, 168n12, 175, 210–11n5, 215; R. Harvey Fleming and, xli, 125; Williams Papers at, 125, 147n1 168n12, 175, 187, 200, 201, 215, 212–13n21

Dickens, Risa, xvi

Dillon, Richard N., lxxxi–lxxxii, cviii n. 154

Dictionary of Canadian Biography, lxxii

Dixon, Captain George (1748–1795), 119

Dobie, R. (Richard), 33, 96, 136

dogs ribs (Dogrib people), 76

Dorchester, 1st Baron KB (Carleton, Guy), 116, 120

Dougall, H.E. (Herbert Edward), 194n19

Doughty, Sir Arthur George KBE CMG FRSC, xxxiii, xxxvi–xxxvii, xci n. 41, xciv n. 72, xcvii n. 93

Douglas, Thomas 5th Earl of Selkirk, xlix, xcii n. 56

Drache, Daniel, lxxxiv n. 1

drainage basin, xxvi–xxvii, li, lix, lxvi, xcv n. 75; Columbia River, lxv, 155; Hudson Bay, xxvi, xxxv, lii, lx, 101, 111, 114, 179–80; in Innis, civ n. 130; Mackenzie River, xxxv, xxxix, li, lx, 26, 28, 29, 49, 95, 101, 104, 106, 107, 108, 114, 176, 179–80; Mississippi River, lx, 66, 114, 176, 179–80; Pacific Coast, 176, 179–80; Richelieu River, lii; St Lawrence River, lviii, lix, 39, 66, 176, 179–80

Duckworth, Harry W., lxxx

Dunbar, Carl Owen (1891–1979), 165, 170n25

Dunlop, W.J. (William James), 178, 194n15

Dunn, Judge Thomas (1729–1783), 131

Dyer, Allan and Co., 8

Index

East India Company, xix, lxii, cviii n. 158

Edgar, Oscar Pelham (1871–1948), xxix, xxxiv, xciv

Edgar, William, 115, 140

Elk River (AB), 91, 100, 111

Ellice, Alexander (baptized 1743–1805), 25, 32, 88–9

Ellice, Alex., and Co., 127n5

Ellice, Edward, 43

Ellice, James, 88

Ellice, R., 8, 95

Ellices, 96, 122

Elliot, T.C., xlvii

Ellis, W., 29, 114

Ells, Sidney Clarke, xcv n. 75

Encyclopedia Britannica, 177

Encyclopedia of the Social Sciences, lii, xv–xvi, xcii n. 53

English River, lxxx, 11, 17n20, 38, 91, 132; Fort, lxxviii, 38. *See also* Churchill River

Ermatinger, Lawrence (bap. 1736–1789), cii n. 120, 148n7; canoes assigned, 5, 32–3, 136–8; and NWC, 5; and Oakes and Co., 97; papers of, 147

Evenden, Matthew, lxx

exploration, xxvii, lvi, lvii, lxiii, lxxiv, lxxv, lxxvii, lxxviii, cvii n. 145, 20, 48, 93, 100, 120, 150–4; Bolton and, lvi–lvii; Brebner and, lvi–lvii; Burpee and, xxxvi; Chapin, lxxiv–lxxv, lxxvii–lxxviii; Gough and, lxiii, lxxvii, lxxviii; Henry and, 48; Innis and, xxvi, xxxviii, xlv, lvi, lxi, lxiii–lxiv, lxvi–lxvii, 93; Mackenzie and, lxiii, lxiv, 149, 150–2; Nute and, xlvi; Pond and, xxvi, xxxviii, xli, xiv, lxi, lxiii, lxiv, lxvi–lxvii,

lxii–lxiv, lxxv, lxxvii–lxxviii, 28–31, 48, 100, 104–5, 108, 119, 122, 153, 162, 184, 198; Thompson and, lxiii, lxiv

Falconer, Robert Alexander (1867–1943), xxxiv, 194n17

Farnum, J.L., xci n. 44

Federal Writers project, lcii

Fidler, Peter (1769–1822), 131

Finlay, Jacques (Jacco) (son), 104

Finlay, James (d. 1797), 5, 23, 84–5, 104, 131, 136, 200

fisheries, xiv, l, lv, lxix

Fleming, Ada Sitzer (1866–1935), 191–2n2

Fleming, Eva (1893–1980), 191–2n2

Fleming, R.H. (Robert Harvey): archival research of, xlii, xcviii n. 94, cii, 125, 135, 175–220; biographical note on, 191n2; and Innis, 176–8, 180, 193n8; "Trading Ventures of Peter Pond in Minnesota" of, 168n12, 188–91, 196n31, 195n25, 195n26, 195n27, 197n41, 197n42, 198–220; at University of Chicago, ci n. 117, 193n7, 193–4n10; writings of, 147n1, 180–7

Fleming, Robert Harvey (Sr), 191–2n2

forestry, timber lumber, xiv, xxvii, lv, lxix, lxxi, lxxxii, 43, 46, 67, 81

Forsyth, John (1762–1837), 8

Forsyth (John), Richardson (John) and Co., 8–9, 43, 181, 195n26

Fort de Lévis (QC), 21–2, 48

Fort des Prairies (AB), 5, 17n20, 38, 87

Forte Eadward (Edward) (NY), 52

Fort Erey (ON) [Fort Ontario], 56
Fort George (NY), 21, 52, 151
Fort Maurepas (MB), lxii–lxiii
Fort McMurray (AB), lxiii, cvi n. 143
Fort Sturgeon (SK), cvi, 171n39, 186
Fox people, 65, 70
Fox River, 66, 70, 83, 195n30
France, l–li, 9, 40, 125;
    explorers/traders of, 72; govern-
    ment of, lviii, 68, 135; military of,
    52–4, 57, 100; religion and, 61, 68
Franceway (François Jérôme, Shash
    or Saswee), 135–8
Franklin, Sir John, cviii n. 157
Fraser River, lxiv, 150–1
Freeman, Donald, 190
Frobisher, B., and J., 96, 101, 200;
    canoes/shares assigned, 6, 18, 111,
    136, 144
Frobisher, Benjamin (1742–1787), 4,
    5, 45 n. 18, 144, 200n;
    canoes/shares assigned, 5, 136–7,
    200; death of, 4, 180
Frobisher, Joseph (1740–1810), 25,
    45n18; canoes/shares assigned, 4, 5;
    and Henry, 24, 32; and Primeau,
    136–7; wintering of, 85, 136, 200
Frobisher, Thomas (1744–1788),
    xxxviii, 200; canoes/shares as-
    signed, 137, 142; and Henry, 5,
    152; and Isle à la Crosse, 32, 90–1;
    and Pond, 6, 24, 33, 85, 94, 164;
    wintering of, 25, 32, 90
Frobisher and Patterson, 34
Frobisher letter book, 4, 8, 45n18
Frobisher/Frobishers, 7, 16n6, 24, 85,
    137, 145, 200; and Henry, 87, 90,
    96, 196n37, 213n28; and Pond, 97,
    103; wintering of, 138

fur trade/traders: xxviii, xxxi, xxxviii,
    xli, xlv, xlvi, l–li, lvi, lx, lxii, lxxiv,
    lxxvi–lxxvii, lxxxvii n. 12, xciii n.
    59, xcv n. 75, xcvii n. 93, cii n.
    117, civ, 6–7, 9, 16n7, 20, 22, 24–
    6, 29–30, 32–3, 35, 39, 45n4, 47,
    48, 59–63, 68–71, 73–7, 82, 85,
    87–9, 91, 94–7, 99–100, 102–5,
    107, 109, 112, 117–19, 122,
    128n10, 132, 135–7, 139–42, 145,
    148, 181–2, 184, 186, 202

Gates, Charles, Innis and, xlvi–xlviii,
    60, 71, 75; on Northwest Fur
    Traders, lvii, lxi, lxxiv, cviii n. 152,
    47, 179, 171n36, 185
genealogy, xviii–xxi, xxiv, lxii,
    lxxxviii, lxxxvii n. 20, lxxxvii n.
    21, lxxxviii n. 22
Gentleman's Magazine, cviii n. 158,
    133
geography, xiv, xxxi, xxxix, lv, lix, lx,
    lxv, lxix, xcv, ciii n. 127, 29, 42,
    114, 198
Gerrard, Samuel, 180, 194n22
Gibb, Captain John, 59
Gibosh (Gibeau?), 44n4, 142–3
Gillespie, George, 194n22
Gillespie, John, 194n22
Gillette, Martha (1810–1831), 160
Giraud, Marcel, cvii n. 145, 46n25
Godsell, Philip, liv, cii n. 120, 147
Goodrich, Abigail, 50
Goodrich, Bartholomew, 50
Gordon, H.K., xcvi nn. 81–3
Gordon, J.S., 23
Gosselin, Amédie, 10
Gough, Barry, xli, lxxii; and other ac-
    counts of Pond, lxxiv, lxxviii,

lxxxii, cvii n. 149, cviii n. 151, cviii n. 156; approach to Pond of, lxxv; and Innis, lxxiii, xc n. 35; on Pond's character and activities, lxxvi, lxxvii, lxxxvii n. 15; writings on Pond of, lxxiii

Graham, Felix, 201, 206; and Pond, 22–3, 31n2, 32n2, 60–1, 73, 84, 125–7, 127–8n5, 152, 168n12, 187, 199–200, 215; Pond partnership documents of, 185–6, 125, 201, 206–7

Graham, George, 137

Grand Portage, xlvii, 12, 117, 137; boundaries and, 145; exploration and, 21; licences issued for, 4, 5, 6, 33, 136, 141–2; meetings at, 10, 14–15, 105, 181, 182; Pond and, 7, 18, 21–8, 30, 31n3, 35–7, 84–8, 93, 95, 97, 99–100, 102, 104, 105–6, 109, 117, 126–7, 130, 139–40, 144, 149, 152, 188, 189, 196n34, 200, 208, 210n5; traders and, 5, 10, 17n20, 26, 32–3, 35, 38, 40, 49, 89–90, 96, 102, 104, 105, 114, 117, 136–40, 144, 155, 181

Grant, Campion and Co., 9

Grant, Charles, 16n11, 33

Grant, Cuthbert (d. 1799), lxxx, 35–6, 45n11, 105

Grant, Robert, 9, 10, 15, 44n4; canoes/shares assigned, 4, 36; retirement, 46n20; wintering of, 10

Grant, R., and Porteous, 17n22, 33

Grant, Ruth, xliii

Gras, N.S.B. (Norman Scott Brien), 193n7

Graves (Greves), Booty, 44n4, 210n5; canoes/shares assigned, xxxviii, 95,

144; information on, 218, 210n5; Pond and, 27, 34, 140, 188, 200; traders and, 44n4, 45n8, 139, 141–3; travels of, 43n2

Gray, John, 43

Great Britain (England), li, cviii n. 158, 41, 169n15; colonies and, cvi n. 146, 155; economy of, 20, 41, 43; government of, 130; MacKenzie and, 149–50; military of, lxxiii–lxxiv, lxxvi, cviii n. 158, 20, 40, 51–3; Pond and, 106; Royal Society of, cviii n. 158; Thompson and, 154–5; trade with, 10, 11, 42, 87–8

"great fleet" of 1630, xix, 50

Great Lakes: Pond and, xviii, xx, lxxv, 183–5; routes to and over, 61, 210n5, 211n10

Greenfield, Bruce R., lxxix, lxxxiii

Gregory, Armstrong, and Kemp, xlii

Gregory (John) and McLeod (Normand), 8, 28, 38

Gregory, John (1751–1817), 3, 10; canoes/shares assigned, 36; and fur trade organization, 11, 15, 104

Gregory, McLeod and Co., 37, 104

Gregory, Oscar T., lxxxix n. 30

Grimsby (ON), 177, 191n2

Groseilliers, Médard Chouart des (1618–1696), lix

Hage, Anne A., 47

Haldimand, Sir Frederick, 16n11, 45n18, 103, 134n4, 211

Hamilton, Hon. Henry, 114, 123

Hammond, Melvin, xcvii n. 93

Hansom, Joseph, 137

Harper, Lawrence A., lix

Harris, Robert, xxxii

Harris, T.W., xli, xliii, c n. 104

Harrow, Captain Alexander, 18

Hartford (CT), xxii, lxxxix n. 26, lxxxix n. 27, 50, 165

Harvard University, 176, 193n7

Harvey, D.C., xxxvi, lxxxv n. 11, xciii n. 59

Hearne, Samuel (1745–1792), xxxi; and Cumberland House, 24, 86, 138, 152; expeditions of, 101, 111, 119, 128n10; journals of, 4, 8, 13, 43n2, 44n4, 45n8, 131, 147, 148n2

Heilbron, Bertha Lion (1895–1972), 175, 192n5

Henry, Alexander (the elder) (1739–1834), 115–16; biographical notes on, xli, xciv n. 70, xcvii n. 92, 48; canoes/shares assigned, 4, 43n2; and colonies, 87, 122; and fur trade, 4–5, 96, 139–40; letter of to Joseph Banks, 1781, lxxvii, cviii n. 158, 90, 108, 123; and Pond, xli, 4, 21–5, 29, 35, 48, 84–5, 94, 96, 115, 133, 200; travels of, xxxi, lxxxviii, xli, 16n6, 22, 32, 49, 63, 85, 86, 87–8, 92, 93, 97, 126, 128n6, 138, 152, 168n9, 188, 196n37, 200, 208, 214; views on geography of, 29, 116

Henry Kelsey Papers, xxvii

Heyer, Paul, ix, xii, lxxxiv n. 4, xiii, xiv, lxviii, lxx, lxxiv n. 4, lxxxvii n. 16

Holland, Captain Samuel Johannes (1728–1801), lxxxv n. 11, 31, 118–20

Holliday, E., xci n. 39

Holmes, Oliver Wendell, 213n25

Holmes, William (d. 1792), 110; canoes/shares assigned, 4–6, 8, 14, 17n23, 33, 34, 36, 84, 102; misconduct of (alleged), 210n5; travels of, 44n2, 44n4, 45n8, 85, 97, 138, 139, 141–2

Holmes (William) and (Robert) Grant, 5, 8, 85, 97; canoes/shares assigned 6, 33–4, 143–4

Holmquist, June D., 47

Horn, Alfred Aloysius, xiv, c n. 109

Howay, Judge Frederick William, xciii n. 59, xciv n. 69, 230, 241; and Innis, lxii, lxiii, xcv n. 74, cv n. 132, cvi nn. 138–41; and Northwest coast history, 46n26, 70n74

Howe, George Augustus, 3rd Viscount (ca 1725–1758), 53, 55

Hubbard, Mary, lxxv, 21, 50

Hubert, Henri, xxxiii

Hudson Bay, 107; aboriginal people trading at, xxxix, 24, 27, 87, 99, 101, 145; drainage basin of, xxvi, xxxiv, 110, 117; export of furs from, xxxix, 42, 89, 117; routes to and from, 30, 108, 118–19; Thompson and, 155

Hudson Bay Railway, xxvii, lxx, xcvii n. 99, 231

Hudson's Bay Company, 150; aboriginal people and, 100; employees of, 35, xciv n. 66, c n. 104; Innis and, xxxviii; Mackenzie and, 150; NWC and, 24, 26, 35, 88, 145, 149–50, 176, 193n7; organization of, 23, 30, 41; Thompson and, 155; traders and, 117–18, 136–7; trading posts of, xxxix, li, 88–9, 119, 132, 155; Western Arctic department of, 93

Hudson's Bay Record Society, 191–2n2; archives of, 123, 135, 191–2n2

Index

Hunter Rose Co., xliii
Hurd, William Burton, lxxxv n. 8
Hutchins, Robert, lxxxv n. 9

Igor I. Sikorsky Bridge, 171n32
Imperial Conference of 1923, l
Innis, Harold: biographical work by,
xiii–xvi, lxxxv n. 12; on Canadian
Pacific Railway history, xv, xxvi,
xxxix, 178; Coats and, 194n14;
communications writings by, xiii,
xv, lxxxiv n. 4; Diamond Jubilee of
Confederation and, xxxiii–xxxiv;
"dirt" research of, xxvi, lxx, lxxiv;
document collections edited by,
178; on explorers, xxxiv, 149–52;
on fisheries, 193n8; fur-trade writings of, xvi, xxv, xxvi–xxxix, l, lvi,
lviii, xciv, xcv n. 80, civ n. 130, 32–
42, 178, 194n13, 194n16, 195n28;
and Gras, N.S.B., 193n7; on
McPhail, xv; memoir of, xv; on
newspaper history, xv; on NWC, 3–
17, 49, 96; obituaries written by,
xv, lxxxvi n. 12; on Perkins, xv; and
possibilist cultural geography, xiv;
and public history, xiv; resignation
of, 194n18; reviews by, xxxvii, lii,
lvi, lviii, lxxxv n. 10, 195n24; and
Royal Society of Canada, 20, 49,
xcv n. 77; and Ryerson Press, xcix
n. 101, xcix n. 102, xcix n. 103,
xcix n. 104; and Sage, Walter, cv n.
132; staples writings by, xlii, xcix n.
101, c n. 103; and Tyrrell, c; at University of British Columbia, cv n.
132; and University of Toronto Extension, 177; on Veblen, xv
– on Pond, xcv n. 73, xcv n. 74, 32,
191–2n2, 192n3, 192n6; archival

documents, 125–6; background to,
xvi–xxv, xxvi, xxxiv, lxvii, lxxxi,
lxxxii, 47, 49; biographical aspects
of, xxxix–xlvii; in Florence Cannon
correspondence, lxxxix n. 31, 157–
71, 175; and commemoration, lix–
lxiii, cv nn. 136–7; and (Canadian)
Confederation, xxxiv, l, ci n. 117,
49; and continentalism, xlix–lix,
c n. 117, and Les Explorateurs
Célèbres, lxiii–lxv; evaluative aspects of, xiii, lxxvii, lxxxiii; Fleming
on, 195n28; and murders (alleged),
ci n. 112, 126; in the Innis oeuvres,
xxv–xxviii, xxxv–xxxix, xc nn.
35–6; and Peter Pond's publishing
history, xxxix, xl, xli, xlii–xlix,
130–1
Innis, Mary Quayle, lxxi, 159, 193n8
Innis, Wendy, 159
Irving, Washington, xix–xx, xxii
Irwin, John S., xcvi n. 84
Irwin and Gordon Ltd: bankruptcy
of, xli; correspondence with Innis
from, xcvi nn. 81–4; Innis's claims
against, xcviii n. 95; as Peter Pond
publishers, xxxix, xl

Jackson, Mrs K.B. See Reid, M.G.
Jarvis, Julia I., xci n. 40
Jay Treaty, 9–10, 41, 145
Jefferys, Charles William, xxxii, xliii,
xcix n. 100
Johnson, Sir William, 59; The Papers
of Sir William Johnson, 127n1,
210n5
Johnstone, Colonel John, 56
Journal of American History, 122,
167n3

Kaministiquia (Fort William), 40
Kamschatka, 214
Kane, Lucile M., 47
Kay, J., and D. Rankin, 33, 142
Kay, William, with John Kay, 140, 201; canoes/shares assigned, 33–4, 141–4
Keast, Ronald, 194n19
Kelley, Geoff, xxxi, xciii n. 55
Kellogg, L. (Louise) P., lxxii, 127n2
Kemp, Frederick, xlii, xliii, xcviii nn. 95–6
Kennedy, W.P.M. (William Paul Mc-Clure), xxxvii, xci n. 40; *Constitutional History of Canada* (1922), xciv n. 72
Keynes, John Maynard, lxvii, lxxxv
King, Horace H., xcv n. 78
King, William Lyon Mackenzie, xxxi
King George's Sound, 29, 114
Klinck, Carl F., et al., xxix, xci n. 50, ci, cii
Krum, G.B., xcii n. 46

La Baie des Puants (Green Bay), 23, 60, 62, 64, 152, 202, 212n14
Labrador, lxxxi, 110, 146, 176, 193n8
Lac Isle à la Crosse, xxxviii; T. Frobisher at, 5, 25, 32, 90–1; Henry and, 90, 92; Mackenzie at, 149; Pond at, 27, 100, 152; Primeau at, 141
Lac la Pluie (ON) (Rainy Lake), 3, 16n17, 36, 94
Lac la Ronge (SK), xlviii, 6, 18, 26, 35, 108, 152; Pond and, 168, 178; Waden and, 166–8
Lahontan, Louis Armand, Baron de (1666–prior to 1716), cvii n. 150, 107, 121

Lake Champlain, 53, 55, 61
Lake Erie, 23–4, 88
Lake George (NY), 52–3, 55, 61
Lake Huron, 23, 60–1, 88, 168n9
Lake of the Woods (ON), 37, 82
Lake Ontario, lii, 24, 61, 183
Lake Winnipeg, 40; Blondeau at, 138; Buoys and, 136; Frobishers and, 90; Henry and, 24, 49, 90; Innis on, lxii, 186; Pond and, 24, 49, 85, 90, 94, 186
Lake Winnipegosis, 86, 138–9
Landon, Fred, xxxiv
Laurentian school, cii n. 127
La Vérendrye, Pierre Gaultier de Varennes, sieur de (1685–1749), xxxi, li, lxiii, lxxxvi, lxxxv n. 11
Lawson, Murray, lix, cii
leather, xiv, lxix, 1, 14, 69, 77, 79, 109, 207, 216
Le Comte, Eustache, 127, 131
Lecuyer, J., 34
Leroi-Gourhan, Andrè: on celebrated explorers, viii, lxiii, 149–56
Leroux, Laurent (1759–1855), 36, 104, 45n11
Lesueur, (Le Sueur) Toussaint Louis (1727– ?), lxxxv n. 11
Lewis, Ethelreda, c
Linsley, John, 50
London, U.K., 30, 123, 133; Fleming and, 191n2; Phyn Ellis and, 23, 42, 88, 182–3; MacKenzie and, 119, 150; traders and, 198
Long, John Alexander, xcvi n. 90, c n. 104
Longmoor, Robert, 44n4
Lowenthal, Max, liii
Lower, A.R.M. (Arthur Reginald Marsden), ci n. 117, ciii n. 126; on

Canadian timber and lumber trade, 46n29

Mabane, Judge, 131
MacDonald, John A., xcviii n. 93
MacDonell, Rev. J.A., lxxxvi n. 12
MacGillivray, Duncan, lxxxv n. 11
MacIver, R.M. (Robert Morrison), 178–9, 194n13
Mackenzie, Alexander, lxxxv–lxxxvi n. 10, 95, 97, 195n23; as author, xxxiv, lxiv, lxxviii, 6, 27, 44n3, 45n14, 16–17, 90, 95, 98, 123, 150; commemoration of, xxxiii–xxxiv, l, xciv n. 64; explorations of, xxxiv, lxiii–lxiv, 6, 119–20, 149, 152; Fleming on, 179; and Pond, xxxvii, lxxvii, cvii n. 149, 27, 105–7, 110–11, 118, 144; and Small Patrick, xlv; as trader, 7, 9–10, 14–25, 27, 104, 123, 181, 195n23; and Turnor, 30; writings on, xxx, xxxv, xxviii–xxix, xlix, xci n. 50
Mackenzie, Roderick (1761–1844), ci n. 113, 36; and Alexander Mackenzie, 3, 16n17, 105–6, 116–17; and Pond, 129n15, 131; reminiscences by, 15n3, 104–5
Mackenzie, Sir William, 231
Mackenzie River, xxvi, xxxv, xxix, li, lx, lxiv, 26; as *De Cho*, cviii n. 156; delta, liv, xcvi n. 90; district, 100; and Mackenzie, 149; and NWC, 36, 145; and Pond, 28–9, 100, 105, 108, 116–17, 119, 152; as River Disappointment, 29, 116, 149; and trade, 118
Mackenzie's Rock, xxxiv
Mackintosh, W.A. (William Archibald), ciii n. 127

MacMechan, Archibald, xv, xxix
MacNaughton McArthur, Duncan, xliv, xlv–xlvi
Mail and Empire (Toronto), xliv, c n. 108
Makers of Canada series (George M. Morang version), xci n. 52
Makers of Canada series (new version), xxviii–xxxii, xcii n. 55
Mandan people, 112
Manitoba Free Press, xliv
Maritimes, xciii, l, 176
marketing, lii, lxviii, 177, 182–3
Marshall, Thomas M., ci n. 122
Martin, Chester Baily (1882–1958), xciii n. 59, 192
Martin, Ged, xxxii, xcvii n. 93
Masson, L.R. (Louis Rodrigue), history of NWC by, xxviii, xxxi, 3, 5, 15, 16n6, 17n22, 45n9, 46n19, 106
Matonnabee (Matonabee), 101
McBeath, George (1740–1812), 6, 14, 25, 31n4, 101, 136, 142–4; canoes/shares assigned, xxxviii, 4, 5, 7, 8, 32
McBeath, Pond, and Graves, 27
McBeath and Co., 6, 34, 95–6, 143
McBeath and Wright, 33, 142
McCord, David Ross, xviii, lxxxvi n. 18, 5
McCormick, Charles, 142–3, 211n5
McDonald, Bill, cv n. 134, cvii n. 147, 171n32
McGill, Jas, 33
McGill, James (1743–1813), 5, 23, 43, 62; canoes/shares assigned, 33, 137
McGill, John, 5, 33
McGill, John, and Thomas Frobisher, 5, 142

McGill, Frobisher, and Blondeau, 137
McGill (John) and Paterson (Patterson?), 34, 144
McGillivray, William (1764–1825), 42; canoes/shares assigned, 106; and Pond, xlix; and NWC, 9–10
McGills, 96
M'Gillivray, Duncan, lxxxv n. 11
McKindlay, John (d. 1833), 33, 96
McKinnon, C.S., xcv n. 75
McLachlan, R.W. (Robert Wallace), biographical notes on, lxxxviii n. 23, 170n28; David McCord and, lxxxvii n. 18; and Pond/NWC, xx, xxi; and Sophia Pond, xvii, xviii, lxxxviii n. 22, 165
McLeod, Normand, 3, 14, 17n23, 36, 105, 45n11
McLoughlin, John, 146–7
McMaster University, xxvi, xcvi n. 90, 171n37
McNamara & Co., 207
McPhail, Alexander James, xiii–xiv, xvi, lxviii, lxxxvi, lxxxvii n. 14
McTavish, Simon (1750–1804): canoes/ shares assigned, 3–4, 6, 10; and Frobishers, 7; house of, 11; and NWC, 7; and Pond, 127n5, 138; trading activities of, 5, 6–9, 11–12, 14–15, 22–4, 87–8, 96, 122, 211
McTavish and Bannerman, 33, 140, 208, 211
McTavish and Co., 6, 143
McTavish and J.B. Durocher, 33
McTavish and McBeath, 25
McTavish, Frobisher and Co., 4, 7–9, 14, 36, 181–2; canoes/shares assigned, 3, 7, 17n22
McTavish, McGillivrays and Co., 182
Memorial of the Northwest Com-

pany, 1785, 28, 45n18, 103, 114, 123
Menominee (people), 64
merchants, 39, 41, 46n18, 114, 143, 167, 170n27, 181, 199
Merriman, Robert Owen, xxviii, xci n. 42, civ n. 131
Methye Portage, xcv n. 75, 35, 42, 99, 108, 117; commemorative plaque of, lxiii, cvi n. 143; Pond and, xxxv, lxxv–lxxvi, 26, 28, 93, 106
Meyrowitz, Joel, lxxxiv n. 1, 237
Miami people, 9
Michigan, Lake, 62, 80, 154, 202
Michilimackinac, Fort (Mackinac), 5, 168n9, 206, 211n7, 211n10; as commercial and military centre, lxxiii, lxxvi, 8, 59, 60, 64; Henry, Alexander and, 49; McBeath and Corry at, 88, 136; Pond and, lxxiv, 18, 22–3, 24–5, 31n5, 59, 61–2, 72, 75, 80–2, 87–9, 96, 125–6, 130, 152, 162, 167n8, 195n29, 198–9, 201; route to, 40, 195n30; trade at, 5, 9, 16n7, 61, 63, 71, 104
Michipicoten, 43n2, 45n6
"middle ground," lxxix, 243
Milford (CT), cvii n. 147; First Congregational Church of, 171n33; memorial bridges of, lxi; Peter Pond Society of, cv n. 134; and Pond, lxxvii, cvi, 20–1, 27, 30, 51, 56, 58–60, 106, 119; Pond (Charles Hobby) and, 167n2; Pond (Dr Nathan) and, xvii–xxii, lxxxviii; Pond (Peter L.) (1933–2000) and, 171n33; tercentenary of, lxii, cv n. 136
minerals, lxxxiii, 42, 169n20

Index

259

Minnesota, xlvii, cii, 168n9, 175, 197–9, 201, 203, 207, 209, 211–13

Minnesota Historical Society, xxviii, ci n. 117, 47; Archives of, 175, 184; Innis and, lxi, xxvii, 15n5, 166; Peter Pond papers of, 168n12, 175, 188, 192n6, 200

Minnesota Society of the Colonial Dames of America, lvii

Minneto [Manitou], 75–6

mining, xxvii, lv

Mississippi River (upper), lvii, lix; aboriginal people and, 65, 83, 94; geography of, 66, 70, 78, 81, 110; navigation down, 117; Pond on, xxv, xlvii, lxxvi–lxxviii, xciii n. 153, 4, 23, 48, 60, 64, 70, 71, 82–5, 87, 94, 109, 112, 113, 120, 121, 125–6, 152, 183, 184–6, 195n29; Thompson and, 154; trading on, 59, 61, 62, 126, 136, 138

Missouri River, 64–5

Mitchell, Mrs Sydney Knox (Mary), 163, 169n15

Mitchell, Sydney Scott (1876–?), 162, 169n15

Mohawk River, lii, 61, 183

Montcalm, Louis-Joseph de (1712–1759), xxxi

Montgomery, Richard G., cii n. 120, 109n4, 146, 238

Montour, Nicholas (1756–1804): canoes/shares assigned, 4, 36, 101, 144; and early NWC, 9–11, 15, 43n2

Montreal, xviii, xxxii–xxxiii, liii, lxxxviii, 5, 18, 90, 98, 104, 115; and Albany, xxviii, li, 7, 87; Beaver Club in, xxi; fur trade and, xxviii, xxxix, xlvii, lii, liv, lx, lxii–lxiii, lxvi, 4–5, 9–10, 14, 60, 87, 95,

138, 143, 183; Mackenzie and, lxiv; NWC at, xxxix, 8, 27, 152; Phyn and Ellice in, 22–3, 182; Pond and, xxix, lxxv, 18, 21, 26, 29, 57, 61, 88, 95, 99, 106, 114, 123, 133, 173, 214; Thompson and, xxxii, 154

Montreal Star, xlv

Morang, George M., xxix

Morton, A.S. (Arthur Silver) (1870–1945), xiv, xlvi, xlvii, lxxxv n. 11, xc n. 35, 130–1, 171n38, 210n1

Morton, W.L. (William Lewis) (1908–1980), xcv n. 76

Mount Royal Cemetery, xxxii

Mure, John, 194n22

Nadeau, François, ci, 127, 131

Nathan, George Jean, lxvii

Nef, John U., lviii, 193n10

Nepean, Sir Evan, 30, 119–20, 133

Nettleton, Dr De Witt Baldwin, lxii, cv n. 137

New Caledonia (BC), 28, 40

New Defence, xx

New England, xix, l, lxxxix n. 29, ciii n. 128, 40–1, 50, 137, 167

New France, 67, 170n31; conquest of, 20–1, 57–61, 120, 184

New Haven (CT), xlix, lxxxix n. 27, 20, 130, 159, 167n2

New Haven Colony Historical Society, 163–5, 169n16

New Haven Museum, lxxvii n. 18, lxxxviii n. 22, 169n16, 170n29

New Ontario, xxvii

New Orleans, lxxv, 71–3, 143, 145

New York (city), xvii–xviii, lii, liii, lxxxvii n. 17, 160; Felix Graham and, 22, 60, 73, 127n5, 199; Pond and, 51, 56, 60, 62, 73–4, 115; traders and, 30, 61, 88, 183, 199

Niagara, Fort, 6, 22, 56–8, 152

Niagara Portage, 127n5

Nicolet, Jean, 202n

Nolin, J.B., 43n2

Nooth, J. (John) Mervin, lxxx, lxxxii–lxxxiii, cviii n. 155, cviii n. 157

North America: aboriginal people of, 109; Britain and northern half of, 20, 40; HBC and NWC in, 41; Pond and, 114, 152, 182; Thompson and, 154–6

North Saskatchewan River, 9, 25, 88–9. *See also* Saskatchewan (River and region)

Northwest: Frobishers and, 87, 141–2; Graves and, 184, 189; Ogden and, 117; Phyn and, 182–3; Pond and, 94, 96, 101, 107, 114, 116, 118, 120, 123, 152, 212n21, 213n24; Primeau and, 141; trade in, 4, 104, 143, 145, 213n28; trade in, 4, 104, 143, 145, 213n28; unification in, liii; Waden and, 95

North West Company: Askin and, 248n15; and Athabaska, 9, 26, 28, 35, formation of, lvi, 4, 6–8, 15n1, 16n11, 95, 144; Mackenzie and, lxiii, 114, 150; McTavish and, 210n5; organization of, 20, 27–8, 117, 142, 145, 184; on the Pacific Coast, 28; Pangman and, 149; Peche and, 131; Pond and, xvii, xx, xxv, xlvii, lxxiii, xcvii n. 93, cviii n. 158, 98, 101, 104, 106–7, 158, 173; precursors to, xvi, xxviii, xl–xli, l, 135, 170n31; on the

Saskatchewan, xxxviii, xiv, 85; studies of, lii, xcv n. 76, civ n. 129

Northwest Passage, xlvi, lxxiii, lxxvi, 36, 111, 118–19

Nottawaseas Notawaysease, 71–2, 76, 83

Nova Scotia, xvi, lxviii, cvii n. 146, 193n8

Numismatic and Antiquarian Society of Montreal, lxxxviii, 170n27

Nute, Grace Lee, xlvi–xlvii, 47n; and Canada, cii n. 117; and *Les Explorateurs Célèbres*, cvii n. 145; and Fleming, 175, 185, 191n2; and Innis, xlvi–xlvii, xci n. 47; and Pond map, 133–4

Oakes, Forrest (d. 1783), 33; shares of, 141–4

Oakes and Co., 6, 97, 143

Oakes (Forrest) and Ermatinger (Lawrence), 33

Ochapawase nation, 75, 78

Ogden, Judge David (1707–1798), lxxx–lxxxi, cviii n. 154, cviii n. 155, 116, 118, 123, 133

Ogden, Isaac (1739–1824), lxxx–lxxxii, cviii n. 154, cviii n. 155, cviii n. 158, 30, 105, 116–18, 123, 134

Ogilvie, John, 180

Old Establishment, 111, 120

Ostenso, Martha, xciii n. 60

Oswego, 22, 56–7, 61

Ottawa people, 136

Ottawa River, 22, 40, 43, 62–3; route, 140, 152, 183, 211

Overland telegraph, lxiii, cv n. 132

Owen Sound, 177

Index

Pacific Coast, xxvi, xxxiii, 28–9, 114, 118

Pacific Ocean: aboriginal people and, 112; and fur trade, 20, 41; Mackenzie and, 150; North, 102, 115–16; routes to, lxiv, 117; Pond and, 120–1

pageants, xxxi–xxxii, xcvii n. 93

Pangman, Peter (1744–1819), xlviii, 3, 149; locations of, 15, 36, 43n2, 44n4, 141–2; organizations in, 10–11, 14–15, 35, 37, 102, 104, 139; and Pond, 36, 103, 149; and Ross, 37–8, 102–4; retirement, 46n20; shares of, 9–10, 14, 34, 36, 38, 138, 143–4

Parker, William, 180, 194n22

Pasquia (MB), 137–8, 141

Paterson, Charles, 32, 137, 201

Paterson and Frobisher, 34, 144

Paterson, Holmes, and Franceway, 137

Patterson, 4, 23, 85, 87

Patterson & Kay, 201

Peace River, 105, 112–13; and Mackenzie, 149; and Pond's maps, 100, 104; and Pond's posts, 27, 114, 152; and Thompson's mapping, 154

Peche, ci n. 112, 131

Pelletier, Yves, xcvii n. 93

pemmican, xxxix, lviii, xxviii, lx, civ n. 131, 26, 35, 39, 94, 128n8

Perkins, Simeon (1735–1812), xiii, xv, lxvii, lxxxiv n. 2

Peter Pond monument, civ n. 134, cv n. 137

Peter Pond Newsletter, cvii n. 147, 171n32

Peter Pond Society, civ n. 134

petrifaction (petrafaction), 165, 169n20

Phillips, P. Lee, 123

Photostat Corporation, lxxxix n. 30

photostatting, lxxxix n. 30

Phyn, G., 110

Phyn, James, 88

Phyn (James) and Ellice (Alexander): and Canadian banking, 42; Fleming and, 182–3; locations of, 8, 22, 88; and G. McBeath, 96; shares held by, 7–8; and S. McTavish, 23

Phyn (James) Ellice (Alexander) and Porteous, 125

Pierce, Lorne, xlii, xcviii n. 95, xcix n. 101; Innis and, xliii, xcviii n. 96

Pink, William, 135–6

Pinnashon (old) (WI), 220

Pioneer Histories series, lvi

Pollock, Duncan, 104

Pollock, Mr, 38

Pond, Captain Charles (ca 1744–1832), xvi, xix, lxxxviii, cv n. 137, 125, 159

Pond, Hon. Charles Hobby (1781–1861), xvi, xix, 159–60, 167n2

Pond, Charles Hobby, Jr, 159, 161, 165

Pond, Harold Gillette, 9, 159, 161

Pond, John, xix, 49

Pond, Joseph Lawrence, lxi, 171n34

Pond, Mary Hubbard, lxxv, 21, 50

Pond, Nadine Lawrence (1869–1950), 169n17

Pond, Dr Nathan Gillette (1832–1894), xvii–xx; and Florence Cannon, 160; and Pond's memoir, xx, xxii; Pond-related projects of, xix–xxi, lxxxvii n. 20, lxxxvii n. 22

Pond, Peter (1718–1765), 99, 132
Pond, Peter (son of Peter, b. 1718) (1740–1807), 7, 50; and aboriginal people, 22, 26, 28, 40, 109–11; achievements of, 107; and Albany-Montreal trade, 23, 26, 36, 94; ancestry of, 49; and Athabasca, 5–7, 14, 18, 24, 26–9, 31n5, 90, 94, 97, 100, 102–5, 111, 116, 133, 142–3; as author, lxxxii; Beaver Club medal of, lxxxviii n. 23; bibliography of, lxxxii, 122–7; biographical studies of, lxx–lxxxiii, lxxxiv n. 2, xciv n. 70, cv n. 137, cvii n. 146–cviii n. 158; birth, cv n. 137, 21, 50; business acumen and organizational skills of, lxxvi, lxxx, 26, 175, 184, 198; character of, lxxxvii n. 15; concern with appearance and style, 190, 197n45; and Cook, xxxv–xxxvii, 20, 29, 114; culinary objects of in personal chest, 191, 215–19, 247n49; as diplomat, lxxvi–lxxvii; early army life of, lxxvi, 28, 49–50; and exploration, lxxxii, 107–8; as father of Canadian Confederation, xvi, xxxv; final days of, 31, 107; geographic knowledge of, 198; Graham and Williams partnership of, 21, 31n1, 31n4, 168n12; and Grand Portage, 6, 24, 26–7, 29, 31n3, 36, 97, 101, 104, 130; and Greves (Bootsy), 43n2, 44n4, 185, 186; and HBC, 24–6; and Henry (Alexander), 24; in Lake Winnipeg region, 23, 86, 89, 138; at Lake Superior, 156; and Mackenzie (Alexander), xxxiv, cvii n. 149, 28–30, 105; as mapmaker, lxxvii, lxxxii, 27–8, cvii n. 159; map of

1785, 29, 87, 99–100, 108, 114, 116, 123, 198; map of 1790, cviii n. 158, 104, 134; and McBeath and Co., 26, 31n4; medicinal items in personal chest of, 191, 215–19, memoir (journal) of, xxxix–xl, lviii, lxiv–lxvii, lxxiv–lxxvi, lxxxvii n. 21, xc n. 34, xcvi n. 88, cvii n. 146, cvii n. 150, cviii n. 152, 120–1, 130, 160, 192n6, 196n36, 210n3; and Methye Portage, 26, 28; and Michilimackinac, 24, 31n5, 130, 167n8, 195n29, 195n30, 198; in Milford, 20, 22, 28, 30, 58, 106, 119; on the Mississipp, upper, i, 4, 94, 200, 213n29; murder, accusations of having committed, 184; and Northwest, 28, 198; relative obscurity of, 21; and NWC, 4, 8, 10, 27–8, 49–50, 67, 98, 101, 106–7, 198, 213n24; and Ogden (Isaac), 107, 117–18; as peacemaker, 75; and pemmican, 26; reputation of, lxxvii; and Ross, 36, 99, 104–5, 141; on the St Peter's (Minnesota) River, 22, 198, 213n23; in Saskatchewan region, xxxviii, 5, 26–7, 28, 43–4n2, 87–8, 93, 97; scholarship on, lxx–lxxxiii, 81–2; as scientist and collector, lxxxii; scientific training, lack of, 28; and Slave Lake, 27, 29, 105; spelling, idiosyncratic, by, xxvi; and 1785 memorial, 28, 45–6n18; Thompson (David) on, 28, 94; and Waden, 97–8, 102n5, 130, 144; and West Indies, 28; and Yale University, xlix, 119, 134, 168n14, 169n19. *See also* Innis, Harold, on Pond
Pond, Peter (III) (1763–1813) (son of

Peter b. 1740), xix, lxxxvii–lxxxviii n. 21, lxxxviii n. 22

Pond, Rev. Peter Lawrence (1933–2000, son of Joseph Lawrence Pond): biographical note, 171n33; and 1939 Milford Tercentenary, cv n. 136; and Nettleton, cv n. 137; and Peter Pond (b. 1740), lxi; and 1955 Peter Pond monument, cv n. 134, cv n. 137, 171n39

Pond, Samuel, 21, 50

Pond, Samuel II, 50

Pond, Samuel III, 50

Pond, Sebastian, 163, 169n17

Pond, Sophia (Mrs Nathan Gillette Pond) (1836–1909), xxv, 161, 165; and Florence Cannon, 161; and McLachlan, xvii, lxxxiv n. 18, lxxxviii n. 22, lxxxviii n. 23, 165; papers of, 165; and Pond's journal, xvi–xxii, 159–60, 190

Pond, Susanna (Newell), xxiv, 22, 58; Newfoundland and Labrador, 50–1

Pond, William, xix, 21, 50

Pond, Winthrop, 130, 159, 161

Pond (Peter) and (Booty) Greves, 126, 144, 188, 200

Pond (Peter) and (George) McBeath, 8, 31, 89, 127

Pond (Peter) and (Thomas) Williams, and Pond/Graves, 204, 252n40; ledger, 207–8; items of, 186, 206

Pontiac (1720–69): wars of, 22, 59

Portage la Loche. *See* Methye Portage

Porteous, John (d. 1799), 8, 9; papers of, 126, 168n12, 175, 188, 208, 215

Porteous, Sutherland and Co., 34, 143

potash, lxxi

Pouchot, Pierre (1712–1769), 57

Prairie du Chien (WI), 23, 71–2, 74–5, 76, 82, 195n30

prairies, xxxviii, l, liii, lxvii, xciii n. 59, 135

pre-Cambrian shield, 39

Prévost, Sir George, 1st Baronet, 39

Prichard, James H., 194n14

Prideaux, Brigadier-General John (1718–1759), 55–6

Primeau (Primo), Louis (ca 1749–1800), 137–8, 141

Prince Albert (SK), lxi, lxxxvi, cv n. 134, cvi, 25, 90, 171n39

Prince William Sound, 29, 114, 118

Printer's Guild Ltd, xl

Prudden, Rev. Mr, 124

P.S. King & Son Ltd, xl

Puans (people), 64, 66

pulp and paper, xxvii, xcviii n. 98, 42

Quaife, Milo M., lxxxvi, ciii n. 120, 213n27

Quebec, cviii n. 155, 14, 119, 123, 143; Innis, Fleming, and, 175; politics and, 40, 104; Pond and, 106, 127; trade of, 41. *See also* New France

Quebec Act, 41

Quebec City, lxxx, xxxviii, xcvii n. 93, 16, 28, 33, 40, 43, 45n18, 103, 106, 114, 117–18, 123, 133, 136, 143, 184, 201

Quesnel (BC), lxiii, cv n. 132, cvi n. 141

Raddall, Thomas Head (1903–1994), cvii n. 146

Radisson, Pierre-Esprit (1636/40–1710), lix

Radisson Society, xxxv

railways, xxx, liii, xcviii n. 99, 135
Ray, Arthur J., 190, 197n40
Red River, 11, 38, 117; Department, 38; District, 17n20, 94, 135–6
regionalism, 135
Reid, M.G., 20, 46n22
Rich, E.E. (Edwin Ernest), lxxvii, 191–2
Richardson, John, 8, 16n15, 43
Riddell, William Renwick, xxxiv, xci n. 45
River Disappointment, 30, 106, 150. *See also* MacKenzie River
Robitaille, Abbé Georges, xciii n. 59
Rocky Mountains, 111–14, 118
Rogers, Robert (1731–1795), lxxiii, lxxvi
Ross, George W., xxx, xci n. 50, 223
Ross, John, 3, 27; Athabasca and, 35; Mackenzie and, xxix; murder of, xl, xlii, xlviii, lxxvii, ci n. 112, 28, 36, 105, 127–31, 149, 195n28; Pangman and, 102–4; Pond and, ci n. 112, 28, 35–7, 103, 105, 130–1, 149; shares of, 3, 6, 34, 38, 102, 141, 143–4, 195n28; as trader, 35, 37–8, 97, 102–4
Ross (John) and Co., 6, 97, 143
Ross (John), and (Peter) Pangman, 34, 38, 102–4, 144
Roy, Pierre-Georges KCSG, FRSC, 3
Ryerson Press, xli–xlii, xcix n. 100, xcix n. 102, cii n. 125
Russia, empress of, 30–1, 106–7, 115, 124

Sage, Walter Noble, ciii n. 128, 192; dissertation of, ciii n. 128, cv n. 132
St Ann (church of), 62

St Fee (Santa Fe) (NM), 68
St Germain, Venant Lemaire: canoes and licences, 32, 34, 96, 138, 141, 143–4; and Cumberland House, 142; Pond and, 33; as trader, 36, 97
St John de Crèvecoêur, 123, 125
St Lawrence River, xxvi, li, lix, 135, 193n8; fur trade and, 183; geographical aspects of, lxv, lxvi, liii, 145, 179; Pond and, 48, 125, 195n30; trade and, 39, 43, 146, 182
St Peter's (MN) River: Pond's arrival at, 71; Pond's description of, 80–1; Pond's exploration of, 108; Pond's leaving forever, 81; Pond's trading ventures in, xlvi, 75, 152, 195n30, 213n23; Pond's wintering on, 23
Salem (MA), xix, 21, 50
Salter, Liora, xiv
Saskatchewan (River and region), 117; Cumberland House and, 26, 138, 144–5; HBC and, 26; Henry and, 24, 85–6; NWC and, iii, xxxviii, lxii, 49; Pond and, xlv, lxxvii, 85, 132, 141, 144, 152; traders and, lxii, lxxii, 5, 17n20, 35, 44n4, 90, 115, 170n31; Thompson and, 155; wintering on, 23, 136–7, 142. *See also* North Saskatchewan River
Saskatchewan Wheat Board, lxviii
Sarschew, 136
Sauk people, 67–8
Sault Ste Marie, 85
Schenectady, 61, 182, 184, 201
Scott, Duncan Campbell, xxix
second Connecticut regiment, 21, 52
Selkirk, Lord, xlix, xcii n. 56

Index

Semple, Andrew, xliii, c n. 105
Sevestre, Neveu, 98
Shiell, Doris, 134n4
Shortt, Adam, xxxvii, xciv n. 72, 185
Shotwell, James Thomson, lvii
Siegfried, André, lxxxv n. 5
Sieur, (Le Sieur) Toussaint, ci n. 112, 27, 98, 99, 131–2
Sikorsky Bridge, 171n32
Silliman, Benjamin, 169n19
Simpson, Sir George, 146
Sinclair, Lieutenant-Governor Patrick, 5, 16n7
Siouan (language) people, lxxxiii
Sioux people, xlvi, 23, 74, 76, 84
Sisseton division (of the native American Sioux), 76
Slave (Slavey) people, 113
Slave Lake, 27; geographical aspects of, 106, 116; Pond and, cviii n. 156, 100, 105, 117–20, 152; posts on, 27, 104
Slave River, 27, 35, 100, 104, 119, 131
Small, Patrick (1759–1846): and Mackenzie, 29, 105; and NWC, 9, 15; and Pond, 106; shares of, 4, 36, 101, 144; wintering of, 13, 143
smallpox: aboriginal epidemic of, lxxv, 35, 37, 112, 115, 99, 100, 144; Chapin on, lxxv; Gough on, cviii n. 151; Pond's warning of, 7, 27, 99; traders' death of, 45n6
Smith, Donald Alexander, 1st Baron Lord Strathcona and Mount Royal GCMG, GCVO, PC, DL, FRS, xvi, xxx, 146–7
Smith, Goldwin, ciii n. 126
Society of Colonial Wars, lxxxvii n. 21

Society of the Cincinnati, lxxxvii n. 21
Solomon, 137
staples industries, xiii–xiv, xxvi, xliii, lxix, xcix n. 100, 12, 42, 120–1, 179
Stedman, John, 127
Stephen, George, First Baron Mount Stephen, lxxxvii n. 13
Sternberg, Amy, xxxi
Stevens, Wayne, cii, 15n5, 21, 46n23; on Northwest Fur trade, 21
Stiles, Reverend Dr Ezra (1727–1795): biographical note on, 168n14; as copier of Pond's map, 87–8, 119–20, 124, 133–4; literary diary of, xlix, 120, 123, 162–3, 165, 169n20; meetings of with Pond, cvii n. 150, 31, 82n1, 119, 120, 169n20
Strathcona, Lord. See Smith, Donald
Sturgeon River, lxi, 88, 142
Sturgeon River Fort (Canadians' lower settlement), 43n2, 142
Suffolk County (NY) Regiment, 21–2, 50, 55
Superior, Lake, 37; aboriginal people and, 74; McTavish/ Bannerman and, 24, 88; Pond and, lx, 6, 18, 84–5, 117, 196n34; Thompson and, 154; trade on and with, 40, 62, 74, 120, 138, 181; Umfreville and, 37
Sutherland, Daniel, 10–11, 17n22
Sutherland (Daniel) and Grant, 8
Sutherland (Daniel), Grant, and Porteous, 17n22

Tanghe, Raymond, lxxxv n. 5
Thodey, Colonel Michael, 56

Thompson, David, biography of, 154–6; commemoration of, xxxii–xxxiii, l, xcii n. 57; in *Les Explorateurs Célèbres*, 154–6; *Narrative* of, xli, 101, 119; and Pond, 50, 124

Thomson, Robert Boyd, xliii, xcviii n. 98

Thwaites, R.G. (Reuben Gold): and Burpee, xcvii n. 91; as editor of history of Wisconsin volumes, xxiii; as editor of Pond's journal, xxv, xxiv, xli, xcvii n. 91, 47, 56, 122, 167n3, 188, 199, 210n3, 210n5, 212n12, 213n22; and Fleming, 188, 210n3; and Innis, xl, 47

Ticonderoga (Fort): attack on, 61, 151; Pond at, 21, 51, 53, 58, 61, 121, 151

Todd, Isaac (1742–1819): Askin and, 148n15; canoes and licences, 59, 61; and Lord Dorchester, 89; and early fur trade, 96, 127–8n5, 143; Pond and, 59, 61

Todd (Isaac) and McGill (James), 5–6, 34, 96, 127, 143–4, 148n15

Tomison, William (1739–1829), 25

Toronto, xxxi–xxxiii, xxxix, l, lvi, xcvi n. 90, ciii

Toronto Globe, xliv, xlv

Toronto Star, xlv

Trader Horn, c n. 109

Trotter, Reginald George, xciii n. 59, xcv n. 75, xcvi n. 93, ci n. 117, ciii n. 128, civ n. 242

Turlington's Balsam of Life, lvii, 132, 197, 206, 210, 212n20, 218

Turnbull, Captain George, 59, 64

Turner, Frederick Jackson, lii

Turnor, Philip (ca 1751–1799 or 1800): and HBC, 107, 161, 188,

207; journal of, lxxxv n. 11, lxxvi–lxxvii n. 12, 43n2; and Ross, 131; and Thompson, 154

Tute, Captain James, 44n4, 137–8, 141, 143

Tyrrell, J.B. (Joseph Burr) (1858–1957), xlix, cii n. 121, 199; and Hearne/Turnor journals, lxxv n. 11, lxxvi n. 12, 148n2, 148n4, 148n8, 148nn13–14, 148nn16–18; and Innis, lxxxvi n. 12, ci n. 113; and Royal Society, xciv n. 69; and Thompson (David), xxxiii, xlii, xcii n. 57, 124, 130–2

Umfreville, Edward, 37, 45–6n18; *Nipigon to Winnipeg*, 45n18

Underhill, Frank Hawkins, OC FRSC (1889–1971), xci n. 59, ciii n. 126

United States, lxiv, 111, 115, 215; Civil War of, 41; Congress, 5; government, 120; Library of Congress, 123; secession states of, 41

University of British Columbia, ciii n. 128, cv n. 132, cvi n. 138, cvi n. 141; History Department of, civ n. 129

University of California, lvi, lviii–lix, ciii, civ n. 129

University of California Press, civ n. 129

University of Chicago, 175, 191–2n2, 193n9; Department of Economics of, 176

University of Toronto, lxi, xcviii n. 99, 171n37, 191–2n2; Archives of, 167n7, 171n35; Bachelor of Commerce Degree (B.Comm.) of, 191–2n2; Baldwin House of, 17; Commerce and Finance program of,

176–8, 191–2n2; Commerce Club, 176; *Commerce Journal* of, 176; Department of Botany of, xcviii n. 98, 26; Department of History of, xcvn79; Department of Political Economy of, xxv, xxxix, xciii n. 58, 190–1n2; Department of Political Science of, 177; Extension Department of, 177; Faculty of Arts of, 176, 194n21; fourth-year seminar course of, 176; Hart House, xxxii, xcix n. 100; Innis at, xv, xvi; Innis Papers of, 167n13, 170n30; Library, 31, 85n5, 192, 195, 196n39; Thomas Fisher Rare Book Room of, 159, 170n24, 170n26; Yearbook (*Torontoensis*) of, 176
University of Toronto Press, xxvii
Upper Settlement (on the Saskatchewan), 44n4, 133, 141–2
Urwick, Edward Johns, lxxxv n. 8

van Dyke, W.S., c n. 109
Van Horn Dewitt, Garrett (b. 1793), 59
Van Veghte, Captain Dirck, 56
Veblen, Thorstein, xvi
Vermilion Falls, 28, 37, 105
Voorhis, Ernest, *Historic Forts and Trading Posts*, xlix
Voyageurs, 68, 72, 117–18, 120

Wade, M.S., xxxv, xciii n. 64
Waden (also Vuadens, Wadins, Waddens, Wadin), Jean Étienne (1738–82): biographical note on, 170n31; canoes, licences, and shares of, 6, 32, 34, 96, 137–8, 141–3; death, xl–xli, xlviii, lxxvii, ci n. 112, 7, 16n13, 27, 35, 95, 98–103, 127,

130–3, 166; Pond and, 18, 27, 31n5, 33, 96–7, 99–100, 130, 144, 152; trading activities of, 18, 26, 27, 44n4, 95, 97, 137, 144; wintering, 18, 35, 96, 130, 152
Waden, Josette, 96, 131
Waden and Co., 6, 96, 143
Waden and St Germain, 34, 96–7, 144
Walker, Thomas, 136
Walker, William, 133
Wallace, J.N., *Wintering Partners on Peace River*, 45n16
Wallace, W. Stewart, xxix; biographical note on, 171n37; as editor of *Dictionary of Canadian Biography*, xxviii; and national feeling, xxxiii, xcii n. 55, xciii n. 60; and new Makers of Canada series, xxix, xci n. 52; on the NWC, cii n. 120; and University of Toronto library, lxi
Walton, Dr George Rutherford, xliii, xcviii n. 99
Wappenassew (Wapinesiw), 136
Ware, Sarah, 50
War of 1812, 20
water transportation, li, liii, xcv n. 75, 25, 43, 106, 163
Watson, A. (Alexander) John, lxxxiv n. 2, xc n. 37, 179
Waugh, W.T. (William Templeton), xciii n. 60
Webster, J.C. (John Clarence), xciii n. 60
Welcome (His Majesty's armed sloop), 18
Wentzel, W.F. (Willard Ferdinand), 38
West Coast, cv n. 132, 119
Western cooperative movement, xvi, lxviii

West Indies, li, 217; Pond and, 22, 28–9, 59–60, 108, 121

wheat, xiv, lxviii n. 14, 42–3

White, Richard, lxxiix

Whiting, Colonel Nathan C. (1724–1771), 21, 52–3

Williams, Thomas (d. 1785), 126, 187; accounts of, 126, 188, 207, 212–13n21; papers of, 125, 147, 168n13, 175, 200, 201, 212n21, 215; Pond and, 31n2, 140, 141, 187, 197, 199

Williams (Thos.) and Fleming, 140

Williams-Taylor, Sir Frederick, xxxiii

Winnett, Frederick, xliii, c n. 106

Winnipeg, xxxvi, xii, xli, lii, xcii n. 56, 45n18

Winslow, General John (1703–1774), 51

Wintemberg, W.J., xciv n. 69

Winthrop, John (1588–1649), xix, 21, 50

Wisconsin: *La Baie des Puants* in, 202, 202n; history of, xxii; Pond and, 185–6; state-centred collectivities of, xxv; trade routes in, 198

Wisconsin Historical Collections, xxiv, 16n8, 21, 47, 49, 122, 210n3, 210n5, 210n6, 212n14, 213n22

Wisconsin portage route, 68, 112

Wisconsin River, 66, 195n30

Wisconsin State Historical Society, xxxiii, 47

Wissler, Clark (1870–1947), xxviii, xci n. 43, civ n. 131

Woollacott, Arthur P., xciii n. 64

World War I, xcvii n. 99, civ n. 129, 171n137

Wright, Chester Whitney (1879–1966), 176, 193n7, 193n10

Wright, Donald, ciii n. 126

Wrong, G.M. (George MacKinnon) (1860–1948), xxxiii, xcvii n. 93

Wrong, H.H. (Humphrey Hume) (1894–1954), xciv n. 64

xerox or xeroxing: lxxxix n. 30

X Y Co., 9, 10

Yale University, xlix, 123, 167, 169, 168n14, 171n33; Divinity School, 171n33; Graduate School of, xxii; University Library, 47, 123–4, 134; Museum of Yale College, 163–4; Peabody Museum, 165, 169n19, 169n21, 170n25; Pond's memoir and, xxiii, 47, 161; Stiles and Pond, xlix, 31, 120, 124, 133

Yale University Press: and Innis's *Fur Trade in Canada*, xci n. 38, xci n. 39, xcv n. 80; Canadian-American series of, xliii

Yankton people, 76, 79–80

Yeoward, Thomas, 194n22

York Fort (Factory), 111, 135, 137

Yukon, c n. 108, cv n. 132, 117, 146